Also by Donald S. Passman

The Amazing Harvey
The Visionary
Mirage

All You Need to Know About the Music Business

TENTH EDITION

Donald S. Passman

Illustrations by Randy Glass

Simon & Schuster
New York   London   Toronto   Sydney   New Delhi

Simon & Schuster
1230 Avenue of the Americas
New York, NY 10020

This Simon & Schuster hardcover edition October 2019

SIMON & SCHUSTER and colophon are trademarks of Simon & Schuster, Inc.

For information about special discounts for bulk purchases,
please contact Simon & Schuster Special Sales
at 1-866-506-1949 or business@simonandschuster.com.

The Simon & Schuster Speakers Bureau can bring authors to your live event.
For more information or to book an event contact the Simon & Schuster Speakers
Bureau at 1-866-248-3049 or visit our website at www.simonspeakers.com.

Manufactured in the United States of America

5 7 9 10 8 6 4

Library of Congress Cataloging-in-Publication Data is available.

ISBN 978-1-5011-2218-7
ISBN 978-1-5011-0490-9 (ebook)

Did You Know That . . .

- Most record deals don't require the record company even to make a record, much less to release it?

- You don't have to register in Washington to get a copyright?

- If we write a song together, and you write only the lyrics and I write only the music, each of us owns a piece of the music and each of us owns a piece of the lyrics? And that neither of us can use just the music, or just the lyrics, without paying the other?

- Prior to 1972, the United States had no copyright law prohibiting the unauthorized reproduction of records?

- Some film music composers can't even write music, much less create the arrangements for each instrument of an orchestra?

- A brain surgeon and a rock star have something in common?

To my precious Shana, and our growing family:
Danny, Soundis, David, Rona, Josh, Lindsey,
Jordan, Dorianne, Benjamin, Talia, Billy, Noa, and Leo

Acknowledgments

PLEASE READ MY THANK-YOUS. I KNOW IT'S A BUNCH OF PEOPLE YOU'VE PROBABLY NEVER HEARD OF, BUT THINK HOW MUCH YOU'D WANT OTHER PEOPLE TO READ IT IF YOUR NAME WAS HERE.

No creative work is ever the product of one person alone (no matter how tempting it is to believe my own hype), so I want to acknowledge and thank all the following people for their inspiration and help:

Payson Wolff and Bruce Ramer, my mentors and spiritual brothers.

Bea Shaw, my mommy, who helped edit the first edition, and who paid for my first soft-drink stand.

Snuff Garrett, for believing in me early on.

Mike Gorfaine and R. Diane McKain, for their invaluable advice on film and TV music.

Gene Salomon, for his invaluable input and strategic thinking ("always study the endgame").

Ethan Schiffres, the rock star lawyer.

Rob Light, for help with the touring section.

Ed Ritvo, for the confidence to do all sorts of things.

Larry Apolzon and Steve Bigger, for help with protecting the rights in names.

Peter Anderson, for the copyright infringement section.

Dave Dunton (in the very beginning) and Stephanie Frerich, for getting this book into the hands of readers.

Alan Garner, for his extraordinary communication skills and advice on conversation, books, and salesmanship.

Kim Mitchell, my incredibly indispensable assistant.

Jules Levine and Corky, for having bulldogs.

Michael Cannon Jr., for his cleverness in updating the royalty chart.

In addition, the following people (in alphabetical order) generously shared their expertise: David Altschul, Jill Berliner, Don Biederman, Kevin Breen, Nancy Chapman, David Cohen, Gary Cohen, Glenn Delgado, Bruce Eisenberg, Steven Fabrizio, Gary Ford, Russell Frackman, Dell Furano, Steve Gawley, Neil Gillis, Mark Goldstein, Lauren Gordon, Trudy Green, Jeff Hill, Zach Horowitz, Cathy Jacobson, Howard

Kaufman, Larry Kenswil, Steve Lyon, Jay Morgenstern, Jay Murray, Michael Ostroff, Ed Pierson, Peter Reichardt, Bruce Resnikoff, Jack Rosner, Tom Ross, Joe Salvo, Rose Schwartz, Joel Sill, Patricia Smith, Lon Sobel, Mike Steinberg, Sandy Tanaka, Lance Tendler, Ray Tisdale, Tracie Verlinde, Wayne Volat, Lenny Waronker, and Ron Wilcox.

FOR THIS TENTH EDITION, special thanks to (alphabetically): Olivia Barton, Lenny Beer, Ken Bunt, Tom Cavanaugh, Gary Cohen, Patti Coleman, Peter Edge, Paula Erickson, Richard Feldstein, Marc Geiger, Lee Goforth, Wendy Goldstein, David Israelite, Joe Kluger, Albrecht Klutmann, David Kokakis, Dennis Kooker, Michael Kushner, Tom MacDougall, Alli Macgregor, Brian Meath, John Meglen, Irwin Nachimson, Brad Prendergast, Bobby Rosenbloum, Andrew Ross, Steve Schnur, Sarah Scott, Cary Sherman, Mike Steinberg, Helen Stotler, Scott Swift, Lisa Thomas, Jake Udell, Mat Vlasic, Emily White, Ron Wilcox, Pat Woods, Simon Woods, and Matt Young.

IMPORTANT

Contents

PART IV

Group Issues

PART V
Touring

PART VI
Merchandising

All You Need to Know About the Music Business

TENTH EDITION

I

First Steps

STATE OF THE UNION

This tenth edition is the most extensive rewrite of my book since the first edition.

That's because the music industry has changed more radically in the last few years than at any other time in its history.

Let me explain:

Since the 1890s, music has been monetized by selling something: wax cylinders, piano rolls, shellac records, vinyl records, cassettes, CDs, and cheesy merchandise (well, I guess we're still doing that). But the business is no longer based primarily on sales. Spotify, Apple Music, Amazon Music, YouTube, and similar services have revolutionized how people consume music, so that streaming is now the dominant revenue source for recorded music. And this change is WAY more drastic than you might think.

Consider this:

1. In the past, when record sales were the mainstay of the recorded music business, you could go to a record store and buy two or three records at a time. Today, you can only stream one song at a time. That may not seem like a big deal, but . . .

2. In the days of sales, an artist was paid the same money for each record sold, regardless of whether a buyer listened to it a thousand times or never took it out of the shrink wrap and used it as a doorstop. But today, the more listens you have, the more money you make. However . . .

3. In the old days, if my records sold big numbers, it didn't make any difference to the number of sales you had. Your fans would buy your albums, and my fans would buy mine. In fact, if you had a big seller, it would bring a lot of people into record stores,

and that increased the chances of selling my records. But in the streaming world, that's no longer true. For reasons we'll discuss later, the more listens you get, the less money I make. A truly radical change.

The good news is that, after fifteen years of music revenue falling like buckets of rocks, we had our first earnings increase in 2016. And every year after that, we've had double-digit growth. All because of streaming.

We still have a ways to go—at the time of this writing, the recorded music business is less than 60 percent of what it was at its peak in 1999. But I predict it's going to be bigger than it's ever been in history. Why?

In 1999, the historical peak of the music biz, an average CD buyer spent about $40 to $50 per year on CDs; let's call it $45. Today, with subscriptions priced at $10 per month, the average per-subscriber fee is about $7 (because of student and family discounts). So let's use $7 per month, which means a music fan spends about $84 per year. That's almost double the $45 of CD purchases we got from each fan in the good ol' days. On top of that, the number of subscribers is growing all over the world.

But wait . . . there's more! In the heyday of the music biz, the average CD buyer stopped going to record stores (or even listening to much music) in their early twenties. Today, people of all ages subscribe to streaming services (oldsters listen to Lawrence Welk, and youngsters want stuff like "Baby Shark," a song that can mercilessly eat your brain). Which means streaming is not only generating more money per user (the $84 vs. $45 in the above example), but it's also bringing in a wider range of consumers than ever before. How can the industry not be bigger than ever?

Another radical shift in the last few years is how the concept of an "album" is being challenged. What does an "album" mean in the streaming age, when you can listen to just the tracks you like? Why should artists even bother to make albums when they can release individual songs as soon as they're ready? And if albums go away, what does that mean for recording contracts that have always been based on the delivery and release of albums? For example, if your contract requires you to deliver three albums, but nobody wants albums anymore, how do you ever finish the deal?

And that's just a taste of what's new in this edition. There's also an update of all the current industry figures, a new section on the recent copyright infringement cases, an overview of the Music Modernization Act, and much, much more. All waiting for you just inside the tent.

So step right up, folks, and lemme show you how the music business is shifting around like a Rubik's cube.

OPEN UP AND SAY "AHHH"

For many years I taught a class on the music business at the University of Southern California Law School's Advanced Professional Program. The class was for lawyers, accountants, record and film company executives, managers, agents, and bartenders who want to manage groups. Anyway, at the beginning of one of these courses a friend of mine came up to me. She was an executive at a film studio and was taking the class to understand the music biz as it relates to films. She said, "I'm here to open up the top of my head and have you pour in the music business." I loved that mental picture (because there's a lot of stuff I'd love to absorb that way), and it spurred me to develop a painless way of infusing you with the extensive materials in this book. So if you'll sit back, relax, and open up your mind, I'll pour in all you need to know about the music business (and a little more for good measure).

HOW I GOT STARTED

I really love what I do. I've been practicing music law for over thirty years, and I represent recording artists, songwriters, producers, music publishers, film music composers, industry executives, record companies, film companies, managers, agents, business managers, and other assorted mutants that populate the biz.

I got into this gig on purpose, because I've always loved creative arts. My first showbiz experience was in grade school, performing magic tricks for assemblies. I also started playing accordion in grade school. (I used to play a mean accordion; everyone applauded when I shook the bellows on "Lady of Spain." I gave it up because I found it impossible to romance a girl while wearing an accordion.) In high school, I graduated from accordion to guitar, and in college at the University of Texas, I played lead guitar in a band called Oedipus and the Mothers. While I was with Oedipus, we recorded a demo that I tried to sell to our family friend, Snuff Garrett (more about him later). Snuff, a powerful record producer, very kindly took the time to meet with me. That meeting was a major turning point in my life. Snuff listened to the record, smiled, and said, "Don . . . go to law school."

So I took Snuff's advice and went to Harvard Law School. While I was there, I played lead guitar with a band called the Rhythm Method. But it was quickly becoming clear that my ability to be in the music business and eat regularly lay along the business path. When I graduated, I first did tax planning for entertainers. Tax law, like intricate puzzles, was a lot of fun, but when I discovered there was such a thing as music law, the electricity really turned on. In fact, I took the USC class that I later taught, and it got me so excited that I left the tax practice for my current firm. Doing music law was so much fun that it wasn't even like working (I'm still not over that feeling), and I enjoyed it so much that I felt guilty getting paid (I got over that).

My first entertainment law experience was representing a gorgeous, six-foot model, referred to me by my dentist. (I promised him I would return the favor, since most of my clients had teeth.) The model was being pursued (I suspect in every way) by a manager who wanted a contract for 50% of her gross earnings for ten years. (You'll see how absurd this is when you get to Chapter 3.) Even then, I knew this wasn't right, so I nervously called up the guy to negotiate. I still remember my voice cracking as I said his proposal was over the industry standard, since most managers took only 15% (which was true). He retorted with "Oh yeah? Who?" Well, he had me. I wasn't really sure what managers did, much less who they were. So I learned my first lesson in the art of humility.

As I began to really understand how the music business worked, I found that my love of both creative arts and business allowed me to move between the two worlds and help them relate to each other. The marriage of art and commerce has always fascinated me—they can't exist without each other—yet the concept of creative freedom, and the need to control costs in order to have a business, are eternally locked in a Vulcan death match. Which means the music business will always need lawyers.

Anyway, I now channel my creative energies into innovative business deals, and I satisfy my need to perform by teaching, lecturing, and playing guitar. Just to be sure I don't get too straight, however, I cycle through my weird assortment of hobbies: magic, ham radio, weight lifting, guitar, dog training, five-string banjo, karate, chess, poker, backgammon, and real estate investment. I also write novels, which you are all required to buy.

BRAIN SURGERY

Speaking of marrying creativity and business, I've discovered that a rock star and a brain surgeon have something in common. It's not that either one would be particularly good at the other's job (and I'm not sure which crossover would produce the more disastrous results), but rather that each one is capable of performing his craft brilliantly, and generating huge sums of money, without the need for any financial skills. In most businesses, before you can start earning big bucks, you have to be pretty well schooled in how the business works. For example, if you open up a shoe store, you have to work up a budget, negotiate a lease, bargain for the price of the shoes, and so forth—all before you smell that first foot. But in entertainment, as in surgery, you can soar to the top without any business expertise.

Making a living from a business you don't understand is risky. Yet a large number of artists, including major ones, have never learned such basics as how record royalties are computed, what a copyright is, how music publishing works, and a number of other things that directly affect their lives. They don't know this stuff because (a) their time was better spent making music; (b) they weren't interested; (c) it sounded too complicated; and/or (d) learning it was too much like being in school. But without knowing these basics, it's impossible for them to understand the different aspects of their professional lives. And as their success grows, and their lives get more complex, they get even more lost.

While it's true that some artists refuse to even listen to business talk (I've watched them go into sensory shutdown if you so much as mention the topic), others get very interested and study every detail of their business lives. The vast majority, however, are somewhere in the middle. They don't really enjoy business, but they want to participate intelligently in their career decisions. These artists are smart enough to know one simple thing: No one ever takes as good care of your business as you do.

It was for my moderately to seriously interested clients that I developed a way to explain the basics in simple, everyday language. With only a small investment of time, these clients understood the essential concepts, and everyone enjoyed the process (including me). It also made an enormous difference in the artist's self-confidence about his or her business life, and allowed them to make valuable contributions to the process.

Because the results of these learning sessions were so positive, several clients asked if we could explore the subjects more deeply. Thus the conception of this book. I had just finished teaching my class on the music biz at USC and realized that my class notes were the outline of a book. So after some more research to flesh it out, I sat down and knocked out the first edition.

The book is designed to give you a general overview of the music industry. You can read it as casually or intensely as suits your interest level, attention span, and pain tolerance. It's not written for lawyers or technicians, so it doesn't include the minutiae you'll find in a textbook for professionals. Instead, it gives you a broad overview of each segment of the industry, then goes into enough detail for you to understand the major issues you're likely to confront.

JUNGLE MAPS

When I was in high school, a policeman named Officer Sparks spoke at an assembly. Mr. Sparks hyped us on the life of a crime fighter, seeming sure we all secretly wanted to be cops. In the process, he showed us something I'll never forget.

Officer Sparks ran a film in which the camera moved down a street. It was a grainy black-and-white movie, only about thirty seconds long, filmed by a camera bobbing along a sidewalk. When it was finished, he asked if we'd seen anything unusual. No one had. Apart from a couple of people bouncing in and out of the doorways, it looked pretty much like pictures taken by a camera walking past a row of boring shops. Mr. Sparks then said that a "trained observer" who watched the film could spot six crimes being committed. He showed the film again and pointed out each of the incidents (there was a quiet exchange of drugs, a pickpocket, etc.). This time, the crimes were obvious. And I felt like a doofus for missing them.

Any time I learn a new skill, I go through a similar process. At first, things either look deceptively simple, or like a bewildering blur of chaos. But as I learn what to look for, I see a world I never knew was there.

From my experience, the best way to become a "trained observer" is to have a guide to the basics—a framework in which to organize the bits and pieces. So that's the purpose of this book—to be a map through the jungle, and show you where the crimes are. (Officer Sparks, if you're out there somewhere, I hope you're proud.)

DETAILS

There is no way one book (even one filling several volumes) could poke into every nook and cranny of a business as complicated as the music business. So the purpose here is to give you the big picture, not all the details. (Besides, for some of those details, I charge serious money.) Also, even if I tried to lay out all the little pieces, as fast as everything moves in this biz, it would be obsolete within a few months. So the goal is to give you a broad overview (which doesn't change nearly as quickly, or at least it didn't until this edition). The idea is to give you a bare tree on which to hang the leaves of your own experience. Oddly, it's easier to pick up details (from the Internet, gossip at cocktail parties, etc.) than it is to learn the structural overview, because few people have the time or patience to sit down and give it to you. In fact, giving you the overall view turned out to be a much bigger job than I thought when I started. But you're worth it.

SOME RESULTS

Since this is the tenth edition, I now have feedback from experiments using this book on actual human subjects. Of all the responses I got, I thought you might enjoy hearing about two in particular:

First, I received an irate call from a music lawyer, who was upset because he charged thousands of dollars to give clients the advice I had put in the book.

Second, I received an equally irate call from a manager, who said that most of the artists he'd approached kept pushing my book in his face.

Way to go! Keep shoving.

And if you'll permit me a momentary lapse of modesty, my favorite compliment was from someone who said this was the first book he'd ever finished in his life.

STAPLE, SPINDLE, AND MUTILATE

When you go through this book, forget everything you learned as a kid about taking good care of books, treating them as sacred works of art, etc. Read this book with a pencil or highlighter in your hand. Circle or star passages you think you'll need, fold over pages, mark them with Post-its, paper clips, or bong water—whatever helps (unless you're reading an electronic edition, in which case you might want to lose the bong water). This is an action book—a set of directions on how to jog through the music biz without getting mugged. So treat it like a comfortable old pair of shoes that you don't mind getting dirty. It doesn't matter what they look like, as long as they get you where you're going.

CHOOSE YOUR OWN ADVENTURE

When my sons, David, Josh, and Jordan were little, their favorite books were from a series called Choose Your Own Adventure. They work like this: You start reading the book on page one and, after a few pages, the author gives you a choice. For example, if you want Pinocchio to go down the alley, you turn to page fourteen, but if you want him to go to school, you turn to page nineteen (my boys never picked school). From there, every few pages you have more choices, and there are several different endings to the book. (The boys liked the ending where everyone gets killed, but that's another story.) These books are not meant to be read straight through; if you tried, you'd find yourself crashing into different plots and stories. Instead, you're supposed to skip around, following a new path each time.

This concept gave me the idea of how to organize this book. You have a choice of reading for a broad overview or reading in depth, and the book tells you where to skip ahead if you want to do this. However, unlike the Choose Your Own Adventure books, you can read straight through with little or no damage to the central nervous system.

Here's how it's organized:

Part I deals with how to put together a team to guide your career, consisting of a personal manager, business manager, agent, and attorney.

Part II looks at record deals, including the concepts of royalties, advances, and other deal points.

Part III talks about songwriting and publishing, including copyrights and the structure of the publishing industry, as well as a section on protecting your name from people who want to pirate it.

Part IV explores things you'll need to know if you're a group.

Part V deals with concerts and touring, including agreements for personal appearances, and the role of your various team members in the process.

Part VI, on merchandising, tells you how to profit from plastering your face on posters, T-shirts, and other junk.

Parts VII and VIII explore classical music and motion pictures. They're the last sections because you need to understand all the other concepts before we can tackle them.

Now, to choosing your adventure. You have four mouth-watering ways to go through this book:

1. **EXTREMELY FAST TRACK**
   If you *really* want a quick trip, then:
   (a) Read Part I, on how to pick a team of advisors;
   (b) Get people who know what they're doing;
   (c) Let them do it;
   (d) Put this book on your shelf to impress your friends; and
   (e) Say "Hi" to me backstage at one of your concerts.

2. **FAST TRACK**
   Short of this radical approach, if you want a broad-strokes over-view of the business, without much detail, skip ahead each time you see the FAST TRACK directions.

3. **ADVANCED OVERVIEW**
   If you want a more in-depth look, but less than the full shot, then follow the ADVANCED OVERVIEW directions. This will give you a solid overview, plus some detail on each topic.

4. **EXPERT TRACK**
   For you high achievers who want an in-depth discussion, simply read straight through.

Feel free to mix and match any of these tracks. If a particular topic grabs your interest, keep reading and check out the details. (Amazingly, top-ics that grab your interest tend to be things currently happening in your life.) If another topic is a yawn, Fast Track through it.

So let's get going. Everybody starts with Part I.

PART I

Your Team of Advisors

2

How to Pick a Team

GETTING YOUR TEAM TOGETHER

Let's talk about the professionals you'll need to maximize your career and net worth. The main players are your:

1. Personal manager
2. Attorney
3. Business manager
4. Agency
5. Groupies

With respect to number 5, you're pretty much on your own. As to the others, let's take a look:

BUSINESS PHILOSOPHY

Before we talk about the specific players, let me share a bit of personal philosophy. (If "share" is too California for you, try "Let me tell you some of my personal philosophy," or the New York equivalent, "Yo, listen up, I'm talkin' to *you*.")

Take a hard look at some facts:

1. **You are a business.**
   Even though your skills are creative, you're capable of generating multimillions of dollars, so you have to think of yourself as a business.
2. **Most artists don't like business.**
   This is not to say you aren't good at it. Some artists are unbelievably astute in business. However, those folks are the minor-

ity, and whatever their love and skill for business, their love and skill for creating and performing are much bigger. So even if you've got the chops to handle your own business, it's not the best use of your time.

3. **Success hides a multitude of sins.**

   This is true in any business, from making widgets to making music. If you're successful, you can get away with sloppy operations that would bankrupt you if times were bad. For example, putting all your pals on the payroll, buying lots of non-income-producing assets (such as houses, jets, and other things that cost you money to maintain), as well as an overindulgence in various legal and illegal goodies, can easily result in a crash and burn if your income takes even a small dip, much less a nosedive. You can make more money by cutting costs than you can by earning more income (see page 394 for proof of this), so the time to operate efficiently is NOW, not later.

4. **Your career is going to have a limited run.**

   Don't take offense at this—"limited" can mean anything from a year to fifty years, but it's going to be limited. In most other careers, you can expect to have a professional life of forty-years plus, but as an entertainer in the music business, this rarely happens. And the road is strewn with carcasses of aging rock stars who work for rent money on nostalgia tours. So take the concentrated earnings of a few years and spread them over a forty-year period, and you'll find that two things happen: (a) the earnings don't look quite as impressive; and (b) this money may have to last you the rest of your life.

It's certainly possible to have a long, healthy career, and to the extent you do, the need for caution diminishes radically. However, even the best entertainers have slumps, and very few have really long careers. So it's best to plan as if your career isn't going to last, then be pleasantly surprised if it does. Setting yourself up so that you never have to work doesn't stop you from working all you like—it just becomes an option, not an obligation.

HIRING A TEAM

The way you pick your professional team will either set up your career and finances for life, or assure you a place on the next Electric Prunes tour. So be very careful and pay attention *personally* to the process of assembling them. I know you don't like to deal with this stuff, but it's your career and your money, and you have to do it every now and then. If you pick the right people, you can set your life on automatic pilot and just check up on it periodically. If you pick the wrong people and set it on automatic pilot, you'll smash into a mountain before you know what happened.

Pre-team Strategies

Since you wouldn't open a store without something to sell, before you start assembling a team, you want to be sure your music is ready for the big time. And how do you know when it's ready? You ask your tummy. Do you believe, in your gut, that your music has matured to the point that you're ready for a professional career? If the answer is yes, then you're ready. (Tummies are reliable indicators once we learn how to listen to them and dismiss the goblins that yell, "You're a phony and nobody wants you." Even the superstars have these goblins; they've just learned to ignore them.)

The first thing is to record your music. The recording doesn't have to be expensive or elaborate—with the advent of relatively inexpensive computer software, you can get a very professional sound in your bedroom. The important thing is to capture your energy, enthusiasm, and drive. You know what I mean.

A word about what kind of music to make. It's simple—you make the music that moves your soul. No one has ever had a serious career by imitating others, or trying to guess what the public wants. And I'll tell you a secret: What the public wants is someone whose music resonates from their heart. Doesn't matter whether you're the commercial flavor of the month, or an obscure blend of reggae and Buddhist chants. All the superstars I've known have a clear vision of who they are and what their music is.

Okay, you got your music. How do you get a fan base (besides your Mom)?

A lot of artists start by playing whatever local gigs they can get. This is not only to attract fans, but also to tighten up your musical chops and get experience playing live. When you do this, get your fans to sign up for your email list at every show. It's crucial to build a database (as we'll discuss in a minute), and a lot of artists give away something as an incentive to build one. For example, everyone who signs up gets a pin or sticker. Even if you only add a few new folks at each gig, you can eventually build a following that helps spread the word about your music and grow itself virally (assuming your music doesn't suck). You can then organize the list using FanBridge, MailChimp, or a similar service.

Another way to add to your database is by giving a free song to anyone who signs on to your email list for the first time. There's software to capture email addresses in exchange for songs at places like CASH Music (www.cashmusic.org), FanBridge (www.fanbridge.com), and Bandcamp (https://bandcamp.com). Of the three, CASH Music has the advantage of being open source (and free), as it's based on the principle that everyone donates resources and uses the platform to help other artists. You can also offer a song in exchange for a fan post on Twitter, using "Tweet for a Track" (www.tweetforatrack.com). And check out blogs like Hypebot for the latest and greatest DIY marketing and promotional tools in real-time.

The idea is to build a fan list that you own. The lists of fans who follow you on Facebook, Twitter, Instagram, etc., are owned and controlled by Silicon Valley folks, not by you, which means they control if and how you can reach them.

Once you have a list, stay in touch with your fans on a regular basis. Direct them to your sites on YouTube, Facebook, Twitter, SoundCloud, Medium, Bandcamp, Instagram, etc., as well as your own website. Promote yourself through email or texting (I'm told there are some services that manage mass texting, though I don't have any experience with them).

When you contact fans, have something interesting to say, and the more personal you make it, the better. Which of these would hit you harder?

1. "We're playing in Schenectady tonight" or
2. "Hey, Clarence, did you know we're in town tonight? Come see us." (Assuming your name is Clarence and you live in Schenectady; otherwise, it's not quite as effective . . .)

Another way that artists engage fans is to run a contest. For example, if fans re-tweet or share a post about one of your shows, they can enter a drawing for free tickets. That makes your promotion easily shareable and viral by nature. (Technically, there could be some issues with the laws that govern sweepstakes, lotteries, and things like that, but artists do quite a lot of this, and I'm not aware of anyone getting hassled for small-scale stuff. NOTE: the key word in the prior sentence is "aware." Sweepstake laws are way outside my wheelhouse, so don't take my word on it. You should talk to your lawyer if you're going to do this.)

I'm told Patreon (https://www.patreon.com) can be useful in creating a relationship with your most hard-core fans (and developing revenue opportunities with those folks). The key is (a) to create unique opportunities for your fans (maybe they get a free ticket if they buy one, a chance to meet you after a gig, or you volunteer to help clean their garage—well, maybe not the last one), and (b) to create unique content, such as exclusive video chats, access to new recordings, or exclusive videos of you in the studio. However you handle it, make sure you're giving as much as you're getting, so the fans don't feel ripped off. Also, it's important that what you give away or sell them is consistent with your image, so you don't come off like Chuck E. Cheese.

When you send out blasts to your database, don't be afraid to tell your fans what you want them to do. For example, tell them to come to a show with a friend. Ask fans to tweet at clubs saying they want to see you. Encourage fans to listen to you on Spotify to increase your play count numbers. Ask them to tell their friends about your music. Write to bloggers and Spotify playlist curators and offer them an exclusive premiere of an unreleased track.

And speaking of bloggers, it's important for you to personally write them. A lot of bloggers love to hear from artists who genuinely like their blog (insincere kissing-up doesn't work, unless you're *really* good at it). If you can connect, try to cultivate a genuine relationship. Send music early, offer to put them on your guest list at shows, help clean their garage (still kidding about that one). I've been told (but have no experience with this) that SubmitHub (www.submithub.com) is another way to get music to the bloggers, though there's a charge for it. If you're big enough to have a publicist, they can sometimes help with bloggers, but tastemakers usually know that those folks are getting paid to pitch your music.

While blogs might be a bit less relevant than they were a few years ago, because fans are looking more to playlists to find new music, the blogs are still important. And if you're featured on one, you can add that to your press kit, which you can send to promoters (the people who book live gigs), streaming services, record companies, garage cleaners, and so forth.

You can get free, basic data from Facebook Insights, Google Analytics, and Spotify Artist Insights. And when you get that data, it can put your booking strategy on steroids—for example, you'll be able to see where your fans are clustered, so you can strategically target those markets rather than just booking gigs in East Bumbleton and hoping the farmers show up.

Another great way to build visibility is by getting your songs placed on TV shows or in commercials. Sites like Music Dealers (www.music dealers.com), Pump Audio (www.pumpaudio.com), Jingle Punks (www.jinglepunks.com), Secret Road (www.secretroad.com), and Zync (www.zyncmusic.com) can help with that. A sincere email to these folks is a great way to start, and it's worth some homework to find out who's the key person at each organization. Since they get a lot of these emails, try to differentiate yourself from the masses by pointing out something you've got going ("I've got 100,000 followers on Instagram"), or if there isn't much happening, mention something about the person you're writing to ("I saw you recently got an award for your sponge collection. Congrats!"). If they do bite, you won't likely get much money for the use of your recording, but you'll spread your music to a wider base. If by some fluke you land a really big use, you still may not get much money up front, but you can earn some decent songwriter monies from airplay of the TV show or commercial (these are called **performance royalties,** which we'll discuss on page 225).

If you're a writer, this kind of activity can also get you noticed by a music publisher, who may give you money for your songs. (We'll talk about publishers in Chapter 16, but essentially they handle the business of songwriters, as opposed to the business of recording artists.) In the meantime, sign up for an organization like SongTrust, who will collect music publishing income on your behalf. This is critical to have in place when you land such placements. You'll also need to affiliate with a performing rights organization, which we'll talk about on page 226.

If you get noticed by a "tastemaker" (an important blogger, journalist, radio station, etc.), be sure to say thanks. You can do it on social media, but try something else to make your "thanks" unique. For example, instead of email, call them on the phone (that's what people did in the old days before texting). Or send a handwritten card. Or mail them a piece of Tupperware with the word "Thanks" written on the lid. This kind of follow-up not only builds goodwill with the tastemaker, but it hopefully also spreads your name to their audience. And keep the tastemaker's info on file for future use, to let them know what you're up to.

Similarly, it can help expand your base if you're able to connect with other artists on Instagram or Twitter and start a tweety love fest. Fans love to eavesdrop on artists talking shop, and you can also get exposed to their fans.

Similarly, if you can get support for your videos and music via channels with large followings on YouTube and SoundCloud, you'll expose your music to an even wider audience that was handpicked by that channel. Reach out to these channels and try to start relationships. Offer them premieres and exclusive content. Or to clean their garage.

When you're more established, give your database fans a chance to hear your music ahead of everyone else. Tell them about a secret show or webcast. Let them have first crack at your tickets. Some bands do lifecasting, where they communicate with fans a number of times each day. For example, they might get on Facebook Live while headed to a gig; blast out backstage updates through Instagram or Twitter; send pictures and video teasers of themselves onstage through Instagram; forward videos of themselves in the bathtub with rubber duckies, etc.

It's great if you can post every day on your social media (primarily Facebook, Twitter, and Instagram, plus Snapchat if your fans are there). Mix up your posts and don't use auto-share or posting programs because those put the same content everywhere. You want to engage your fans, not spam them with the exact same posts on all networks.

There are obviously tons of additional ways to market yourself, so let your imagination take flight and go for it. A number of websites can help with marketing, both in terms of specific tools and general advice, but because I don't use them myself, I can't really recommend any particular one. Some of my friends have suggested CASH Music, BandPage, Bandcamp, Hypebot, Digital Music News, and Midem's blog.

Of course, with all these techniques, be sure to stay on the right side of the line between keeping people intrigued and becoming the pushy egomaniac at the party.

Back to a forty-thousand-foot view: Make sure you stay focused on creating your music as the first priority, with marketing as the second. Some people recommend that you spend no more than an hour a day on social networking/promotion, so that you don't use up all that creativity and have none of it left for your music. Others prefer going in streaks of posting, and then holing up in the studio when they need to create. Or mix and match.

Okay, so you've got a killer recording and you're ready to boogie. Next question is whether you want to sign to a record company or do it yourself. We'll discuss later, on page 75, whether you actually want to sign or not, but for now, let's assume you do.

In this day and age, before a label will sign you, they expect you to have a decent-size fan base and hopefully one or two other goodies in your story, like high streaming numbers on SoundCloud, Spotify,

Apple Music, or YouTube with a low **skip rate** (meaning people don't move to the next song a few seconds after yours starts), or positive words from an important tastemaker. And even after you've done that, and even though most labels have scouts monitoring the Internet for hot new artists, unless a lot of people are going nuts over you, it's not likely anyone will call out of the blue. As with most things in life, you gotta make it happen yourself.

And now, ladies and gentlemen, a bit of a bummer: The major record companies (not so much the independents) don't listen to new artists' material unless they're submitted by someone in the business. It's usually a manager or attorney, though it could be an agent or a respected tastemaker. (I hate delivering bad news, but look at the bright side: I just saved you two months of waiting for a form email that says they won't consider your stuff because it didn't come from someone in the biz.) The reason is that record companies can get more than a thousand submissions *per week*, so restricting who can send in material is one way to regulate the floodgates. However, it's also a Catch-22: How can you get your music heard if you're not already connected in the business, and how do you get connected in the business if you can't get heard? Don't despair; I'm going to give you the key to the door. Namely:

The key is to get yourself a lawyer or manager to shop your music, which leads nicely into our next topic.

Who's on First?

The first person on your team is almost always a manager or a lawyer. In your baby stages, the manager is not likely to be someone in the business; it's more likely a friend or relative with a lot of enthusiasm. While this can be a major plus (as we'll discuss in more detail when we talk about managers on page 32), it may or may not get your music to the record companies. So if you have an inexperienced manager, or if you have no manager at all, a music industry lawyer can really help. Record companies prefer to deal with people they know, meaning your music will get heard much faster, and by more important people, if it's submitted by an industry lawyer.

It's much easier to get a music lawyer than a manager. Why? Because the time required of a lawyer is minimal compared to the time a manager has to devote. The manager is expected to help you with songs, image, bookings, babysitting (you, not the kiddies), etc., but the lawyer only has to spend a few hours getting people to check out your music. It's the lawyer's relationships—not their time—that count.

A word of caution about hiring a lawyer to shop your music. of the lawyers consider it important to maintain their credibility with the record companies, so they'll only shop artists they really believe in. Unfortunately, there are a few who will shop anything that walks in the door as long as they get paid a fee. Being shopped by one of these slime-bags is no better than sending the music yourself, and maybe worse, because the record companies know these lawyers don't screen out any of the garbage. So their clients' music goes to the bottom of the pile.

To prevent your music from being thrown out with the tuna cans, you should carefully check out the references of any lawyer you're considering. Ask them for the names of people whose music they've shopped (both successfully and unsuccessfully, so they don't just give you the few success stories that slipped through the cracks), then contact the references and find out how it went. You can also check around other industry sources to see who's legit. (We'll talk more about checking references later on.)

You'll of course need a lawyer and manager even if you don't go the record-company route, and the criteria for hiring them (which we'll discuss in the next chapters) is exactly the same.

A business manager (the person who collects your money, writes your checks, oversees investments, etc.) is usually the last on board for the opposite reason of why the lawyer is first: It's expensive (in terms of staffing and labor) for a business manager to take you on, and new artists need a lot of work just to keep financially afloat. Another reason they come on last is that very few business managers are willing to "take a flyer" with a totally unproven, unsigned artist; the business manager's potential upside is not nearly as great as a personal manager's or agent's, but they have to run up substantial expenses from the beginning. (As you'll see in Chapter 4, business managers aren't paid as much as agents or personal managers.) But don't sweat it. Until you have some decent money coming in, you don't need a full-fledged business manager. A good accountant can take care of your tax returns and answer basic questions.

The Search

Where do you find warm bodies to begin assembling your team? Well, start with the age-old ploy of asking every human being you know for a recommendation. Talk to people involved in music, even if it's only your high school choir's piano accompanist. You can lead yourself into any unknown area by diligently following your nose, and the music business is no exception. You'll be amazed how many things fall into your life when you open yourself up to the possibilities. The only frustrating part is that the people you really want don't have time for you in the beginning. (Be assured, as soon as you're successful, they'll fall all over you and say they "knew it all along.")

The major players are almost all in Los Angeles and New York, with a good number in Nashville, though of course that leans heavily to country. I don't mean to say there aren't qualified people in other places—there most certainly are—but the music industry is centered in these three towns, and the people who live there usually have more experience. On the other hand, major managers are increasingly popping up in other places. For example, I've dealt with managers of world-class artists who live in Atlanta, Austin, Vancouver, Philadelphia, and Boston. However, the better ones spend a lot of time on airplanes visiting Los Angeles, New York, and/or Nashville.

Here are some specific suggestions for building your list:

1. **AllAccess**
   There's a website called www.AllAccess.com that has a pretty comprehensive online directory of people in the music biz. I'm told it's updated often, and it has the major advantage of being free. You'll need to register for the site (don't be intimidated by the radio station questions—anybody can register), then click on Industry Directory.

2. *Hits* **Magazine**
   Hits is the *MAD* magazine of the music biz. It's full of current news and gossip, reported with a college-humor-magazine style, and is very funny reading (www.hitsdailydouble.com).

3. *Billboard* **Magazine**
   Billboard is an industry trade magazine, with lots of news, interviews, charts, and other goodies. (www.billboard.biz). Note the **.biz** ending. Billboard.com is consumer oriented, while .biz is for the industry.

By no means are these three an exhaustive list of sources; they just happened to be the ones that first came to mind. Frankly, I've been doing this long enough to know everybody I need to get to, and I don't use references on a routine basis. So don't take my suggestions as gospel. Check the Internet for more sources.

Here's some more ideas for developing your list of potential team members:

1. Read interviews with industry figures online and in music publications, and note the names. In addition to the industry sources above, here's some major *consumer* publications (meaning they're geared to fans, as opposed to trade publications that are geared to business people), in alphabetical order:
   (a) *Music Connection*, www.musicconnection.com.
   (b) *Spin*, www.spin.com.
   (c) Pitchfork, www.pitchfork.com.
   (d) *Rolling Stone*, www.rollingstone.com.
   (e) *Vibe*, www.vibe.com.
2. Watch for quotes, stories, or blurbs about music industry people online, on radio, and on TV.
3. Try these online places: TAXI (www.taxi.com), Music Business Registry (www.musicregistry.com), RecordXpress (www.record xpress.net), and Songwriter 101 (www.songwriter101.com).
4. Some artists list the names of their professionals, together with their jobs, on their websites, on the info page of Facebook, or in tour programs.
5. Or simply Google artists you respect, together with "manager" or "agent," to find out who's behind the magic.

Using the above and anything else you can think of, write down the names and develop a "hit list." Just keep moving forward—follow any lead that seems promising.

Once you assemble a bunch of names, prioritize who you want to contact first. If you've heard any names from two or more sources, the odds are you are on to a person who is "somebody," and he or she should move up in priority. Also look for the professionals surrounding people whose music you admire and whose style is similar to yours. While this is less critical with lawyers and business managers, it's important to make sure that agencies, and especially personal managers, handle your kind of music. For example, the agent who books Wayne Newton is not likely to book Lil Wayne, and I guarantee you they have different managers. On the other hand, you may be surprised to find that acts just as diverse are represented by the same agency (with very different individual agents). And the legal and business management lives of different artists are a lot alike. Rock 'n' rollers (like Green Day, the Rolling Stones, etc.), rappers (like Kanye, Jay-Z, Kendrick Lamar, etc.), and divas (like Adele, Beyoncé, Barbra Streisand, etc.) all have similar needs in music publishing, record royalties, touring, merchandising, sponsorship, etc.

Once you've prioritized your list, start trying to contact the people on it. It's always better to come in through a recommendation, friend of the family, etc., even if it's only the person's dry cleaner. But if you can't find any contact, start cold. You can try calling people on the phone, but expect a lot of unreturned phone calls, or at best to be shuffled off to an underling. That's okay—talk to the underling. If you get someone on the phone, be brief and to the point because these folks are always in a hurry. It's a good idea to rehearse your rap with a friend in advance.

You can try emailing folks, with a story about yourself and a link to your music, or maybe attach an MP3 file. Again, be short and straightforward—good people are always busy, and you'll be lucky to get five seconds of their attention. If you can't grab 'em fast, you're off to the digital trash bin. Repeated emails to the same person help get their attention, and may even have the subliminal effect of making your name sound familiar if anyone ever asks. But it can also be annoying and get your name into their spam filter, so don't overdo it.

You could also use that old-fashioned thing you may remember, the "U.S. Mail." Since so few people do that anymore, a physical letter might even get more attention. In this case, include a CD or a USB stick, pictures, hundred-dollar bills, and anything else to distinguish yourself. (I once had someone send me a recording stuffed inside a rubber chicken. For real.) If you've gotten any local press, that's a good thing to add. Use a yellow highlighter so they don't have to search the page for where you are. And just like the emails, be short and sweet, or you're off to the round file.

However you approach it, expect a lot of unanswered emails and unacknowledged letters. Don't get discouraged.

If you successfully snag someone's attention and they politely (or not so politely) blow you off, ask who they would recommend. This is valuable for two reasons: First, you've got a lead from someone who's actually in the industry. Second, when you reach out to the recommended person, you can tell them "So-and-so" told you to contact them. If "So-and-so" is a big enough name, it should at least get your email or phone call returned. (Maybe.)

Someone, somewhere will nibble, and you can parlay it into real interest by being persistent. All the superstars I've known have heaping helpings of drive and they'll continually hound people to further their careers. So hang in there and keep following up, despite the discouragements thrown in front of you. Virtually every record company in America passed on Taylor Swift, the Beatles, and Elton John, so don't expect people to be any smarter about your music. And don't get discouraged—it only takes one enthusiastic person to get the ball rolling.

Screening the Sharks

So you've honed your list, run up hours of chasing people, and hopefully found two or three nibbles on your line. At this point, you should fly, drive, bus, or hitchhike to meet these people in their natural habitat. You can't tell everything from a phone call; you want to see their body language, meet their associates, see if they work out of a dog kennel, etc. Basically, use your instincts to feel how they vibe you, and don't be afraid to trust your gut. If you think you're meeting with a piece of slime, you probably are. But if they dazzle you, *be even more cautious*—charming crooks are the most dangerous!

The fact that someone works with a lot of big names is helpful, but not a final determination. There have been a lot of big names associated with disasters over the years. Here's a bit of personal history to illustrate:

When we first got married, my wife and I decided to buy a vacuum cleaner. For reasons I still don't understand, we called a door-to-door salesman. This buzz-cut, square-jawed man bounced into the house and showed us how the vacuum's suction could pick up a seven-pound metal ball. Then Buzz poured some blue gunk on our carpet and used the vacuum nozzle to slurp it up. Finally, he started bragging about how he'd sold vacuum cleaners to the wives of several celebrities and started rattling off a list of big names. At that point, I said, "Excuse me, but do these people know anything about vacuum cleaners?"

The point, as I'm sure you see, is that a big-name celebrity isn't necessarily a good recommendation. It may just mean the celebrity pays no attention to his or her business, or that the celebrity is an imbecile.

So how do you protect yourself? Like this:

References. Have the potential team member give you references. And check them out carefully.

In asking for references, it's important to get people at your level of success. The fact that someone takes good care of their biggest client doesn't mean he or she will give you the same attention, or even have the time to take care of you. Odd as it seems, some people don't even pay much attention to their big-name clients, usually because they're too busy. There's an old joke (based on truth) about a major artist who couldn't get his lawyer on the phone to fire him. Also, try to get the reference from someone who's been using this professional for a while, so you don't just get a report on their honeymoon period.

Although it may seem obvious, be sure the professional's expertise is in music. There are brilliant real estate accountants who would be lost in the music business, just as the opposite is true. In fact, even people with extensive film, television, or book expertise may not understand music. So be sure you're talking to someone who does.

Use Your Other Team Members.   You should consult the other members of your team anytime you hire someone. First, you want their input and suggestions, and second, these people have to work together, so you want to be sure you're hiring someone who can get along with the team. But beware of this: Benjamin Franklin once said (and I'm too lazy to look up the exact quote, so I'll paraphrase it) that when you gather a group of people for their collective wisdom, you also gather their collective prejudices and hidden agendas. In other words, there will almost always be a political reason why your other team members want something, and this may or may not coincide with your best interests. For example, a business manager may have just referred a very important client to a personal manager. The personal manager may therefore be pushing you toward this particular business manager in order to pay back the favor, regardless of whether the business manager is right for your situation. (I don't mean to make you paranoid; most people are ethical and won't recommend someone unless they genuinely believe he or she would be the best person for the job, even if it's a payback. But a great deal of politicking goes on in the music business, just like any other business, and you should be aware of it—particularly because we're a small business and deal with each other so much.) So, always ask people *why* they're making a recommendation, rather than just the bottom line of who you should use. Make them give you specific, factual reasons. Facts are something you can evaluate yourself, and you should make the final decision.

Look Beyond the Sales Pitch.   Everybody looks great when they're selling. When you interview someone, all the seller's attention is focused on you, and you are absolutely the most important creature on the planet. That's almost never the case when you actually get down to business; the realities of other people's needs take their toll. It's *extremely* difficult to know this in your first meeting, as "giving good interview" can take people very far in their professions.

So how do you protect yourself from this? Once again, you have to check their references very carefully. Ask the references about their experience of working with this person, such as whether they quickly return phone calls and emails, how fast he or she gets work done, what's their zodiac sign, etc. It's a good idea to make a list of questions in advance, so you don't forget anything.

Don't be lulled by promises that sound unbelievably fantastic. If they sound too good to be true, they probably aren't. Some people will promise things they can't possibly deliver, just to get the job. They figure you won't fire them when they don't come through, because they know most artists don't like to make changes in their lives. (These are the same people who will stop returning calls if your star fades.) They also figure they have to lie just to ace out the next guy, who they assume is also lying to you.

The truth is that there are no real miracle workers. The secret of success in the music business is no different from that in any other business—intelligent planning and hard work. Promises of "shortcuts" usually don't come through.

Who Does the Work? Ask exactly who is going to be involved in your day-to-day work. It may not be the person you're meeting with. This isn't necessarily bad, but you should be aware of it from the start, and you should meet the people who will be involved. All professionals use staff people, some to a greater degree than others. In some firms, the staff people divide and multiply like paramecia, so the people you're meeting today may be gone in six months. Other places are more stable. So ask, and also ask your references.

Fees. Never hesitate to ask what someone is going to charge you. I know it's an uncomfortable subject, but bring it up anyway—you can be in for a seriously rude surprise if you don't. And when you do raise the topic, be wary of someone who gives you a vague answer. (If you really can't stomach a fee discussion, have another team member do it for you.)

Personality. It's a myth to think any one personality style is more effective than any other (assuming you don't hire a wimp). Screamers and table pounders, if they're smart and knowledgeable, can get a lot out of a deal, but no more than those who speak quietly, if they're smart and knowledgeable. Some people work with a foil, and some with a sabre. Both styles can be effective.

Remember, you're hiring people to guide your professional life, not to hang out on the tour bus. It's nice if you strike up a friendship with your professionals, but it's not essential. (However, with your personal manager, I think you need at least a solid rapport, if not a true friendship.) I'm not suggesting you hire someone you really dislike, or someone who has the personality of a salamander, but I am saying these folks don't have to be your pals. In fact, some amount of distance is often helpful. Just as doctors can't operate on their own relatives, one of the main things a professional does is bring some objectivity to your life.

There is a wonderful story about Genghis Khan, the great warrior. In the midst of a pivotal battle for his empire, involving thousands of troops on both sides, an aide went into Khan's tent and was surprised to find Khan himself sitting there. The aide said, "How can you be in your tent? The battle is at a critical point and the troops need your command." Khan replied, "I found myself getting angry over a turn in the battle, and I can't think straight when I'm angry. I came in here to cool off before deciding the next move."

Think about that. If even ol' Genghis had to detach from his emotions to do the best job, who are you and I to do any better? When I have legal problems, I hire a lawyer. This may sound strange to you, but I get emotional about my own problems, and I don't trust my judgment when I'm too close to the situation. So I hire someone who isn't.

In sum, a bit of distance from your professionals is not a concern, but you should feel comfortable enough to have an easy communication with your team. If you think you'll dread talking to one of them, look for someone else.

Decide Now—Confirm Later. Make a decision reasonably quickly, but confirm it slowly. In other words, once you've hired somebody, continue to watch them carefully (to the extent you can stand to do it). The fact that someone came in with rave reviews doesn't mean they'll be right for you, so consider them "on probation" until you've seen enough to merit your trust. And don't just take another team member's word that it's working. Force yourself to follow their moves in the beginning, and you'll earn the right to relax later. Remember: No one pays as good attention to your business as you do.

CHANGING A TEAM MEMBER

Here's what to do if something goes wrong on your team:

Even if they never pay much attention to business, I've never met an artist who doesn't have a built-in radar that tells them when something is wrong. So if you're feeling weird, then, "Houston, we have a problem."

It may be that things aren't being handled right. Or maybe you just don't feel comfortable talking to one of the team members. Ignoring the issue doesn't help any more than turning up the car radio to drown out a rattle in the engine. It's like a quote I once heard attributed to Dick Gregory: "I read so much about the bad effects of smoking that I got scared and gave up reading."

So deal with problems head-on.

Talk About Your Problems

I know confrontation is difficult. I have never known an artist (or anyone else, for that matter, other than a few ornery jerks who've been divorced five times) who enjoys confrontation. But for your team members to do an effective job, you must have an open communication with them. If you can't bring yourself to talk directly to the person who is bugging you, talk to another team member and make sure they carry the message. *Fast.* Nothing is worse than letting small things snowball to the point that they build into a major drama. If you discuss them when they're small, they can usually stay small. Often they're just innocent misunderstandings.

If you talk frankly about your problems, and they still aren't getting solved, make a change. No one has the right to expect a lifetime contract with you. People and circumstances change over the years; those who were spectacular for you at one point in your life may no longer be interested in you (for example, if they've lost interest in their job, or your career has taken a nosedive, etc.). Or they may no longer be capable of handling you (for example, they were unable to grow with you and your career is soaring, or you've changed careers and their expertise is in the wrong area, etc.). I respect and admire loyalty, but blind loyalty does no one a favor. To me, loyalty means you don't turn your head and run off with every pretty face that walks by (and as you get more successful, pretty faces come out of the woodwork to try to seduce you, literally and figuratively). But loyalty is a two-way street, meaning you're entitled to the same commitment from your professionals. You're only obligated to stick with someone as long as they're doing a good job for you. If you're not getting the service you want, then loyalty means you discuss it with them and tell them what needs to be changed. (Again, if you don't want to do it directly, do it through another team member.) If things still aren't being done right, and you're sure your complaints were clearly communicated, make a change. But do it for the right reasons, not the wrong ones.

Lost Confidence

It pains me a bit to give you this next piece of advice, but you should have it. Once you've lost confidence in someone, it's almost impossible to continue with them. It's like falling out of love—it isn't easy to fall in again. I say this sadly, because many times we lose confidence in people for the wrong reasons. It may be that someone with a political ax has buried them unjustly; it may be that they're doing a terrific job, but they have the personality of a stop sign and treat you rudely or bore you to death; it may be they have just delivered bad news to you (firing such a person is known as "shooting the messenger," from ancient Greek times, when a messenger bringing bad news was killed); it may be they've done a terrific job on everything important in your life, but screwed up paying your bills one month, so you had no electricity and your spouse refuses ever to see their face again; or it just may be an uneasy feeling in your stomach that you don't trust them. When you find yourself in this situation, again, I urge you to talk to the person openly (directly or through another team member) and tell them how you feel. (I know this is easy for me to say, and I admit it's difficult for me to do as well. But I force myself, and most of the time I find that the problem is a simple mistake that's easily fixed. And even if it isn't, I always feel better just from processing it.) If you talk things out, and the situation doesn't get any better, split.

COCKTAIL PARTY TALK

Let me say a word about cocktail party talk. In college, we used to play a kind of poker called "roll your own." In this game you get five cards, then draw additional cards (like in regular five-card draw). Finally, you arrange your cards in any order you want before flipping them over one at a time and betting on each card. After flipping the first three cards, everybody at the table looks like they have a spectacular hand. There appear to be straights, flushes, straight flushes, three of a kind, high pairs, and every other imaginable configuration to make you want to drop out and give up the pot. However, when it comes to flipping over the last couple of cards, most of the hands are mediocre.

I've always thought cocktail party talk is the same as flipping only the first three cards. Everyone sounds like a genius; everyone has just pulled off the greatest deal since the Louisiana Purchase. The truth, however, is in the last two cards, which you never see. The million-dollar deal turns out to be a hundred-thousand-dollar deal, with the other nine hundred thousand being there only if the artist achieves massive success (not that a hundred thousand isn't a decent amount of money, but it ain't a million). Nobody talks about their screwups, because self-aggrandizement is part of the Hollywood dance of the sand crabs.

The whole point of this is to say that you shouldn't take casual talk at face value. Especially if someone has an editorial point of view, like a manager trying to convince you to leave your current manager for the terrific things he or she can do for you. (Lawyers, of course, would never do such a thing. And if you buy that, I have some land in Florida that would be perfect for you.) So make your own evaluations in the realistic light of day.

3

Personal Managers

ROLE

The personal manager is the single most important person in your professional life. A good personal manager can expand your career to its maximum potential, and a bad one can rocket you into oblivion. When the job is done properly, a personal manager is the general manager and chief operating officer of your enterprise. (There are, of course, some artists without managers, but they are very much the exception, and they usually have one or more other team members filling this role.)

The most important aspects of the manager's job are:

1. Helping you with major business decisions, such as deciding whether to do a record deal, and if so, which record company to sign with; deciding whether to make a publishing deal (we'll talk about what those are on page 220); figuring out how much to ask for; etc.
2. Helping you with the creative process, such as deciding which songs to record, selecting a producer (we'll talk about who producers are on page 125), hiring band members, selecting photographers, etc.
3. Promoting your career by managing social media, coordinating your marketing and publicity, and otherwise hyping you to everyone the manager meets.
4. Assembling your professional team by introducing you to lawyers, business managers, and agents, and overseeing these people's work.
5. Coordinating your concert tours by working with your agent to make the best deals with promoters, routing the tour, working with your business manager to develop a budget, assembling

your road crew, supervising the tour personnel to make sure everything runs smoothly, etc.

6. Pounding your record company to maximize the advertising and marketing campaigns for your records, making sure your records are treated as priorities, screaming at them when they do wrong, praising them when they do right, etc.

7. Generally being a buffer between you and the outside world, such as fielding inquiries for commercial endorsements, personal appearances, charitable requests (both for money and for your smiling face), taking the rap for tough decisions that you make but don't want anyone to think you did, etc.

Let's first take a look at the structure of your deal with the personal manager, and then we'll talk about picking one.

COMMISSION OVERVIEW

Managers typically get from 15% to 20% of earnings from new artists. Established artists can sometimes knock them lower, as we'll discuss in a minute.

These percentages are generally applied to your *gross* earnings, meaning your earnings before deducting any expenses. That means:

1. If you're an individual artist, the fee is pretty much what it sounds like for songwriting, publishing, records, etc. We'll discuss some of the finer points later, but basically, if the manager's deal is 15%, they get 15% of what you take home. However, when it comes to touring, the 15% means much more than you might think. You'll learn, when we discuss concert appearances (on page 369), that you're lucky to take home 40% to 50% of your gross income. That means a manager's 15% of gross can take a big bite out of your net. For example, if you earn $100,000 and net $45,000, your manager gets 15% of gross ($15,000). Since you're only taking home $45,000, the manager's 15% is one third of your money. Not so good if you're the artist (though awesome if you're the manager).

2. If you're a group and you have more than five members, 15% of gross equals almost the same as, or more than, any one of you earns (assuming you're dividing equally). For example, if there are seven of you, everybody gets one-seventh; that's 14.28%,

which is less than the manager's 15%. In fact, since the manager's percentage comes "off the top" before you divide up any monies, you only get one-seventh of the 85% left after the manager's 15%, which is 12.14%. And for touring monies, a manager's 15% of gross can be many times your individual share of *net*.

Because artists have found it, shall we say, "uncomfortable," to pay managers more than the artist makes, the classic "15% to 20% of gross" has softened over the last few years. Here's what's going down:

NEGOTIATING THE MANAGER'S DEAL

Despite the powerful personality of many managers (carefully designed to keep you in your place), it is possible to negotiate with your manager. However, just like any other negotiation, the result depends on bargaining power. If you're a major artist, bringing in $10 million plus per year, the managers will follow you like floppy-eared puppies, delighted to take whatever treats you care to drop in front of them. On the other hand, if you're a brand-new band negotiating with a powerful manager, you're the doggy.

Here are the points to discuss:

Compensation. The first and most obvious issue is the manager's percentage. You should try to limit the percentage to 15%, although some managers argue that the risk of taking on a new band is worth 20%. They say it will be years—if ever—before they get paid for a lot of work (which is true). A compromise is to say the manager gets 15%, but it escalates to 20% when you earn a certain dollar amount (such as 15% of the first $2 million and 20% of the excess). I've also seen the opposite, where the manager gets 20% up to a certain level, and then 15% after that. The theory is that the manager gets a bigger percentage when you're young and the manager can't make as much, but his or her cut drops to the 15% norm when you're successful. This seems a bit weird at first, because it looks like the manager has no incentive to make you more successful (the more success, the lower the manager's take). But that's not really true—all managers would rather have 15% of a big number than 20% of a small one. This kind of deal is much better for you with success (though of course it's worse if you flame out).

Sometimes managers share in the *net* of an artist's earnings (meaning your earnings *after* deducting expenses) rather than the gross. This is WAY better for the artist—for starters, the manager won't get paid if the artist loses money, which is not the case in gross deals. In one deal I'm aware of, the manager got 20% of the net of a four-piece band. Another deal paid the manager on the gross for records and publishing, but on the net for touring.

When a manager has a deal on the net, they will often ask for limits on the expenses. For example, artists who decide to go on the road and charter jets, throw parties in every city, put inflatable pools in their hotel suites, etc., can easily eat up the net while having a great time with their pals. Managers don't enjoy these parties quite as much. Thus the agreement might be that the manager is paid on net touring proceeds, but that the expenses of the tour can't exceed a negotiated percentage of the gross. Or that the manager has the right to approve expenses, which I don't love as much because you could often end up fighting with your manager about expenses.

A variation on this theme is that the manager gets a percentage of gross for touring, but the commission is capped at 50% of the net. In other words, the manager will never make more than the artist actually puts in his or her pocket. For example, if your gross is $1,000, and you have $800 in expenses, your net is $200. If the manager got 15% of the gross, he or she would earn $150. Under this arrangement, the maximum would be 50% of the net (50% of $200, or $100), so the manager gets $100 and the artist gets $100. Note, however, that if you're a group, you all have to share the artist's 50% of the net, which means the manager makes more than any one of you.

In a few situations, where the artist is a superstar, the manager sometimes gets 10% or less, and occasionally just a salary (no percentage). These salaries can run well into six, or sometimes even seven, figures.

You could also try to reduce the manager's commission for endorsement earnings (meaning money you get to hype a product), and for film and TV appearances. The argument is that you have to pay an agent to bring you these opportunities (more about agents in Chapter 6), meaning you're paying two people for the same gig. If the manager won't reduce their commission, you can sometimes get them to agree they'll only commission the amount left after you pay your agent for those deals. For example, if an agent brings you an endorsement deal for $100,000, and the agent charges 10%, the manager would get 15% of $90,000 ($100,000 less the agent's $10,000). If the manager agrees to this, they'll want to cap how much you can deduct for the agent (usually 10%).

Exclusions. It's sometimes possible to reduce (or even exclude) certain types of earnings. For example, if you're a major songwriter who's hiring a manager to help you become a recording artist, the manager might get 15% of your earnings as an artist, but only 10% (or even 7.5%, 5%, or 0%) of your songwriting monies. Or maybe the manager gets 15% of your songwriting monies from records on which you appear as an artist, and a reduced (or no) percentage on other songwriter earnings. Another example is an established motion picture actor who hires a manager to help with his or her music career. In these cases, you normally exclude (or reduce the percentage for) the area where you're already established.

If you exclude any of your earnings from commission, the manager won't be obligated to do any work in the excluded area (though they often do as a practical matter).

Money-Losing Tours.   You can sometimes get managers to agree that, if a tour loses money, they'll take no commission on it. This is the same concept we discussed above, when we talked about capping your manager's commissions at 50% of your touring profits. If you can't get your manager down to zero on money-losing tours, then try for a reduced commission (meaning, for example, instead of 15%, they'd only get 7.5% on a losing tour), and at the very least, get them to defer their commission until you're more successful (meaning you agree they're entitled to a commission, but they have to wait and get paid later, when you have money coming in). Another variation is that the manager doesn't get paid for dates where you make a small amount, such as $1,000 per night (or a similar negotiated figure).

Repayable Monies.   Sometimes you have to pay back money you got under a deal (for example, under some merchandising deals, as we'll discuss in Chapter 24). In this case, ask the manager to repay their commission on monies you have to shell out.

Deductions.   Certain monies are customarily deducted before computing the manager's percentage, even when a manager is paid on gross. Most managers don't take commissions on these, even if their contract says they can, but some try. So it's always a good idea to spell things out and avoid any misunderstandings.

Here's the list of no-no's:

1. **Recording costs.**
    If the record company pays you money, and you spend it on recording costs, you shouldn't pay a commission on those mon-

ies. This is because the funds only pass through your hands (i.e., you don't keep them), and so they aren't really "earnings."

2. **Monies paid to a producer of your records.**

   Producers are the people hired to put together your recording, as we'll discuss in detail on page 125, and you pay them advances and royalties. Just like recording costs, monies you have to fork over to a producer aren't really earnings, for the same reason we just discussed in connection with recording costs.

3. **Co-writers.**

   When you write songs with somebody else, the manager shouldn't get paid on the other person's share of the song's earnings, even if you collect them first.

4. **Tour support.**

   This is money paid by a record company to offset your losses from touring (see page 180). Whether managers should commission tour support is a bit controversial. Some managers argue this is money you get from the record company, just like any other money, and they helped you get it, so they should commission it. Most of the time, however, they'll agree it isn't commissionable, because it only compensates you for a loss.

5. **Costs of collection.**

   If you have to sue someone to get paid, the cost of suing them to collect the money (called **collection costs**) should be deducted before applying the manager's percentage. For example, if a concert promoter stiffs you for $50,000, and it costs you $10,000 in legal fees and court costs to collect, the manager should only commission $40,000 (the $50,000 recovery less the $10,000 collection costs). Another way to look at this is to say the manager bears his or her proportionate share of the collection costs.

6. **Sound and lights.**

   It's common in personal appearance contracts for the artist to supply his or her own sound system and stage lighting. The promoter then "rents" the sound and lights from the artist for a specified dollar amount. Customarily, this rent money is considered an expense reimbursement (as opposed to a fee paid to the artist), so the manager isn't paid on the amount allocated to sound and lights. But you gotta ask for this one.

7. **Opening acts.**

   When you get to the superstar category, your deal for a personal appearance may also include monies you pay to an opening act. Again, since this money just passes through your hands, it shouldn't be commissionable.

8. **Related entities.**

More and more often, managers now own record labels, and sometimes publishing companies, film production companies, concert promotion businesses, or even festivals. If you make a deal with a company owned by the manager, you shouldn't pay a management commission on the earnings from that company. Managers don't always agree to this, arguing that they're wearing two hats (for example, manager and record label) and therefore they should be paid for both. They also say, if you had another record company, you'd be paying them on the record company earnings. In response, you argue that they can't be expected to beat up their own company the way they would beat up a major label. You also argue that they're getting paid much more through that entity than they would as a manager, so they shouldn't "double dip" and get paid twice on the same earnings: they'd get paid once as a label when you sell records, then again as a manager when you get paid for those sales. Also, if you leave them as a manager, they'll still get paid as your record company if that deal continues.

Term

The term of a management agreement (meaning the period of time that the manager will work for you) is usually three to five years. If you're an artist, you want to make it as short as possible; if you're a manager, you want it as long as possible. Historically, most managers tied the term of their deals to **album cycles** (meaning the time from when you start recording an album through the end of touring and promotion of that album), and some managers still operate on this basis. However, the concept of an "album" is challenged in the streaming world, because artists release more and more of their recordings in non-album bunches (both bigger and smaller than albums), and the recordings aren't always at the same time. So the definition of an "album cycle" is becoming problematic, and the trend is now to set the term of a management agreement as a specific number of years.

Be very careful when negotiating the term of a management deal. Many artists have lived to regret being tangled up in long-term contracts with lousy managers. Yet there's a balancing act that has to work for both sides. Managers don't want to put their sweat into launching your career, only to see you waltz off at the first sign of success, and you don't want to be married to a moron who's holding you back.

The most common compromise is to say that if the artist doesn't earn a minimum amount, he or she can terminate the agreement early. For example, the deal might be for four or five years, but if the artist doesn't earn $200,000 over the first two years, he or she can terminate the deal.

I hesitate to give you specific dollar figures for the earnings, because (1) they'll probably be out of date by the time you read this, and (2) they also depend on who you are. If you're a heavy touring band, the numbers are much higher than if you sing folk songs in coffeehouses. But here's an example from a beginning pop artist's contract: The deal was for two years, and the manager could renew for an additional two years if the artist earned $300,000 over the first two. The manager could then renew for another (third) two years if, during the second two years, the artist earned $500,000.

The manager, if he or she has any sophistication, will also say that the "earnings" have to include offers you turn down. The theory is that you can't refuse to work and then get out of the deal because you didn't earn enough. I usually agree to this, but require that the offers must be similar to those you have previously accepted. So an offer to appear nude at the Moscow Circus wouldn't count (unless that's your act).

Another approach is to say you must have a record deal (or a publishing deal if you're a songwriter) within a year or eighteen months after the start of the term, and if not, you can terminate the deal. If you get this kind of provision, you should also provide that, if the record or publishing deal ends, the manager has to get another one within that same time period (twelve to eighteen months). If you don't have this second provision, you could get a deal in the beginning, never make a record, get dropped by the label, and be stuck with the manager for the balance of their term.

Termination for failing to clear the hurdle can be done two ways. One is a letter from the artist to the manager containing legal words that translate as "You're fired." The other is a shorter management deal that gets renewed if the artist achieves certain earnings (for example, the term of the agreement is two years, but if the artist earns at least $200,000, the manager continues for an additional two years). The only difference between these two arrangements is whether the artist has to remember to send the manager a notice.

Earnings After the Term: "The Gift That Keeps On Taking"

One of the most important points you have to negotiate is what your manager gets paid after the end of the management deal. Even though the term may end after a few years, virtually every management contract says the manager gets paid on earnings *after* the term if those earnings are generated under "contracts entered into or substantially negotiated during the term." This language means two things:

1. As to records made during the term of the management deal, the manager gets a commission from income earned by those records after the end of the management deal; and
2. The manager is paid on records made *after* the term of your management deal, if the records are recorded under a contract signed during the term.

All of this could mean—and I've seen it happen—that a manager is still getting paid seven, ten, or more years after he or she finished rendering services. For example, suppose six months before the end of the management deal you sign a five-album deal. Under this clause, the manager gets paid forever on sales of these five albums, most of which will be recorded after you've parted company.

I think this clause is way overreaching, and these days most every manager will agree to cut it back. Let's take a closer look:

The major things to worry about are records and publishing. Unless you're in a television series, long-term product endorsement deal, or some other nonmusical commitment that could run for several years, records and publishing are the only areas where you're likely to have significant earnings from activities after the term under agreements made during the term. The other contracts you make during the term, such as personal appearance engagements, may be completed after the term, but this happens in a relatively short period (although it can represent millions of dollars). And if a manager is involved in setting up a tour, it's not unreasonable for him or her to be paid something for the tour (at least for dates happening within six to twelve months after the term). So if you're going to dump your manager, do it before the tour gets set up.

Sunset Clauses.   Here are some of my better strategies to cut this back. These are known as **sunset clauses,** because they end the day for commissions.

1. **Records.**
    (a) The manager gets paid only on records recorded and released during the term (and not on any others). This is the best for you.
    (b) If (a) doesn't work, a compromise is to pay the manager for records that are recorded during the term and released within three to six months after the term ends. If they're released later than that, the manager doesn't get any commission on their earnings.
    (c) Another solution is that the manager gets a half commission (e.g., if the manager has 15%, it's reduced to 7.5%) on records recorded during the term but released afterward. The theory is that the manager only does half the work—overseeing the recording, but not overseeing the release and promotion. (As in (a), records made after the term aren't commissionable at all.)
2. **Publishing.**
    (a) The manager is paid only on songs recorded and exploited during the term. This is the best for you.
    (b) The manager gets a half commission on songs recorded during the term and exploited after.
    (c) The manager gets a half commission on songs written during the term but recorded afterward. This at least cuts off participation in songs written after the term under contracts made during the term.
3. **Post-term reductions.**
    You can often reduce the commissions while you're waiting for them to die. For example, there might be a full commission for the first two years after the term, a half commission for the next three years, then over and out.
4. **Final cutoff.**
    I try to have some date after which all commissions end, no matter what. Try three to five years after the term; settle for no more than seven.

Feel free to creatively mix and match the above three approaches. For example, the manager could get a full commission on records recorded and released during the term, but only for a period of three years after the term. Or they might get a commission for a period after the term equal to the term itself (for example, if the term were three years, the period afterward would be three years; if it were four years, the period would be four years, etc.), and thereafter nothing else. If it's a period equal to the term, you should ask for a "cap" (meaning a maximum number of years, no matter how long the term is) of say, five years. If the manager agrees, they'll also want a "floor," meaning a minimum number of years, such as two. The limits are only your imagination and the manager's patience.

A particularly thorny problem (and another reason you should pay so much attention to the commissions after the term) is the fact that, after the term, you'll need to hire a new manager. As you can imagine, there aren't too many managers who want to work for free, and there are even fewer artists who want to pay 15% of their gross to two managers (30%!). Thus, it's very important to limit or eliminate commissions after the term. In truth, most new managers will take a reduced (or even no) commission on earnings that another manager is commissioning. But they're only going to do this for, say, the first album or the first tour, and they'll only do it if you're pretty successful. If they can't start making money relatively soon, managing you isn't going to be worth their time. So while you can live with paying a prior manager something on after-term projects, you should limit it as much as possible.

Key Man

Another important aspect of your management deal is called a **key man** clause (hopefully soon to be called a "key person" clause). Although you have a relationship with a particular personal manager, your contract might be with their corporation or a partnership. Thus it's possible that "your person" could leave the company, and since your deal isn't with that manager personally, you can't just get up and go with them. Accordingly, you could find yourself managed by a stranger. Or someone you know but who smells like the Cuyahoga River.

To prevent this, you should insert a clause that says the person with whom you have a relationship (the *key person*) must personally act as your manager, and if not, you can terminate the deal. If the company buys this concept (some bigger ones won't), it will only be for one of the owners of the company or a very senior manager, not the day-to-day people who stream in and out of the company's revolving door.

If you do get this kind of clause, you can easily say that you can terminate if the key man dies or is disabled, and you can sometimes get the same right if he or she is no longer employed by the management company. Much trickier is the situation where they're alive and kicking, still employed by your manager, but taken off your account. It's much harder to say the key man must be "actively involved" in managing your life, because the manager worries that, even if the key man is working on your career, you'll try to use this clause to get out of your deal—you'd argue that the manager is doing a mediocre job (and thus is not "actively involved"), and therefore the management company is in breach of your contract. (For exactly this reason, from your point of view, the broader you can make the language, the better.)

Double Commissions

If, for tax planning or otherwise, you set up a corporation or other entity to conduct your entertainment activities, you want to be sure this doesn't trigger a **double commission.** (See page 189 for a discussion of using a corporation in record deals, and page 355 for corporations used by groups.) Observe:

Management contracts say that the manager's commission is based on your earnings at the corporate level. This is perfectly reasonable— otherwise you could easily pay the gross monies into the corporation, pay yourself only a small salary, and claim the manager only gets his or her commission on the small amount that comes out to you. For example, if your corporation gets $100,000 for your appearance at a show but only pays you $10,000, it wouldn't be fair to pay the manager only 15% of the $10,000. However, it's not reasonable for the manager to take a second bite at the money. Once he or she has commissioned it at the corporate level, there should be no further commission when it comes out to you in the form of salary. (In the previous example, this means the manager can't commission both the $100,000 and the $10,000.) Most management contracts would technically allow the manager to do this "double dip" (after all, the salary is your gross income), but in practice it isn't done (by reputable managers). Still, it's a good idea to specifically say so.

Power of Attorney

Another provision to watch for is one that says the manager has a **power of attorney** (meaning the power to act for you), such as the right to sign your name to contracts, hire and fire your other representatives, approve use of your name and likeness, cash your checks, etc. I like to wipe out most of this nonsense. You should hire and fire your own representatives, and definitely cash your own checks. The only time I let a manager sign for an artist is if (a) the deal is for personal appearance engagements, of no more than one or two nights, which will be performed within the next four to six weeks; (b) you're unavailable to sign the agreement yourself; and (c) the manager has your verbal approval of the deal. If it doesn't meet these criteria, bless the piece of paper with your autograph.

As you get busier, you may want the manager to handle routine approval of the use of your name and likeness. If so, make sure it's only for certain uses (publicity for your own career is okay, but major things like commercial endorsements are definitely not okay), and that they can only authorize use of a likeness that you previously approved.

The Best Deals

Now that you've studied managers' contracts, you're ready for a well-kept secret.

Shhh. Go close the door before I tell you.

Okay, here's the secret: Many of the top managers have absolutely no written contracts with their artists. It's all done on a handshake, and the only discussion is the percentage. Their feeling, and I respect them for it, is that the relationship is more important than any piece of paper, and if the artist isn't happy, they're free to go at any time. Also implicit in this arrangement is that the artist needs the manager as much as (or more than) the manager needs the artist.

Please don't misunderstand this point. Many legitimate and well-respected managers require written contracts, and there is nothing wrong with this. But there are also a number who "fly naked" (without a written deal), and ironically they are often the ones who keep their clients the longest.

Even with these folks, I generally do an email outlining the terms. It spells out the percentages, states that the term can be ended by either party at any time, and deals with the post-term earnings (see the above discussion). It never hurts to make sure there are no misunderstandings.

PICKING THE RIGHT MANAGER

So how do you pick a manager? First, review Chapter 2, which applies to picking everyone on your team. Then take a look at these specific tips.

Let's start with the absolute best. This is the yardstick to use in measuring your candidates: The absolute best is a powerful, well-connected manager, with one or more major clients, who is wildly enthusiastic about you and willing to commit the time required for your career. If you're a superstar, you can easily find such a person. If you're not, this situation hardly ever exists. The reason is that, when a manager is powerful and successful, he or she is usually not interested in anything other than a major money-earning client. The analysis is simple—it takes as much (or more) work to establish a new artist as it does to service an established artist, and guess which one pays better (and sooner)? (Yes, every once in a while, a powerful manager gets genuinely revved up over a new artist. But this is rare, and you have to be extraordinarily lucky even to get such a person's attention.)

So let's look at more down-to-earth alternatives, not in any particular order:

1. A major manager with a young associate who is genuinely enthusiastic about you.
2. A midsize manager who is wildly enthusiastic about you.
3. A major, powerful manager who is taking you on as a favor (either personal or professional) to somebody who is *very* important to him or her.
4. A young, inexperienced manager who is willing to kill for you.

There are of course endless combinations of the above, but those are the major categories.

Unless you can get the best possible situation described above, you'll have to make some kind of compromise. The compromise is between power and clout on one hand, and time and attention on the other. The reason a manager is powerful is that he or she has at least one major client who takes up most of the manager's time. This means you're going to get less of it, and thus less personal attention (although these people can often do more in a five-minute call than a newcomer can do in a week). At the other extreme, a young, bright manager with no other clients will lack clout and experience, but will spend all of his or her waking hours promoting your career. And in between lies a rainbow of choices.

I personally like young managers a lot. If they're bright and motivated, I've seen their energy overcome the lack of experience and political clout with superb results. And to help you understand why, let me give you the Passman Treatise on Managers' Careers.

Managers' careers go something like this:

1. The manager is young and enthusiastic, and attaches himself or herself to a promising young act.
2. By doing whatever it takes, the manager promotes the artist into major stardom, at which point, (a) every other manager tries to steal the artist, (b) the manager is offered twenty-seven other acts to manage, and (c) one of the larger management companies tries to buy all or a part of their company.
3. After a few years, the manager is exhausted from having worked so hard on the first act (back when he or she had nothing else to do and could literally live with the artist). So the manager wants to cash in on the fame and fortune while it lasts, and, accordingly, starts hiring associates and taking on superstars.
4. This is the point at which many managers begin to lose it because they're too successful. Some of them have such huge egos that they won't take on associates of their own caliber (for fear the associate might steal the artists). So they hire less capable people and give the artists lousy service. Others hire good people, but pay them so poorly that their employees get frustrated and go out on their own (usually stealing the artists in the process). As things unravel, the manager begins to lose artists who are no longer getting the personal attention they once did.
5. After these batterings, the manager decides it was a mistake to have tried to get so big, breaks up with his or her partners, keeps one or two key artists, and starts a record label or goes into the movie business.

   Of course, a few managers have been able to pull off large, successful management companies, but they're the exception. Also, most of these big companies are really just a collection of managers who essentially share expenses and some central services (such as marketing, digital, etc.), meaning the managers are operating on their own for the most part.

At any rate, every major manager was a nobody at one time. While I don't suggest that a superstar take on an inexperienced manager, I do think many new artists are well advised to hire a bright, aggressive young manager. Obviously, you shouldn't do this if you have the opportunity to go with an established manager who is (or has someone in his or her organization who is) genuinely enthused about you. But if this isn't an option, the right young manager can be a real asset.

4

Business Managers

ROLE

The business manager is the person on your team who handles your money. He or she collects it, keeps track of it, pays your bills, makes sure you file your tax returns, oversees your investments, etc.

Listen to me!!! Did you know that in California, a person needs no credentials whatsoever to be a business manager? Contrary to popular opinion, you don't have to be an accountant (much less a certified public accountant), and you don't even have to be licensed by the state. Technically, business managers who give certain kinds of investment advice need to be "registered investment advisors" (like stockbrokers, who are licensed by the federal government before they can sell securities to the public). However, very few are.

What this means is that you could be turning your money over to someone who has no more financial training than you do. And when you stop to think about it, that's pretty scary.

I know you wouldn't have gone into the music business if you wanted to be a financial whiz—if you were good with numbers, you'd be in some cubicle manipulating an electronic spreadsheet instead of winning your way into the hearts of millions. I also know that numbers make you nervous and may even intimidate you. On the other hand, there are parts of all of our lives that we don't like, and, while we can get other people to deal with them day to day, we have to be sure we choose good people to do it. For this reason, I urge you to *personally* spend some time investigating all of the people on your team, AND BE ESPECIALLY CAREFUL WHEN IT COMES TO BUSINESS MANAGERS. They can range anywhere from superb to sleazoid, with all variations in between. And their bedside manner and office space may tell you very little about what they're really like—the bad ones can be like a shiny used car that's rusting underneath a new paint job.

Financial disasters can come from someone who's an out-and-out crook, or they can come from an honest person who is just a boob. My doctor once told me a story about an orderly he had when he was in the army. One day the orderly decided to go that extra mile and do something on his own initiative. So, with the best of intentions, he sterilized all of the thermometers by *boiling* them. SO BE EXTREMELY CAREFUL WHEN YOU PICK A BUSINESS MANAGER!

Hopefully I've now got your attention, so let's look at how to find the right person.

Oh, and did I mention you should be careful?

HOW TO PICK A BUSINESS MANAGER

References

The other professionals on your team can be a great help in choosing a business manager. But remember, they may have their own agendas. For example, a personal manager may have referred a lot of important clients to a business manager and therefore has a lot of control over the business manager. This is a two-edged sword—it means you may get a lot of attention from the business manager, but it also means that, if you have a fight with your personal manager, the business manager is not necessarily on your side (if the business manager loses you, it's only one account; if they upset the personal manager, it could mean their whole career). This is particularly true when the business manager also does the personal manager's work. With reputable personal managers and reputable business managers, I have rarely found this to be a practical problem, but it's a sign to be extra careful.

Family, Friends, and Hangers-On

Barring very unusual circumstances, inviting family members into your financial life is extremely dangerous. Most of them aren't qualified to do the job, and even when they are, it's difficult for them to be totally objective about you. It's the same reason that doctors won't operate on their immediate family, because they're too involved emotionally. And not only that, (A) it's very difficult to fire your brother, and (B) if something goes wrong, Mom may stop speaking to you.

Friends are also dangerous, for exactly the same reasons. This is an area that really needs a professional.

BUSINESS MANAGER CHECKLIST

When interviewing business managers, take another look at Chapter 2 for general questions, then add these specifics:

1. What kinds of financial reports are you going to get, and how often? (You should get monthly reports.) Ask to see samples of the reports. Are they clear? Can you understand them?

2. What is the business manager's investment philosophy? Will they only keep your money in conservative, short-term paper (meaning bank deposits or government notes of thirty-days to one-year duration), or in highly speculative pork belly futures? Don't settle for the gobbledygook that says, "We tailor our services to every individual's needs." Ask what they'd do for *you*. And why.

3. Is he or she a *CPA* (certified public accountant)? Accountants who are certified have passed rigorous exams and at least have that part of the job down. Whether they have the other skills to be good business managers is a different question, but at least they're true professionals who have trained extensively and are required to follow the CPA's code of ethics.

4. How much do they charge? (This is discussed in detail below.)

5. What's the business manager going to do besides paying your bills and keeping track of your income?

   Will they do your tax returns? (Some charge extra for tax returns or send them to outsiders who charge.)

   Are they going to handle your investments or hire an outsider? In either case, are they paid for investments?

   Do they do projections, budgets, and forecasts of your income and expenses?

   Do they coordinate wills and estate planning? Oversee buying and selling houses? Monitor your insurance needs? Oversee divorces?

6. Do they have a dedicated tax staff? As you get more successful, you're going to need specialized tax advice. For example, when you tour in the United States, you may have to file tax returns in every state you play. And international touring gets even more complicated tax-wise.

7. What security systems do they have in place to safeguard your money? How strictly do they screen their employees? What checks and balances keep a bookkeeper from turning up on a yacht in Venezuela, lighting cigars with your money?

8. Does the business manager want a written agreement? Most business managers require written agreements, although some don't. It isn't a bad idea, because it spells out exactly what's going on. However, don't ever agree to a deal that locks you in to them for any period of time—you should be free to leave whenever you want. If there's a written agreement, be sure you see it in advance and have your lawyer look it over.

9. Does the business manager represent music clients? This may seem like a silly question, but some very talented business managers—even those who do film and television—have no expertise in the music industry, and you don't want one of them. The music industry is very specialized, and you need someone who understands its intricacies. For example, if they don't understand music publishing, they can't do a good job of making sure you're getting paid everything you're owed by the publisher. Good business managers know when something should have come in but didn't; someone without industry expertise may not.

10. Have they handled people with your particular problems and challenges? If you're a new artist, you want to be sure they know how to watch every penny so you can survive. You also want to be sure they have time for you. If you're a superstar, you want to make sure they've handled, for example, mega tours, which require massive financial controls (as we'll discuss in Chapter 23), as well as knowledge of how much venues should be charging, what you should pay for a truck rental, how to minimize taxes, etc.

11. Do they have *E&O* (**Errors & Omissions**) *insurance*? E&O insurance pays you if the business manager mishandles your affairs. If they have insurance, how much do they carry? Also, ask if their insurance only covers accounting, or does it also cover investing advice.

12. If you live outside the United States or plan any extensive touring or other activities outside the U.S., do they have international experience? I probably don't have to tell you that meshing the tax laws between several countries (much less understanding the tax laws in any one of them) is a major pain, and if you have (or think you'll have) these kinds of problems, you need someone who's been down that road.

13. Do they get **referral fees** from any place they might put your money (such as buying insurance, putting your money in a

specific bank, running your investments through a particular stockbroker, etc.)? A *referral fee* is an amount paid to the business manager for sending your business to a particular place, as compensation for referring you there. Ideally, they shouldn't get any such fee because it could affect the advice they give you— they might be inclined to put your dough with someone who gives them a fee, even if it's not in your best interests. However, if the existence of the fee and the amount are fully disclosed up front, and if the business manager is willing to credit it against their fees, and if you get independent advice about the particular transaction, this could be okay. Maybe. Put your radar up if you see it; it's a serious red flag.

14. How do they handle check signing? It's now possible for artists to see and approve checks online through a secure system, so ask if the business manager has that capability. If not, you may want to sign the bigger checks.

15. Will the business manager object to your auditing them periodically? (An **audit** means you send in an independent person to see if the business manager has properly handled your money.) A lot of people are reluctant to audit their business managers. They think it's awkward because it looks like they don't trust them. In fact, the ethical business managers welcome it—they have nothing to hide, and they understand it gives you peace of mind to know everything is as it should be. (You can figure out which ones don't want you to audit.) Auditing a business manager is expensive ($25,000 plus), so it's not worth it unless you earn substantial monies. However, when you get to the big leagues, an audit is important to consider. If you raise the issue up front, there won't be any hassles later on.

16. Be sure the business manager wants to educate you, rather than just pat you on the head and say, "Trust me, kid." Most decisions can be condensed down to a fairly simple summary, and you should make all the significant decisions yourself. Be wary of someone who just wants to tell you what to do and seems offended if you question it.

FEES

How you pay your business manager varies, depending on your circumstance. The custom is for them to work on either a percentage basis

(5%), an hourly rate, a flat fee, or a combination. Some people earn tons of dough and have uncomplicated lives. If this is you, go for an hourly rate or a set fee. Others earn much less and always seem to have financial troubles. If that's more your style, go for a percentage. (Ironically, if your finances nose-dive, you may need more of your business manager's time than when you're doing well—he or she has to keep the wolves away from the door and turn pennies into nickels. This, of course, comes at a time when you can least afford to pay.)

With percentage deals, a lot of business managers want a minimum fee, because they have legitimate costs to set up their systems for you. So, unless they're willing to take a flyer in the hope that you'll someday be hugely successful, they want their downside covered. These minimums are in the range of $2,000 to $5,000 a month, but can be much more for superstars. Sometimes the minimum fee is a discounted hourly rate (for example, two-thirds of their normal rate). Under these arrangements, they get more dough if they do a lot of work, but you pay less than if they were on an hourly rate. Whatever minimum you work out, it will be against (meaning a prepayment of) the percentage.

If you do a percentage deal, many business managers will accept a maximum fee (called a **cap**). You should always ask for this, particularly when they're charging you a minimum. The cap will vary with the amount of money you earn and the amount of work you require. They're generally around $150,000 to $300,000 per year (which means, if you're paying 5%, you're earning $3 million to $6 million a year). Minimum fees for people in this range are about $30,000 to $125,000 per year.

When you make a percentage deal, it should only apply to money **received** (not **earned**) while the business manager is involved. Also, ask if it applies to investment income. With some business managers it does, while with others it doesn't. If the business manager is farming out investments to independent advisors (as most of them do these days), I would try not to pay a percentage of investment income.

If you don't do a percentage fee deal, most business managers charge an hourly rate. In this case, spell out what the rate is, and be sure they tell you the rate for everyone involved, not just the top people.

Sometimes, if the business manager is young and hungry, or if you have a lot of clout, he or she may be willing to take a **flat fee** for all services, regardless of the amount of work. Often it's a flat fee for normal services, plus an additional amount for touring work (which is reasonable, because touring takes an enormous amount of time and resources).

Listen again! Let me say this one more time: BE EXTREMELY CAREFUL in picking your business manager. More careful than you are with anyone else on your team. This is the person who can make sure you have a cozy old age, or leave you playing supermarket openings in your fifties.

YOUR HALF OF THE JOB

Just as important as picking the right business manager is your own attitude. I remember seeing one of Elvis Presley's bodyguards at a press conference. A reporter asked why he didn't stop Elvis from taking drugs. His answer: "How do you save a man from himself?"

That answer really hit me. I've always felt it was one of the most telling statements about an entertainer's life. If you don't care about your financial future, it's difficult for anybody else to. If someone is constantly telling you not to do something (like spend money), and you really want to do it, you'll probably get rid of them rather than listen. Remember Dick Gregory's quote (see page 29). If you're going to spend everything you make, then start spending money you don't have, you're going to end up broke. It's that simple. And it doesn't matter how much you earn. So don't do it, unless you subscribe to my partner Chuck Scott's philosophy: "The best way to build a small fortune is to take a large one and dwindle it down."

Few things last forever, and an assured stream of earnings at your highest level is not one of them. So even the best business managers can't help you if you overspend on jets, yachts, houses, cars, and controlled substances.

I know: You're reading this and saying it will never apply to you. But only you can make sure it doesn't.

5
Attorneys

GREGORY

*"We've got Tom O'Brien on bass, Nick Weber on
drums, and Jonah Petchesky on contracts."*

©*Alex Gregory/The New Yorker Collection/www.cartoonbank.com*

Now for a subject close to my own heart. It's hard for me to be totally
objective about this one, but I'll try.

PICKING A LAWYER

Role

Attorneys in the music business do much more than just look over
contracts and advise clients about the law. They're very involved in
structuring deals and shaping artists' business lives.

Lawyers have evolved into one of the most powerful groups in the music industry, odd as that may sound to you. The reason is that the power bases in the music business aren't concentrated in any one group. (For example, in the film business, the major agencies are the most powerful players. In the music biz, the agents are powerful but limited in their sphere of influence, as we'll see in the next chapter.) Personal managers are very powerful, but the nature of their job limits the number of clients they can take. Business managers can have a lot of major clients, but they deal only in limited financial areas and are therefore not power bases. Lawyers, on the other hand, are involved in all areas, and because the time required for each client is less than that of a personal manager, they can handle more clients. This means the attorneys end up seeing more deals than anyone else, and therefore have more knowledge of what's "going down" around town. Consequently, they can be influential in determining which company will get a particular deal, which means the companies want to keep them happy. They can also influence which personal manager and which business manager get a client, which means these guys also want to keep the lawyers happy. This means lawyers have power (and are happy).

Style

There are distinctly separate styles of attorneys in the music business. Some are into "hanging out" and acting as if they're one of the band members, while others stick to the business side. There are power broker/agent types, who are good negotiators but not particularly good lawyers, and excellent lawyers who lose sight of the big picture. And of course there's a whole spectrum in between.

Using the techniques in Chapter 2, first assure yourself you're talking to a good, competent lawyer. After that, the match-up of style is mostly a matter of your personal taste. For example, if you like flash, you may want a flashy lawyer (although I find more often that flashy artists like their lawyers to be staid and solid). If you're honest and straightforward in your business dealings, be sure to get an honest and straightforward lawyer (your references will tell you who is and isn't). If you aren't, there are unfortunately lawyers to match you.

Clout

It's true that a lawyer with clout can get through to people that other lawyers can't (or at least they can get through faster). Indeed, one of the major things to look for in a lawyer is his or her relationships in the industry. Let me illustrate with a story about remodeling my house: Over the years, I went through a number of house remodels, always looking for the cheapest possible price (which meant dealing directly with the workmen). I finally got sick of that process, so I broke down and hired a contractor. During this job, for the first time, I realized the value of a general contractor. In the past, whenever I called up a tile man, electrician, plumber, etc., these people couldn't have cared less about me. They came to my job when it was convenient for them (if ever). If my sink leaked for a few days, they didn't care because they had a lot of other customers. On the other hand, when the contractor called, they jumped. The reason was pretty simple: If they didn't satisfy the contractor, they didn't just lose one job, they lost their next year's work.

The same applies to lawyers. Record companies can't ignore phone calls from important lawyers, nor can they afford to treat them shabbily in any particular transaction. The reason is the same as with the contractor—they're going to be dealing with the lawyers over and over, and they don't want to make enemies of them. So a lawyer with good relationships will get your deals done quicker, and if they know what they're doing, will get you the maximum that can legitimately be had.

You should also know what clout doesn't do. There is only so much you can get from any particular deal, regardless of who is asking. If a record company doesn't like your music, they're not going to sign you because of your lawyer. If they're hot for you, you'll get a deal even if you're represented by Kim Jong-un. Put another way, the real "clout" is your musical talent. (Note, I'm not talking about a lawyer's experience and knowledge—that is truly valuable, and will indeed get you the maximum from the negotiation. But you should have a perspective on the hyped-up importance of "clout.")

Loose Lips

Be especially wary of a lawyer who tells you about other clients' lives. Some lawyers, for example, will tell you exactly what deal they got for a specific client. Apart from the fact that this violates the attorneys' Canon of Ethics, it also means they will be telling other people about your deal. It may appear that these people trade confidential information for secrets they wouldn't otherwise have, but in fact the opposite is almost always the case—everyone knows they have a big mouth, so they're only told things that people want spread around.

FEES

Most lawyers in the music business don't charge on just an hourly basis. For the ones that do, the rates are from $300+ per hour for new lawyers, up to $1,000 or more for biggies. Some of us charge a percentage (usually 5%) while others do something known as **value billing**, often with an hourly rate or **retainer** against it. A *retainer* is a set monthly fee (like the business manager's minimum fee discussed on page 52), and it's either credited against the ultimate fee, or it's a flat fee covering all services. *Value billing* means that, when the deal is finished, the lawyer asks for a fee based on the size of the deal and his or her contribution to it. If the lawyer had very little to do with shaping the deal, but rather just did the contract, the fee should be close to an hourly rate (though I'll get heat for telling you this, because it's usually more). On the other hand, if the lawyer came up with a clever concept or strategy that made you substantial money, or the lawyer made the introduction, or created the deal from scratch, he or she will ask for a much larger fee. If your lawyer value-bills, you should ask in advance what the fee is likely to be, so there won't be any rude surprises. Sometimes you can pre-negotiate the fee, based on results. (For example, if I get you X, you'll pay me Y. If I get you two times X, I get Z.) At a minimum, get a ballpark range.

CONFLICTS OF INTEREST

A lawyer has a **conflict of interest** when his or her clients get into a situation where their interests are adverse (i.e., opposing each other). This is easy to see, for example, when two clients of the same lawyer want to sue each other. However, it's also a conflict when two clients of the same lawyer make a deal with each other.

Lawyers are ethically required to disclose their conflicts of interest to you. Your choice is either to hire another lawyer or to **waive** (meaning you "choose to ignore") the conflict and continue to use the same lawyer.

Because the entertainment industry is a relatively small business, those of us who practice in this field are continually bumping into ourselves when our clients make deals with each other. Most of the time these situations are harmless and can be handled simply, in one of several ways:

1. Each of the clients gets another lawyer (rare unless it's a pretty serious conflict).

2. One of the clients gets another lawyer (much more common).
3. The clients work out the agreement among themselves (or else the manager, agent, or business manager negotiates for them), and the lawyer merely draws up the paperwork, not representing anyone's interest.

When interviewing attorneys, you should ask if they have or foresee any conflicts of interest. Most ethical lawyers will bring it up before you do, but you should ask anyway. For example, your lawyer might also represent your record company, your merchandiser, your personal manager, producer, publisher, etc. It's not uncommon for a personal manager to recommend his or her own lawyer, business manager, etc., and thus it's not uncommon for lawyers to represent both the personal manager and an artist. Most of the time, this isn't a problem. However, if you get into a fight with your personal manager, the lawyer will probably have to resign (or at least resign your side if the manager was there first). And you can't expect him or her to represent you vigorously against the personal manager in making your management deal.

In short, there are no hard and fast rules about conflicts. If the lawyer is straight and ethical, you can usually live with their representing a few other people in your life. But if you have a problem with another of your lawyer's clients, you must seriously consider getting separate counsel. And if you just don't like the idea of your lawyer having these conflicts (which is a perfectly reasonable way to feel), get someone who's independent.

Conflicts, by the way, are not limited to lawyers. Business managers can have conflicts when they represent both a personal manager and an artist (for example, when there's a dispute over commissions). Managers can have conflicts when they act in some other capacity (such as becoming the producer of the artist's motion pictures and negotiating a fee for themselves that affects what the artist gets paid). Managers can also have conflicts when they have two artists vying for the same gig. Like I say, it's a small business. But we generally work things out amicably.

A disturbing thing that's happened over the years is that some lawyers are selling conflicts of interest as a benefit to their clients. For example, they might suggest that you'll get a better deal with a certain record company or publisher because they also represent them. I'll give you my subtle opinion of this pitch: It's utter nonsense. For one thing, if the lawyer is being paid by a record company or publisher for work on other clients, it's human nature to think twice about how hard they want to beat them up and jeopardize a profitable relationship—especially for an artist who will pay them much less. Second, it's unethical for them to use any information they gain representing a company when negotiating against that company, and you can bet the company is neither going to like it nor permit it. So be wary of any pitch along these lines.

As I said earlier, it is certainly possible for you to live with a conflict, if you're fully informed and are comfortable that the lawyer will be in your corner. But a conflict is a reason to be careful, not a plus. Accordingly, the issue must be left to the tummy test. In other words, ask yourself whether your tummy feels like it's okay, or whether you're concerned about it. If you're concerned, get another lawyer.

ATTORNEY CHECKLIST

Here are some questions to ask your potential lawyer:

1. Do you have expertise in the music business? What kind of deals have you done?
2. What do you charge?
3. Do you have a written fee agreement? In California, lawyers can't enforce their fee agreements unless they're in writing, which is obviously a major incentive to have a written contract. If your lawyer requires one, ask for a copy, so you can review it.

   It's unethical in California for lawyers to have an agreement that can't be terminated at any time. If it's a percentage arrangement, be careful about what happens to the percentage after the term. See the discussion of this under management deals, on page 38.
4. You should ask if they object to your having the fee agreement reviewed by an independent advisor, preferably a lawyer, but at least a personal manager or business manager. No legitimate lawyer will object to this, and in fact they should encourage it. If it's at all possible, you should have your lawyer's fee agreement reviewed independently—especially if it involves a percentage. If it isn't possible to do this, make sure the lawyer explains it to you in detail, and that you understand it.
5. Do you have or foresee any conflicts of interest?
6. Ask for references of artists at your level and check them out. Does the lawyer return phone calls? Do they get deals done in

a reasonable period of time? "Reasonable" in the music business is not going to be anywhere near the speed you'd like. It's not uncommon for a record deal to take two to four months to negotiate, especially if you're a new artist and can't force the company to quickly turn around their contract drafts. Two to four months is a realistic time frame, but if it goes beyond that, someone isn't doing their job. I've always been amused by a story I heard from a new client when I was a young lawyer. He had been represented by another lawyer and, as he handed me his record deal, he said, "I know this is a good deal. It took over a year to negotiate."

6

Agents

ROLE

Agents in the music business are different from agents in the film business. While agents in the film business are the major power brokers in the industry, controlling most aspects of it, agents in the music industry are involved primarily in booking live personal appearances (concerts). Music agents are often involved in commercials, endorsements, tour sponsorship, television specials, and other areas, but they don't participate in (or get paid for) records, songwriting, or merchandising. Thus, they aren't involved in every area of the artist's life in the way that managers and lawyers are. So even though agents are extremely powerful players, their sphere of influence is limited.

FEES

Because agents aren't involved in your recording or songwriting (with the possible exception of film music, as we'll discuss on page 63), or your merchandising, you should never give them a piece of the income from these areas. Usually agents don't ask for this, but be careful of union forms, as noted in the next paragraph.

Agents are regulated by the unions: **AFM (American Federation of Musicians)** for musicians; **SAG-AFTRA,** a union formed by merging **AFTRA (American Federation of Television and Radio Artists)** for vocalists and actors on live and digitally recorded media with **SAG (Screen Actors Guild)** for film; and **Actors' Equity Association** for live stage.

The unions put a cap on how much the agents can charge, namely 10%. (For certain personal appearances under AFM jurisdiction, it can be more than 10%. However, the agents readily agree to a 10% maximum if you ask.) The AFM and AFTRA printed forms have a place for you to initial if the agency gets commissions on your earnings from records. *Watch out for it and NEVER do this.*

The union regulation of agencies is called **franchising,** and unions only allow their members to be represented by "franchised" agents, meaning those agents who agree to the union's restrictions. One of those restrictions is that the agency can only use contracts approved by the union, which results in each union having its own pet form, spelling out that union's particular requirements. So your agency contract looks like a fat coffee-table book. Actually, it's a stack of separate contracts: three for SAG (one for films, one for filmed TV, and one for filmed commercials); one for AFM; one for AFTRA; one for Actors' Equity; and two (called "General Services" and "Packaging") to pick up everything that isn't covered by a union.

Don't tell them I told you, but some agents will discount their percentage to as low as 5% for artists generating major revenues. (This is only for concerts. They stay at 10% for films, TV, etc., unless you're a major hitter in those areas—and even then, they may not budge.) Sometimes there's a sliding scale, so that as your income goes up, the percentage goes down. The industry goes through cycles as to how easy it is to get this discount, so you have to check out the situation when it's relevant to you.

DEAL POINTS

The major things to negotiate in your agent's deal are the following:

Term

The agency will ask for three or more years, and you will want to give them only one year. Shorter is better for you, because you can split if things don't work out, or squeeze their commission down if things do. The result of this wrestling match depends on your bargaining power.

If you give more than a year, you should have the right to get out after each year if you don't earn minimum levels. (See the discussion of this under personal managers' deals on page 38; agency deals work the same way, except the numbers are lower because they don't represent all areas of your life.)

If you have some clout, you may never sign any papers at all (although some agencies get snippy about this).

Scope

If you're involved in the film business (for example, if you're a musical artist and also an actress, screenwriter, director, etc.), and if the agency is in both the film and the music business, the trend is for agencies to insist on representing you in all areas. Thus, an agency representing you in the film business will require you to sign with them for your musical concerts, and vice versa. This may or may not be to your advantage, and it becomes more negotiable as your bargaining power increases. Some agencies have a firm policy and won't let you in the door without a full package. Others are more flexible.

Exclusions

Similar to personal managers' deals (see page 35), you can exclude certain monies from commission:

1. As we just discussed, you can exclude earnings from records and songwriting without any difficulty. However, some agencies try to commission your soundtrack album royalties if the album is derived from a film in which they got you work as an actor or actress. I try to resist this, and I've been pretty successful for established artists. The agencies' main argument is that, if you have no career as an actor or actress, and the agency is instrumental in creating one, they should get paid on everything you get from being involved in the film. If you do agree to this, make sure it only kicks in if you're getting a major part in the film. It isn't fair for an agent to commission your earnings from musical performances (for example, your fee for singing the title song, your soundtrack album royalties, etc.) just because you're on-screen for ten seconds to tell the doctor she has a phone call. Your argument is that you don't need the agency to get your music into motion pictures (unless, of course, you do), so they shouldn't be commissioning an area in which you already have a career. Their argument is that, if they move you into a new arena (acting), and the soundtrack album is merely an aid to doing it, they should get paid on everything. Results vary with bargaining power.

   There are agencies that specialize in getting motion picture musical work for artists. In that case, of course, the agency will get commissions on your fee for writing music and/or singing, and your record royalties as well. They normally don't commission songwriter performance royalties, which are monies we'll discuss on page 225.

2. You should exclude things like book publishing (if you're so inclined), merchandising, and record producing. You should also try to exclude commercials, though this is getting harder. Even in excluded areas, however, the agents will want to get paid if they find you work. I like to say they can't look for employment in these areas without your consent. That way they don't come running in with a basketful of offers if you aren't in the market, or if you just don't want them involved.

3. You can also exclude costs of collection before applying the commission (as we discussed in managers' deals on page 37). In other words, if you have to sue a deadbeat to get paid, you should deduct the cost of the lawsuit from your recovery before the agent gets his or her commission.

Termination of the Agency

As we discussed above, your agency deal is a stack of union forms. Each of these union agreements has a clause saying you can terminate if the agent doesn't get you work (or an offer of work) for ninety days. Since these are separate agreements, with separate terms, you want a provision that says you can get out of all these deals if you have the right to terminate any one of them. Without this, the agency would represent you in some areas but not others, because they all have different termination criteria.

This clause is a bit hard to get if you only work in the music area. Since you've never had a film career, the agency can reasonably argue that they can't be expected to produce one in ninety days. The usual compromise is to say that, if the AFM or AFTRA agreement (the ones covering the music area) can be terminated for failing to get you work, then you can get out of everything.

Territory

If you're a new or even midlevel artist, and you're based in the United States, it's difficult to give an agency less than worldwide rights. If you're a non-U.S. artist, and already have a deal outside the U.S. with another agency, this isn't so difficult. Even for U.S. artists, however, you can sometimes exclude territories outside the United States if you have enough clout. This is often beneficial, because you can hire agents in Europe or elsewhere who specialize in those markets. In fact, some U.S. agencies use a local sub-agent for foreign territories, and you can thus eliminate the middleman. The major U.S. agencies, however, all have their own shops "over there."

At a high enough level, you might even eliminate a foreign agent altogether and deal directly with the concert promoters through your lawyer and personal manager (if they have the expertise).

On the other hand, even if the U.S. agency uses a sub-agent, they don't just sit there idly while the sub-agent does all the work. The American agency oversees the foreign agent and makes sure the shows are properly promoted, that you get paid on time, etc. It's also easier to deal with someone locally than to get up at strange hours and call around the world.

Double Commissions

Just like personal management deals, there should be no double commissions if you have a corporation (see page 43).

PICKING AN AGENT

If you have a personal manager, you'll have only occasional contact with your agent. You may meet when you first set up your tours, and you'll see them at your shows, where they'll tell you it's the best performance they've ever seen. The rest of the time, he or she talks to your personal manager and, to a lesser degree, to your lawyer and business manager. Thus, picking an agent should be primarily handled by your manager (since he or she deals with the agent most of the time), but you should make the final decision.

If you don't have a manager, the agent will report directly to you. In this case, the criteria for picking your agent should be the same as picking a manager. So take another look at page 44.

As always, make sure you get a good vibe from whoever you're hiring.

PART II

Record Deals

7

Broad-Strokes Overview of the Record Business

INDUSTRY STRUCTURE

Before we get into the various moving parts of record deals, and discuss whether you even want one, let's first talk about how records make their way from the oven to your table (well, tablet . . .). There are several designer methods to choose from:

Major Record Companies

There are three major record companies in the world today, and each owns a set of labels. They are Universal (Interscope, Republic, Capitol, etc.), Sony (Columbia, RCA, Epic, etc.), and Warner (Atlantic, Warner, Elektra, etc.). In addition to these mainstream labels, all three of the majors own "independent" distribution companies (more about those later).

In prior editions, I included a snappy little chart that showed the major divisions of record companies. Maybe I'll bring it back in the next edition, but currently several of the record label departments are shifting around like staircases at Hogwarts. That's because the transition to streaming has caused traditional jobs to morph into new ones, as well as morph into each other. Meaning everyone is still scrambling to figure out what the record company of the future looks like.

In particular, the line between what used to be the **sales** department (getting retail stores to buy physical records, plus making sure they're displayed prominently) and the **marketing** department (getting consumers to go into stores and buy the records) has gotten fuzzy in the digital world. For example, when someone places an ad for your song on the front page of a streaming service, it took a relationship with the streaming service to get that ad in a prime location (traditionally a "sales" job), but the ad is directed at consumers (traditionally a "marketing" job). So is that under the sales department or the marketing department? Moreover, the departments doing these jobs aren't the same at the different labels, either in name or function. So I ditched the record company org chart.

Okay. With all that in mind, let's move on to the promised lesson in record company anatomy.

Let's start with the departments that haven't changed in the new world, meaning jobs that aren't related to how music is delivered or marketed:

A&R.   These are the people with "ears" who find and nurture new talent, and who work creatively with the artists (see page 126 for a discussion of A&R people). Nowadays, they also work with the company's data geeks to catch new music that's starting to trend.

Promotion.   These folks live solely for the purpose of getting your records played on the radio. They spend their days "jamming" radio stations, and saying, "Dude," "Baby," and "Sweetheart" a lot. In the digital world, radio is less important than it used to be, but it still matters. Radio helps build an artist's visibility in general, and the streaming companies are more open to featuring your music if you're "happening" on the radio.

Finance.   They compute and pay your royalties—bless their little hearts—and keep track of the company's income and expenses. They also deal with audits, which we'll discuss on page 164.

Business Affairs/Legal.   These folks are responsible for the company's contracts, not only with artists, but also with digital service providers, foreign licensees, and more. Historically, business affairs people negotiated the deals and, in conjunction with other executives, decided what to give and what to hold. Then the legal department gave legal input and negotiated the contracts. Due to industry cutbacks, business affairs and legal are now almost always the same people.

International.   As the name implies, the international department coordinates the release of your records around the world and oversees everything happening in foreign territories. With some companies, marketing is now global, so there's not a separate international division.

Catalog. There is a separate marketing department for older product (called **catalog** product).

Film/TV. This department hounds people to use the company's recordings in movies, TV shows, and commercials. (It's also called a **sync department**, which we'll discuss on page 242.)

So much for the survivors. Now let's take a trip to Fuzzy Valley.

Historically the other record company departments were **Sales** (selling and shipping records to stores, making sure your product is displayed prominently), **Marketing** (publicity, album cover artwork, promo videos, ad campaigns, etc.), **Production** (manufacturing, printing covers, etc.), and **Product Management** (a point person in charge of making sure the other departments all did their jobs for your record).

This worked nicely when we were dealing with physical product, but as you know, physical product is now a vampire with a wooden stake in its heart, throwing off a few last twitches. So here's what these jobs look like today:

As we discussed, "Marketing" departments traditionally reached out to consumers, and "Sales" people reached out to record stores. Since the "stores" of today are the **digital service providers** (called **DSPs**) such as Spotify, Apple Music, etc., Sales and Marketing departments are now divided on the basis of who they're going after. Specifically, Marketing people deal with consumers, and Sales people deal with the DSPs (like they did with stores). Here's some more detail:

The marketing departments have different names at different companies but are usually called something like **Digital Marketing.** Their job is to hype your music to consumers through website design, social media marketing, etc. They also track social media engagement and collect data on how your music is trending (Are more and more people streaming it? Is it falling off a cliff?).

Similarly to the way Sales departments shipped physical records in the past, today's Sales departments are responsible for all the technical functions around digital files, such as correctly encoding **metadata** on the masters (*metadata* is the embedded information that tells the name of the song, artist, album, who to pay, etc.) and delivering digital files to hundreds of DSPs around the world. Most important, however, is that Sales people push the DSPs to maximize streams of your music. For example, Sales folks try to get you featured on the DSP's home page. They also try to get you on playlists, and as I understand it, playlisting is a pretty complex area. For example, you don't want unknown music too early in a playlist (listeners skip it, and DSPs keep track of which songs are being skipped so they can dump them), but you don't want your song too late in the playlist (because people stop listening before they get to it). Their goal is to drill your music deep enough into a subscriber's brain so that it ends up on their personal playlist. That way, they keep listening to your music (and making you money) long after the record was released. This is known in the industry as **lean back,** meaning that someone is listening to their own playlist (or a DSP-created playlist), as opposed to **lean in,** where they're actively searching for new music.

As for other departments:

Product managers now handle the logistics of things like TV appearances, or Facebook and Spotify promotions.

Production now plans releases, meaning they get together final edits of the music, credits, delivery to the DSPs, etc.

Some companies also have a **Strategic Marketing Department** that finds endorsement and sponsorship opportunities for artists (and takes a percentage of the deals).

Finally, we come to **Distribution.** The major record companies' records are all distributed by **major distributors,** which are gigantic distribution networks that are owned by the major labels' parent companies. These distributors coordinate digital distribution and move physical records from manufacturing plants into the stores. They also report streaming data to the record labels.

Independents

Independents are record companies that aren't owned by a major, and they come in two main flavors:

True Independents.   A true independent is not owned by a major label, either in whole or in part, and is a fully functioning record company on its own. Examples are XL, Merge, Epitaph, and Victory. True

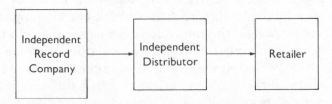

Figure 1. Independent record company distribution.

independents generally distribute their records through **independent distributors**, which are set up to deal with the specialized needs of independent companies (though some larger independents distribute through major label distributors in a few situations).

Strange as it sounds, most of the big independent distributors are owned by the same companies that own the major labels. Specifically, RED and the Orchard are owned by Sony; Caroline is owned by Universal; and ADA is owned by Warner.

Major-Distributed Independent. This is an independent entity that has little or no staff, but rather signs artists and makes a deal with a major label to perform many (sometimes all) of the functions beyond recording the records. These companies may be truly independent in ownership, or they may be owned in whole or in part by a major record company, such as Sub Pop, which is partially owned by Warner.

The primary thing these companies bring to the party is the ability to find talent and then mercilessly beat the distributing company to make sure their product gets promoted. Product released by these companies may be on the independent's own label, or it may be on the distributing company's label (in which case the public may never know the independent company exists). This type of entity is discussed in detail on page 191, in connection with independent production agreements.

Here's a chart, and note that "Retailer" means streaming services like Spotify and Apple Music, digital stores like iTunes and Amazon, and the disappearing physical retail locations (which are called "brick and mortar" locations, like Walmart).

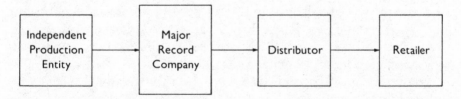

Figure 2. Major-distributed independent record company.

A WORD ABOUT RETAILERS

At the time of this writing, brick-and-mortar record retailers are on the endangered species list, waiting for their appointment with Dr. Kevorkian. The pure record store is virtually extinct, because there's not enough CD and vinyl business left to support it. A few independent stores are hanging on, but even they have to sell posters and other merchandise to stay afloat. There are some oddball places, like Urban Outfitters, that sell vinyl and even cassettes, but overall vinyl is less than two percent of the business. And as the CD's heartbeat continues to slow down, it's hard to see how anyone (other than maybe a few specialty shops) can survive in the long run.

Today, most of the CDs and vinyl in the United States are sold by Amazon and **big-box retailers** (so named because their stores are in the shape of gigantic boxes). Specifically, Walmart and Target handle the biggest chunk of the physical business (I use "chunk" in the smallest possible sense). As CD sales continue to shrink, these big boxes keep cutting back the number of CDs they're willing to carry in their stores—in fact, as I write this, most of them only carry the top-selling titles. In addition, these stores are cutting back the amount of floor space they're willing to devote to CDs. That's because they want to get the most money from their real estate, and if selling vacuum cleaners is more profitable than selling CDs, the dirt suckers win. All this, of course, becomes a vicious cycle: If the stores carry less product, CD sales drop even more, because there's less available to buy. Which means the big boxes cut more floor space. Which means even fewer sales.

There's of course no doubt that streaming is the game of the future. At the time of this writing, streaming accounts for more than 75% of recorded music revenue in the United States and is growing rapidly both in (a) overall dollars, because of added users, and (b) as a percentage of overall sales (because, in addition to streaming dollars getting bigger, physical sales and downloads are shrinking fast).

If you want the most current figures, take a look at the **RIAA** website (*RIAA* stands for **Recording Industry Association of America,** which is an industry group formed by the record companies): www.riaa.com/u-s-sales-database.

You might ask why you need a distributor for streaming. Can't you just license your music to Spotify and be done? Well, you'd have to license all the services, and there are quite a lot of them floating around the world. And even if you did, it takes a lot of effort to stay on top of all those licenses—the major labels have hundreds of employees to do that. However, you can easily get your music on all the DSPs through services like TuneCore or CD Baby (more about them on page 76), and they'll handle the licensing and tracking. Which makes an artist wonder if they need a record company at all.

And which happens to be our next topic . . .

DO YOU NEED A RECORD LABEL?

Historically, record companies held the keys to the kingdom. It took a large organization (and a lot of money) to manufacture and ship records to stores (you needed manufacturing plants, warehouses, sales forces, shipping people, freight charges, financial controls, etc.). Also, in order to really sell records, you had to get your music on the radio, which took a promotion staff and a lot of money.

In those days, the record retailers were so big that they wouldn't bother with small players. That meant, if you didn't come through a major record company, it was hard to get your product on their shelves at all. Also, frankly, the big record companies paid retailers a lot of money to position their product prominently in the stores. So even if an artist managed to get their records into the retail bins, they'd likely get buried in the back. If, somehow, an independent artist's records started selling anyway, the retailers would pay the artist late (if at all), since one little player didn't matter to them. On top of all this, the artist would have to put up the money to manufacture the records. And if the stores didn't sell them, they'd be returned to the artist, who'd lose the manufacturing costs, plus the freight costs in both directions.

So, putting this all together, you can see it took a big player to absorb these risks.

Well, Dorothy, we're not in Kansas anymore:

1. While it's still difficult to get your physical product into stores (now it's because the stores carry so few titles), brick-and-mortar retailers are way less significant, as we just discussed. And, as we also discussed, it's easy to get your music distributed digitally.

2. Radio is still important for mainstream artists, but less so than it used to be. Also, radio has become a very narrow channel—in other words, it plays only a limited range of music genres, and not a lot of different titles. That's because radio stations aren't in the music business; they're in the advertising business. And their sweet spot is attracting 16 to 24 year olds, so they only want to play music that brings in those folks. Because of this, alternative ways for people to discover music have become more important, and streaming playlists are quickly becoming the new radio.

3. As we discussed on page 15, a direct relationship with fans is the next generation of marketing, and young artists are proving savvier in this area than a lot of established companies.

On top of all this, as you'll see shortly, when you make a deal with a record company, you give up control of your recordings (as well as other aspects of your life, such as the ability to do music for films, commercials, concert videos, etc.), and you also give up a chunk of your income from both record *and* non-record areas (which we'll also discuss in a bit).

So, why would you want a record company?

Well, if you're a niche artist (for example, a jam band or backpacker), and you're happy staying in your niche and selling to a small group of fans, you may not need or even want a record deal. As we discussed, it's easy to get your music to Spotify, Apple Music, Amazon, Pandora, and other digital outlets (through outfits like TuneCore and CD Baby, who we'll discuss in a minute), and you can make a living doing gigs, promoting yourself directly to your fans, and selling your tracks. Because your genre limits your potential audience, you'll often make more money by doing it yourself than you would if you signed to a record company. For a record deal to make sense, the company has to generate more money for you (after they take their piece) than you would get by going it on your own. With niche artists, that's often questionable.

If you're more mainstream, such as hip-hop, pop, or country, this is a much tougher question. You can set up a killer Web presence, build a fan base, and market to them. Since your music has a wide appeal, if you break through, you'll make far more money by keeping the record company's share of the pie, not to mention keeping all of your non-record income. But here's the problem: The same way that it's easy for you to set all this up, it's easy for *everybody* to set this up. At the time of this writing, there are more than ten million artists on SoundCloud and Facebook, and who knows how many on YouTube. How's anyone going to find your music?

There are some "virtual" record companies who can help. These companies were started by talented people who left record company jobs when the industry melted down, and they'll do everything from sales to marketing, promotion, etc., under a deal that lets you keep complete control. However, they charge pretty heavily for these services, which most new artists can't afford. Thus, they've mostly been successful with artists who've already released a few albums (and therefore have a decent-sized fan base).

DIY, or Not to DIY?   If you decide you want to release your own music (known as **DIY** in the biz, for **Do It Yourself**), you can easily get it on all the digital services through sites like TuneCore and CD Baby, who charge a flat fee per year. TuneCore provides only digital distribution, but CD Baby will sell physical product for a flat fee per CD (at the time of this writing, CD Baby charges $4 per CD; you set the price to the public and keep the balance. However, they have a minimum order of 50, so you're taking the risk that they don't sell, meaning you pay $4 per CD whether it goes out the door or not). And unlike TuneCore, CD Baby also charges a percentage of the money from downloads. The Orchard (owned by Sony) will also do both digital and physical, but they are much more selective about what product they take. The Orchard takes a percentage of revenue, and they also charge a setup fee. For the most current pricing and services, check out their various websites.

When your music is available, it doesn't help much if no one knows about it. And there's a LOT of competition for consumers' attention, as we just discussed. So you have to get the word out by using the same techniques and online resources we discussed on page 15 (in the section on "building your buzz"). You might want to take another peek at those if you're going DIY. Hurry back. Don't leave me dangling here . . .

As of this writing, most mainstream artists still want to sign to a record company. Apart from guaranteeing you money (so you can avoid sleeping on park benches while creating your music), the record companies have the resources to get your music heard above the noise of all the other artists out there. They have staffs of people with experience in marketing and promotion, relationships with streaming services that can get your music featured, and radio relationships that can get you airplay. Also, the major labels have massive amounts of data from all over the world, which they use to develop strategies. So for these reasons, a lot of artists choose to go the label route, and this even includes artists who do quite well on their own. A common pattern is for an artist to get to a certain level, then move to a label because they feel they need the company's resources to take their careers to the next level.

Having said that, more and more artists are doing extremely well on their own and may decide to stay that way. The future in this area will be very interesting, so stay tuned.

Assuming you want a contract with a record company, lemme show you what those babies look like.

WHAT'S A RECORD?

Let's start with a real basic: What's a **record**?

Interestingly, in virtually every record agreement, the contractual definition of *record* includes both **audio-only** *and* **audiovisual re-**

cordings (meaning recordings with both sound and visual images, such as music videos). Surprisingly, this language has been in deals since the 1960s, which is before videocassettes and DVDs were even invented.

Also dating back to those early days, the definition of records has also included (and still does) any other device *now or hereafter known* that is capable of transmitting sound alone, or sound with visual images. And even more important, the current deals define "records" to mean *any kind of delivery of your performances for consumer use,* whether sound alone or with visuals. This language is designed to ensure that the company has rights to mobile, Internet, and whatever else comes down the pike.

As you'll see later, these broad definitions in record deals can make life a bit tricky if you're a recording artist and also an actor or actress in films. Stay tuned (or peek at page 140 if you can't wait).

By the way, did you know that, originally, records were made by having the musicians and singers perform for each record sold? That's because there was no mass duplication process in those days, and thus the recordings were made directly onto the wax that was ultimately sold (meaning every record in a store contained a unique, one-time performance). Can you imagine how sick you'd be of a song that sold a million copies?

MASTERS

The word **master** has two meanings:

1. The original recording made in the studio is called a **master,** because it is the master (meaning the original) from which all copies are made.

    Master recordings are now almost entirely done on computer hard drives, and the recordings are **multitrack,** meaning that each instrument and voice part is recorded on a separate track: the drums on one track, guitar on another, voice on another, etc. When the recording is finished, the master is then **edited, mixed,** and **EQ'd.** As in films, *editing* means cutting out the parts you don't like and splicing in the parts you do. *Mixing* means getting the right level for each track, so that the drums are the right volume during each particular part of the song, the voice is raised a bit on the chorus, etc. Also as part of mixing, the sounds may be enhanced through processes I have never completely understood. *EQ'ing* stands for **equalizing,** and means that the bass, midrange, and treble are each adjusted to the right level (so that no one of them overpowers the others). The mixed multitrack is then reduced down to a two-track stereophonic master, which is ready for the duplication process.

You may have also heard the term **stems.** *Stems* are the individual track recordings of each instrument and each vocal, usually in the two-track stereo mix form that's used in the final record. You need stems for **remixes,** which means, not surprisingly, a new mix of the original record (such as a dance mix, club mix, radio mix, etc.). You also use stems when you perform live to the track, or when you use a different version of the master, for example without the vocals in an audiovisual work).

So there are two masters—the original multitrack, and the finished two-track.

2. The word **master** also means a recording of one particular song. Thus, you might say an album has "ten masters" (meaning ten selections) on it. These individual recordings are also called **cuts,** because of the historical process of cutting grooves into vinyl for each song.

ROYALTY COMPUTATION

Enough about art; let's talk about money.

We'll start with your royalties.

Basic Concept

My brother-in-law, Jules, was in the used car business. He was famous throughout the West Valley because he'd trade cars for anything. At one point, he traded a car for a silver tea set, a set of golf clubs, and a mule. (Honest.) He then traded the mule, along with a stained-glass window of Daffy Duck, for an English bulldog named Rosie.

About that time, my wife and I were looking for a dog. It was before we had children, and we wanted to test our parenting skills on something that wouldn't use drugs if we failed. In trying to decide what kind of dog we wanted, we used to take Rosie for outings on weekends. In a perverted way, we began to think of her gnarled face and drooling as cute. Anyway, Jules decided he was going to breed her, and we wanted a puppy. So I helped him find a stud dog, through a sophisticated referral system—the Yellow Pages (for you young 'uns, Yellow Pages were the Internet in those days). I called a place named Royal Family Bulldogs, which conjured up images of some country squire's dogs lounging around on velvet pillows. It turned out to be a dilapidated house in Pacoima, the most impressive feature of which was its bulldog smells. But Royal Family had a brown-and-white champion stud named Winston, so Jules hired Winston, and Rosie got pregnant.

After a few weeks of this, Jules decided he wasn't interested in the headaches of small puppies. So he enlisted the help of his friend Corky. Corky's deal was that she would take care of Rosie and the puppies, then when each dog was sold, she'd get half of the sales price. So if a dog sold for two hundred dollars, Jules would get a hundred dollars, and Corky would get a hundred dollars.

What does this have to do with records? Well, your record royalty is very much like Jules's share of the bulldog proceeds. In the case of records, the artist (Jules) turns the recordings (pregnant Rosie) over to the record company (Corky), who then monetizes the finished product (puppies). For each record (puppy) sold, the artist gets a piece of the money, and the company keeps the rest to cover its costs and make a profit.

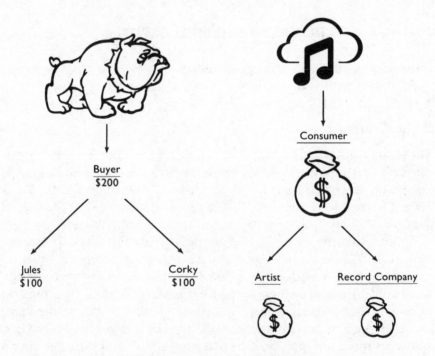

Figure 3. Bulldogs and royalties.

Basic Royalty Computations

The division of proceeds between the artist and record company is a bit more complicated than the puppy deal. In fact, for many years, this process was more complex than NASA's formula for getting the space shuttle home. But then, in a surge of *Why can't we all just get along?*, the companies shifted to a much simpler system. You get off easy—I had to learn all the complicated crap. (I included a section on how it used to work in Appendix A at the back of the book, titled "Ye Olde Royalty Calculations." It's only included because (1) there are a number of older deals written this way, (2) I spent hours writing that section and hate to see it go to waste, and (3) even though I know nobody ever reads anything titled "Appendix," I thought you might need it some night if you have trouble sleeping.)

And now, we return to our regularly scheduled programming.

To follow this next part, we'll need to use a little math. Don't worry if numbers aren't your strong suit—I'll go slowly. I explained these concepts to my cousin David, who has to take off his shoes and socks to count to twenty, and he understood them.

Here's how it works:

1. For streaming, it's just like the bulldogs. The artist gets a percentage of what the record company receives for streaming your recordings. This is really as straightforward as it's ever been in the business (the early accounting magicians, who found many ways to screw artists while smiling at them, must be rattling in their graves). In other words, if the company gets $100 from your recordings, and you have a 10% royalty, you get $10.

    There are, however, a few bumps along the way to figuring out how much money your percentage applies to, and one particularly important issue around foreign streaming that we'll discuss in a minute.

    The basic streaming economics work like this:
    a. Each month, the streaming services count their total streams. Just to pick an easy example, assume that all the music on Spotify had a total of one million streams last month (they actually have billions, I'm just using numbers that make for simple math).
    b. Next, they look at how many of those streams were your record company's masters. If your company had 300,000 streams that month, it would be 30% of the one million total streams.

    c. Spotify next looks at their total revenue for the month (subscription money and advertising revenue). Let's say that was $1 million. They divvy that up among the record companies on the basis of how many plays came from each company's masters. In our example, since your record company had 30% of the total streams, they'd get 30% of the $1 million, or $300,000. (By the way, there's some controversy around this calculation, which we'll discuss on page 145.)

    d. The record company then looks at the number of streams of each of their artists. Using our example of 300,000 streams for your company, if you had 60,000 of those streams, you'd be 20% of the record company's streams for that month.

    e. Accordingly, 20% of your record company's $300,000 revenue from Spotify would be allocated to your masters ($60,000).

    f. The record company then applies your royalty rate to the $60,000 attributed to your masters. So if you had a 10% royalty rate, you'd get 10% of $60,000, or $6,000. (Again, these numbers have nothing to do with reality; they're just simple numbers to make the math easier. Major streaming artists can make multi-millions from streaming, even after taking out the record company piece.)

2. For downloads and CDs, which of course are quickly shriveling into raisins, the artist royalty is a percentage of the **wholesale price.** The companies also call this price the **published price to dealers** (**PPD** to its friends), or sometimes (mostly outside the United States) the **base price to dealers (BPD).** So if the PPD for an album is $7 (which is about right these days), and you have a 10% royalty, you get 70¢ for each unit sold or downloaded.

    In either ease, each royalty percentage is known as a **point,** so if you have a 10% royalty, you have 10 *points*.

Physical Peculiarities

When it comes to physical product, there are a few wrinkles in computing royalties that don't apply to digital. Physical is of course rapidly becoming irrelevant, but these provisions are still in every record deal, so you should take a look. Or skim through. Or skip to the next chapter. Or go walk the dog. Your call.

Free Goods

CD royalties are paid for each record *sold*. Why do I emphasize the word *sold*? Well, the companies give away some CDs to retailers, which are called **free goods,** more specifically **special campaign free goods**. This practice started when the companies wanted to push out large numbers of a particular artist's album. To get stores to stock more of it, they gave away 10% or more of all records shipped. Originally, these were short-term deals (a few months), but they've evolved into a near-permanent arrangement.

Because record companies don't get paid for these free goods, they don't pay royalties on them. In reality, they are just a discount of the price. If you have some clout, you can limit these free goods to 10% of total CDs shipped.

Promotion Copies

Records given away for promotion, such as radio-station copies, contest giveaways, etc., are also free goods and don't bear royalties. They are known as **promotional** or **promo** (pronounced "pro-moe") records. These don't go to retailers and the physical ones are marked "not for sale." They are also disappearing, as radio now gets everything digitally. Besides, what contest winner wants a CD?

Return Privilege

To understand this next part, you need to know that physical records are sold with a **100% return privilege**. This means, if a retailer orders one hundred records from RCA but can't sell them, it can bundle them up, ship them back to RCA, and get credit for (or a refund of) the price it paid. This practice is pretty unusual. In most businesses, if you buy a load of plastic flamingos and can't sell them, you eat them.

To see why the return privilege is important, let's go back to Rosie's puppies. A customer comes to Corky's house and wants to buy one of the dogs. But she isn't sure the puppy will get along with her children, so she says, "I'll give you a check for the puppy, but hold it while I take the dog home to play with the kids. If, after a week or so, everything is going well, you can cash the check. If not, I'll bring the dog back for a refund." Corky agrees, willing to do anything to move the little nippers out of her living room.

Later the same day, she tells Jules about the deal. Jules then asks for his half of the check (which of course Corky can't yet cash), and Corky suggests he have intercourse with himself. She says he can have his share when the buyer decides to keep the dog.

Reserves

The **reserves** used by record companies work exactly the same way (usually without the suggestion for self-intercourse). Because CDs are sold on a 100% return basis, the companies don't know, particularly with a new artist, whether the records will sell to customers, or get returned by the retailer. Because the records may come back, the companies (like Corky) keep a portion of the royalties that would otherwise be payable to the artist (Jules) until they know whether the sales to the retailer are final. This holdback is called a *reserve* against returns.

For example, if a company ships 10,000 CDs of an artist, they may only pay the artist on 6,500 of these and wait to see if the other 3,500 are returned. At some point in the future (usually within two years after the shipment), the monies are paid through to the artist. The technical term for this pay-through is called **liquidating** the reserve. Of course, if the records are returned, the reserves are never paid to the artist because the sales are canceled, and the royalty is never earned.

The size of your reserves varies with how well the company thinks the CD will sell, and also with how well it thinks your *next* CD will do. For example, if they think your next CD will sell extremely well, they'll be less concerned about holding big reserves—if they hold inadequate reserves and overpay you, they can take the money back from your next album. However, if you're a new artist and they're not sure there is even going to be another CD, or if this is a "one-off" record such as a soundtrack album, or if this is the last album under your deal, you can anticipate healthy reserves and a record company attitude along the lines of "If you don't like it, stuff it." (As your bargaining power grows, you can put caps on reserves. See page 161 for more on this.)

8

Advances and Recoupment

ADVANCES: THE BASIC CONCEPT

Back to Jules and his bulldogs. Our friends at Royal Family charged him a $300 stud fee for the services of Winston. Let's suppose Jules didn't have the $300. Corky (who's agreed to raise the puppies in exchange for 50% of the sales price) comes up with an idea: She says she'll pay Jules the $300, or pay it directly to Royal Family, and then take her money back from Jules's share of money from the puppies. For example, if the puppies sell for $200 each (so that Corky gets $100 and Jules gets $100 for each dog), Corky would keep Jules's $100 share of the first three puppies ($300) to get back the stud fee.

This is exactly how a record company **advance** works. The company pays a sum of money to the artist (the $300 stud fee) and then keeps the artist's royalties (the proceeds from selling the puppies) until it gets its money back. So if a company gives an artist $10,000 to sign a record deal, it keeps the first $10,000 of royalties that would otherwise be payable to the artist. The process of keeping the money to recover an advance is called **recoupment,** and we say an advance is **recoupable** from royalties. The amount of **unrecouped** monies is called your **deficit** or **red position** (from the accounting use of red ink to signify a business loss), since this is the amount that has to be recovered before you get paid. So if you got a $100,000 advance and earned $75,000 in royalties, you have *recouped* $75,000 of the advance, and your *deficit* is $25,000 (you are $25,000 *in the red*, or $25,000 *unrecouped*). Once you recoup, you're said to be **in the black.**

Here's another way to look at it:

When I grew up in Texas, it was a big deal to drive just outside the city and look at the huge water tanks with the names of towns painted on the side. (It takes very little to make me happy.) In fact, Farmer's Branch, a city outside Dallas, had a water tower that was a major local site. (Not as famous as its post office, however, because the sign there said FARMER'S BRANCH BRANCH. Honest.)

Anyway, picture a water tower with a big ol' connecting pipe that runs deep into the ground. The connecting pipe feeds into a dry well that needs a thousand gallons of water to fill it up to ground level. If there wasn't any other access to the water, you'd have to wait until it filled the well up to ground level (that is, until a thousand gallons had been poured in) before you could get any water. If there were only five hundred gallons, you couldn't reach it (see Illustration A in Figure 4), but when another five hundred gallons was added, you could (see Illustration B).

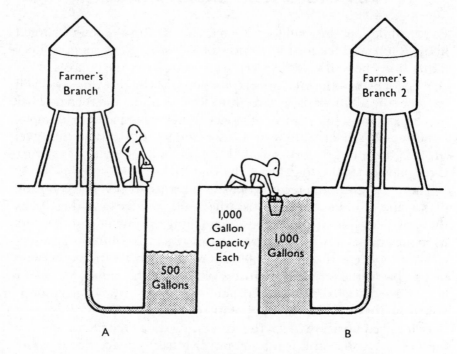

Figure 4. Deficit and recoupment.

Recoupment works exactly the same way. The water represents your royalties, and the ditch is your deficit account. If you got a $1,000 advance from the record company, your account is $1,000 unrecouped. Until you earn $1,000 of royalties (i.e., until you have enough water to fill the well), you don't get anything. In other words, just like the hole needing a thousand gallons of water before you can get a drink, the record company needs to keep the first $1,000 of royalties before you get any money.

Other Goodies

Monies paid directly to you are not the only recoupable monies. Recording costs are also recoupable from royalties, and so are some portion of costs for video production, independent publicity, independent promotion (see page 175 for what that means), advertising campaigns, website creation and hosting, monies paid on your behalf (for example, to buy equipment or to support a personal appearance tour, wardrobe, vocal coaching, choreography), and anything else that isn't nailed down.

Recoupable recording costs include everything you can think of, which is often a page-long list in your record deal. It's not just studio time; it includes equipment rental, travel, arranging, instrument transportation, etc. It also includes **union scale** (**scale** means the minimum amount a union requires everyone to pay its members) that's paid to you and others to perform at recording sessions.

In addition to a specific list of recoupable stuff (like cash to you, recording costs, and video costs), every contract has a general provision that says all amounts "paid to you or on your behalf, or otherwise paid in connection with this agreement" are recoupable unless the contract specifically provides otherwise. You can feel the history jumping from the pages on this one—Charlie Artist asked his company to advance the cost of a trip to see his mom, and then argued the money was non-recoupable because the contract didn't say it was recoupable. This of course is wrong, but the broad language that the companies now use is overkill—sort of like using a sledgehammer to squash a fly (which is effective, but messes up the kitchen). In practice, the companies don't abuse this language, but I like to add my own broad language, saying they can't recoup amounts that are "customarily nonrecoupable in the industry."

Risk of Loss

What happens if you don't sell enough records to get back the full amount of the advance? With very rare exceptions, such as your failure to deliver product or otherwise seriously breaching your contract, advances are **nonreturnable,** which means it's totally the record company's risk. So if you don't sell any records, it never gets back its advances. (This nonreturnable aspect is also significant because it means advances are taxable income when you get them, as opposed to when they're recouped.)

CROSS-COLLATERALIZATION

An important concept tied to recoupment is that of **cross-collateralization**. Remember the illustration on page 86, with the two towers side by side, and two 1,000-gallon wells? The water tank for one of the wells contains exactly 1,000 gallons, which means the well is full and the water usable. The other tank has only 500 gallons, so you can't reach the water. Suppose we dug a hole underground that connected these two wells. In that case, the same 1,500 gallons (500 from Well A and 1,000 from Well B) would be distributed equally between the wells (750 gallons in each), and you couldn't reach the water in either of them (see Figure 5 below).

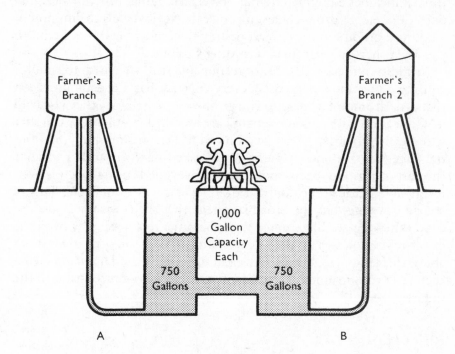

Figure 5. Cross-collateralization.

Cross-collateralization in record deals works exactly the same way as the connected wells. And it's built into every deal.

Let's assume you get a $100,000 advance for album number 1, plus another $100,000 for album number 2. Now suppose album number 1 earns royalties of $10,000, and album number 2 earns royalties of $120,000. If the two albums were *not* cross-collateralized (the two wells were not connected), you would get nothing for album number 1 (it only earned back $10,000 of the $100,000 advance, so it's $90,000 unrecouped), but you'd be paid $20,000 for album number 2 (the $20,000 earned in excess of the $100,000 needed to recoup the $100,000 advance). However, except for very rare circumstances, this only happens in Fairyland. In the real world, the two albums are always cross-collateralized (i.e., the wells are always connected), which means the entire $200,000 deficit ($100,000 for each album) gets recouped from the entire $130,000 earnings ($10,000 from album number 1 plus $120,000 from album number 2). Accordingly, your account is $70,000 unrecouped ($200,000 less $130,000), and this deficit carries forward against the next album(s).

Cross-Collateralization of Deals

Cross-collateralization can also apply to different *agreements*. These can be simultaneous agreements (for example, an artist signing a recording and publishing agreement with the same company), or they can be sequential (such as an artist who, at the end of a record agreement, signs a new deal with the same company). In either case, the concept is that advances under either agreement can be recouped from royalties under both. This is *never* good for the artist. NEVER.

Most companies include language in their form contract that automatically cross-collateralizes the deal with all other deals. Major record companies don't try to cross-collateralize a record deal with a publishing deal, but small labels may (see page 291). However, everyone tries to cross-collateralize *sequentially*, meaning that advances under your current recording deal are cross-collateralized with royalties under past and future record deals. The language that does this is buried innocently in the recoupment language and can easily be missed by the untrained eye. It says that advances and costs can be recouped from royalties payable, and royalties can be used to recoup advances and costs paid, "under this *or any other agreement*." (Your eye is now trained—so don't miss it!) I've been reasonably successful in knocking this language out of artists' first deals by arguing that the issue should be discussed later, if and when there is a second contract. My argument is that there is no other deal to cross-collateralize with, and until there is, the language is meaningless. That reduces the point down to who is more likely to forget about it—the artist or the company—at the time of the new deal. (Don't worry: The company won't forget.)

9

Real-Life Numbers

OVERVIEW

Let's start to plug some real industry figures into these concepts.

What's Your Clout?

Well, I basically chucked the section on determining your clout that was in the prior editions because it dealt with album sales levels, which are almost irrelevant in the streaming age.

Weirdly, the industry still translates today's streaming numbers and single-track downloads into album sales equivalents, since that's what they're used to. For example, the U.S. industry uses the following criteria to determine whether an album is gold (historically, the sale of 500,000 units) or platinum (one million units):

1. 10 single-song downloads equal the sale of one album. This is known in the biz as a **Track Equivalent Album** (or **TEA**—pronounced one letter at a time, not like a drink in the English countryside).
2. 1,500 streams equal the sale of one album (known as a **Streaming Equivalent Album,** or **SEA**—also pronounced one letter at a time, not like the . . . you get the idea).
   TEAs and SEAs are referred to collectively as **STEAs.**
3. And of course a CD sale and a full-album download each count as one album sale.

I predict at some point we'll switch to a pure earnings formula to determine gold and platinum, like the movie industry box-office reports, but we're not there yet. If we do, the figures may only be available inside the industry, not publicly. I could see it being a bit touchy for an artist's fans to see multi-millions in earnings (especially since it's at retail, and the artist only gets a fraction of it). Publicly reporting an individual's earnings feels different from a movie studio's reporting box-office earnings. But logically this is how things should be measured, so we'll see what happens.

At any rate, when determining your clout, it's now based on what the company thinks of your streaming potential in the future. Your genre of music is also very important to your deal size. For example, at the time of this writing, the biggest streaming numbers are in hip-hop and pop, while rock bands are having a tough go. In addition, hip-hop artists tend to put out a lot of product, certainly more than pop, and that of course drives up your numbers.

But when it's all said and done, just as it's always been, the more record companies that are chasing you, the better deal you're going to get.

So here's some categories I've made up, just to have a frame of reference. These aren't industry terms, just things I pulled out of my esophagus to give you a general idea of how things break down. Also, these aren't precise points on a map; most folks would fall above, below, and in between these categories. But we gotta start somewhere, so let's use these:

1. *Minor heat.* New artist, who's not in the hip-hop space, with some social media activity, and one, maybe two, labels interested.
2. *Moderate heat.* Good social media presence, strong Sound-Cloud numbers, moderate amount of streaming. Two or more labels chasing.
3. *Heavy heat.* Most likely hip-hop or pop, with almost every label frothing over you. Usually your current product is showing strong streaming numbers, and the record label wants to distribute that current product as well as future recordings. Add a good deal more degrees of heat if you're an artist with a track record of prior releases getting bigger each time.
4. *Superstar.* Streams and social media in the stratosphere, with consistent performance over time, or, even better, growing numbers.

ROYALTIES

Range of Royalties

Using the above categories, the following is the current industry range of U.S. royalties:

1. **Minor Heat:**
   15% to 17%
2. **Moderate to Heavy Heat:**
   17% to 20%
3. **Superstar:**
   20% plus, often higher on streaming. At this level, with an enormous amount of clout, you can sometimes make an off-center deal like a joint venture/profit split (see page 200), or even a distribution deal where the artist owns the masters (see page 197).

Let's go deeper.

1. **Streaming.**
   Sorry, what did you say? Oh, yeah, I wondered how long it would take you to ask . . .
   What's each stream worth?
   The answer is, "It depends." It depends on:

   (a) Is it streamed on a service that is subscription only (Apple Music, for example)?
   (b) Or is it on a service that is both subscription and advertiser supported (in other words, some users don't pay a monthly fee but instead listen to commercials, like Spotify)?
   (c) Is it on YouTube, where it's only advertiser supported?
   (d) Is it on Pandora, which has a whole different calculation?
   (e) Is it outside the United States? If so, the amount you get varies from territory to territory.

   We'll discuss all this in depth a bit later (on page 232), but you can see there are so many variables that there's no easy rule. For example, you'll get much more per stream on Apple Music than you will on Spotify, because the advertising generates much less per subscriber than a subscription does, and the vast majority of Spotify users don't pay a subscription fee. And in last place, because YouTube is only advertiser supported, it generates substantially less per stream.

As a *VERY* rough rule of thumb, I've heard figures thrown around in the range of $3,500 to $5,000 for each million streams, again depending on where the streams are. This is the amount that goes to the record label, meaning your share of that is equal to your royalty percentage. For example, if you had a 10% royalty, you'd get $350 to $500 for each million streams.

Please don't put a lot of stock in these figures, as they may well be out of date by the time you read this, and even more importantly, there's no accurate way to answer the question without plugging in your specific streaming situation.

The major concern for artists in calculating streaming income has to do with an issue we call **at source.** "At source" came from a game that was played years ago in the publishing world. It had mostly died, or at least was handled openly, but has been spectacularly resurrected for the streaming era.

We'll talk about this more in the publishing section (on page 256), but the essence of the "at source" issue is that a multinational company's foreign affiliates take a percentage of the streaming income before it comes back to the United States, and therefore the artist isn't paid on 100% of what the streaming service pays. For example, Apple Music pays $100 to your company's affiliate in France. The French company takes 25% of the money, and sends $75 back to the United States. When the company applies your rate to the streaming money, you only get a percentage of the $75, not the $100. And as you'll see in Chapter 12, you may also have a reduced royalty rate in foreign territories. So it's a double hit.

The companies argue that this deduction is for the profit margin for their affiliate, which is doing marketing, promotion, etc. in that market. Not entirely untrue, but then again, it's one big company and all the money ultimately ends up in one pocket. And even without the deduction, the company gets the majority of the money.

More and more, the majors are moving to pay streaming "at source" worldwide for new deals, but you should be sure that's in your contract. If you're signing to an independent label, who doesn't own the foreign company, or signing with anyone else who won't agree to an "at source" royalty, you should limit the percentage that the foreign company can charge. For example, say that the affiliate can't take more than 15% to 25% before it sends the money back to the United States.

The other exception to "at source" is legacy artists, with old contracts. In the olden days, record companies paid artists 50% of their net receipts from licensing masters to third parties. At that time, it really only covered licensing songs for movies, TV shows, and the like. However, since streaming is a license, these old deals entitle artists to 50% of the company's net receipts from streaming, which is much higher than their royalty rate for CDs. In response to this, the labels take a very large intra-company reduction (like 30% to 50%, sometimes even higher) before applying the artist's 50%. As you can quickly figure out, that reduces the artist's royalty substantially.

2. **Downloads/CDs.**
At the time of this writing, the wholesale price of digital downloads is 70% of the retail price (so if it's $9.99 retail, the wholesale price is just under $7.00; if it's $10.99 retail, wholesale is about $7.69). Most top-line CDs sell for a wholesale price of $8.50 to $10.00 or sometimes more (the higher end is for superstars or albums with bonus material, such as extra tracks). So to figure the number of pennies you'll get, multiply your royalty rate times those amounts. For example, if you have a 15% royalty, and the average wholesale price of your album is $9.00, then:

PPD (wholesale price)	$9.00
Royalty rate	× 15%
ROYALTY (ROUNDED TO PENNY)	**$1.35**

Remember (as we discussed on page 83) that this can be reduced by 10% or more for special campaign free goods.

Historically, the royalty rate for physical singles was lower, on the theory that record companies made very little profit on singles (which was true). The singles rate was normally three-quarters of the album rate, but it topped out in the 10% to 12% range, occasionally up to 14% for superstars. This is now almost irrelevant, as physical singles have essentially disappeared, but some contracts still reduce your royalty for singles. That's truly not fair when most of the world is single-song streaming, or single-song downloads, so the key thing is to make sure your contract limits the reduced rates to *physical* singles.

Escalations

It's common to escalate royalties based on sales. And yes, the contracts still say that the escalations are based on album *sales*, even though actual sales are falling like fruit flies. To determine escalations, they use the STEAs we just discussed on page 90.

Typical escalations are .5% (sometimes you can get 1%) at some level between 250,000 and 500,000 album equivalent sales, and another .5% (or 1%) at 250,000 to 500,000 albums beyond that point. So, for example, if your royalty is 15%, it might escalate to 15.5% for sales over 300,000, and to 16% for sales over 600,000. The lower your royalty rate, the sooner you can expect the escalations to kick in, and in fact you may even be able to get a third bump. These escalated rates usually top out around the 18% range for artists with minor heat, 18% to 20% for moderate to heavy heat, and 20% to 21% or more for superstars.

These escalations only apply to sales occurring after the level is reached, and are called **prospective** escalations. For example, if you have 16% on the first 300,000 units, escalating to 16.5% thereafter, you don't get 16.5% on the first 300,000. If you have enough bargaining power, you can sometimes get the escalations on prior sales (called a **retroactive** escalation). This is extremely rare, and if you can get it at all, it's usually for stratospheric sales. For example, at sales of 2 million units, you might get an increase on the first 500,000.

In a standard contract, escalations apply only to **full-priced sales** (as you'll see later, there are reduced royalties for sales at less than full price, and of course the company's profit margin is also reduced). Typically, escalations are also limited to sales in the United States, but as your bargaining power goes up, so does your ability to get escalations in other major territories (such as Canada and certain European markets) based on sales in those markets. Because these are smaller markets, the escalation sales levels in each are lower.

As noted above, one element of determining gold and platinum albums is that a download of ten single tracks equals one TEA (track equivalent album). You, of course, want to make sure these also count for escalations. The labels now all agree to this, but some contracts say that you only get one TEA if you sell the number of tracks on your album. In other words, if you have twelve songs on your album, it takes twelve downloads to equal one album sale for purposes of escalating your royalty. Usually you can knock this down to ten, because the price of ten single tracks equals the price of a digital album, and also because the industry uses ten tracks as a TEA for gold and platinum status. But some companies are stubborn. If you have to agree that it's the number of tracks on your album, be sure to say it's the number of tracks on the "standard version" of your album. It's common to do special versions of albums with **bonus tracks** for a particular retailer (for example, an exclusive piece of product for Target with two tracks that aren't available anywhere else). These special versions shouldn't be the standard for your TEA.

SEAs (streaming equivalent albums) should also count toward escalations, and it's either (1) based on a number of streams (e.g., 1,500 streams equal one album sale, as we discussed for gold and platinum status), or (2) with some companies, an album SEA is the number of streaming dollars that equal the PPD of one album. For example, if the album PPD is $7.00, then $7.00 of streaming royalties is the equivalent of one album sale.

"All-in"

The above royalties are known by the technical term **all-in,** which means the artist is responsible, out of his or her royalty, for paying the record producer, the mixer, and any guest artist. (Producers' and mixers' roles, and how they're paid, are discussed in Chapter 11. However, I suggest you wait 'til we get there before tackling the subject unless you're already familiar with royalty calculations.)

The practice of paying artists an *all-in* rate began in the early 1970s and is now the industry norm (excluding a few oddball situations, like in classical and sometimes in country music). Accordingly, the all-in rate is not what the artist puts in his or her pocket; that amount is the all-in rate *minus* the amount paid to the producers and mixers (and any guest artist), which is called the **net rate**.

ADVANCES

In the 1950s, artists would go to the studio, sing their little hearts out, and have almost no other involvement in the creative process. In those days, companies paid the artist a set amount of money as an advance (for example, $10,000 for an album). The record company paid all the recording costs (which are recoupable from royalties, just like an advance), and everybody went their separate ways. It took maybe two weeks to do an album; three if you were a perfectionist; four if you were a pain in the ass. (A fast-track album today takes six to eight weeks, and more typical is three or four months. More established artists, who are busy touring, promoting, or generally being persnickety, can take a year or more to finish an album.)

Funds

Today, most recording agreements are structured as **funds.** A fund is a set amount of money, which includes both recording costs and any amounts that may be payable to the artist as an advance (the term *recording costs* also includes the producer's advance, which we'll discuss later). Whatever the artist doesn't spend on recording costs goes into his or her pocket. For example, if the recording fund for an album is $200,000, and the recording costs are $150,000, the artist pockets $50,000 as an "advance." On the other hand, if the recording costs are $200,000, the artist pockets nothing.

Here's a rough range of all-in recording funds:

1. **Minor Heat, Signing to Independent Company:**
   Zero to $100,000, occasionally even more, though most new artist/independent company funds are in the range of $25,000 to $75,000. If that sounds like a big range, it is—the amount of the fund is proportionate to the number of people chasing you. It's also based on whether you want to take a big check and a smaller royalty, or a small check (or nothing) and a big royalty, or even a share of the company's profits from your records.
2. **Minor Heat, Signing to Major:**
   A fund in the range of $100,000 to $200,000, occasionally running up to $500,000 if you're really hot. If you're urban/ hip-hop, or a pop artist, the deals (at least for the first album) are often advances plus recording costs. (We'll discuss the range of those advances in the next section.)
3. **Moderate/Heavy Heat:**
   $300,000 to $750,000, with a few particularly hot artists kicking way up.
4. **Superstar:**
   $1,000,000 and up. A really big artist's fund can run into multimillions of dollars. At this level, funds are computed on the basis of past track record and future expectations, as well as the bidding in the marketplace.

Advances

Fund deals are the norm in the record biz, except for hip-hop artists, and for pop artists (balladeers, crooners, adolescent boy bands, etc.). (Bizarre to think those two worlds have similar deals, but hey, it's showbiz.) For the urban/pop deals, it's common for artists to have pure advances plus a mutually approved recording budget. How come? Well, as you'll see when we discuss producer deals (on page 125), hip-hop and pop producers get truckloads of money, and the albums get very expensive. This means contractual funds (if they're within the orbit of the earth) won't be enough to record an album, much less leave any money for the artist. So, at least for the first album, some companies give hop-hop artists an advance plus mutually agreed recording costs. These advances are typically in the range of $50,000 to $200,000, but can go way higher if there's heat.

After the first album, hip-hop deals are usually funds.

Pop artists are in the same range of advances, though their deals are often advances plus costs throughout the entire contract.

Budget Woes

If you have a fund of $200,000, what keeps you from recording a super-cheapo album for $25,000 and pocketing $175,000? In all of these deals (unless you have a lot of bargaining power), the record company has to approve the budget for your recording costs, precisely for this reason. Well, partly for this reason. Actually, they're more worried about the other end—that you'll set an unrealistically low budget and not be able to finish your album for less than the fund. This is particularly common with new artists, because their contractual recording funds are lower. For example, albums can easily cost $150,000 or more, and that could be the entire fund. Moreover, if you're using producers of any note, that can radically jack up the price. As we'll see when we get to Chapter 11, top producers can get advances of $25,000 or more per *master*, and I'm sure you can see how quickly this turns into a giant sucking sound.

So what happens when you've spent your full recording fund and have three-quarters of an album? Historically, most of the record companies paid to finish the record, under the age-old business strategy of "What the hell are we going to do with three-quarters of an album?"

But this is about to change radically.

In recent years, companies are more and more "testing the market" by releasing product before committing to a full album, and in the pop world, this is already close to becoming the norm. For example, they might release one song, or submit a song to a test group, to see what kind of reaction it gets. If it's only moderate, they might rinse and repeat. Or hit the garbage disposal button.

It's also becoming common in the pop world to release a few singles or an **EP** (standing for **extended play**), which is five to seven tracks. If they like the way things go, they'll do an album. If not, it's back to Poughkeepsie.

In hip-hop, the trend is to release a large number of tracks at the same time (for example, some artists have released twenty-four songs at once). It's also common to release multiple albums per year, particularly including **mixtapes.** *Mixtape* has a fuzzy meaning. Originally, mixtapes were (a) mixes of other people's records with your music, (b) given away for free, and (c) called **underground** because they didn't bother to get permission from other people to use their music (we'll talk more about what you're supposed to do in connection with sampling on page 250). Since the people who created that other music weren't exactly happy, and they had a nasty habit of suing everyone, including the record company, there are very few true (if any) underground mixtapes anymore. Instead, mixtapes are now released only after the label has cleared the rights, meaning there's no real difference between a mixtape and any other album (except that you decided to call it a "mixtape"). The occasional, truly underground, uncleared mixtapes usually come from artists acting on their own (at least until they get slapped a few times).

So looking at the big picture, you can see that the model of the past—record an album every few years, get an advance—is falling apart. Nowadays, it's a few tracks in the pop world, then maybe an album (at least in the beginning), and in hip-hop, it's releasing massive product as fast as you can get it out. This is particularly relevant to the question of how much product you're required to deliver under your record deal, which we'll cover on page 108. In reality, this area is still a work in progress, and we don't yet know exactly how it will work out. But we're getting there . . .

Formulas

If you know enough to ask for it, most record companies will agree to something called a **formula** for advances. This is a mechanism designed to automatically increase (or decrease) your deal if you're successful (or a flop). It works like this:

Your advance for the second album is equal to a percentage (usually 60% to 70%) of all royalties *earned* (as opposed to paid) by the first album under the agreement. For example, if the first album earns $1,000,000 in royalties and you have a 60% formula, the advance for the second album is $600,000.

The advance for album number three is a percentage of album number two's earnings, and so forth. Sometimes the formula is an average of the prior two albums' earnings, which is better for the company because if one album spikes and the other is so-so, the formula is reduced.

Formulas only use earnings in the United States, plus other territories if you can negotiate that (try to add Canada and the United Kingdom at least). Also, it's only earnings in those territories from (a) the streaming of tracks included in the album, (b) sales of the album (physical or download), and (c) single-song downloads of tracks from the album. Can you figure out what's missing? We haven't really covered it yet, so don't feel bad if you can't. The answer is at the end of this section (on page 101).

Formulas only count earnings that happen within a certain period of time (usually twelve to eighteen months after release), so that sales trickling in over a two- or three-year period won't increase the advance for an artist who is slow in delivery. The last thing a company wants to do is reward late delivery.

If you can't get a formula right away, try to get it on the third or a later album.

But what happens, you say, if the first album is a dismal failure, and earns only $20,000? How can anyone make an album for $12,000 to $14,000 (60% to 70% of the $20,000)? Well, you can't, so this is handled by establishing a **floor** in the formula. A floor means that no matter how lousy the earnings of the previous album, your fund will not be less than an agreed amount (the *floor*). Not surprisingly, as soon as record companies hear the word *floor,* they think of a concept called a **ceiling,** which means that no matter how wildly successful the prior album, the fund won't exceed an agreed dollar figure. (The prospect of owing you $4,000,000 for an album makes them nervous.)

Some companies want to reduce your fund if you're unrecouped, by deducting the unrecouped balance from your formula advance. They argue that this saves them from disaster if you have a big album after a series of losers. For example, suppose the formula for your next album has a floor of $200,000, and a ceiling of $600,000, and your last album earned enough to hit the maximum $600,000. However, all your albums before that last one were turkeys, so you're $450,000 unrecouped. Under this provision, the company deducts $450,000 from the $600,000 formula advance and pays you $150,000 (even though your floor was $200,000).

One slight problem with this clause: If you were $800,000 unrecouped in the above example, subtracting that amount would eat up your entire $600,000 fund, and you'd get zippo. The same thing would happen if you were $300,000 unrecouped and only qualified for the floor advance of $200,000 (from which they'd subtract the $300,000). Since it's pretty hard to make a record for zero, you have to tell the company you need something called a **subfloor** (meaning a floor below the floor). For example, your contract might say you get the formula advance, less any unrecouped amount, but not less than a subfloor of $125,000. (We'll discuss a similar concept in songwriter deals on page 291.)

Historically, both the floors and ceilings escalated for later albums, varying with the bargaining power of the parties. A recent trend is for companies to keep the floors at the same level (with maybe slight increases) and only escalate the ceilings, to protect the company's downside. Here's a recent new artist deal:

Album No.	Floor	Ceiling
1	$175,000	(no formula)
2	$175,000	$400,000
3	$200,000	$450,000
4	$200,000	$600,000
5	$250,000	$750,000

Don't get excited about the big numbers for the last albums. The company isn't really committed to them, as you'll see on page 110.

When the deal is for an advance that goes directly into the artist's pocket (*not* a recording fund), the formula percentage is of course much less, usually in the 15% to 20% range. The floors and ceilings for option years would go up in roughly the same percentages as the funds. For example, a formula for the third album might be 15% of the prior album's earnings, not less than $125,000, or more than $250,000.

Answer to question: So what earnings are missing from the formula? Licenses to use your masters in commercials, or in movies or TV shows (we'll talk about this on page 150). The reason it's not included is that these can be one-off types of things, and therefore skew the formula for your next album over something that may not repeat.

360 RIGHTS

Welcome to the land of **360 deals.** You may not like the climate.

The name comes from the 360 degrees in a circle, because record companies now want to share in the total pie of an artist's income (or maybe it's because they want to corral you). Under these deals, the companies get a piece of an artist's earnings from touring, songwriting, merchandising, fan clubs, sponsorship money, motion picture acting, modeling, garage sales, and so forth. (Okay, I made up the garage sales part to see if you're paying attention. Don't tell the record companies, or they'll include them in their next contract.)

These deals started because the record industry was in such financial distress that the companies couldn't survive on their record business alone. So they grabbed pieces of other income. Their argument (the sugarcoating on the 360 grab) goes like this: "In this new world, we are no longer just a record company, confined to a narrow lane. We are now an artist brand-building company. Of all the players in your life, we are the only ones who spend substantial money to make you a household name. Then, thanks to our rocket launch, you make tons of money by touring, songwriting, selling your face to teenagers on T-shirts, etc. This isn't right. We should share in all the businesses we help build for you. Besides, we'll have a much bigger incentive to spend money on you if we know we have an upside beyond records. Oh, and one other thing. We won't sign you if you don't agree."

It's true that record companies are the only ones spending substantial money to break an artist's career, so their argument has some merit. On the other hand, many people see this simply as a land grab, arguing that the company brings no value to the party beyond their record business expertise.

Whatever you think of these arguments, 360 deals are here to stay because record companies like making more money (as do most of us). Thus, from the major labels down to the independents, virtually all the companies are insisting on some kind of 360 rights. Meaning, if you want to sign a record deal, you gotta live with it. Maybe this will change as streaming grows massively and the companies are again flush with cash. Maybe my dog will learn to play the bagpipes.

With enough bargaining power, you may be able to trim back the 360 pie. Sometimes (actually, it's becoming "rarely") you can get a "180 deal," meaning the company only gets a share of one other income stream (songwriting, touring, or merchandising [selling merchandise with your name or likeness on it]) or two of the three streams (called a "270"). Sometimes, for real superstars or other extremely hot artists, it's just a record deal. Or a minimal 360 participation. But it's getting harder and harder.

Record Company Share

How do 360 deals work? Well, they vary quite a bit from company to company. Because of antitrust laws, record companies can't talk to each other about these deals, so there's no "industry custom"; instead, we have a patchwork of practices. Most companies want from 10% to 25% of the artist's net income from non-record sources, with the majority of deals falling in the 10% to 20% range (touring is different, as we'll talk about below). I know that's a big range, but it varies a lot with bargaining power, and from company to company. It can also vary by category (e.g., 20% for publishing, but 15% on merchandising). And it can go away in some areas if the company takes "active" rights, which we'll discuss in the next section.

If you already have a non-music career before making the deal, say as an actor or model, you should exclude that altogether.

The definition of your "net income" (against which the company's 360 percentage applies) is the source of some debate in making these deals. Artists want to deduct as much as possible before paying the record company, and, shockingly, the record companies want to limit these deductions. Except for tours (which we'll discuss in a second), the language is usually something like "gross receipts less customary, third-party, arm's-length expenses." They say "third party" to keep you from cutting your brother in for a chunk, which he gives back to you in a brown paper bag. They say "arm's length" to make sure the expenses aren't any higher than you would pay in the open market.

Most companies put a limit on the total commissions you can pay your representatives (manager, agent, lawyer, and business manager) in computing "net income." This cap is usually around 30% to 35% of your gross earnings, though at least one company tries to cap commissions at 35% of *net* (meaning 35% of your gross income after deducting all expenses other than commissions). If the cap is based on your gross earnings, 35% is probably okay, figuring 15% for a manager, 10% for an agent, and 10% to cover both the attorney and business manager. (Note: If your lawyer and business manager are not on a percentage, make sure the language allows you to deduct their cost. Some contracts only say you can deduct "commissions." Of course, if the company agrees to your deducting fees that are not commissions, the 30% to

35% limitation on deductions still applies.) If you go over the cap—for example, if you're paying your manager 20%, and you can't keep the others down—you should ask the record company to increase their cap to reflect reality. Results will vary with bargaining power.

You can of course pay commissions that exceed the cap, but you don't get to deduct the excess in computing what you owe the record company. So it's a double hit.

If the commission cap is 35% of your *net* earnings, that's much more of a fight, because there's a good chance you'll go over it. This is less of a worry for non-touring income, because the expenses aren't as significant. For example, the money you get from a publishing company is after they've already taken their expenses, so your "gross income" is already a kind of "net." Thus, you can probably craft some variation of this that's livable.

The "net income" discussion gets particularly thorny when you talk about tours. The companies have two worries:

1. As you'll see when we discuss touring (in Chapter 23), artists are lucky to take home a fraction of their gross income, and when you're a new artist, you'll likely lose money. So the record company is worried that their share of net will mean little or nothing. (Of course, you're not doing so well, either.)
2. At the other end, when you start to make some real dough on the road, the companies worry that you'll charge lots of questionable goodies against your tour income, for the purpose of reducing the amount you have to pay them.

To keep you from playing games, most companies now insist on a percentage of your *gross* income from touring, before you deduct any expenses or commissions at all (the same way an agent is paid). The gross percentage is of course smaller (from 5% to 10%, occasionally less if you have some clout), and sometimes it's a minimum: for example, the company gets 20% of net, but not less than 7.5.% of gross. And just like our discussion of management commissions that are paid on tour gross income (on page 33), this could mean the record company gets paid when you lose money.

The companies are usually willing to accommodate new artists by not taking their percentage for monies under a certain dollar amount. For example, they don't get paid on the first $100,000 to $500,000 of your touring income, which is called a **shelter.** The shelter can sometimes mean you keep that amount of money every calendar year (meaning, for example, they don't participate in your first $100,000 of touring income each year), which is best for you. But companies often want the shelter to apply to each period of the term of your record deal, which can be much longer than a year (as we'll discuss on page 114). When you earn more than the shelter, you pay the company a percentage of the excess.

Even if your touring is profitable, paying the company on gross could mean they make more from your tours than you do. And of course if you're not profitable, it's a seriously heavy burden. As a practical matter, if you can't afford it, they will usually work with you. But you should get the best protections you can up front.

Another compromise is to pay the company on "adjusted gross" tour income, which means you're allowed to deduct certain expenses, but not others. For example, they might allow you to deduct your agent, true road expenses (like sound and lights), and maybe accounting fees, but not things such as legal fees, management commissions, and the like. Or they may not allow you to deduct any costs other than commissions, which will be subject to the commission cap we discussed. The specifics vary with your bargaining power.

Besides their financial interest, most labels will also want to approve deals that involve any rights in which they share. This could really put a crimp in your life, having to go back to them all the time, waiting for their blessing. If you can't knock this out of the deal, the usual compromise is to say they get **consultation rights,** meaning you talk to them about what you want to do before you actually make the deal, but the final decision is yours.

Now speaking of the label getting into your other deals . . .

Active and Passive Interests

The record company's 360 share is usually what's called a **passive interest,** meaning the company has no control over the rights involved (other than any approvals or consultation rights we just discussed). In other words, you make whatever kind of deal you want with someone else, collect the money, and then write them a check for their share.

Some companies, however, actually take some of the rights involved, as opposed to just getting a piece of an outside deal. This kind of deal is called an **active interest.** For example, they might insist that you (as a songwriter) sign with a publishing company they own (or, more commonly, it's a publishing company that's owned by the same company that owns the record company—the company at the top is known as the *parent company*, because both the record company and publishing company are its "children"). If the record company or its parent company also owns a merchandising company (a company in the business of selling artist-branded T-shirts, posters, etc.), they may insist that you give your merchandising rights to that company. And even if you don't sign a merchandising deal with them, they will want the exclusive merchandising rights to the album cover and a couple of other designs for each contract period.

Some companies also want the right to operate your fan club and/or VIP ticketing (see page 386 for what that is).

And a few companies also want to act as your **promoter,** meaning produce your live concerts in some territories.

Try to keep the active rights for yourself. That way you can shop them around and drum up competition. However, if your label is being pushy, instead of giving them active rights, try to only give them right of **first negotiation** (meaning, for example, you talk to them before you make a publishing or merchandising deal with others) and a **matching right** (meaning you can look for another deal but have to let them match it, so they have the option to take you on), which is also known as a right of **first refusal.**

If you make an active deal with your company's affiliate, the contract will look just like any other deal in the area, and you should negotiate the same protections covered in the applicable section of this book. The difference, however, is that you may only get a small (if any) advance for these rights, as some companies consider it part of your dues to make a record deal.

Okay. So you fought the good fight but have to give them active rights. When you get paid under that deal, do you also have to write them a check for it, under the 360 provisions of the deal? In other words, if you sign with their merchandising company and get $5,000 under the deal, does the record label get 15% of that?

First of all, congrats if you thought of this question before you read it. Second, why should the record company be making money on both sides of the deal, when the active rights money and the passive money both go into the same parent company's pocket? Third, get ready for disappointment . . .

Labels argue they're entitled to this money because they are playing two different roles (for example, record company and merchandiser) and therefore should be paid for each. They argue (correctly) that if you made a merchandising deal with someone else, the merchandiser would make money for what they do, and the record label would get their passive money as well, so you're in the same boat. And why should they be penalized?

What they don't tell you is that the affiliate company has a separate profit center from the record company. That means the record company executives don't get a bonus if your merchandising soars, unless you give them 360 rights to the merch income.

With some clout, you can get rid of the record company's passive obligation if you sign with an affiliated company. But if you can't do this, try to reduce the 360 percentage. For example, if your deal gives the record label 15% of your merchandising money, maybe you only pay them 5% or 10% if the deal is with an affiliated company.

If you're on the *Fast Track* and
haven't decided to leave the
music business, go to Chapter 11 on
page 125. Everyone else, forward ho . . .

IF YOU DON'T UNDERSTAND THE WORDS IN THE BOX, IT MEANS YOU SKIPPED PAGES 8–9. IT ALSO MEANS YOU NEVER READ THE DIRECTIONS WHEN YOU BUY A NEW ELECTRONIC DEVICE.

10

Other Major Deal Points

The other major things you'll want to know about your record deal are "How much?" and "How long?" The "how much" part of this doesn't mean royalties and advances, which we already discussed, but rather the number of masters you have to record. The "how long" part means the period of time that the deal lasts, which sounds pretty straightforward but has taken some strange twists over the years.

AMOUNT OF PRODUCT

Commitments vs. Options

Record deals are traditionally structured with the company having the smallest obligation it can negotiate, while keeping the option to get as much product as possible. For example, a company may commit to record a few tracks or an album of an artist, then have the option to require an additional four or five albums, each one at the company's election. Albums to which the company is committed are called **firm** albums. The others are called **optional** or **option albums.**

As we discussed on page 99, the whole concept of how much product an artist delivers is changing. As of this writing, we haven't settled on a new norm, and most companies are still writing deals based on albums (even though they privately acknowledge it will be unrealistic to do this in the future). One major label is already shifting its contracts to a specific number of masters rather than albums, but the others have yet to follow. So, while the next section could well be out of date by the time you read this, at the moment it's still the way most deals are structured.

Options in New Artist Deals

With new artists, companies like to commit to a few tracks, an EP, or maybe one album. However, the major companies want the right to get a total of five to six albums over the course of the deal (indies will often agree to a maximum of three or four, sometimes even less). This is an improvement over the past—companies used to insist on options for eight to ten albums.

The company wants the right to these optional albums one at a time. With a lot of clout, you can sometimes make them take two at a time (called **two firm** in industry lingo), but this has become harder for new artists. And if you get it at all, it will most likely be later in the deal. For example, they can pick up albums two and three individually, but if they go on with the deal, they have to take four and five as a package. Can't hurt to ask for this, but don't take it personally if you don't get it.

If you have a lot of heat, and the company does commit to two albums from the git-go, it may ask for the right to bail out if the first album tanks. For example, if the first album sells less than 150,000 units in the United States (based on STEAs and sales; see page 90 for what that means), the company is no longer committed to the second album. Or you could get to the same place by stating it another way: The second album is optional, but the company is required to exercise its option if the first album generates the equivalent of 150,000 units.

As we'll discuss in a bit, I'm talking here about the number of newly recorded **studio** albums (meaning recorded in a studio) you'll have to deliver. This does not include live albums (see page 121), Greatest Hits albums (see page 121), specialty albums (Christmas, Easter, Polka Parade), side projects, duets (because you're not the featured artist), or the like.

Options in Midrange and Superstar Deals

If you're scoring high on the Heat-O-Meter, and lots of hounds are chasing you, the company may commit to two albums *firm*, and get *options* for additional albums (each option would require them to record one or two albums). Even if they actually commit to two albums, however, as noted above, they may want the right to bail out if the first album tanks.

It's rare that a company doesn't have the right to at least four albums from this level of artist, and five is the norm.

At the superstar level, deals of only three albums are possible, and at least two of those albums are typically firm.

A few huge artists (and at the other end, a hot new artist signing to an indie label) have made deals for one album only, but this is rare.

Options Aren't Good for You

I remember a friend of mine from the high school choir who came in one day, jubilant, because she had signed a "ten-album deal" with Capitol Records. In reality, it turned out to be a deal for only one single, and she had merely given Capitol the option to require up to ten albums. While my friend faded from the music biz after recording that one single, her attitude was not unusual. Many artists still think that record company options are good for them (the numbers are so high at the end!). But in fact, options are only good for the record company. If you're a flop, you'll never see the money; if you're a success, it'll probably be less than you're worth. So train yourself to think of options as nothing more than a chance for the record company to get out of your deal. They are never good for you.

Making the Best of Options

Despite my high-minded speech, the reality is that you have to live with options at all but major heat and superstar levels—this industry custom is too well entrenched to buck. However, since you're giving the company a chance to drop you after each album or two (in other words, to protect their rear ends if there's no success), I think you're entitled to more goodies if they keep you. This can be done in two different ways:

Royalties. For optional albums, you should get better royalties. Typically, the increase is around 0.5% to 1%, both in your basic rate and in any escalated rates. For example, I did a midlevel deal that looked like this:

Album No.	Royalty on Sales of 0–500,000 Albums	Royalty on Sales of 500,001– 1,000,000 Albums	Royalty on Sales of 1,000,001– 1,500,000 Albums	Royalty on Sales of 1,500,001– 2,000,000 Albums	Royalty on Sales of 2,000,000+ Albums
1	17%	17.5%	18%	18.5%	19%
2	17%	17.5%	18%	18.5%	19%
3	18%	18%	18.5%	18.5%	19%
4	18%	18.5%	19%	19.5%	20%
5	19%	19.5%	20%	20%	20%

Funds. You should also get increased recording funds for optional albums. Page 101 cites an example of a new-artist deal, and here are the numbers from a midlevel deal:

Album No.	Floor	Ceiling
1	$300,000	(no formula)
2	$300,000	$800,000
3	$350,000	$900,000
4	$350,000	$1,00,000
5	$400,000	$1,200,000
6	$400,000	$1,500,000

Don't the numbers look delicious in the later option periods? What a great deal! What a genius negotiator! DON'T BE FOOLED! OPTIONS ARE *NEVER* GOOD FOR YOU!! They only mean you'll get dropped if you're not worth the price, or you'll get too little if you're a smash. So repeat after me: "OPTIONS ARE *NEVER* GOOD FOR ME!!!" Now write it on the blackboard twenty-five times.

Pay or Play

So you have a deal for an album. Let's hit the studio. Right?

Well, not so fast, pardner.

Virtually no record deal ever requires the company to actually make a record.

Huh?

Yep. And this is not only true for new artists, but also for midlevel ones and superstars.

Almost all contracts contain a provision that says the company, instead of recording an album, can merely pay you a sum of money equal to (in the first draft of their agreement) minimum union scale for an album (see page 87 for what union scale means) or (after negotiating) either the difference between the recording fund and the cost of the last album, or a pre-negotiated set fee. This is called a **pay-or-play** provision, meaning, as the name implies, that the record company has the option either to allow you to "play" your music or to "pay" you off.

The amount you get for pay-or-play is negotiable. Ideally, you want to get your recording fund, less the recording costs of your last album. That's what you'd make if you actually recorded an album and it stiffed (which could only happen because the company didn't do their job, of course . . .). Sometimes the company will agree to that amount, but with a floor and ceiling (we discussed this on page 100). Or sometimes it's just a negotiated amount.

Apart from beating them up for the most pay-or-play money you can get, you also want to be sure that, once they pay you off, the deal is over. This shouldn't be hard to get, but it isn't in a lot of form agreements, and without it, the company could hold on to you without making records. (On the other hand, since they don't want your records, they probably don't want you around either. But it's cheap insurance to add language making sure.)

HOW LONG?

Term

How long the record company keeps you under an exclusive agreement is called the **term** of your deal. Record deals used to be for a term of one year, with options to renew for additional periods of one year each. These segments of the term are also called **terms,** or sometimes **periods,** such as the *initial term* (first year), *first option period* (second year), etc. In the olden days, an artist was usually obligated to deliver two albums during each year. That worked terrifically back when records were banged out like pancakes, since most of the time artists just showed up, sang, then went to the beach. As we discussed, in those days it was not unusual to make an album in a few weeks.

Every contract is a history lesson, and the contractual language dealing with the length of deals has a particularly colorful past. Behind each clause is a story that ends with "I'm going to write something that makes sure, if this ever happens again, I won't get shafted." And unraveling these bits of history can be fun, so let's take a look.

Late Delivery of Albums

As artists took more creative control, albums took longer to make. Indeed, the more successful the artist, the longer (with rare exception) the recording process. Today, for pop artists, periods of years between albums are not unusual for superstars (or for flakes at any level). Many reasons for this are legitimate—if an album is successful, you need to be out touring and promoting it, which means you can't be in the studio. In fact, the more successful it is, the longer you'll be out touring and promoting, and the record company won't even want you to start the next album. (Hip-hop is a totally different story, as we'll discuss in a minute.)

Unfortunately, many of these delays don't have such a noble purpose. I'm convinced (but can't prove) that one of the reasons for delay is that artists, particularly following a major success, are a bit frightened to put out their next record. When it's actually released, they have to find out whether it does as well as the prior one; until then, it's only specula-tion and their fabulous track record stays intact. So, they continue to fine-tune, tweak, poke, re-record, rethink, etc., which delays the day of reckoning. And second albums are particularly troublesome. If you think about it, someone's first album can actually be five years or more in the making. That's because they were accumulating songs for a long time before they ever got a record deal, and thus had a huge catalog to choose from in making the first album. However, when an artist gets to the second album, all the cherries have been picked, so it's a matter of writing new material or going into the second tier of old stuff. And this process has to take place within a year or two, so you don't lose the momentum of the first album. That's in stark contrast to the unlimited time that preceded the first album. So there's much more pressure on the second go-round.

Record companies historically solved this slow-delivery problem by having the right to extend the term of the agreement if an album wasn't delivered on time. In other words, if your album was six months late, the current one-year term of your deal was extended by six months. This worked terrifically until Olivia Newton-John filed a suit against MCA Records seeking termination of her agreement. (The case cite is *MCA Records, Inc. vs. Newton-John,* 90 Cal.App 3d. 18 [1979], for you technical freaks who like to read court cases.) In this case, she argued that her deal should be limited to the actual number of years stated in the contract, without regard to any extensions. In other words, since her contract was for a two-year term with three one-year options (a total of five years), she argued that MCA couldn't enforce the deal beyond five years from the start date, even if she hadn't given them all the product due. To everyone's surprise, the court (sort of) agreed. It reduced the duration of MCA's injunction (meaning the court order that said she couldn't record for anyone else) to the five years, rather than allowing any extensions. However, I said "sort of" because the five years weren't over at the time of the case, and so the court techni-cally didn't deal with the issue in full. Nonetheless, the case's language was strong enough to make all the companies nervous, and it forever changed the way record contracts are drawn.

The result was that, since the Newton-John case, the terms of record deals have not been stated in specific time periods like one or two years. Instead, the contracts say each period ends twelve months after release of the last album required for that period, but that the term is no less than a specified minimum (e.g., eighteen months) from the time it starts. For example, if you're required to record one album, the period might start upon signing your deal and end twelve months after release of that album, but no sooner than eighteen months after signing.

This method of fixing the term of a deal based on delivery of albums has worked swimmingly for many years, but as we've been discussing, the nature of what's going to be delivered under record deals is changing. Albums certainly won't be the only thing required—assuming albums even survive at all in the age of single-song streaming. So how will the term be figured in the future? Will it be just a number of masters instead of albums? If so, will those masters be delivered in bunches, or one or two at a time? And how often will the company want them?

At the time I'm writing this, there's no consensus on how this should work, though as I noted earlier, one major label has already moved to contractual periods based on a number of masters (rather than an album) for each period of the term. But the other labels still use albums, meaning they basically have their fingers in their ears while singing "La, La, La, I Can't Hear You." Interestingly, publishing deals, which are deals for songwriters, were also based on albums historically, but they've changed their model even more radically (as we'll discuss in Chapter 18).

Here's another interesting aspect: All the deals made in the last few years, including for superstars, end after delivery of a number of albums. But if no one wants albums anymore, how do you ever get out of the deal? Just deliver an album, even though you know the company and the marketplace don't want it? The answer is that each deal will have to be renegotiated when a new norm sets in, but the company and artist won't necessarily agree on what to do. In essence, the industry pretty much punted, deciding that we'll have to figure it out when we get there.

Whether it's based on a number of albums or a number of masters, record contracts don't end until a certain period of time following delivery of the last required product. This concept nicely solved the Olivia Newton-John problem, but the companies needed to add additional provisions to deal with this little snippet of history: In 1970, Dean Martin signed an agreement with Warner Records. The agreement was unusual for those days (although it's the norm today) because the term continued until delivery of all the albums. About six years later, after everyone had forgotten about him, Dino came in and announced he was about to start recording a new album (for which he expected the substantial amount of money required in the contract). This sent Warner into a tizzy, since Mr. Martin's star was not of the same brightness as when he signed the deal, and they began scrambling to find a way out. So Dino sued them. Ultimately the case was settled, but it taught the companies a lesson—contracts shouldn't be geared only to delivery of albums, or else they can go on forever.

Because of this, you'll now find contractual provisions that say companies can get out of a deal if the artist doesn't deliver an album within a certain period of time after delivery of the previous album (I'm going to use the term "album" because it's simpler, but the concept applies equally to a specified number of masters, if that's how the deal is written). In other words, if you're late more than a certain amount of time (usually twelve to eighteen months, depending on bargaining power), they can terminate your deal. But they don't have to whack you. Even if you're late, if they want to keep you under the deal, they can sit back and wait.

On top of the right to terminate, record companies also have the right to reduce your advance on the next album. For example, a common provision reduces your advance by 5% for every month that you're late. Note this is 5% of the *recording fund*, not just the difference between costs and the fund (which would be the money you keep). So being late could eat up your entire in-pocket advance. For example, if you're recording fund is $100,000 and it will cost you $90,000 to record, you have $10,000 for yourself. The 5% penalty, however, applies to the $100,000, meaning a $5,000 reduction for every month you're late. Meaning your pocket money is gone after only two months. And of course this also reduces what's left for recording costs.

Here's how we try to soften this penalty:

1. The 5% reduction only applies to unpaid monies, not anything you already got. The form agreement will say 5% of the entire fund, which includes monies you got when you started recording, as well as recording costs. So, for example, if you got $25,000 when you started recording, and there's $75,000 left to pay, the 5% reduction only applies to the $75,000 (not the full $100,000).
2. If there's a formula for the fund (see page 99), try to say that the reduction can't take you below the minimum of the formula.

Of course, if this album's fund is only the minimum under the formula, that means there's no reduction. Labels don't like this; they want something that will hurt if you're late.

Apart from the financial penalty, as we first discussed, the form contract also says that the label can get out of the deal if you're late. We try to soften this by saying the company can't terminate your deal unless you're more than six months late. They can still reduce the advance, starting on the date you're late, but they can't bail on you completely for a few more months.

So . . . because of Dean and Olivia, (a) the term goes on until you deliver, and (b) you're shafted if you deliver late. Does that take care of everything? Not quite . . .

Next comes a history lesson from Frank Zappa (you probably wouldn't think Zappa was the guy to first anticipate hip-hop practices, but . . .).

Mr. Zappa had a four-album deal with Warner Records and badly wanted out. So one day he showed up with four albums tucked under his arm and announced he was delivering all the remaining product required under his deal. Thus, says Mr. Z, "I'm now free to sign with another label."

Warner was not thrilled.

The Zappa lesson is now handled by stating that you can't even start *recording* an album until you've delivered the prior album, and that the new album can't be delivered sooner than six months after delivery of the prior album. This was legitimate enough in the past—historically, you couldn't really market more than one album at a time, and if an artist put an album on the shelf for later release, when it finally came out, it could well be out of touch with the current taste of the music biz (which can change hourly).

But in today's hip-hop world, "more is better," meaning artists release multiple albums at once, and these albums can have twenty or more tracks. And often these batches are released very close to each other. Wherever Mr. Zappa is, he's probably smiling.

In the same way that the album concept is still included in record deals, there's no norm for this kind of blizzard delivery yet. As a practical matter, the companies just sit and figure it out with each artist, depending on the situation. But it's still the Wild West, at least until a new norm emerges. I suspect all the labels will follow the one major that's converted to a number of masters (rather than albums), but whatever happens, it's gonna be interesting . . .

DELIVERY REQUIREMENTS

Apart from the number of recordings, contracts also talk about the kind of recordings you can deliver. **Delivery** is a magic word, because it means more than dumping the stuff on their doorstep, ringing the doorbell, and running off. It means (a) you have to deliver a bunch of other junk along with the recordings (artwork, licenses for the songs, deals with producers, etc.) and (b) the company has to accept the recordings as complying with your deal. Your contract will specify what standards the company can use in deciding whether to accept the recordings, and the definition of these standards depends on your bargaining power. The extremes are:

Commercially Satisfactory

If your contract says you must deliver **commercially satisfactory** recordings, it means the record company only has to take recordings it believes will do well in the market; in other words, recordings it finds "satisfactory for commercial exploitation" (translation: recordings it likes). If your contract has this language and they don't like your record, then (a) at best, they send you back to the studio (at your expense); or (b) at worst, they say you haven't delivered the product required by your deal, which means you're late, in breach of your contract, and they can reduce your advance and/or terminate the deal.

Technically Satisfactory

At the other end of the spectrum is **technically satisfactory.** If you only have to deliver technically satisfactory recordings, then as long as a recording is technically well made, the company has to take it.

Technically satisfactory delivery standards are very rare today because of abuses that I'm sure you can imagine (for example, one of my record company clients got an album that was supposed to be a secret group of superstars but turned out to be a previously released flop from an unknown group).

Newer artists can expect to live with commercially satisfactory. Midrange artists may get a technically satisfactory standard, but it will be subject to the company's approving the songs and the producer, plus the same limits described in the next two sentences. Superstars can expect an even more favorable version of technically satisfactory: The company may not have any approvals, but it will have language saying the recordings must be of a "style" (and perhaps even a "quality") similar to your previous recordings. They will also exclude any "specialty" or "novelty" recordings, so you can't give them a children's record, Christmas record, the Johnny Mathis songbook (unless, of course, you are Johnny Mathis), Gregorian chants, etc.

Other Delivery Criteria

The other requirements for your recordings (regardless of your level) are that they must be:

1. Studio recordings (as opposed to "live" concert recordings—see page 121 for a discussion of "live" albums).
2. Recorded during the term (to keep you from pulling out those old garage recordings).
3. Songs not previously recorded by you or someone else (I'm sure you can figure out the history lesson behind this one).
4. Recordings that feature only your performance (to keep you from bringing in the kids and your aunt Sally as guest soloists).
5. Not wholly instrumental selections (unless you're only an instrumentalist).
6. Material that doesn't cause the company any legal hassles, such as infringing somebody's copyright, defaming someone, or using obscene language (to the extent that's still possible).
7. Songs of a minimum playing time (usually two minutes).

In addition, you also have to deliver all the legal rights they need to exploit your recordings, such as producer agreements (we'll talk about those in Chapter 11), licenses to use the songs (Chapter 16), and sample clearances (we'll talk about samples on page 250).

GUARANTEED RELEASE

As we discussed on page 111, very few record contracts even build in an obligation to *record* your records, much less a commitment to release them.

With even a little bargaining power (and with some companies, as a matter of practice), you can get a **guaranteed release,** which is also called a **release commitment.** Bizarrely, this clause will never obligate the company to release your records. It will, however, let you get out of the deal if they don't.

With more bargaining power, you can sometimes get the right to buy back the unreleased album. After all, if the company doesn't think enough of it to put it out, why not let you take it elsewhere and get their money back?

Guaranteed release clauses basically turn you into a notice factory. If, within a certain period after delivery (usually 90 to 120 days) the company hasn't put out your album, you have earned the right to give it a written notice saying, "You haven't put out my album." After receiving this shocking news, the company has another period (usually 60 days) within which to actually put out the album (if they feel like it). If they don't, you now have the privilege of sending a second notice, usually within 30 days after the 60 days (and if you're late, you lose your rights). This notice says the company has still failed to put out your album; that you really meant it when you said you wanted them to; and that you are now terminating the deal. At this point you can say good-bye. (But note that the company still doesn't have to put out the record.)

By the way, the period after delivery in which the company must release is usually extended if any of it falls between October 15 and January 15. This is because, for the most part, no one other than the major stars release product after October 15. Beginning in early December, the radio stations start thinking about Hawaii, Aspen, or St. Bart's, and they "freeze" their playlists (meaning they add no new records until after January 15). In response, the record industry closes up around the middle of December. If an artist isn't well-known, their record doesn't have time to make its climb before the December shutdown, so everyone has to wait until next year. Thus, the record companies want to extend their release commitment period to make way for this practice. And to make way for their vacations. All of this may change, as streaming becomes more dominant than radio, but for now this clause still lives.

Guaranteed release clauses only let you out of your record deal if the company doesn't release your record in the United States. As your bargaining power increases, as well as your international fame, you may be able to negotiate a similar release provision for foreign territories. Certainly you should try to get a guaranteed release in the "major" territories (see page 139 for what they are) and anyplace else where you sell big numbers.

Normally you can't get out of the entire deal for failure to release outside the United States—you can only terminate for the particular territory where they blew it, and only for the specific album not released (so you can get another distributor to release that album in the territory). However, without massive clout, you won't actually get back the territory. Instead, you'll get the right to find another company to license the unreleased album from your record company. Your company will credit 50% of what it gets from this license to your account, and keep the other 50% for themselves. If you keep pushing, the company may agree that if it fails to release two consecutive albums in a particular territory, you can have back that territory for the rest of the deal. While this isn't likely to be meaningful (if you're that much of a stiff in the territory, odds are no one else will want you), it's better than a sharp stick in the eye.

As the CD's heartbeat slows, an interesting twist to guaranteed releases is starting to poke out its head. Namely, can the record company satisfy its "guaranteed release" requirement by just sticking your songs on a streaming service? That's certainly not the spirit of these clauses, as they historically required the company's financial commitment to press CDs, ship them to stores, and do some level of marketing (there was rarely a contractual marketing commitment, but if the company wanted to see any of their money back, they had to give it a go). However, the company forms don't define the term "release," so dropping songs online would technically do it.

The real goal is to have them market your music with some amount of energy, though that's hard to quantify in any meaningful way, especially if they hate your record. If you have some heat, however, you can sometimes get a guaranteed marketing commitment, or an agreement to spend a certain amount to promote your records. Whatever's in the contract, you have to hope they will want to get back their investment in you, so your interests should be aligned. (Spoiler Alert: From the beginning of the business, almost every artist feels their company should be doing more.)

CONTROLLED COMPOSITIONS

Historically, one of the most important provisions of your record deal was the **controlled composition clause,** which limits how much you get paid as a songwriter. Due to some changes in the copyright law, this has become much less important. But unfortunately, it hasn't become that much less complicated, and to understand it you need a pretty extensive knowledge of publishing, which we're going to discuss later. So let's put it off until you have more background info. (If you really can't wait, flip ahead to page 264, but you'll get pretty confused if you don't have a decent grasp on publishing.)

If you're on the *Advanced Overview Track*, go to Chapter 11 on page 125.
Experts, straight on . . .

GREATEST HITS

A **Greatest Hits** album (also called a **Best of**) is a compilation of songs from your prior albums. (I've always been amused by the term *Greatest Hits*, since the album is sometimes neither.)

Greatest Hits albums are on the endangered species list (somewhere between the hawksbill turtle and the black-footed ferret). As streaming has soared, Greatest Hits albums have nose-dived, and the reason is pretty simple: Everyone is essentially making their own greatest hits by creating playlists on streaming services. However, record company contracts still want the right to make Greatest Hits albums, even though there really isn't anything they can do with them.

If you don't say anything, the company will put out as many Greatest Hits albums as it likes, whenever it likes. You should add a provision in your contract that requires the label to get your consent before they can release a Greatest Hits album, so you can approve the tracks and artwork. If you can't get that, at least get some limitation on what they can do, such as allowing one Greatest Hits album for every three albums you deliver. Or one during the term, and one after.

There used to be advances for Greatest Hits albums. Those days are gone, since there's no longer any market for this product, with the exception of a cousin of the Greatest Hits album called the **box set** (which we'll discuss in detail on page 157).

LIVE ALBUMS

A **live album** is recorded during a live concert (with lots of screaming and applause), rather than in a studio. Their popularity goes through periodic ups and downs (sort of like musical movies). They were historically something a company did to keep the artist happy, because they didn't really make any money. Then, in 1976, Peter Frampton broke all the rules with an album called *Frampton Comes Alive!*, which was not only a live album, but also a *double* live album (double albums were a traditional handicap at retail because they're more expensive).

This album sold multimillions of copies and blew out all the traditional wisdom. After the predictable glut of live albums following Mr. Frampton's, the live album popularity again faded and currently is at a level I'd call "Eh." People who want live music now mostly go to YouTube or the concert festival websites.

Unless you've got a lot of muscle, record companies won't let you deliver a live album (or even one live cut on a studio album) without their consent. On rare occasions, superstars can get the right to deliver one live album during the term of their deal. But it'll usually have a reduced advance, both because of live records' dicey sales history and the fact that most of the songs have been previously released.

INDEPENDENTS DAY

When the music biz started its decline in the year 2000, deals with independent record companies became more prevalent. That's because independent labels became more prevalent.

How come? I like to think it's because majors don't always understand the kind of cool music that indies love. There are, though, a couple of other reasons. People laid off by big companies in the downturn started indie labels, and indies are happy with smaller numbers because they make smaller bets and therefore don't need to score as big as the majors to do well.

I think the spread of indies is incredibly healthy for the biz. It's like the record industry in the 1960s, when independent labels like A&M, Chrysalis, and Island changed the face of music. Great music has always come from doing things out of the mainstream. Keep at it!

As the independents grow stronger, however, their deals look more and more like major label deals. But there are some differences you should understand, so let's take a look. We'll start with "true independents" (see page 72 for what that means), then mosey on over to major-distributed independents that have little or no staff (and rely on a major label to do the heavy lifting).

True Independents

1. As we already noted, you get less of an advance from an independent. Because a deal with them is like shopping in the bargain basement, you should make up for it by giving them the lowest number of albums possible. A few years ago, it wasn't

hard to limit independent deals to one or two albums. Lately, as the independents' muscles grew, so did their desire for more albums. So now they try to get as many as five. See if you can keep it down to three or four. As a general rule, the less money they're guaranteeing, the fewer albums they should get. And with a smaller deal, you can often limit them to two or three.

2. If you're willing to take a very small, or zero, advance, some labels will give you 50% of their profits instead of a royalty. We'll discuss how profits are computed later (on page 201). For now, take my word that a profit share means a lot more money if you're a big success (though it could mean less money at mid level).

3. Most indie labels don't have overseas operations, and therefore you want to make sure that your records get released in those territories. If they're not released, you should get back the rights to those territories (see the discussion of this on page 119). Sometimes you can even limit their rights to the United States only, and make your own foreign deals.

4. Most independents, just like majors, want 360 rights (see page 102 for what those are). They may also want to own some or all of your publishing (your earnings as a songwriter, as opposed to your earnings as a performer on records). Since we haven't discussed publishing, I want to defer the ins and outs of this until we do. The way to protect yourself is on page 291 if you want to look ahead, but I suggest you do it only if you understand publishing pretty well.

Major-Distributed Independents

When you're recording for a major-distributed company that isn't a true independent, you have the same concerns we just discussed, plus a few added goodies. Some of these companies have an overall deal with a distributor, for all their product, while others just make a deal with a major for each artist they sign, one at a time.

If your company doesn't have an overall distribution deal with a distributor, you have to ask whether this company can get anyone to distribute your album. As we discussed on page 75, it's not that hard to get your music out digitally, but of course you could do that yourself. The idea is to get a real distributor, with marketing skills and staff, behind your music. If you have some clout, you should say that the company must enter into an agreement with a *major* distributor, to make sure it's a legit distributor. In addition, and even if the company doesn't agree to a major distributor, you want to say that the indie has to make a distribution deal within a certain period of time, such as six months after execution of the contract or completion of your album (though I've gone as long as nine to twelve months). If the time period is measured from completion of your album, be sure you have an outside date—otherwise, if the company never records you, the date will never arrive. For example, you might require a company to make an agreement within six months after completion of your album, but in no event later than twelve months after execution of your deal.

If they don't use a major distributor, you want to approve who it is. Assuming the independent agrees, it will say you must be "reasonable" in your approval, so you can't use this clause to get out of the deal when some prettier face dangles more money in front of you. (You wouldn't do that, would you?) And by the way, when I represent the independent, I insist that the artist preapprove all the likely distributors (which I then list).

Watch out for this one: Suppose your deal with the independent is for two albums firm, but the distributor drops the company (and you) after one album. How do you make sure the company doesn't hold you for the second album?

Historically, part of your protection is a guaranteed release—if they don't put your album out, you can terminate the deal (see page 118). But nowadays, that just means slapping your masters online, so it's not much protection. Also, as you'll remember from page 111, companies don't even have to make a record to hang on to your contract. And if they don't record any product, the guaranteed release never comes into play. Knowing this, various sleazeballs in our business have sunk their teeth into an artist and not let go if they smelled that somebody might pay them for the privilege.

The way to cover yourself is to say that the independent has six to twelve months after a distribution deal lapses within which to get a new deal, or else you're out.

11

Producer and Mixer Deals

WHAT'S A PRODUCER?

Traditionally, a record producer combines the roles of director and producer in the motion picture field. He or she is responsible for bringing the creative product into tangible form (a recording), which means (a) being responsible for maximizing the creative process (finding and selecting songs, deciding on arrangements, getting the right vocal sound, etc.), and (b) administering the whole project, such as booking studios, hiring musicians, staying within a budget, filing union reports, etc. (The mechanical aspects of administration—actually calling the musicians, doing the paperwork, etc.—are often handled by a **production coordinator,** whose life purpose is to make things happen.)

In the pop/EDM/hip-hop world, there are a number of producers who produce only **tracks**, meaning everything except the vocals. These tracks can be "made to order" for a specific artist, or often these folks produce tracks without any particular artist in mind, then sell them to the highest bidder. It's also common for an artist to record a song with a producer, decide not to use it, and then let the producer remove the artist's vocal and use the track for someone else.

If you get this kind of track, then you would then get a **vocal producer,** who (not surprisingly) produces the vocals to finish the track. Sort of like building a burrito at Chipotle.

The History of Producers

As we discussed earlier, artists in the 1950s were mostly people who just showed up to sing, then left to "do lunch." My friend Snuff Garrett, one of the most important producers of the fifties and sixties, considered it burdensome if it took him more than five days to record an album (and the artist wasn't even there for the whole time). Using this technique, Snuff produced records for Cher, Sonny and Cher, Gary Lewis and the Playboys, Bobby Vee, Del Shannon, and a host of other successes, including such strange choices as Telly Savalas and Walter Brennan.

Snuff started out (as did all the early producers) as an **A&R** man (the letters stand for **Artists and Repertoire**). A&R men (in those days there were no A&R "persons") were executives of record companies whose job was to find, sign, and guide talent, match songs to singers, and run recording sessions (in other words, doing almost exactly what producers do today). A&R executives still exist, and indeed are among the most important industry people. They're responsible for finding and developing talent, as well as finding songs, matching producers and artists, and generally overseeing projects. But today most of them don't actually produce the recordings (although many of the better ones come pretty close to producing).

Anyway, Snuff worked for Liberty Records, which was then run by its founder and chief executive, Simon Waronker (the father of former Warner Records and DreamWorks Records president Lenny Waronker); its president, Alvin Bennett; and its chief recording engineer, Theodore Keep. (Do the first names of these gentlemen sound familiar? Do they remind you of a recording artist on Liberty? See page 137 for the answer if you can't guess.) Snuff, who was one of the smartest business-people I ever met, but hid behind this country cornpone, figured out early on that he was making millions of dollars for Liberty while getting a generous but small salary in comparison to what he was generating. So he summoned up all his courage and asked Alvin for a royalty of one cent per record.

Alvin was not pleased.

The radical idea that a person instrumental in creating product could get a royalty? I'm guessing words like "outrageous" and "treason" got thrown around between the four-letter daggers. Snuff almost got fired for this request, but he stood his ground and was so valuable to Liberty that he won the point. And started a trend that is the reason today's producers get royalties on records.

ROYALTIES

Producers get a U.S. royalty in the range of 3% to 4%. Some producers, who become "superstars" in their own right by producing hugely successful records, can get 5% or (very rarely) 6%. (If there are two producers, such as a track producer and a vocal producer, or a team of two producers, each generally gets half.) However, there are some major distinctions between artists' and producers' royalties, and some fine points that will bite you in the butt if you don't know about them.

"Record One" Royalties

Interestingly, for whatever historical reasons, producers' royalties are computed more favorably than artists' royalties. Specifically, with success, producers are paid for all records sold, meaning recording costs are not charged against their royalties. (As you know, recording costs are always charged against artists' royalties.) These are called **record one** royalties, because they're paid from the first record ("record one") that the company exploits. Producers, of course, have to recoup the advances they put in their pocket, but if you think of those advances as a prepayment of royalties, it's the same as getting a royalty on all records. (Actually, some superstar producers are paid from record one and don't even have to recoup all of their up-front money, as we'll discuss in a minute.)

Producers' royalties are paid **retroactive to record one** after recoupment of recording costs at the **net artist rate.** What this means in English is that (a) recording costs are recouped at the artist's **net rate** (the all-in artist rate after deducting all third-party royalties, which generally means the royalty for the producer, any mixers, samples, etc.); (b) until recording costs are recouped, the producer gets *no royalties* at all (just like an artist); but (c) once recording costs are recouped, the producer gets paid on *all* monies earned, including those used to recoup recording costs. In other words, once recording costs are recouped, the producer is paid from the first monies earned (called *record one* from the days when it meant the first record sold), and this payment is **retroactive** because the company "goes back" and pays on sales previously made that didn't bear royalties at the time of sale.

The concept is easier to see with numbers. Suppose an artist's "all-in" royalty (artist and producer combined) is 12% a record, and the producer's royalty is 2%. (These numbers bear no relationship to reality but make for easy math.) That makes the "net" royalty 10% (the

12% all-in rate less the 2% producer royalty). Here's what happens when the album generates $1,000,000 for the record company, meaning the artist earns $100,000 (the 10% net royalty multiplied times $1,000,000):

Producer's Recording Cost Recoupment Computation		Producer's Royalty Account	
Company Income	$1,000,000	Company Income	$1,000,000
"Net" Royalty	× 10%	Producer Royalty	× 0
Less: Recording Costs	$100,000		
	−$120,000		
DEFICIT	− $20,000	NET PAYABLE	$0

Since the artist's 10% net royalty equals only $100,000, which is short of the $120,000 recording costs, the album's recording costs are unrecouped and therefore the producer doesn't get any royalties. That's why the producer royalty is zero in the above example.

Now let's assume the company generates $1,200,000, which means the artist earns a total of $120,000 at the 10% net rate. At this point, the $120,000 of recording costs are recouped, and the producer is paid on all the money earned (i.e., retroactively to the first dollar, which is called *record one*). Thus, because the producer has a 2% royalty, he or she gets 2% of $1,200,000, or $24,000:

Producer's Recording Cost Recoupment Computation		Producer's Royalty Account	
Company Income	$1,200,000	Company Income	$1,200,000
"Net" Royalty	× 10%	Producer Royalty	× 2%
Less: Recording Costs	$120,000		
	−$120,000		
NET PAYABLE	$0	NET PAYABLE	$24,000

Did you notice that the producer is owed money, but the artist isn't? Stick around . . .

ADVANCES

Producers, like artists, also get advances. These advances fall into two categories. In one corner, weighing in at more than three hundred pounds, you've got the urban/hip-hop producers, and a handful of superstar pop producers. These folks are often considered as important as (or in some cases more important than) the artist—just adding their name to a track can mean hundreds of millions of streams. And in the other corner, we've got rock producers and everybody else.

For rock/everybody else, the range of advances is:

1. **New Producers:**
   Anywhere from zero to $7,500 per master. If the producer is doing an entire album, advances are anywhere from zero to about $30,000 per album.
2. **Midlevel:**
   $10,000 to $15,000 per master, or about $30,000 to $50,000 for the entire album.
3. **Superstar:**
   Up to $25,000 per track, and about $150,000 to $200,000 for the whole album.

For urban/pop:

1. **New Producers:**
   Anywhere from zero to $10,000 per master.
2. **Midlevel:**
   $20,000 to $30,000 per master.
3. **Superstar:**
   $35,000 to $40,000 per master, and up.

For urban/pop, these amounts are generally recording **funds,** meaning they include recording costs (just like the artist funds we discussed on page 97). The important issue with funds is to allocate how much is treated as recording costs, and how much is considered the producer's advance. The higher the recording costs, the worse for the artist—remember, from page 127, only the advance is charged against producer royalties, because the royalties are payable from record one after recoupment of the recording costs. Not surprisingly, producers want more allocated to recording costs, and artists want more allocated to advances.

By the way, in making this allocation, the actual recording costs have little to do with the discussion (in fact, many of these producers own their own studios, so the actual costs are minimal). The negotiation is really about how much gets charged to the producer's royalties.

OTHER ROYALTY COMPUTATIONS

Except for the record-one aspect we discussed on page 127, producers' royalties are generally calculated the same way as the artists' (although audiovisual royalties are different, as noted in the next section). For example, if an artist gets 75% of his or her U.S. rate in England, the producer will get 75% of his or her U.S. producer rate in England. We'll get into the details of how artist royalties are calculated in the next chapter.

In situations where the artist gets a percentage of the company's net receipts (such as a license to use a recording in a motion picture, where the artist gets 50% of the fee paid by the motion picture company), the producer gets a pro-rata share of the artist's earnings, based on the ratio that the producer's royalty bears to the all-in rate. For example, if the artist's all-in rate is 12% and the producer gets 3%, the producer would get three-twelfths (one-fourth) of the artist's receipts. So if the record company gets $20,000 to use a master in a film, and pays $10,000 to the artist, the producer would get $2,500 (three-twelfths [25%] of the $10,000), and the artist would get $7,500 (the remaining nine-twelfths).

Audiovisual Royalties

For audiovisual exploitations (mainly streaming videos these days), producers generally get half of their otherwise applicable rate. The theory is that the master is only half of the product (the video portion is the other half). For example, if the producer had a 3% royalty and YouTube streams the video, the producer would get 1.5% of the revenue. Also, for videos, the payment isn't retroactive to record one, but rather prospectively after recoupment of video costs.

WHO HIRES THE PRODUCER?

At one time, record companies routinely hired the producers. That was in the days when one producer did an entire album (a concept that has almost vanished, since most albums today have multiple producers—other than a few areas like rock, country, and oom-pah alpine bands). As it became common to have four, five, or more producers per album, the companies realized their in-house lawyers were spending so much time negotiating producer deals that it was clogging up their system. So they hit on the brilliant idea that the artist should hire the producer, which has not only shifted the paperwork burden to the artist, but has also shifted the financial burden to them. Let's analyze the issues separately.

Who Actually Hires (Contracts with) the Producer?

Since the artist has a direct contractual relationship with the producer, the producer is answerable to the artist, and the artist has full control of deciding the terms of the producer's deal. That's the good news if you're an artist. And now for the commercial: You bear the legal fees for negotiating the producer's deal.

But wait. There's more bad news.

Who Pays the Producer?

As we discussed, in an all-in deal, you're responsible for the producer's royalties, regardless of who actually signs the contract with him or her. This is a much more serious issue than it may look at first glance. For reasons we'll discuss in a minute, the producer may be entitled to royalties before you're recouped under your deal with the record company. Look back at our example on page 128; you earned zero royalties, and the producer was owed $24,000. In other words, this means you owe money to the producer at a time when the record company doesn't owe you anything. Which means you could have to write a check to the producer from your own pocket. Which majorly sucks.

And the situation can get much worse. Continuing with these same assumptions, let's assume the artist got a $100,000 advance on top of the $120,000 in recording costs. That means the artist won't get any money until *both* the $120,000 in recording costs *and* the $100,000 advance are recouped. Meanwhile, the producer (who didn't share in the $100,000 advance) is owed royalties. For example, if the company earns $2 million, check out this Parade of Horribles:

Artist's Account		Producer's Account	
Company Income	$2,000,000	Company Income	$2,000,000
"Net" Royalty	× 10%	Royalty	× 2%
	$200,000		$40,000
Less: Recording Costs	–$120,000		
Less Artist Advance	–$100,000		
DEFICIT	**–20,000**	NET PAYABLE	**$40,000**

As you can see, you're $20,000 unrecouped (which means you have no money coming in for a while), but you owe $40,000 to the producer. If that $40,000 number doesn't impress you, try adding a zero to make it $400,000. Do I have your attention?

This is one of the times when success can kill you, because the more streams you have, the deeper in the hole you go! (In a sense, I'm misleading you. First of all, at some level of success the artist will recoup and earn enough royalties to pay off the producer. Secondly, part of the reason the artist isn't getting royalties is an advance, which is in his or her pocket. So if you think of advances as prepaid royalties, the artist has already gotten these royalties and has to pay a part of them to the producer. However, unless you're very different from the artists I know, you won't be setting money aside for your producer. Also, much of this problem is caused by the fact that recording costs haven't been recouped, which is not money sitting in your bank account. You can't put those monies aside to cover the producer even if you want to.)

Think that's the worst of it? Nah, we're just getting warmed up. Here's how the above example can get truly miserable:

Suppose the deal we just discussed was the artist's first album, and it earned only $300,000 for the company, meaning $30,000 for the artist. This means the album didn't recoup its $120,000 of recording costs, and the producer didn't recoup his or her advance. So far, the artist doesn't owe the producer anything, and everything is fine (from the point of view of our example, that is—the artist's career is of course in the toilet). When it comes time to do a second album, the artist ditches this turkey and hires a new producer. Let's assume the second album also costs $120,000, and let's assume the artist's recording fund is $200,000 for both the first and second albums, so that the artist pockets $80,000 (the difference between the fund and the $120,000 recording costs) on each album. Also, assume the second album grosses $3 million, and earns $300,000 for the artist. That means the artist has recouped the recording costs of the second album, and the producer of album number 2 is entitled to retroactive royalties. This means he or she is owed $60,000 (2% of $3 million).

Now let's look at how the accounts stack up. First, the artist's account with the record company:

Artist's Account with Record Company

	Royalty Earnings	Charges Against Royalties	Due Artist (or Deficit)
Album 1	+$30,000	−$200,000 ($120,000 recording costs and $80,000 advance)	−$170,000
Album 2	+$300,000	$200,000 ($120,000 recording costs and $80,000 advance)	+$100,000
TOTAL	+$330,000 ROYALTIES	−$400,000 CHARGES	−$70,000 DEFICIT

Now here's the computation of album number 2's producer royalties (album number 1's producer is not owed any royalties):

Album Number 2
Producer's Account with Artist

	Royalty Earnings	Charges Against Royalties	Due Artist (or Deficit)
Album 2	+$60,000		+$60,000 PAYABLE

As you can see from the above, the producer of album number 2 is owed $60,000, but the artist is unrecouped by $70,000. If you add a few more unsuccessful albums prior to the big hit, or add a few zeros after these dollar amounts, the artist is nearing 10 on the Richter scale. And the producer ain't gonna be much happier when he or she doesn't get paid—instead of having a nice solid record company to send out the producer's royalty checks, he or she now has to chase the artist, who was last seen in Moldavia. If either of these people is you, take two Valium and call me in the morning.

So what happens in real life? Any producer who has the slightest idea what they're doing will insist on the record company paying his or her royalties. Any artist who has the slightest idea what they're doing will insist on the record company paying the producer's royalties. Any record company that knows what it's doing will grumble but ultimately do this.

The reality is that producers simply won't produce an artist unless the record company gets into the mix, so you can almost always get the record company to pay the producer when you're unrecouped. (It's easy to get them to pay when you're recouped; they just take it out of your money.) Unless you're a mega star, they won't contractually agree to pay a producer while you're unrecouped. However, they will accept a **letter of direction** (known to its friends as an **L.O.D.**), which is a letter from the artist to the company that says, "Please pay my producer (and deduct it from me)." The letter will attach a royalty schedule that the producer has agreed to accept, so that the company knows how much to pay them. If you're a producer, be sure all your deals require the artist to send the company such a letter of direction; without it, you won't get paid.

When the company agrees to pay under a letter of direction, they will say that they're doing it only as an "accommodation," meaning it's because they love you, not because they have to. In other words, the company has no legal obligation to pay the producer, and the producer has no legal right to sue the company if they don't get paid. The producer can only sue the artist who signed their deal. Neither producers nor artists love this, but it's the best we can do, so they all agree to take it. And as a practical matter, the companies all pay royalties under letters of direction even if the producers are unrecouped.

Before a record company agrees to pay a producer, however, they'll insist on approving the producer's deal. That's to make sure the amount it has to pay while you're unrecouped can't get out of hand. They want to keep the producer's royalty low (not a surprise), but interestingly they want to keep the producer's advance high. Can you figure out why they want a higher producer advance? (See the answer at the end of the chapter if you can't guess.)

Whatever payments the company makes are treated as additional advances under your deal. In our example, this means the company would pay the producer $60,000 and you would then be $130,000 in the red (the original $70,000 plus the $60,000 paid to the producer). This makes you further unrecouped, but it's vastly superior to taking the money from your own pocket (few things aren't).

SoundExchange Monies

If you're a producer, you want a share of SoundExchange monies, which means nothing to you, because I haven't told you about it yet. As we'll see later (on page 140), artists are entitled to monies when their masters are transmitted digitally (like on Sirius XM, Pandora, and so forth), and those monies are collected by an outfit called Sound-Exchange (more about them on page 315).

We'll talk about specifics down the road, but the thing to understand now is that, unlike some other countries, producers aren't entitled to SoundExchange monies unless the artist tells SoundExchange to pay them. So if you're a producer, it's important that your deal with the artist requires them to send SoundExchange a letter of direction (similar to what I described above for the labels) telling them to slide some dough your way.

The producer's share of SoundExchange monies is the same percentage of the artist's money that you get for motion picture licenses: a fraction equal to the producer royalty over the artist's all-in royalty. So if the producer has a 3% royalty and the artist has 12%, the producer gets $\frac{3}{12}$, or 25% of the artist's SoundExchange monies.

Recently, the Music Modernization Act adopted some protections for producers, in a section cleverly named **AMP**, meaning **Allocation for Music Producers**. Those Washington guys are more fun than . . .

Basically, it cleans up some procedural stuff and adds some goodies for old-timers: If you were a producer, mixer, or sound engineer on a sound recording made before November 1, 1995, and you don't have a letter of direction from the artist, you can get 2% of the Sound-Exchange monies if you can't find the artist. If this is relevant to you, check out Title III of the Music Modernization Act, which you can find online. If it's not, don't bother . . .

MIXERS

Closely akin to producers are **mixers,** whose work we briefly discussed on page 96. Basically, these folks take the multitracks, throw them in a blender, and pour out a mystical potion of sublime music. Mixers both create a mix for the original release of a record, and also do remixes for later versions.

Great mixers can make a huge difference in the success of a record, so they're paid handsomely. Top pop mixers can get $7,500 to $12,500 per track, though most are in the range of $3,000 to $5,000. Usually this is a one-time payment, but mixers with clout can get a royalty as well. If there are royalties, they're usually from .5% to 1%, paid exactly like a producer (retroactive to record one after recoupment of recording costs at the net rate).

The per-track money we just discussed (e.g., the $3,000 for mixing) is often a **fee,** meaning it's not recoupable from royalties (*fee*, in industry parlance, means nonrecoupable; as opposed to an *advance*, which is recoupable). For the higher-paid folks, 50% of their up-front money is usually recoupable.

When we enter the hip-hop world of mixers, we walk through the looking glass. The top hip-hop mixers can get $30,000 to $50,000 per remix, and sometimes more. When they also get royalties (and a lot of them do), it can be more than 1% (as high as 2%). As with pop producers, because they're so highly paid, half their money is usually treated as an advance (the other half is nonrecoupable). However, at these levels, it's hard to earn enough royalties to ever recoup, especially since a lot of remixing is done only for specific genres (like a dance remix of a pop song), which means the income is limited.

Answer to question on page 126:

The Chipmunks.

Answer to question on page 135:

Record companies want you to pay the producer a higher advance so that the producer isn't owed royalties until as late as possible, after which you've recouped more of your deficit.

If you're on the *Fast Track*, go to Part III (Chapter 15) on page 211.
Everyone else, read on . . .

12

Advanced Royalty Computations

ROYALTIES FOR THE UNITED STATES

We'll start first with United States royalties, because, if you're signing to a U.S. company, all other royalties are based on (i.e., a reduced percentage of) the rate for the United States.

The royalties we discussed in Chapters 7 and 9 are for exploitations of masters in the United States (meaning streaming, downloads, and CDs). For downloads and CDs, however, those royalties only apply to sales at **full price** (sometimes called **top-line** price), because there are reduced royalties for other prices (as you'll see in a minute). Your U.S. rate for full-price exploitations is called, in most contracts, a **base rate,** or **basic rate.**

By the way, in most contracts, *full price* means 80% or more of the company's highest wholesale price for the format involved (you'll see why they use 80% in a minute). So if a CD wholesales for $10, full price means anything priced at $8 or more.

Let's assume you have a base rate of 10%, to make the math easier for the next topic, which happens to be . . .

FOREIGN ROYALTIES

Even though we Americans think the world stops at our borders, it turns out that people on the rest of the planet actually like music. But if you're a U.S.-based artist, you'll get less money in those other places. If it makes you feel any better, UK artists signed to a UK company get less in the United States.

Feeling better?

As streaming takes over, at least one record company now makes a worldwide deal at the same rate for streaming. But other than this outlier, unless you are the most super of superstars, you're going to get a smaller royalty for exploitations outside our border wall, certainly for physical product and possibly downloads. The reduction varies widely from company to company, and artist to artist, but as a broad rule, companies give a higher rate in "major" territories, and in territories where they have an ownership interest in the foreign distributor (today the majors all have worldwide operations). Conversely, they give a lower royalty in "minor" territories and in territories where they're only licensing their product to a wholly independent third party (**licensing** means they give someone else the right to exploit the masters and get a royalty from those folks).

Here's the most common pattern:

Canada

Canada has evolved into 85% of the United States rate with most companies, although some still treat it like any other "major" foreign territory (see the next paragraph). Using our example of a 10% U.S. basic rate, an 85% rate means you'd get 8.5% for normal retail sales in Canada. With clout you can sometimes get 90%.

Major Territories

There are a number of markets in which American product sells particularly well, and these are known as the "major" territories. They of course vary from artist to artist, but in general they are (in no particular order): United Kingdom, Australia, Italy, Japan, Holland, Germany, and France.

The remaining European Union countries (Western Europe) and Scandinavia can be treated as "majors" if you have some clout.

The royalty for major territories varies for the same reasons set forth above (ownership versus licensing, artist clout), but it's generally 70% to 75% of the U.S. basic rate, or 7% to 7.5% in our example. With clout, you can get this up to 80%, and sometimes a bit higher for the United Kingdom (like 85%).

And in all these places, you should push for a higher royalty on streaming.

R.O.W.

R.O.W. stands for **rest of world** and means the grab bag of countries left over, which I'll leave to you and Google Maps to figure out. The royalties for these territories generally run around 50% to 66.66% of the U.S. basic rate, or 5% to 6.66% under our assumption. If you have bargaining power, you can sometimes edge this up a bit, to 70% or so. Again, try to do better on streaming.

While those are the general rules, if you're an artist with a huge following in any particular territory, you can usually negotiate a better royalty for that country.

ELECTRONIC TRANSMISSIONS

To record companies, every delivery of music that isn't physical is an **electronic transmission**. As you'd expect, this means streaming and downloads, but it includes much, much more. Typical contract language defines *electronic transmissions* as something like this: "Any transmission or delivery to a consumer, whether audio or audiovisual, and/or with other data, by any means now known or hereafter discovered, whether on demand or not, and whether or not a charge is made for the transmission or delivery."

So . . . can you tell what all it picks up besides audio streaming and downloads?

Certainly YouTube, and any new delivery services that are later invented. But did you notice it also sweeps in radio, TV, and motion pictures (at least when they're streamed or broadcast)? More about that later.

Before we hit the royalties for electronic transmissions, let me give you:

The Passman Theory of Technology Cycles

There are predictable patterns that take place every time a new technology hits the record industry. It goes something like this:

1. Because the technology is so new, no one (including the record companies) really understands its economics. Also, when it's first introduced, the thing is usually expensive, and it's a small market. For example, when digital started, the companies had

to take all their analog music and turn it into digital, as well as add metadata (see page 71 for what that is), and set up systems to keep track of the billions of digital uses. All this while the music earned zippo.

2. The result is a grace period during which royalties on these new-bies are not particularly favorable to the artist. This is to give the technology a chance to get off the ground, and to help the record company justify the financial risk of going into it.

3. Invariably, this grace period goes on far beyond its economic life, during which time the companies make disproportionate profits.

4. As artist deals expire or are renegotiated, the rates go up.

5. Finally, an industry pattern develops and royalty rates stabilize.

OK, it's showtime.
Welcome to the world of Electronic Transmissions.

On-Demand Streaming

On-demand streaming, also called **interactive streaming,** means you can listen to any songs in a digital service provider's database, any time you like, and you can pause, skip, rewind, and create playlists. Examples of DSPs offering this service are Spotify, Apple Music, YouTube, Amazon Music, and SoundCloud. This is by far the biggest segment of the recorded music business, and it's growing strongly.

For these uses, you get your royalty rate applied against the record company's receipts from the DSP, so if they get $10,000 and you have a 10% royalty, you get $1,000.

On these services, you're not allowed to permanently download; just listen. Some of the services let you download and listen offline, but the download goes away if you stop paying for your subscription. This is called a **tethered download,** which we'll discuss in a minute.

As of this writing, Spotify, SoundCloud, and YouTube are the only major companies that offer on-demand streams for free (if you don't mind listening to annoying ads). Pandora offers a free service, but it's not interactive. As we'll discuss in a minute, there is pressure on these services to move to a subscription-only basis, meaning the users have to pay a monthly fee to get the music. Services that are subscription-only sometimes offer a free introductory period to try it out, but it's for a limited time. Spotify and YouTube are currently unlimited, but

Spotify's free mobile service, which is where the vast majority of the users are, is not fully on demand. YouTube, however, is fully interactive for mobile, and is therefore one of the biggest problems in our industry, as we'll discuss.

May I See Your ARPU?

An important aspect of streaming is something called **ARPU** (pronounced R-Poo). That may sound like a character on *The Simpsons,* but it means **Average Rate Per User**. In other words, what's the average amount of money that the streaming service gets from each user? For Apple Music, that's easy. Every user pays a subscription fee (other than for a thirty-day free trial period), so if the average subscription fee is $7 per month (the headline $10 per month reduced by student and family discounts), then Apple Music's ARPU is $7.

However, Spotify's ARPU is much lower. Can you figure out why?

Remember that Spotify offers a free ad-supported service, then hopes you'll pay a subscription fee to lose the ads. At the time of this writing, Spotify's free users outnumber paid subscribers more than two and a half to one. And the ad-supported free users bring in *way* less money than paid subscribers.

Why do ads generate a lot less money than subscribers? Over-the-air radio has about 14 to 16 minutes per hour of advertising, while Spotify has much less. That means: (a) Spotify ads can't generate as much money (there's not as much time sold); (b) their rates are cheaper than over-the-air ads; and (c) because there's less advertising time, there aren't enough ads to annoy people into paying a subscription fee.

Accordingly, the ARPU is majorly diluted by the freebie users. In other words, for every $7 per month from a Spotify subscriber, there's two and a half ad-supported subscribers who bring in far less money. Which means the average earnings per stream come out to a much smaller number than they would on a pure subscription service (like Apple Music).

This is easier to see with an example (though I'm making up numbers). Assume Spotify had only two paid subscribers and five free users (that's roughly the ratio that now exists). Also assume that the total ad sales for the free users are $3, and that Spotify gets $2 from each of the two paid subscribers, for a total of $4. If you add those together ($7) and divide by the total number of subscribers (seven), you get an average rate per user (ARPU) of $1, which is obviously far less than the $2 it gets from each paid subscriber. And a lot lower than Apple Music, where they get a full subscription fee from every user.

So, now you understand why the music biz is pressuring Spotify to push its users away from free and into paid subscriptions. Spotify argues that the free service is necessary to get people into the "funnel" that leads them to paid subscriptions, which is true to some degree, but I understand there are a lot of people who never convert to subscription. This game is still in progress, so stay tuned.

The Biggest Streamer in the Known Universe

Here's an even bigger problem than Spotify's dilution:

Can you guess who delivers more music than any other service? In fact, delivers more music than all the other sites put together, including pirate sites? It's . . .

YouTube.

YouTube lets consumers call up their favorite music and listen to their little hearts' content, totally free to the user (though they have to put up with ads). In essence, this means the paid subscription services have to compete with "free."

In the prior section, you saw how Spotify's free, ad-supported service substantially reduces Spotify's ARPU, and this problem is on steroids when it comes to YouTube. First, as we discussed, there's a lower revenue base because ads generate far less than subscription money. Second, YouTube is the only service that offers consumers a free, unlimited, fully interactive service on mobile (which is where almost all the users are).

Huh?

The biggest streamer of music pays less per user than the others? How could anyone let that happen?

It's because of a quirk in the copyright law, which I'll explain on page 318, but for now just know that the labels can't really stop them. Accordingly, YouTube pays WAY less than Apple and Spotify. Put this together with the fact that YouTube delivers more music than anyone else, and you can see that a huge portion of the potential music audience has an abysmal ARPU.

Recently, YouTube started a premium service that, although it doesn't release numbers publicly, I'm told is still very small compared to Apple and Spotify. And even as it's growing, the vast majority of *all* music still goes through their free service.

Streaming Royalty Calculations

So what's all this mean to you as an artist? As we discussed, your royalty rate is applied to what the company gets. So now it's time for Toto to pull back the curtain and let you see the Wizard. Well, mostly pull it back; the deals aren't actually public. But I'll show you the outline of his face.

Essentially, the streaming services (remember they're called **DSPs,** meaning **Digital Service Providers**) pay a portion of their income to the record labels. As I said, the percentages aren't public, but I understand they're in the mid 50% range For our discussion, I'm going to refer to the percentage of income that the DSP pays to the record companies as the "Record Company's Percentage." That's not an industry term, I just made it up because it seems like a reasonable way to refer to a vague percentage. Cool?

As we discussed a while back, the Record Company's Percentage is applied to the DSP's total subscription fees and advertising revenue each month, then pro-rated for each master based on the number of streams that month. In other words, the DSP computes your company's percentage of the month's total streams, multiplies that percentage times their revenue, then pays out the Record Company's Percentage of revenue to your company.

When your company gets the dough, they then figure out your share of it, which is the percentage that your streams bear to your record company's total streams that month. Finally, they take that money and apply your royalty percentage to it. (If this isn't clear, take a look back at page 81 for a more detailed example.)

For subscription services, in addition to this formula, most of the record company deals have a **per-subscriber minimum,** also called a **per sub minimum,** or **PSM.** That means the company gets a certain amount for each of the DSP's subscribers, regardless of what the DSP actually collects. For example, the deal might say that payment for the service's use of master recordings can't be less than the Record Company's Percentage of $7 per subscriber. This is to discourage the DSPs from dropping their prices too low; the companies are worried the DSPs might do this just to build up subscribers. Or to drive traffic to another product, like Walmart in the old days, when they discounted CDs just to bring in people who buy refrigerators.

Here's how it works, using the example of a $10 per subscriber minimum (to make the math easier):

Let's say the Record Company's Percentage is 50%, meaning the

DSP is obligated to pay 50% of its revenue to the labels. If there is a $10 per subscriber minimum (I'm using an easy math number; this is much higher than any real PSM), the DSP can't pay less than 50% (the Record Company's Percentage) of $10 (the PSM), meaning it has to pay out $5 for every subscriber. This payout is to all the labels licensing content, so if your company's masters were 30% of the DSP's total streams in a month, they'd get 30% of the $5 per subscriber minimum, meaning $1.50 for each subscriber. This $1.50 is then pro-rated over all your company's artists, based on each master's number of plays. So if your masters were streamed 200,000 times in a month, and all of your record company's masters were streamed 1,000,000 times, your streams were 20% of the company's streams (200,000/1,000,000). Accordingly, 20% of $1.50 (30¢ per subscriber) would be allocated to your masters. You'd then get your royalty rate based on that 30¢. Meaning, if you had a 10% royalty, you'd get 3¢ per subscriber. (Of course, if 50% of the DSP's revenue that's allocated to your company is more than the PSM, you'd get the higher amount.)

Per Stream vs. Per User

There's a developing controversy over the current system (which I just described) of allocating money based on the number of streams. It certainly sounds fair on the surface—if you get more streams, you get more money. But is it?

The argument is whether it would be more equitable to allocate the money on a **per-user** basis, as opposed to the current system of allocating **per-stream.**

Let me explain.

I'm a niche artist, with an avid (but small) group of fans. My fans subscribe to Spotify and listen to my music a lot. Because I'm such a small player, my streams are a tiny percentage of the total streams, which means I get a very small piece of the pie under today's system of allocating *per-stream.*

What if, instead, I got a share of my fans' specific subscription money (meaning the money was allocated *per-user*)? Would that be more fair?

Here's a very simplified example:

Let's assume there's a streaming service with just two artists, you and me. Also assume there are only two subscribers (Billy and Leo), and they each pay $10 per month, for total subscription fees of $20. And assume the labels get 50% of that money, meaning $10.

In the first month, Billy listens only to me, and streams my songs

100 times. In that same month, Leo listens only to you, but streams your songs 900 times. Under today's per-stream system, since you had 90% of the listens, the DSP allocates 90% of the $20 total subscription fees to your label (meaning it gets its share of $18), and my label is allocated the remaining 10% of the fees (meaning it gets its share of $2). Since labels' deals with the streaming service are 50%, your label would get 50% of the $18, meaning $9, and my label would get the other $1. Thanks a lot . . .

However, if the allocation was based on per-user rather than per-stream, the payout would look very different. Since Billy listened only to me, my label would get 50% of Billy's subscription money, meaning 50% of $10, or $5 (instead of the $1 under today's system). And your label would only get $5 of Leo's subscription money instead of $9. You're welcome . . .

This would of course benefit the smaller artists, and I think it has the ring of extreme fairness. But it's a lot more complicated than my example. Subscribers listen to billions of streams, and I doubt if more than a handful listen to only one artist, if any. So setting up systems to reallocate like this would be incredibly complex and expensive. A recent article I came across said that the differential could be about 4% of the total money, meaning that 4% would go away from the top streaming artists and be spread around the rest of the system. However, this was based on a very small study in Finland, so I have no idea how accurate it would be overall. (If you want to see the article, which will likely be out of date by the time you read this, it's online at Music Business Worldwide, titled "Spotify Still Pays Artists Out of One Big 'Pot.' Should the Company Change Its Policy?")

Streaming services acknowledge that a user-based allocation could be fairer, but they argue that the cost of setting up and implementing new systems would eat up the differential. Not to mention the politics of taking money from top-selling artists who benefit from the current system.

So stick around; this could get interesting.

Breakage

Another issue around subscription services today is **breakage.** Which doesn't mean a coffee mug you knocked over in a souvenir shop and now have to buy. It means . . .

Newer streaming services (and new business models that use music) have to get licenses to use masters or they can't be in business. Unfortunately, a lot of newer companies have this nasty habit of going broke and stiffing record companies. So to protect themselves from *Sorry It Didn't Work, I'm Outta Here, Incorporated,* the labels get advances up front against future income and/or nonrecoupable money. In addition, record labels sometimes get stock in the new business as part of their license, or they might get the right to buy stock as part of their license deal.

Let's assume your record company gave a two-year license to a start-up DSP and got a $1 million advance (I'm making up numbers for the example—they actually get much more than that). At the end of the two years, the deal is over, so the DSP can no longer use the music. However, the record label only earned $600,000 over the two years, meaning $400,000 of the $1 million is unrecouped. Since this was a nonreturnable advance, the record company doesn't have to pay back the $400,000 that wasn't earned. This unearned amount (the $400,000 in our example) is called *breakage*. "Breakage" also includes nonrecoupable money, which of course is never earned back, and arguably the stock they got in the company.

So the question is, do artists share in breakage?

The companies argue that it's not payment for use of your masters, so you haven't earned a piece of it. And it's true that, unlike royalties, this money isn't earned by any specific master. But we who represent artists argue that there wouldn't be any breakage if there weren't any artists in the catalog. So all the artists should share in it.

It's worth asking for a piece of breakage in your deal, and many companies are willing to agree if you have some clout. As a practical matter, all the majors, and some of the big independents, share breakage with artists even if they're not contractually required to (for example, they share with artists who are under older deals that were done before breakage became a big thing).

Most (if not all) companies will now also share the profit they make from taking stock in a new business that licenses their catalog, though this is also almost impossible to get contractually. By "profit," I mean they'll deduct whatever they paid for the stock and share the excess.

Each of the majors has a different way of distributing breakage to their artists. In general,

1. They first look at how your masters performed during the term of the license to which the breakage relates.
2. Next, they compare the results of your performance to the performance of all the company's masters for that time period.

3. The company then computes your percentage of the total per-formances by dividing the result of number 1 above by the result of number 2.
4. Next they multiply that percentage times the breakage money, to determine the share of money that's allocated to your mas-ters.
5. Finally, they multiply the money determined under number 4 above times your royalty rate, and the result is your share.

This is a little easier to see with numbers. Using our breakage figure of $400,000, if your masters streamed 1 million times during the rel-evant period, and all the company's masters steamed 10 million times, you'd be allocated $\frac{1}{10}$ (10%) of the $400,000 breakage ($40,000). If you have a 15% royalty, you get 15% of the $40,000 ($6,000).

While that's generally the formula, there are differences between the companies in the computations. For example, some labels allocate based only on your streams over the service that generated the break-age, while others look at your streaming numbers on all the services. Some labels also factor in your overall track record with the company, including downloads and CDs. Also, some companies pay your share of breakage as a royalty, meaning it's used to recoup your advances and costs, while others pay it to you whether you're recouped or not. And some won't pay if you're no longer signed to the label when the break-age happens.

Downloads

A **digital download,** which is also called a **DPD** (standing for **digital phonorecord delivery**)**,** is a transmission to the consumer (via Inter-net, satellite, cell phone, mental telepathy, etc.) that allows the buyer to download music for later use. Examples are songs sold via the iTunes download store and ringtones.

Sales of DPDs are falling quickly, but they're still around as I write this, so let's take a few minutes to understand them.

There are two kinds of downloads:

1. **Permanent downloads.** As the name implies, it's yours forever, and you can copy it, burn it, stomp it, or do anything else your heart desires. Well, actually not "anything." When you sign up with a digital retailer, the fine print you never bother to read be-

fore you click "Accept" contains something called an **End-User License Agreement** (her friends know her as **EULA**). In that hot little piece of literature, buried among exciting words and phrases, it says that the downloads are only for your personal, non-commercial use.

2. **Tethered downloads. Tether,** which is a fancy word for *leash,* means the service provider doesn't give you complete control over the download. These are also known as **conditional downloads.** For example, Spotify allows you to load songs onto your phone so you can listen offline, but if you stop paying your subscription, they send little gnomes over the Web to eat your music.

For iTunes-type *permanent downloads,* the record companies get what they call a "wholesale price" equal to 70% of the retail price (the other 30% is kept by the platform, such as iTunes, that sells the download).For example, the labels get about 91¢ for a 1.29¢ download, so if you have a 10% royalty, you'll get 9.1¢.

Tethered downloads are treated exactly like interactive streaming, meaning you get your royalty rate applied against the company's receipts.

Non-Interactive Streaming and Satellite Radio

Non-interactive streaming (also called **webcasting**) means you can only hear what the programmer decides to play (just like over-the-air radio stations). Pandora is by far the biggest non-interactive streamer, and another example is iHeartRadio. Also, there are tons of local radio **simulcasts,** which means a broadcast that's streamed on the Internet at the same time that it's broadcast over the air. A service called Tune-in aggregates the local stations and lets you access them on the Internet through your app. (On a personal note, I kinda got hooked to a small town station in Texas, where I particularly like the local ads. I'd never before heard a children's chorus singing a happy tune to advertise a crematorium. Honest.)

On an even smaller scale, there are individual webcasters who put together music they think is cool and send it out to the world.

Most of these webcasts are advertiser supported, but they can be paid subscription as well (for example, Pandora offers both).

Satellite radio, not surprisingly, sends music over a satellite rather than the Web. The biggest player in this area by far is Sirius XM, which is subscription based. Sirius XM is *non-interactive*, meaning you have to listen to whatever they decide to play. And unlike Pandora, you can't skip songs or customize the content (other than by changing channels, which has been a form of interactivity ever since a second radio broadcaster started transmitting in the 1920s).

For non-interactive webcasting and satellite radio, the copyright law requires record companies to license their masters at a rate set by the government. This is called a **statutory rate,** because the rate is set by a statute (a law). The money is not paid by the broadcaster directly to the labels, but rather is collected by an outfit called **SoundExchange.** Exactly what gets paid is pretty complicated, and I want you to stay awake for the moment, so I stuck it further back in the book (on page 316 if you can't wait).

Video Streaming

Video streaming deals are the same percentage (mid-50%) as the audio deals *if* the video is produced by a record company. All other videos that use music (such as a little old lady moshing to a punk rock track) are called **user-generated content** (known in the trade as **UGC**), because they're created by a user of the video service rather than a company. Record companies get a lower rate for UGC than they get for a record company–created video. The only exception is a UGC video that really does nothing more than showcase the music (for example, a video that plays a song all the way through while showing a picture of the album cover, pictures of the artist, lyrics, etc.). These showcase videos are paid at the same rate as a video made by the record company.

If the UGC is a video of someone sitting at a piano and playing a song, then the record company gets nothing because there's no use of their master. Only the songwriters get paid, and we'll talk about what they get later (on page 237).

MASTER LICENSES

When masters are licensed by a record company for motion pictures, television shows, and commercials, the company gives you 50% of their net receipts, meaning the company's gross receipts, less any third-party payments, the company's direct costs for duplication, shipping, etc.

The amount of money that the companies get for master licenses is almost always the same amount charged by the publishers for use of the song, which we'll discuss in detail on page 242. If you flip ahead, don't forget to come back.

SAMPLES

Sampling means using a part of your master in someone else's record (or licensing someone else's master for use in your recording). Sampling is a bit legally complicated, so I'd like you to have a few more concepts before we tackle it. When we get to it on page 250, I'll tell you what you can expect if someone samples your master (which is also what you have to pay if you sample someone else's master).

GUEST ARTISTS, FEATURED ARTISTS, AND JOINT RECORDINGS

A **joint recording** (keep the puns to yourself) is where more than two or more royalty artists get together on the same song, such as a duet. *Joint recording* is the term we use in contracts; in the real world, these are called **guest artist** deals, because one of the artists is "guesting" on the other artist's record. Or they're called **featured artist** deals, or **collaborations**, or **I'm more important than you are, so you're lucky to have me on your record** (well, maybe not the last one).

These deals are becoming more and more common, particularly in hip-hop and pop. A major guest artist can generate visibility for a lesser-known artist's track, which of course translates into a lot more streams. Which translates into more visibility for the artist.

How everyone gets paid really isn't covered in your record deal, because it's figured out case by case. When artists decide to collaborate, they negotiate with each other for the royalties and any advances. If you and the other artist aren't signed to the same label, the two labels also have to make a deal with each other before the record can go out.

Here's how it works:

Guest Artist Royalties

Historically, the most common arrangement for guest artists was to split the royalty among the artists in proportion to their numbers. So if it was a duet, each gets half; if there are three artists, each gets a third; etc. This is still the case when two artists of about equal stature get together, but most commonly, the guest artist gets a specific royalty rate. We'll talk about the range of those in a minute.

If it's a straight split of royalties, watch out for the following:

1. If you do a duet with a five-piece group, be sure that the group only counts as one entity. Otherwise, the company might say there are six royalty artists instead of two (you and the group), and you'll only get one-sixth of the royalty instead of one-half.
2. Whose royalty gets divided, yours or theirs? If you're the star, and you're on someone else's record, you want a share of *your* royalty, because it's likely to be higher than the other bozo. If you're new and singing with a star, try for a piece of theirs.

   Whatever gets divided, it's after deducting third-party royalties, like producers, mixers, and samples. Also, it's paid after recoupment of all costs charged by the record label in connection with the masters, such as recording costs, videos, promotional costs, etc.

If, instead of splitting, you negotiate a specific guest royalty, it can run anywhere from a few points (3% to 4%) if you're just singing a small part on the record, up to 10% for major stars. If the deal is for a negotiated royalty, you shouldn't be reduced for producer or mixer royalties.

Sometimes artists do what's called a **swap,** where the guest takes no royalty in exchange for a future performance by the other artist. For example, if Benjamin appears on Talia's record and takes no royalty, Talia agrees to sing on one of Benjamin's records for no royalty. The problem with swap deals among bigger artists is (a) it's hard to schedule the second recording because there's a tight delivery date and major artists are slammed; (b) you're in the middle of promoting your own records and your label doesn't want your voice on someone else's record during that time frame, and (c) creatively, you may not like the future track.

Guest artist deals get even more complicated in hip-hop and EDM. For example, some guest artists take a tiny royalty but want a huge advance that they can't possibly recoup. Also, some producers think they're artists, so they ask for more points than they'd normally get as a producer.

If the guest artist is also a writer, the main artist should require the guest to go along with their controlled composition clause. That means nothing to you because we haven't talked about it yet, but it's an important point, so make a note of it if you're doing a guest deal. We'll get to this baby on page 264.

As noted above, often the guest artist and the primary artist are signed to different labels. In this case, you can't do anything until the labels work out a clearance, which we'll discuss on page 172. So it's essential to alert your label as soon as you get a case of "guest-itis," and certainly don't start recording until the labels have signed off.

APPS

Here we're talking about apps that use music as the primary purpose of the app (such as Garage Band, TikTok, Beat Fever, karaoke apps, instructional music apps, etc.) or that use music as an important element of the app (like Flipagram, video games with music in the background, fitness apps such as Peloton, Aaptiv, and Soul Cycle). I'm not talking about apps that just let you access streaming music, such as Spotify, Apple Music, or iHeartRadio, which we already covered.

The payment for music in apps is a bit all over the place, mostly because the apps are all over the place. If an app isn't primarily a music product (for example, a game where you chase turkeys around the barnyard while listening to death metal), the deal is usually a flat fee in the range of $500 to $10,000 per song, depending on how much of it's used and the stature of the song. These licenses are always short—generally one year to eighteen months—so if the app succeeds, the company can ratchet up the money on the next round.

If an app is *monetized*, meaning it generates money after the initial download (for example ad sales, subscription fees, in-app purchases, emoticons, virtual currency, etc.), there may be a revenue share on top of the fee, running anywhere from 15% to 35%, depending on usage and the song. In computing these percentages, the app developer wants to deduct the fee that's charged by the platform where consumers get it (e.g., the iTunes store charges 30% of every purchase), and they also want to deduct the cost of ad sales. These are negotiable by the label, depending on bargaining power, but the norm is to at least allow them to deduct the 30% platform fee. For example, if an app sells for a dollar, iTunes takes 30¢ for selling the app, and the app developer gets 70¢. If your company's share of the money is 20%, it gets that portion of the 70¢, meaning 14¢.

If the app is subscriber based, there will usually be a per-subscriber minimum (we discussed this concept on page 144).

In revenue sharing deals, there's almost always an advance against the royalty. The amount is totally dependent on the specific situation, importance of the song, and the nature of the use. It can run from a hundred dollars per song into the thousands. Sometimes these are deals for all the masters in the company's catalog (subject to the artist's approval where required), and in that case, the advance can be really big bucks.

Even if the app has no revenue after the initial download, the record companies sometimes charge a yearly fee (a flat fee or a minimum per user) for as long as your music is in the app. Note this means the app developers are paying these fees out of their own pocket, because there's no additional money coming in. They're willing to do this because they're building up a user base (which makes their business more valuable), and that's more important to them than making a profit in the short term.

Another variation is called a **step deal,** where there's an initial fee, and an additional fee for a certain number of downloads.

A recent trend is for record companies to ask that app developers link to a Spotify or Apple Music account. In other words, the music isn't embedded in the app, but rather linked to a DSP that streams the music. That way, each time the song is streamed, the label gets paid under its deal with the streaming service.

You might be surprised to hear that song identifiers like Shazam and SoundHound don't pay for music at all. That's because they don't actually have any music in their apps. All they do is digitally fingerprint the music (meaning they break it down into little digital chunks), then match those identifiers against what they're "hearing." The labels all have deals with these apps, because they view the service as highly promotional (for example, Shazam lets you add a song to your Spotify playlist when you identify it). Even more important, the labels want the app's data of which songs people are chasing down.

If you're on the Fast Track, skip ahead to page 164, starting with Accountings

RINGTONES AND RINGBACKS

Ringtones are short clips of songs that play when your cell phone rings. **Ringbacks** happen when you call someone and instead of hearing an annoying ringing signal, you hear an annoying song. Ringtones are something you download and own, while ringbacks are held on the server of the phone service provider, so you're only "renting" them. Ringtones and ringbacks were at one time a surprisingly strong business (doing sales in the billions per year), but they took a major nosedive when it became easy to make your own for free. Currently they're not a big source of income.

Ringtones started out as **polyphonic,** which means the song was played by a synthesizer, but nowadays almost all of them are the actual master recording by the artist (called a **mastertone** or a **truetone**). If it's polyphonic, you have nothing to do with it as an artist—the only one who gets paid is the songwriter (we'll discuss how much the songwriter gets on page 217). If it's a master recording, the record company gets paid by the ringtone company, and then pays you a share equal to your royalty rate.

For mastertones, the companies get about 50% of the retail price charged to the customer, sometimes with a minimum amount per sale (the minimum puts a floor on what the record company gets, no matter how low the consumer price drops). So if a ringtone is $2.00, the record company gets $1.00, and if you have a 10% royalty, you'll get 10¢.

VIDEO GAMES

Here we're talking about true video games (think Grand Theft Auto), rather than apps, which we just discussed.

Except for games where music is an essential part (like Guitar Hero, R.I.P.), the licenses are on a flat-fee basis. And the fees are low, because the video companies don't believe that any particular song means more people will play the game.

The fees that labels get for these deals are the same amounts that songwriters get, which we'll discuss later (on page 248).

BUNDLES

A **bundle** is a combination of stuff (a "bundle" of products, so to speak . . .) that you get for a single price. For example, if you buy a concert ticket and get a code that allows you to download the album for free. Another example is where you get a basic music streaming service when you subscribe to Amazon Prime.

What you get for bundled services are all over the map, so unfortunately I can't give you a lot of specific guidance. It depends on what music is offered, whether a consumer automatically gets the music as part of the purchase or whether they pay more for it (called an **add-on**), what the other product is, how much the service is getting for the bundle, what the executives had for breakfast, etc.

In the broadest of strokes, the record company and bundler agree on a percentage of the bundle's price that's allocated to the music. The bundler then pays that percentage to the record company and you get your share of it. Or sometimes the music payment isn't a percentage of the price, but rather a flat fee for each bundle (for example, every time the bundler sells a widget, the record label gets $3). Sometimes it's a bundle of $100 bills in a leather satchel (just kidding about the last one, in case we're being wiretapped).

TELEVISION ADVERTISING

A number of years ago, record companies figured out (only in Europe at the time) that they could sell a lot of records by doing short bursts of television advertising. In fact, this worked so well that it quickly exported itself to America and other territories. Today, it's not really the case in the United States at all, and driving "sales" is a disappearing game. However, these provisions are still in contracts for the time being.

If your company decides to do any TV advertising, their form contract says they can recoup the costs of it from your royalty, meaning if you're successful, you're paying for it.

With some clout, you can push back. Usual compromises are to let them only recoup a portion (50%) of the costs, or to reduce your royalty on the advertised album to 50% for as long as they can get away with. They love to get two years, and I love to give them much less. Here are some things to ask for:

1. Get approval of the campaign before they can deduct anything.
2. Try to restrict the reduction to the income earned during the quarterly or semiannual accounting period during which the campaign is launched and the following period (maybe a third

period after that, if you have to). The idea is to keep the reduction period close to the campaign, so the reduction is only of money generated by TV ads.

3. The total amount taken from your royalty shouldn't exceed half the cost of the campaign.
4. Make certain they can only reduce the royalties in those territories where the campaign is running—you'd be surprised what their little forms say about taking reductions everywhere.

PODCASTS

Not much money in podcasts. Usually they're free to the user, as they're ad supported.

Licenses are generally done on a flat-fee basis, though sometimes the labels get a percentage of the ad revenues. The fees are small, and there aren't really any standards. Moreover, some podcasters seem to just go ahead and use the music without asking anybody, hoping they're small enough that no one bothers. I don't recommend this . . .

MULTIPLE ALBUMS/BOX SETS

The **multiple album** went through an enormous change when vinyl first fell off a cliff years ago. Originally it meant an album that couldn't fit on one vinyl disc, since vinyl discs were limited to a maximum of fifty-some-odd minutes of playing time. Then it meant more than one cassette. When CDs appeared, they could hold substantially more music than a vinyl disc or single cassette, so it took a lot of material to require two CDs. Thus *multiple albums* (in the classic sense of a two-CD package) were rare.

When they existed, there was a complicated royalty formula, because the increased manufacturing and packaging costs (as well as increased payments to songwriters) meant the company had a smaller profit margin, even with a higher price. Prior editions of the book had the formulas, but they're now pretty much irrelevant, so I'll spare you. And frankly, they bored me, too.

But like any good zombie movie, multiple albums came back to life, ironically in part because vinyl has come back to life. In this new life form, they are **box sets,** meaning a collection of multiple vinyl or CD records, and usually a career retrospective. They may contain reissues of old albums, unreleased cuts, alternative versions of well-known songs, demo recordings, posters, compromising photos, etc. They can also be a retrospective of a company (for example, Capitol or Motown) or a genre (the Blues, the Definitive Chicken Dance), etc. And they're very high-priced, which means their sales potential is limited.

The royalties on box sets are always negotiated at the time the product is being put together, and are very specific to the particular package. They'll depend on the selling price, manufacturing costs, number of selections (which affects the songwriters' royalties—we'll discuss those later), cost of licensing tracks from other labels, size of the artist's original royalty rate, and your leverage. Unfortunately, there are no real guidelines, since each deal is so unique, except that there's usually a reduced artist royalty and almost always a reduced songwriter royalty.

If you're on the **Advanced Overview Track,** go
to the Accounting section on page 164.

DEARLY DEPARTING CONTRACT CLAUSES

Cue the somber Funeral March. You're now entering the Dying and Truly Dead section of the music biz. Please speak softly.

Despite the fact that these contract clauses are almost irrelevant, either because they deal with physical and downloads, or because the practice they cover has disappeared, virtually every record contract still has these provisions.

So let's hit them briefly. If you find yourself yawning, skip to the Accounting section on page 164 (which isn't exactly riveting . . .).

Mid-Price Records

After a record has had its initial run in current release, it's known as a **catalog item,** meaning it's listed in the company's catalog of available titles but isn't being currently promoted. Some catalog items are issued at **mid-price,** meaning a reduced price that's designed to encourage consumers to buy older titles. The contractual definition of a mid-price record (with slight variations from company to company) is one "with a PPD between 66.6% and 80% of the price for newly released top-line records." Some companies go as high as 85% for mid-price. A lower percentage of the top-line price is better for you, because your royalty goes down when you get there, as you're about to see:

Royalty

The royalty for mid-price is usually from 66.66% to 75% of the U.S. basic rate (if you have a 10% royalty, that means 6.66% to 7.5%). Note this is a double whammy—not only is the royalty rate lower, but the PPD on which it's based is also lower. The record companies justify this because their wholesale price is less, and accordingly so is their profit margin.

As you gain clout, you can negotiate a period of time after initial release before a record can be sold at mid-price (usually twelve months, moving up to eighteen with some clout), or sometimes even a flat prohibition without your consent.

If you do get restrictions, it'll only be for the United States. That's because, in some foreign territories, mid-price is customary for the first release. Presumably, your interests and the record company's are the same, since they want to maximize their profits in that territory. Thus they won't put something out at mid-price unless they believe the reduced price will promote enough extra sales to justify the lower profit margin.

Presumably . . .

Budget Records

The next step down from mid-price is **budget,** which means the company doesn't think it can sell the stuff unless it knocks the price way down. The contractual definition of budget records is one with a price of less than 66.6% of the top-line price, but sometimes there's no mid-price definition and the contract says everything under 80% of the top-line price is a budget record.

Royalty

The royalty on budget records is usually 50% of the top-line royalty rate, or 5% in our 10% example. With some clout, you can hold back budget records for a period after initial release. Because your being on a budget line is a statement about what the company thinks of your career, you can usually get a longer holdback than you can for mid-price. For example, in the United States, the company might agree to wait twelve to eighteen months after initial release (which you can push to two years with some clout). Again, foreign markets have their own peculiarities, and there will be little you can do unless you're a major artist in a particular territory.

As your muscle increases, you may be able to get a flat prohibition against budget, at least during the term of your agreement. And, if you can't get the right to consent to budget records after the term, a compromise is to say they can't do it as long as your account is recouped. The idea is that, if they've lost money on your project, they can do whatever they want to get even, but otherwise they should keep you off the budget line.

Deletes, Scraps, and Other Food For Bottom Feeders

When a company finds that an album isn't selling at mid-price or budget, either because nobody cares about it or because the company over-manufactured and/or had gigantic returns, it looks for a way to bail out for whatever it can get. These used to be called **cutouts** because they were cut out of the company's catalog of available recordings, but since the days of streaming, nothing gets cut out—it simply sits on the services, lonely and still tucked in some cobwebbed corner.

When the company decides physical product isn't going to sell, the leftovers are sometimes sold as **scrap**, to be broken up for their component parts. If not, they're sold as **schlock**, which means they're put in the bins for 99¢, $1.50, etc. Artists get no royalties whatsoever for these, as the company says (correctly) that they're sold at cost or below, just to get rid of them. Also, most forms say that any sales under 50% of the top-line price don't bear royalties at all.

With negotiating power, you can say that the company can't schlock your records sooner than eighteen to twenty-four months after initial release, or with some clout, twenty-four to thirty-six months after release. (Note you can do this for schlock, not scrap. You can't restrict their ability to sell records as scrap because the public never knows about it; schlock, however, tells the world that your records are fit for lining parakeet cages.) You can also get the right to buy these records at the best price offered to the record company, but I've never felt this is of any practical value. You're not likely to be able to sell them at a better price than the company, and what are you going to do with 10,000 dogs?

Reserve Limitations

Reserves are money that the company holds back in case your physical product is returned (as we discussed on page 84). Limiting reserves used to be a big deal, when CDs were the only game. But as CDs bite the big one, this clause is becoming less and less relevant. At least for the moment, however, CDs are still alive, so reserve limitations are worth asking for.

You should ask to limit your reserves to around 35% to 50% of the records shipped, which was historically the norm. But even though CD sales are dropping, and they're only a fraction of the dough, reserve limits have interestingly gotten harder to get—the falling sales increase your record company's risk of overshipping product that won't sell. So these days, the companies don't like specific percentage limitations; they just want to say "reasonable reserves." That language is better than nothing at all, because it at least gives you the right to argue with them if you think they're taking too much.

In any event, you should make sure that your agreement says they can't take reserves on digital exploitations because digital sales are what the industry calls **one-way,** meaning that they can't be returned. Therefore there's no reason to hold a reserve. Most companies won't take digital reserves, even if their agreement says they can, but you should say so anyway.

At mid-level and up, you can also force the company to **liquidate** (meaning "pay out") the reserves over a set period of time, usually two years. Try to make the liquidation **ratable,** meaning they have to pay an equal amount each time. For example, if the company has to liquidate your reserves over two years, that means four six-month accounting periods. If they're required to liquidate *ratably*, they have to pay you one-fourth of the reserves in each of the four periods. If you don't say this, they could pay you a small percentage in the first three periods and hold the bulk of your money until the end.

Coupling and Compilations

The practice of putting your performances on records with perfor-mances of other artists is known as **coupling,** and albums with a bunch of different artists are called **compilations.** In days of yore, compila-tions such as the NOW series sold multi-millions, but in the streaming age, people can just listen to the tracks they like, or create their own playlist compilation. To the extent compilation albums exist, they're almost exclusively soundtrack albums from motion pictures with diverse music (*O Brother, Where Art Thou?*; *Pulp Fiction*; etc.).

Royalties

The royalty on coupled products sold by your record company is pretty much what you'd think—if there are ten cuts on the album and you did one of them, you get one-tenth of your normal royalty; if you did two cuts out of ten, you get 20%, etc. This process is called **pro-ration,** and you are said to have a **pro-rata** royalty (meaning your royalty is in proportion to the number of cuts on the album). Sometimes, however, your company will want to negotiate a specific royalty for the compilation, and guess which way they want your royalty to go?

If your company doesn't release the compilation album, but rather licenses your track to another company who releases it, your royalty is usually 50% of the company's licensing receipts from your track, though a few labels just pay a lower royalty for compilations (pro-rated by the number of cuts). Remember, in an all-in royalty deal, your share includes the producer's royalty (we discussed the producer's share of this on page 126).

Control

You should always try to control coupling, and while this used to be a fight because the record company could make money from licensing you out, the digital age has made this way less relevant (some would say irrelevant, though we're not quite there yet). I would still ask for it, both for (1) the artistic reason that you don't want to be on a record with someone you hate; and (2) the financial reason that you can make sure you think the deal is worthwhile. With moderate bargaining power, you can control coupling during the term of your deal, but the companies carve out things like playlists on streaming services, jukeboxes, in-transit uses (like in-flight programs), and similar stuff. With more bargaining power, you can control it after the term, at least if you're recouped.

If you get control, it's normally just for the United States, unless you have incredible bargaining power.

Even as a new artist, you should at least be able to get a limit on the number of couplings. A common provision is to say the company can't couple more than two of your selections per year, and can't put you on more than two albums per year. Note the difference between these two concepts: If the company's only limit is two selections per year, they could put one of your hits on thirty-seven different compilation albums. Control is getting easier and easier to get these days because there are so few compilations still around.

"Greatest Hits" Albums

The royalties on Greatest Hits albums used to be a big deal (see page 121 for what a Greatest Hits album is, and see the obituary section of your local newspaper if you want to know how well they're selling). Since they're virtually nonexistent today, it's not worth saying much. Essentially, you get pro-rata royalties (see page 162) for each track, based on the royalty rate of the album they come from. For example, if your first two albums were 12%, and the others 13%, and if half the Greatest Hits album was from the first two albums (12%) and half from the others (13%), your royalty on the Greatest Hits album would be 12.5% (50% times 12%, plus 50% times 13%).

DVDs

The royalties on DVDs, another near-death configuration, are the same as your audio record royalties.

Record Clubs

Record clubs are truly dead and buried. Except they don't seem to know it, because every record deal still has a provision for them.

Record clubs are (were) mail-order "clubs" that you join by agreeing to buy a certain number of records. The companies give you 50% of their net receipts from the record club, and since they don't exist, just take it.

I would make them get your consent before they include you in a record club, so if they ever come back to life, you can figure out a deal.

Premiums

Premiums are records sold or given away in connection with a sponsor, such as getting a free CD when you buy a new car. Nobody really cares about getting CDs anymore, and in fact new cars don't even have CD players. But contracts still mention premiums, so at least you now know what they are.

The only thing you need in your contract is to say the company needs your consent to use any of your music in a premium. You should really push for this, because premiums use your music to sell another product, and you shouldn't be associated with any product without your consent. That's a valuable right.

If the company can't do anything without your consent, and premiums make a miraculous recovery, you can decide if you want to play.

ACCOUNTINGS

When do you get your royalties? Twice a year, within ninety days after the close of each calendar six-month period (except for some companies that use weird, noncalendar six-month periods). As I write this, however, some companies are talking about moving to a quarterly system, meaning you'd get paid every three months. Let's encourage them!

Objections

Your contract will say that each accounting becomes "final" (meaning you can no longer argue it's wrong) one or two years after the statement is sent to you. If the companies didn't say this, you'd have until four years after the statement (in California) or six years after (in New York) within which to sue them. That is, of course, precisely why they say it.

You can increase the objection period to two years, and often three years, with minimal clout. Superstars can sometimes get four years. Always get the longest period you can, because it's uneconomical to audit unless you can cover a number of years at once.

What's auditing? Funny you should ask . . .

Audit Rights

Closely following the accounting clause is an **audit** clause, which says you can *audit* (meaning send in an accountant to verify) the record company's books. This is a way of ensuring that you're getting a fair reporting, and if you have any success, you should do it. Audits are expensive ($25,000 to $50,000 or more), so you'd better be recouped (or close to recoupment in the near future) before you start. There's not much joy in proving that, instead of being $1,000,000 unrecouped, you're only $900,000 unrecouped. Most reputable auditors will give you an indication of whether an audit is worthwhile before you engage them. They do this by looking at your contract and your accounting statements and knowing what the various record companies do.

Nowadays almost every record contract has a built-in right to audit, although in the past you had to ask for it. The audit clause will also say you can't audit more than once in any twelve-month period; that you can't examine any particular accounting statement more than once; and that you can only audit before the period to object has expired (see the above section).

13

Advanced Record Deal Points

EXCLUSIVITY

I'm sure you won't be shocked to learn that every record contract includes a provision that says the deal is **exclusive**. In other words, during the term of the agreement, you can't make records for anybody else. However, just like a TV commercial for prescription drugs, here's a list of side effects (pretend there's soft orchestral music playing while we talk about nausea, shortness of breath, and oily residue):

Motion Pictures

Remember, as we discussed on page 78, that companies now define "records" so broadly that the term includes motion pictures, television appearances, webcasts, and Ninja blenders (maybe not the last one). Put that together with the fact that you can only make "records" for your label, and you'll quickly see that your company can stop you from singing in motion pictures or on television, even where there's no audio-only record involved. They can also stop you from being streamed when you appear at a festival. And they can stop you even if there's no music involved, like the case when you're the actor in a film. Or appearing on a TV talk show without singing. Nice, huh?

You can usually negotiate some slack in these, if you know enough to ask. Here's a map.

If there's no music involved, most companies will easily agree that you can be an actor and let you keep all the money (though they may want their 360 share of that money). When you start performing music, things get stickier. You'll need the label's permission, and if they let you, they'll want a chunk of your money to let it happen (as we'll discuss in a second). With respect to films, the most common compromise is that they let you perform one or two songs in a film with a laundry list of restrictions, such as keeping the size of your name the same as other artists, requiring a credit to the company, not granting any audio-only rights, etc. With more leverage, you can do more songs as long as you don't give the film company audio-only record rights.

In either case, the record company will be looking for money. They usually want 100% of what you're paid to perform in the film, of which they keep half (for releasing you from your exclusivity) and credit the other half to your account (meaning it's paid to you if you're recouped, or it's used to recoup your deficit if you're not). If you've got some clout, you may be able to knock down their percentage (say to 25%), or even keep the entire fee yourself.

But what about audio record rights, you ask? You've seen lots of artists with recordings on soundtrack albums, often on different labels. How does that happen? Short answer: with difficulty.

Record companies don't want you freely dropping recordings on others because (a) they want to be exclusively identified with you; (b) they don't want someone else releasing a record at a time that would conflict with one of your own singles or albums (incidentally, neither should you, as you normally make a lot less on soundtrack recordings than your own label's recordings); and (c) if they bend on these mighty principles, they want to get paid.

So how do people get on soundtrack albums? Well, it's handled one of two ways in your record deal:

Forget It. At some record companies, this is an absolute "religious issue" ("sacred cow," "irrefutable principle," etc.—you get the idea), meaning you have no right to let anyone else put out a soundtrack album with your recording on it. In these cases, the artist throws himself or herself on the mercy of the record company each time a film company asks them to perform a song in a movie. The record company either agrees to let the artist perform (with restrictions—see below), or it refuses and the issue is closed (unless your manager can yell loud enough to reopen it). The other choice is to force the film company to give the soundtrack album to your record company, because there is then no conflict. If you're important enough, you can do this, even if you're only on one track.

Contractual Exclusions. If you have clout, you can negotiate an automatic contractual soundtrack album exclusion in your record deal, at least with some companies (or even with the sticklers if you're King

Kong). These typically have some or all of the following laundry list (which will also apply if you have no exclusion but get the company's consent at the time):

1. You can't perform on more than one (or two at most) selections for inclusion in the album.
2. You can't do recordings for more than one soundtrack release during any one-year (or two-year) period of the term. Sometimes it's an overall limit, such as a maximum of three cuts over the term.
3. You must not be late in delivery of your product at the time.
4. All the royalties and advances must be paid to your record company. (Note that here we're talking now about advances against your royalties, as opposed to a fee that you may get for using your recording in the film, which we already discussed.) Just like the film fee, after the company gets your royalties and advances, it'll want to keep 50% for releasing you from the exclusivity and credit the other 50% to your royalty account.

   If the soundtrack album is being released by your own company, you should be able to get 100% of the monies credited to your account, either to reduce your deficit, or to be paid out if you're recouped. If you really have a lot of bargaining power, you can get 50% or more of the royalties paid to you even if you're unrecouped. Your argument is that the film recording is in addition to the product they're entitled to get under your deal, and thus should be treated separately.
5. You must try to get the right to use the recording on one of your albums. The film company, if it gives these rights, will ask for a holdback period before you can do it. (This is discussed on page 442.)

An interesting issue has come up around soundtrack albums in the streaming age. Namely, if someone streams a single song, does the money go to your label or to the label distributing the soundtrack? I'll give you the answer later (on page 429 if you want to cheat and look ahead).

Streaming, TV, and Radio Broadcasts

There are four flavors of streaming/broadcast rights that are swept up by your exclusivity clause:

1. On-demand streaming of audio and/or videos on the Internet (Spotify, Apple Music, Rhapsody, YouTube, Vevo, etc.; see page 234);
2. Non-interactive streaming (see page 233);
3. TV, radio, and film appearances; and
4. Streaming of your concerts

Numbers 1 and 2 are not surprises. Those are the company's primary business; they obviously need these rights.

Numbers 3 and 4, however, snag artists who aren't careful, because these uses don't feel like they have anything to do with "records." But under your contract, a "record" is any reproduction of sound and/or video, and these uses are "electronic transmissions" (see page 140 for the definition of those). Which means your company has the exclusive rights. Which means, if you want to do any kind of broadcast, motion picture, or streaming, you have to go to your label (a) to get their permission, and (b) if they say okay, pay them a chunk.

If you're doing a purely promotional radio or TV appearance (*Saturday Night Live, Howard Stern, Jimmy Kimmel,* etc.), they want to be in the loop but won't get in the way—in fact, they usually help set these up. Their major concern is the afterlife of those performances, such as on-demand streaming. Because artists are so regularly on these shows, the major labels have standard contracts with the TV producers concerning these rights, so this is rarely a fuss. The usual deal lets the TV show stream your performance as part of the show, but not apart from it. They may also limit the amount of time they can make your performance available online.

For concert webcasts, which have become very common for festivals, things get more intense. Superstars may be able to pre-negotiate some very narrow exceptions, but record companies have become increasingly touchy in recent years. They view concert streams of your performances as competitive with their streaming of your music. Meaning they want to get paid.

This is usually worked out by the promoter sliding money to the record company. The deals are negotiated case by case, though if it's a big enough festival and they regularly do business with your label, the promoter may do an overall deal that covers the label's roster.

Motion pictures are far more complicated, so we'll hit them down the road in Chapter 28, when you've got some more concepts under your belt.

Re-recording Restrictions

All contracts say you can't re-record any song you recorded during the term of a deal for a certain period of time *after* the term. This is known as a **re-recording restriction**. When you think about it, it's perfectly logical—without it, you could go out the day after your deal is over and duplicate your masters for somebody else.

The usual restriction period is five years from the date of recording, but with a minimum of three to five years after the end of the term. The minimum keeps you from re-recording an album delivered in the first year of a six-year deal immediately after the term, even though it's been more than five years since you recorded it. While the five years from recording is pretty much carved in stone, you can almost always get the period after the term down to two years. Some companies also add a period beyond this date (seven years, or sometimes less) during which you can't re-record more than four songs on any one record.

Trivia Fun Fact: The world's record for re-recording restrictions belongs to Decca Records, who structured a deal under which Bing Crosby had a *perpetual* re-recording restriction for the song "White Christmas."

In the early days of the business, re-recording restrictions applied only to "records," and those were defined as audio-only consumer products. Which meant there was no restriction on re-recording for motion pictures, commercials, etc. So a lot of classic artists started re-recording songs for movies and commercials, instead of using the original master (for which the record company could have charged a fee). In response, the companies changed their contracts like this:

1. As we've discussed, the companies expanded the definition of "record" to include everything imaginable, so you can't re-record for any purpose during the restrictive period.
2. Most companies now say you can *never* re-record your songs to sound just like the masters you've given them, whether it's for records, commercials, or any other purpose. So nowadays, even after your re-recording restriction expires, you can only record a wholly different arrangement of the songs.

Note this dragnet also picks up performing on television and concert webcasts. That means you can't go on TV and perform any song that's under a re-recording restriction even *after* the term of your deal is over. If you know enough to ask, you can usually to carve out TV and concert webcasts. I strongly suggest you do this. It'll be hard to do a festival show without your old songs, unless you want the audience to spend a lot of time in the bathroom.

Side-Artist Performances

Isn't it nice how all the superstars seem to be playing instruments or singing background on everybody else's records? (I'm not talking about duets and featured guest artists; we covered those on page 151. These are things like a guitarist who plays on the record without singing, or a background singer.) These nonfeatured appearances are known as **side-artist** performances (they were historically called *sideman* performances, and still are by some folks, but I'm sure you agree that term is past its sell-by date. So let's put a nail in it).

Now that you're educated, don't you wonder how this is possible? Doesn't it violate the exclusivity provisions of the superstar's agreement when she sings background for her pals on another label?

The answer is yes, it violates their exclusivity. However, there's a strong custom in the industry (and you can usually add a provision to your contract just by asking) that allows side-artist performances on the following kinds of conditions:

1. The performance must be truly a background performance, without any solos, duets, or "stepping out."

2. You can't have a "featured" credit; you can just be in the liner notes (those things that used to be inside records that list the producers, musicians, and florists).

3. Your exclusive company must get a "courtesy credit" in the form of "[Artist] appears courtesy of _____ Records." (Before I started in the music biz, I always thought they did that just to be nice.)

4. You can't violate your re-recording restriction (see page 170), even as a background performer.

5. If you're a group, no more than two of you can perform together on any particular session. That's because your record company doesn't want your distinctive sound showing up on another label.

6. Some companies require you to get the other artist's label to give up a side-artist clearance in exchange for letting you go (sort of like a future draft pick).

Unless it's carved out of your contract, meaning you don't need your label's permission, the labels clear side-artist rights with each other by exchanging emails (rather than doing a formal contract). This is usually a "rubber stamp" process, unless one company is having a fight with the other about something unrelated to the side artist. After all, if one of the companies makes an issue of it, they won't have such an easy go when the other company's artist shows up as a side artist on their label. The process is something like porcupines dancing carefully with each other.

Guest Artists and Featured Artists

If it's a true duet, or featured performance on another label, clearing your exclusivity gets more complicated. A featured recording really has the ability to interfere with your company's plans for you.

We discussed the artist deals for featured performances on page 152, but because of your exclusivity, the two record companies also have to make a deal with each other before this can happen. You won't be directly involved in the deal, but if they get into a fight, no one can use the track. So you should understand the principles in case you or your manager need to referee.

Assuming everyone is cool with going ahead, it's handled with an override royalty to the guest artist's label, or if the guest artist is really big, there may be a profit share between the labels. The deals vary from situation to situation, depending on the bargaining power, stature of the artists, and whether the labels are getting along with each other at the time.

WEBSITES

Back when websites were strange and unknown creatures, the companies registered the website names of all their artists without bothering to ask. And without regard to the fact that most of their record deals, which were made before websites existed, probably didn't give them the right to do this.

After the predictable shouting, gouging, and five-finger death blows, most deals now provide that, during the term, the company will have the exclusive right to set up the artist's website and control social media (Twitter, Facebook, etc.). Their argument is that they want to present a coordinated marketing campaign across all platforms and, oh by the way, we're the big record company and you're not.

You can't really stop this without massive clout, but you should be able to limit them to one website. If you don't say this, their form contract will give them the right to multiple sites. If they agree, they will also want to have an artist section on their company website, which is fine. You should ask for approval of the look, feel, and content of your section of the company website.

After the term, all the website rights should go back to you, although they'll keep the right to have you on their company website. The contract usually requires you to give the company written notice before they fork over your site. Don't forget. Also, you should ask for the right to continue using their masters on your website after the term.

Some companies, if you ask, will allow the artist to set up an "unofficial" website during the term. You should ask the company to let you use your masters on that as well, but this takes some clout to pull off.

Companies also want to control your social media. You can usually exclude this, based on the argument that your fans believe it's you— whatever is posted reflects on your overall image and therefore has to be authentic. But even when you exclude it, the label won't let you post music on social media. Also, they'll want access to your social media to promote your records.

Some companies want to recoup the costs of creating and maintaining the artist's website and social media, but you should push back and say that it's a marketing expense (marketing expenses aren't customarily recoupable). If you can't get them to eat it, and this is hard with the companies that want to charge you, sometimes you can limit the amount they can recoup to, say, $25,000 over the life of the deal.

SINGLE-SONG VIDEOS

Single-song videos are the ones you see on YouTube, Vevo, and the like. Even though they're monetized these days, they're sometimes called **promotional videos**, because historically they were just marketing tools that lost money.

History

Did you know that music videos (which only became popular in the United States when MTV started in 1981) have been around since the 1960s in Europe? They were invented because it was cheaper for artists to make videos than to tour Europe. But videos have an even longer history than that. There are some great treasures that came from something called a "Scopitone" (pronounced "scope-ih-tone"). This was a jukebox that played videos on 16mm film, and it enjoyed a brief life in the late 1950s and early 1960s. Today the Scopitone videos are collectors' items, and they include a number of color videos from such artists as Sonny and Cher, Neil Sedaka, Dion, Nat King Cole, Bobby Darin, etc. And if you really want to delve into the past, there are black-and-white videos that were shown in cinemas in the 1940s and 1950s, with such artists as Fats Waller, Louis Jordan, Lena Horne, Bing Crosby, Spike Jones, and many others.

But back to this century.

The video issues in your contract are:

Is the Company Going to Make a Video?

This is the first question, because if the answer is no, there's not much else to talk about. Until you have quite a bit of bargaining power, the record company, totally by itself, decides whether or not to make a video. As your bargaining power increases, you can require the company to do one or two videos per album.

Creative Control

Creative control over the content of videos is very limited. Companies don't want to spend $50,000 for a video, then have you say the "vibes" don't hit you right, leaving them stuck with a turkey they can't monetize. So if they give you any approval rights, it'll usually be a bare-bones approval of the story, director, and maybe producer. If you have serious bargaining power, you may be able to get approval of all elements, including the final edit. Some superstars even take over control of making the video.

Recoupment

Historically there was a separation of video recoupment, but now everything goes into one big pot with your audio account. The only exception is a full concert-type video, which would be an entirely separate deal.

Budget

Budgets for shooting a video are typically designated or approved by the company. As your stature grows, you may be able to put in a minimum budget amount. The cost of videos has dropped radically over the years, and most are in the $15,000 to $50,000 range. A real superstar video can cost up to $400,000 or more, some as high as $1,000,000 plus, but videos over $250,000 are rare.

Once a video budget has been approved, record companies get very touchy about your running over the limit. Sometimes they flatly refuse to pay, and the artist (only superstars can afford this "luxury") actually writes a check. Other times they grudgingly, grumblingly, bitchingly pay the excess, but they charge it against anything they can grab—future advances, songwriting monies, etc.

For some artists, sponsors will pay money to have their product included in a video (called **product placement**). It's up to your own personal Cheese-O-Meter to decide if you're willing to hold a soft drink while you're hang-gliding. But if you are, the placement dollars can offset a lot (and sometimes all) of the video costs.

INDEPENDENT PROMOTION AND RADIO CONCERTS

There is an important phenomenon in the business known as **independent promotion.** Promotion people (as noted on page 70) get records played on the radio, and they have relationships with station programmers.

Some of these promotion people are independent of the record companies. Meaning they work for themselves and are hired by the companies on a project-by-project basis. They're cleverly called **independents,** to distinguish them from record company employees who do promotion. And unlike the in-house promotion people, they also have relationships with streaming services (which you may remember is handled by salespeople inside the label).

The independents are paid handsomely for their services by a record company (in most cases) or by the artist (in others). And by handsomely, I mean the costs for multiformat promotion (meaning Top 40, Alternative, Hot AC [Adult Contemporary], AAA [Adult Album Alternative], Rhythm, or Urban) can run $75,000 to $400,000 *per single*, and the prices are heading upwards. By the way, as high as those numbers sound, they're less than they were at their peak. A bit of history . . .

It's illegal to pay a broadcaster to play music in the United States (at least without disclosing they're being paid), and from time to time the government put pressure on independents, going back to the 1980s. When Eliot Spitzer was the attorney general of New York State (and before his hot nights with various ladies), he launched a probe into the record companies' promotion practices. In response, the companies cut back on independent promotion, and consequently the promotion prices came down and stayed down.

With respect to radio, the trend these days is to promote a record in one radio format, get some traction, then spend bigger money to take it to other formats. The initial format is known as a **point of entry,** because the idea is to get it to work in one genre, then move it to others. The art of promotion is knowing which stations will play the record, getting it to be a hit there, and moving it more formats. For example, if it's a cool, tasty track, you might start at alternative, build it up, and then go wider.

Top 40 is the Holy Grail of radio, meaning if they play it, your record has a chance to be massive. For that reason, Top 40 is also the most expensive to promote. So the companies like to see a record doing well in the smaller formats before they spend the big bucks to take it to Top 40. Also, the better your record has done in other formats, the more likely Top 40 will pay attention.

For streaming, it's a somewhat different game, but based on similar ideas. I've been told there are thirty thousand submissions to the streaming services every week, which means breaking through the noise requires a bulldozer on rocket fuel. Some independent promotion folks have relationships with the curators of the playlists, and can at least get you noticed. Whether the curators like your record enough to put it on a playlist is a different story, but you actually have a few bites at the apple (no pun intended). For example, Spotify has New Music Friday, which covers all genres. You can only be on it the first week of release. If you get on, you're a giant step ahead, particularly if you're far enough up that people notice. If you can't get on New Music Friday, then the promotion folks work the genre-specific playlists (rap, rock, pop, etc.) and try to build a buzz that spreads, just like we discussed with radio formats.

Once you're on the list, it's all about the data. The DSPs are very sophisticated with their algorithms; for example, they know what should happen to a record at your spot on the playlist if it's a hit, and they can see very quickly if it's not. If your song is reacting, it moves up, gets on more lists, and explodes. If it's lying there like that new kind of dog food you decided to try out on Muffy, it'll pretty quickly slide into the garbage disposal.

Whatever the company spends on independent promotion will be 50% to 100% recoupable from your royalties. It's worth fighting to keep the company from recouping more than 50% of independent promotion costs. If they're charging 100% to you, they don't have the same incentive to reduce spending as they do when 50% comes out of their own pocket.

Another form of promotion is what's known as **radio-promoted concerts.** Those of you in the bigger cities have seen local radio stations promote gigantic concerts with all kinds of big-name acts (for example, Jingle Ball). Independent promo folks have relationships with the stations, and they often broker deals for artists to do these shows. You probably didn't know that these acts are paid much less than their normal fees (or maybe no fee, just a reimbursement of their costs) to show up. They do it to generate goodwill with the radio station (which makes a large profit on these concerts), in exchange for the hope that these stations will play the artist's music. In essence, the artists are paying for promotion of their recordings by cutting their fees.

MERCHANDISING RIGHTS

Some record companies want to take artists' **merchandising rights,** also known as **merch rights.** These are the rights to put your name on T-shirts, posters, etc., and we'll discuss them in detail in Chapters 24 and 25. (Note: I'm not talking about the rights to put out promotional posters, promotional T-shirts, etc., which are distributed free as a way of marketing your records, and for which all record companies have the rights. This section is about record companies who want the right to sell your merchandise at concerts, in stores, etc.)

All record companies try to share in your merchandising income under the 360 provisions of their deals (as we discussed on page 102). However, some record companies want to get *active* merchandising rights (see page 106 for a refresher of *active rights,* but basically that means you give our merchandising rights to your label, who then is responsible for selling the goods and paying you a royalty for the sales).

Some companies have divisions that actually manufacture and distribute your merchandise. We'll discuss what those deals look like in Chapters 24 and 25. Other companies (usually independents) take these rights even if they don't have any manufacturing facilities. In other words, they're taking active rights, but they don't have the ability to exploit them. Instead, they turn around and license the rights out to a merchandiser, then pay you 50% of their receipts from that merchandiser. So not only do they get a bigger piece of the money, they also *control* your merchandising rights, meaning they can decide which merchandise company gets them (as opposed to you making that decision). That also means you have no direct contract with the merchandiser, which makes it harder to coordinate the business. On top of that, since the record company collects the money, they can try to cross-collateralize your merchandise earnings with your record deal (see page 88 for what that means). If you collect the money and pay them a piece under the 360 provisions, they can't do this.

It's certainly best to hold on to your active merch rights. But if the company is pushing back, try one of these:

1. You keep the active rights, but your company gets a **first negotiation** right. This means you have to talk to them first before you talk to anyone else, but if you can't make a deal, you can go elsewhere.

2. If the company won't agree to just a first negotiation, the next compromise is to give them a first negation followed by a **matching right.** This means, if you don't make a deal during the first negotiation, you can go out and shop around all you like, but you have to come back and give them a chance to make the deal on the same terms as your best offer. If they agree to those terms, they get the deal. If they don't match it, you can give the rights to the company that made the offer.

    This situation isn't ideal: The requirement to come back makes your shopping more difficult. Bidders aren't so interested in negotiating a whole deal if someone else can waltz in and take it away. But it's better than giving away the rights.

3. If all else fails, and you have to give up merchandising rights, make the best possible royalty deal (see Chapters 24 and 25), and don't let them cross-collateralize merchandise earnings with your record deal. You can usually knock out the cross-collateralization just by asking.

Most if not all companies, even if they don't get your overall merchandising deal, will want the right to merchandise one image (usually your album cover). Other companies want even more images but will limit their rights to merchandise sales on their website. If you agree to any of these, try to get a decent royalty (see Chapters 24 and 25 for the royalty range). This should be separate from your record royalty account, so they can't use merchandise monies to recoup your advances. Also, make sure they can only sell this stuff on their website, maybe in retail stores if they push. It's worth trying to limit them to online only, so you can be the only one offering your merchandise in physical retail stores.

Some companies also try to grab **app rights,** and also **digital merchandise.**

App rights means the right to create an app based on you. Many labels want to control these rights, and you don't want them to. If the app uses your masters, they'll have to be involved because you'll need a license for the music. But they try to get these rights even if you aren't using music in the app. So push back.

Digital merchandise means digital use of your image. Examples are **wallpaper** (which means the background on a mobile device or computer desktop) and **voice tones** (a recording of your *speaking* voice that plays through a cell phone, saying things like, "Yo, my main man ain't here"). Another example is a website with avatars, where users can buy virtual T-shirts for the character, or hang a virtual poster in their virtual crib. The last thing is kinda weird, and the business didn't really work, but record companies hang on to all kinds of rights that once meant something, as we discussed in the last chapter.

Because of the exclusivity provisions we discussed earlier, you can't give your voice tones to anyone but your record company—the exclusivity covers nonmusical performances as well as musical, which drags in voice tones and also a lot of other stuff. However, you've got some leverage because the companies can't force you to record voice tones (though that's changing in some newer contracts). What you should do, however, is negotiate an exclusion from your exclusivity for nonmusical film and TV voice-overs, commercials, spoken word recordings, etc.

Wallpaper falls in between. You might be able to license wallpaper on your own, because it's your name and likeness, and it's not for records. However, the exclusivity clauses that companies are now using have gotten broader and broader, so it could get dragged in. You need to look at your specific language, and if it's covered, try to exclude it. If the company insists on those rights, ask for 50% of the profits, and keep it separate from your record deal, meaning it's not crossed with your royalty account. And be sure to build in creative controls for yourself.

TOUR SUPPORT

And now for a bit of my personal finances. When I was a kid, I had a soft drink stand (there's a picture of it in the Appendix on page 486). Here's that summer's take: 250 drinks, at 5¢ each, equals $12.50. Not bad for sweating in the sun for seven days a week over ten weeks, eh? But here's the real coup: I convinced my mother to pay for the drinks, so it was *all profit*. (I hope you're impressed.) If she hadn't, the drinks would have cost me $6.25, and the lumber for the stand was $11. So the expenses were $17.25, and I took in $12.50, resulting in a loss of $4.75. If it hadn't been for Ma, I'd have had to file for bankruptcy.

This is not unlike the situation of a new band going on tour. As you'll see later (on page 369), it's virtually impossible for a new artist to go on the road and do anything besides lose money. Even assuming everyone in the band only has a "share of profits," and therefore you don't have to pay salaries to the musicians, you still have the costs of rehearsal, equipment, travel, hotels, agents, managers, etc. And that's more than most artists can earn in their baby stages. Indeed, even by the time you're midlevel, you'll be doing well to break even on the road.

So why would you ever tour under these circumstances? (As the joke goes, if you buy widgets for $1 and sell them for 50¢, how do you make a profit? Answer: Volume.) The reason, of course, is to become better known, build an audience, get more streams, play bigger concerts, and rocket yourself to stardom. As we discussed, the future of the music biz is to find ways other than radio to reach fans, and touring is still one of the best. On top of that, being on the road builds your performing skills. There are a lot of artists who explode on their first album but have a lousy live show because they haven't spent time getting their act down.

So touring is a good thing. However, if you go out and lose money, who's going to pay for the loss? The answer is usually one of two possibilities: (1) a rich relative; or (2) a record company. Guess which one happens more often.

Monies that record companies give you to make up tour losses are called **tour support.** It's defined as the actual amount of your loss (you'll be required to give accountings to the company), but of course it has a maximum limit, usually in the range of $50,000 to $100,000 per tour for a major record company, and more like $10,000 to $15,000 for an independent label. In this era of 360 deals, the companies say they'll be more generous with tour support if you're more generous with their share of touring income. Maybe that's true . . .

Many if not most record companies are reluctant to commit to any tour support in your contract but are pretty good about doing it at the time of the tour. If you can get it up front, it's great to have; if you can't, the amount of your tour support will depend on how well your manager does the Tijuana Two-Step. But even if you get a tour support guarantee in your contract, it's usually limited to the first album. After that, you'll hopefully be at the point where you no longer need it, or you'll need to come in and grovel.

Record companies have gotten pretty sophisticated about tour support. For example, some companies won't let you charge a management commission in computing losses, on the theory that the manager shouldn't get paid when everyone else is losing money. Also, if you use any of the money to buy equipment, the company sometimes tries to own the stuff. Most importantly, they ask for so many approvals of your deals and expenses that, if they decide they don't really want to pay your tour support, they can make things so difficult that you'll give up.

None of this stops them from wanting some active rights to your tours, such as VIP ticketing packages (we'll talk about what that means in the touring section on page 386, but basically it's higher-priced tickets along with other goodies). Some labels want free tickets to your shows, and many of them want the right to buy additional tickets before they go on sale to the public. You should push back on all of these, especially if you're not getting any tour support. And at least try to limit their right to buy tickets to situations where you're doing a VIP package.

You should control your free tickets because they can be used strategically to move your career ahead, or if you don't need them for that, you could let them go on sale. If your concerts sell out, giving the label free tickets at each show is prime real estate, so giving them away as opposed to selling them is money out of your pocket.

Tour support used to be nonrecoupable. For a while, the record companies bought the argument that it was "promotion" of their records, and wrote it off just like any other marketing. But those days have gone the way of eight-track cartridges. Today, tour support is always 100% recoupable (if you need it, your bargaining power ain't so great).

If you're on the *Advanced Overview Track*, go to Chapter 14 on page 188. *Experts*, read on . . .

TERRITORY

For U.S. artists in the new-to-midrange category (unless there's a massive bidding war), the **territory** of your recording agreement (meaning the countries where your company can exclusively sell your records) is almost always "the world." In fact, the territory is usually defined as "the universe," because some backroom lawyer worried that an artist might argue satellites weren't covered by a contract that only said "the world."

This "universe" wording was the cause of one of my most bizarre negotiations, as well as my initiation by fire to the music business. I had only been practicing entertainment law a few months when a label that my firm represented signed a jazz artist named Sun Ra. This guy said he was a reincarnated Egyptian, and he recorded records in the pyramids (for real). Anyway, his lawyer called me up to say that it was unacceptable to grant the universe, and that our territory must be limited to the Earth Zone. At first I thought he was kidding, so I said I would give him everything beyond our solar system, and maybe Neptune and Pluto, but that the moon and neighboring planets were mine. I also asked if we had to pay him in Earth money. The lawyer, very seriously, said this was not negotiable and would blow the deal. So I added "satellites" to the territory of "the world" and caved in on the rest. (That lawyer owes me one, especially if Elon Musk actually colonizes Mars.)

More routine negotiation of the territory comes at the superstar level, or when the artist isn't based in the United States. In these cases, the artist may divide North America (United States and Canada, but sometimes including Mexico) from the rest of the world, thus making two separate recording agreements.

The advantages of this are:

1. The two territories aren't cross-collateralized (meaning royalties you earn in North America can't be used to recoup advances and costs from other territories, and vice versa); and
2. You can always get a higher royalty outside North America because you're eliminating the U.S. company's share of it.

The disadvantages are:

1. The advances may be lower (because there is no cross-collateralization); and
2. It's a pain for an artist to deal with two record companies. Dealing with two companies means shipping two sets of masters

and artwork, "schmoozing" (hanging out) with two sets of executives, and most important, coordinating marketing efforts (which means getting up very early in the morning, or staying up very late at night, to call around the world). Also, the contracts for split-territory deals are much more complex than worldwide deals, meaning higher legal fees, as you have to work out how the two companies will share the costs of artwork, videos, etc. In addition, if you audit your label (see page 164), which you almost always do with success, it's far more expensive to be auditing two companies.

3. Foreign labels want you to eat the cost of union per-record payments, which isn't the case with U.S. labels. This doesn't mean anything to you, because we haven't yet covered that topic (we'll get to it on page 186). For now, just know it's a decent chunk of change that shouldn't come out of your share.

In recent years, major companies have generally refused to sign you for anything except the entire world. So territorial deals are getting harder to come by. It's a bit easier if you start with an overseas deal, then come back to the United States and tell them you don't have those other territories. However, if you're going to a major label overseas, more and more often they're holding firm for the world.

By the way, if you sign an overseas deal for the world, be sure to ask for approval of the U.S. label that will distribute your records.

CREATIVE, MARKETING, AND OTHER CONTROLS

There are a number of controls you should ask for, some of which you may actually get. These are:

1. Consent to the use of your masters in commercials.
2. Consent to licensing your masters for films, television, video games, and other audiovisual works.
3. Approval of your photographs, biographical materials, and other artwork used in advertising and promotion (see the next section for more detail on this).
4. Approval of using your masters in **samples** (we'll discuss samples in detail on page 250, but basically it means incorporating your track into somebody else's master).
5. Approval of any edits of your masters.

6. Approval of **sequencing**, which means the order of your songs on the album. In a streaming age, this is becoming way less relevant, but as long as physical and full-album downloads are still alive, you should still ask for approval of the initial sequence and any changes (called **re-sequencing**).
7. Consent to coupling and premiums (see page 161 for what those are), but as we discussed, this is also becoming less relevant daily.

If you do get approvals, they may be limited to the term of your deal, and to the United States. As your power grows, so do your territorial approvals, as well as the ability to keep your consent rights after the term. As to foreign, if the label agrees at all, they'll probably just agree to *instruct* their foreign affiliate to get your consent. That means, as long as they've told them what to do, they're not on the hook if the foreigner goes rogue.

If you can't get any approvals, at least try to get consultation rights (see the next section for what those are).

And if all else fails, take some comfort in the fact that even with nothing in your contract, as a practical matter, the labels are pretty good about asking your consent for anything that's important.

ARTWORK

By **artwork** I'm referring to album covers and the photos/artwork used in your advertising and marketing campaign. At any level you can get some involvement in your artwork, but you have to ask for it.

"Involvement" at lower levels means they tell you what they're doing, then go ahead and do it whether you like it or not. This process is called **consultation,** which means they talk to you but don't have to get your approval. *Consultation* is actually more valuable than I'm making it sound, because you can at least make your feelings known before the horse leaves the starting gate, and many companies will actually listen to you.

The next step up is **approval,** which means you can approve artwork that the company prepares. When you have approval rights, the company has to please you or you can stop them from using it.

Top of the line is the right to create your own artwork, subject to the company's approval. You can get this as your bargaining power grows. If you're a superstar, the company's only approval rights may be as to legalities, obscenity, and other major grossness—otherwise it's your show.

When you get the right to do your own artwork, the trick is to make sure you have an adequate budget, or else your creative juices will be severely hampered. So build in a set figure and escalate it over time (for inflation). I hesitate to give you specific figures because they may be out of date by the time you read this, but as of now a normal (no particular frills) artwork budget is in the range of $10,000 to $20,000, which is the most you'll likely get contractually. Major artists can sometimes get a minimum budget for photography in addition to the artwork budget, but it varies so widely that I can't really give you a range. Just know that superstar photographers are *really* expensive. And regardless of what's in the contract, companies will usually spend a reasonable amount for artwork because they know it's a key part of the marketing effort. But they may charge the excess over budget against your royalties.

You should ask for the right to use the artwork on your merchandise, but this is really hard to get. As we discussed (on page 185), the company wants these rights for their merchandise.

If you can get merch rights to the artwork, the company will ask for something in exchange. Typical deals are that you have to reimburse all or part of their costs, or maybe give them participation in the proceeds from merch using their artwork. But note this: when the company hires a photographer, particularly an expensive one, they just get the right to put the photos on the album cover and for advertising and marketing. Photographers usually reserve all other rights, so even if the company lets you use the photos, you'll almost certainly have to pay the photographer for those rights as well.

UNION EXPLOITATION CHARGES

It's important that you not be charged with any union payments based on the **exploitation** (streaming, sales, etc.) of records. These costs are customarily borne by the record company. This is different from union scale—see page 87 for what that is—paid for performances at recording sessions, which has nothing to do with exploitations and is due even if the recordings are never released. Session scale payments are always recoupable as a recording cost, as we discussed on page 87.

As I mentioned earlier, this is different if you're signing to a foreign label—those folks do expect to charge you by deducting it from your royalties.

The most significant of these union charges are what the companies pay to the American Federation of Musicians (AFM), which has two funds—the **Special Payment Fund (SPF)** and the **Music Performance Trust Fund (MPTF)**. This is for musicians, not singers (those are covered by AFTRA, and we'll talk about what they do in a minute). The specific AFM contribution is 0.36% (meaning a little over a third of 1%) of worldwide audio streaming receipts, subject to a ceiling of 0.55% of U.S. receipts and a floor of 0.50% of U.S. receipts. AFM also gets a piece of digital downloads, which is currently 0.55% of the wholesale price for each permanent download, excluding the first 10,000 units.

On physical, through some complex computations that are beyond your and my pain tolerance, these payments total about 4.2¢ per physical album (excluding the first 25,000 units) for worldwide sales during the first five years after release of the album. For sales during years six through ten after release, only the SPF gets paid, which is about 3¢ per album. In addition, these rates escalate after the first 300,000 units, and again after 1 million units. (There's no payment for physical singles.)

The biggest portion of these monies go to studio musicians (people who get a fee for recording, but don't get a royalty), and the balance goes to royalty artists. (If you're a studio musician, you get a bigger piece for working more hours, so be sure the producer or the contractor booking the session fills out the AFM B-4 [session] Report Form properly, so you get credit for your hours.)

If all this turns you on, you can get more info on the AFM at www .sound-recording.org.

For non-royalty singers (as opposed to musicians), AFTRA (which merged with the Screen Actors' Guild and is now called SAG-AFTRA) requires the companies to pay 0.36% of worldwide audio streaming receipts, subject to a ceiling of 0.55% of U.S. receipts and a floor of 0.50% of U.S. receipts. They also pay .07% of their receipts on permanent downloads. Music videos get .55% of receipts for the first ten years after release, then .3% of receipts for the next five years.

For physical, the record companies make a **contingent scale** payment to SAG-AFTRA based on sales, but it's much less money. It's only payable if there are non-royalty background singers on a master, and if the master sells more than 157,500 physical units. (Why 157,500? I have absolutely no idea.) The SAG-AFTRA contingent scale also has a ceiling for physical product, meaning it stops after the union gets a certain amount. The ceiling is a little over ten times scale for a one-hour session record, and since one-hour scale is currently $236.25, that means the maximum AFTRA contingent scale is about $2,375.00 per singer, per side. Through various voodoo computations, you'll hit that ceiling around sales of 3 million physical units, so I wouldn't be holding my breath.

Both unions also get percentages of money from use of the recordings in video games, consumer products (e.g., toys and greeting cards), and new media, such as apps, video games, podcasts, and webisodes. These payments go to a combined union fund (meaning it's for both AFM & AFTRA), which is called by the exciting name of "Intellectual Property Rights Distribution Fund." Those folks collect and distribute the digital revenue to nonfeatured musicians and vocalists for streaming and some international revenue sources.

So as you can see, these babies add up to a chunk of change that shouldn't be charged to your royalty account as a recoupable cost. Make sure your deal says they can't.

Another union oddity is that, each time a record company signs a new artist, they're required to pay SAG-AFTRA Health Plan a Special Minimum Roster Payment for every vocalist in the group. That's the good news. The bad news is that you have to pay SAG-AFTRA a one-time new member fee to become a SAG-AFTRA member (which the company may pay and charge back against your account). The current new-member fees range from $1,150 if you live in Tennessee, to $3,000 if you live in New York or California. Additionally, if you want health insurance, SAG-AFTRA Health will bill you about $300 per quarter for single coverage, with additional charges if you want to cover a spouse or family (though it's way cheaper than you could get anywhere else). The record companies are required to pay SAG-AFTRA Health a fistful of money to subsidize your insurance as long as you're on the active roster of the label.

14

Loan-out, Independent Production, Label, and Distribution Deals

LOAN-OUT DEALS

Loan-Out Companies

As you get more successful, you may want a **loan-out company.** It's called a *loan-out* because the company (not you) enters into the deals, and "loans" your services to others for recording, concerts, etc. This is the entity you see people naming with cute little phrases (two of my favorites are "Disappearing, Inc.," and "I Want It All"). When tax laws changed in the eighties, it became questionable whether it made sense to have a loan-out company, though the latest tax laws may spin the tide the other way.

Even if you don't need a loan-out for tax planning, however, this kind of company can shield you from some kinds of liability if you get sued. For example, if the loan-out company's only assets are your record royalties, and someone sues you over a record-related claim, they can only grab your record money. Not your personal bank accounts, your songwriting income, your stamp collection, etc. (Note I'm talking about your being sued by someone other than the record company. Record companies figured this out a long time ago, so under your record deal, they take the right to grab anything they can find, as we'll discuss in a minute. Also, an entity doesn't protect you from someone who claims you ripped off their copyright because of some technical legal reasons. For the lawyers reading this, it's because copyright infringement is a tort committed by the artist or writer, so you can look past the entity.)

To determine whether or not a loan-out company is right for you, consult your lawyer, accountant, and life coach.

By the way, I'm using the term "company" for simplicity. It is usually an **LLC** [a **Limited Liability Company,** which is something that looks and smells like a corporation, but is treated like a partnership for tax purposes], but it could also be a corporation, a limited partnership, a partnership of corporations, a general partnership (though this doesn't have any limited liability), a cluster of worms, etc. But I'm going to use "company" to mean any of these.

Anyway, for record deals, it works like this: You sign an exclusive recording contract with your own company, on a form that looks like a bare-bones record label deal. Then the record label signs a recording agreement with your company, which agrees to supply your services to the label. It looks like this:

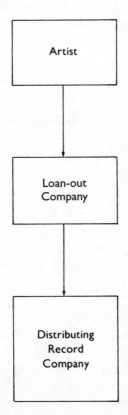

Figure 6. Loan-out deal structure.

Inducement (Side) Letters

As you can see in the above chart, you have no direct deal with the record label. So what's to keep you from walking out on your own company (after all, you could fire yourself), then thumbing your nose at the record label? You personally have no deal with the record label—only your bankrupt loan-out company has a contract, and its secretary/treasurer is now in Uzbekistan with the masters.

Well, you know the labels won't let that happen, so they have you sign something known as an **inducement letter** or **side letter.** This is a piece of paper that says, if your company doesn't deliver your recordings to them, you will deliver them directly to the record label. And you also personally guarantee that, if your company doesn't perform under the deal, you are financially responsible.

So the real picture looks like Figure 7.

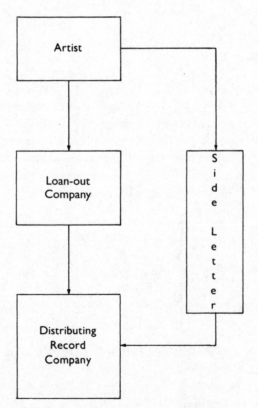

Figure 7. Loan-out deal with side letter.

The side letter is an integral part of these deals. It's like an emergency detour. If the highway is flooded, the company sends a Jeep down a back road to haul your ass back in.

Structure of Loan-out Deals

Loan-out contracts are very similar to contracts directly between the record company and artist (known as **direct agreements**), except that:

1. The parties, of course, are the record label and your company, instead of the label and you;
2. Your company agrees to supply your services and recordings;
3. There are additional legal clauses, which are basically assurances that your company has the right to your exclusive services, that it has the right to deliver your recordings, etc.; and
4. You have to sign an inducement letter saying that if your loan-out tries anything cute, you'll perform directly for the record company, and you'll be financially responsible for anything the loan-out company does wrong.

INDEPENDENT PRODUCTION AGREEMENTS

If, instead of signing a deal with your own loan-out, you sign to an independent company that in turn makes a deal with a record label, that's called an **independent production agreement.** Let's call the independent company the "production entity" (not an industry term), because it "produces" the recordings. Typically, the production entity is owned by a producer or other record mogul whose "magic ears" have found you. The independent company then takes the rights it gets from you and supplies them to a record label for distribution (let's call it the "distributor"). As we'll see in a minute, the inducement letter under these deals is even more critical.

There are two basic flavors of production deals:

1. A **single-artist deal** is where the production entity makes an agreement with the distributor for one specific artist. Note, by the way, that the production entity may have signed more than one artist; we're talking only about the deal between the production entity and the distributor.
2. A **multi-artist deal,** also called a **label deal,** is where the pro-

duction entity agrees to supply the recordings of multiple artists to a distributor. Many of these artists (or perhaps all of them) may have not yet been signed by the production entity.

As you can imagine, this type of deal is way more complicated than a single-artist deal. So let's start with the simpler one.

Single-Artist Deals

A single-artist deal between an independent production entity and a distributor is basically the same as a deal between your own loan-out company and a record label. However, because the production entity isn't owned by the artist, there are a couple of significant differences:

1. The deal between the artist and the production entity is now a real, arm's-length record deal, as opposed to a deal the artist makes with himself or herself. This means there is a true negotiation—i.e., a deal made by parties who are at "arm's length" from each other instead of hugging—and the artist asks for the same kind of things he or she would get from a record company, such as a guaranteed release, creative approvals, etc. (When you sign to a production entity, you should also get some things that you don't need from a record company, which we'll discuss in a minute.)

2. There is a real possibility that the artist can get into a fight with the production entity. This means it's more likely that the record company will exercise its rights under the inducement letter, and thus the terms of the inducement letter are even more critical.

Why Do It?   So why should an artist make a deal like this? Wouldn't it be better to have direct contact with your record company? Well, the answer is "maybe." A production deal has its pluses and minuses compared to a direct deal, and whether it's better for you depends on your specific situation.

Here are the negatives:

1. The production entity takes a chunk of the royalties and advances. Traditionally, distributors pay independent production entities a higher royalty than they pay in direct artist deals (by 1% to 2%) for precisely this purpose. But you still get a lower royalty than you would under a direct deal, and this is especially

so when you're successful and renegotiate your contract. The reason is that, with success, the production entity's deal with the record company "tops out" and leaves no room for them to keep anything without taking it from you. In other words, with success, these deals create a lot of stress.

2. You lose a lot of control. First, the production entity will be making the deal with the distributor, and may not even involve you in the process. Meaning you don't have a say in the terms of their deal, or even a right to approve who the distributor will be. Second, once the deal is done, it will be harder for you to coordinate marketing, promotion, etc., if you and your manager have no direct contact with the distributing record company.

3. There may be problems auditing the distributor directly (see page 164 for what auditing is). The production entity has the right to audit the record company, but you have no deal with the distributor and therefore no right to audit. Distributors understandably don't want two different people (you and the production entity) doing the same audit, so you won't be able to look at their books.

4. The production entity might go south with your money.

On the positive side:

1. The production entity may be owned by a person who really brings something to the party. For example, there are production companies owned by major producers who will only work with a new artist if the artist signs to his or her entity. Other production companies are owned by important managers, promotion people, or industry folks with good track records (translation: They have a lot of clout and can harass the major label better than you can).

2. You may be able to get the same calculation of royalties as the production entity (meaning "at source" streaming rates, foreign reductions, etc.). If you're a new artist and they're an established company, this can be more favorable than what you could get on your own.

3. And I saved the best for last: Nobody else may want to sign you.

On balance, this is not your ideal choice (barring very unusual circumstances, like a major producer), but it can be a desirable alternative to flipping Big Macs.

Artist Deal Points.   If you're making a deal with a production entity, in addition to all the other items we talked about for record deals
(advances, approvals, etc.), you should get the following:

1. You want the same computation of royalties that's in the production entity's deal with the record company. Indeed, you may
   want to ask for a percentage of the production company's receipts. It's not uncommon to do a deal where the artist gets
   75% of the production entity's royalties (with the artist paying
   the producer from his or her share), or maybe 50% or 60% (with
   the production entity paying the producer from its share). This
   percentage should also apply to advances in excess of recording
   costs. If you go this route, try to get a floor of say 15% or so as
   an all-in royalty; otherwise, if the producer makes a lousy deal,
   you're stuck.

   If the production entity doesn't have a royalty deal (for example, they have a share of profits or a pure distribution deal—
   we'll discuss what that means on pages 200 and 205), you'll
   then need to negotiate your own royalty.
2. Try to get direct accountings from the record company. This
   may or may not be possible, depending on the production entity's own deal. Your worry is similar to the situation we discussed on page 131, where we talked about a producer being
   owed money by an artist when no royalties were payable. In this
   case, the roles are reversed: You're the one due money, and the
   production entity may not have any royalties coming in. This can
   easily happen to your production entity—especially if it signs
   several artists (as you'll see in excruciating detail on page 198).
3. Ask for the right to approve the distributor (if one isn't already
   in place), and ideally the terms of the deal (the last one is much
   harder). At a minimum, get consultation rights (meaning they
   have to tell you about it before they make a decision, so that you
   can yell at them if you're not happy).
4. As we discussed, you have no right to audit the distributor. So
   ask for a pro-rata share of any audit recoveries that the independent production company gets. If they agree, and they should, it
   will be after deducting the cost of the audits. A tricky aspect of
   this is that the audit may cover things besides you (for example,
   other artists on the independent company's roster), and even
   trickier is the situation where your interests and the company's
   aren't the same. For example, the audit might uncover that the
   distributor overpaid you and shorted them. This usually gets

worked out with language to the effect that everyone will act reasonably with respect to allocating the audit recovery.

5. And, of course, don't forget the points we discussed on page 123: You should have the right to get out of your deal if the production company doesn't get a distribution deal within a certain period of time, or if that deal goes wonky and they can't replace it.

Production Deal Issues. Now let's jump over the table and get the production entity's point of view. (Come on—it'll make you a better-rounded person.) Here are two major areas of concern:

1. Remember how the artist wants the same computation of royalties as you? (See paragraph 1 of the previous section.) In representing production entities, I've rarely found it worthwhile to recompute the royalties. First of all, it's difficult, complex, time-consuming, and usually given to a low-level bookkeeper who doesn't quite understand what to do. So half the time they end up paying more than you would if you just used the same computation. Second, even when done correctly, the advantage you pick up is often minimal. Third, if the artist finds out you're taking an edge (which will happen if there's a great deal of success), you look like a pig, which is not usually good for artist relations.

2. Make sure you don't give the artist any rights you don't have in the first place. I remember a situation where one production company gave the artist approval of artwork, guaranteed release, etc., when they didn't have those things from the distributor. If you fall into this trap, it'll be embarrassing at best, and at worst the artist can walk away from your deal when you don't deliver. (Note that the artist isn't going very far—if he or she succeeds in walking away from you, they'll still have to record for the record company under their inducement letter. However, this doesn't do you any good because the record company won't pay you any royalties if you lose the artist because of your screw-up. This position is known in show biz as "sucking rocks.")

Multi-Artist (Label) Deals

A **multi-artist deal,** as the name implies, is one where the production entity has a deal with a record company to sign and deliver a number of artists. It is sometimes called a **label deal,** as nowadays the production entity usually has its own label or logo on the product. Sometimes, however, the producing entity has no identification on the records, and the public doesn't even know they exist.

Let's now assume you're the production entity and see what the deals look like.

Differences from Single-Artist Deals.   A multi-artist deal between the distributor and the production entity looks a lot like a single-artist loan-out deal, but:

1. In addition to paying a recording fund for each album, there is often an overhead payment to the production entity. This is usually an advance (although it can at times be nonrecoupable, at least in part) and it's used to pay the entity's rent, payroll, phone, light bills, etc. For bigger deals, there may also be money for marketing, promotion, etc., and the distributor might give the production entity office space in their building (though if the production entity has an indie image, vibe-wise it may not want to be housed in corporate offices).

2. The term of the deal is usually two or three years firm, with the distributor having options for additional one-, two-, or three-year periods.

3. The number of artists the production entity can sign, and whether the distributor can approve these artists, is a matter of major negotiation. A new production entity will maybe get the right to sign one, two, or three artists over the term, but a more established company may get to sign one or two artists per year. More and more, the distributors want to approve the artists before signing, but if you have a lot of bargaining power, you may be able to negotiate (a) no approval (very difficult today); or (b) for each one or two approved artists, you have the right to sign an artist that isn't approved (which is called a **put** because you can "put it to" the company and they have to take it). Getting the label's approval isn't as bad as it sounds, because if you force them to take an artist they don't like, the company won't put resources behind it.

4. The minimum and maximum number of albums the production entity can deliver is also pre-negotiated, both in terms of the overall number per year, and the number per artist (I'm still using "albums" because the industry still is, but it can mean any agreed product commitment). Budget-wise, the distributor doesn't want you delivering more than one album per artist per

year without its consent, though in the hip-hop world, the attitude is *Bring It On!*

5. Speaking of albums, how about this great idea (see if you can find the history lesson): You're a production entity in the last year of your deal with a distributor, and you suddenly have the opportunity to sign a hot new artist. Six months before the end of your term, you deliver an album and say, "Please make this lady into a superstar so that, six months from now when my deal ends, I can (a) beat you to death in a renegotiation; or (b) better yet, take her to another company, leaving you with a gigantic deficit from my prior flops. That way I can take the royalties from this new artist and buy that little pig farm I've always wanted."

   Sound too good to be true? Of course; the deal will require you to deliver a minimum number of albums for each artist—usually three or four—even if the term is over. So your production entity is free to go at the end of the term, but the artists have to stick around for a while. (Note, in essence this means your deal expires for some artists and continues for others.)

6. The recording funds for the artists are spelled out up front. If you're a new entity, you'll probably have to live with something like $75,000 to $150,000 per album. To exceed these figures, you need the company's consent on each specific deal. This means, if you have the chance to sign a major artist, you have to sit down with the distributor and work out a special arrangement. (Sometimes the production entity and the distributor are both bidding for the same artist. You can imagine, since the distributor approves how much the production entity can spend, which one is likely to come out the winner. In this case, unless there's a personal relationship or some other good reason why the artist would rather sign to you, you can pretty well kiss them off.)

7. It's sometimes possible, although difficult, to get ownership of the master recordings under a label deal. Even in this situation, however, you normally wouldn't own the recordings during the term. So even if you win this point, the distributor may own the masters and assign them back to you down the road (usually seven to ten years after the term). The distributor will insist on your being recouped before they'll assign the masters back, and if not, they'll want to extend the assignment date until you are. If this is the case, you should get the right to pay back the

unrecouped deficit at any time during the extension, to trigger an immediate reassignment.

Cross-collateralization.   Remember our story about a producer being entitled to royalties when the artist is unrecouped, and how the artist went further in the hole with every success? (See page 131.) Well, when you get to a multi-artist deal, this scenario gets to be a high-speed drilling rig. It's entirely possible (even easy) to have two or three real losers, together with one smash, but not get any royalties because the record company is using the winner's royalties to recoup the losers' deficit. Here's an example:

Suppose a production entity has signed three artists. Assume the following (*the numbers bear no relationship to reality;* they're just for easy math):

Multiple-Artist Deal

All-in Royalty to Production Entity:	12%
Royalty to Artist A:	10%
Royalty to Artist B:	10%
Royalty to Artist C:	10%
Recording Costs:	$60,000/album
Advance for Production Entity's Operations	$100,000

Sales:	Artist A:	Album 1: Distributor Gross	$300,000
		Album 2: Distributor Gross	$200,000
	Artist B:	Album 1: Distributor Gross	$100,000
		Album 2: Distributor Gross	$200,000
	Artist C:	Album 1: Distributor Gross	$300,000
		Album 2: Distributor Gross	$2,500,000

Under these assumptions, let's look at everyone's accounts:

Artist A's Account with Production Entity

	Charges (Recording Costs)	Earnings	Balance
Album 1	− $60,000	+ $30,000 (10% × $300,000)	− $30,000
Album 2	− $60,000	+ $20,000 (10% × $200,000)	− $40,000
TOTAL	**$120,000**	**+ $50,000**	**− $70,000**

Summary: Artist A is *in the red (unrecouped) in the amount of $70,000* (the $120,000 deficit less the $50,000 earnings), and is thus owed nothing.

Artist B's Account with Production Entity

	Charges (Recording Costs)	Earnings	Balance
Album 1	− $60,000	+ $10,000 (10% × $100,000)	− $50,000
Album 2	− $60,000	+ $20,000 (10% × $200,000)	− $40,000
TOTAL	**−$120,000**	**+ $30,000**	**− $90,000**

Summary: Artist B is *in the red (unrecouped) in the amount of $90,000* (the $120,000 deficit less the $30,000 earnings), and is thus owed nothing.

Artist C's Account with Production Entity

	Charges (Recording Costs)	Earnings	Balance
Album 1	− $60,000	+ $ 30,000 (10% × $300,000)	− $ 30,000
Album 2	− $60,000	+ $250,000 (10% × $2,500,000)	+ $190,000
TOTAL	**−$120,000**	**+ $280,000**	**+ $160,000**

Summary: Artist C is *in the black (and owed) $160,000* (the $280,000 earnings less the $120,000 deficit).

Production Entity's Account with Record Company

	Charges	Earnings	Balance
Overhead	− $100,000		− $ 100,000
Artist A	− $120,000	+ $ 60,000 (12% × $500,000)	− $ 60,000
Artist B	− $120,000	+ $ 36,000 (12% × $300,000)	− $ 84,000
Artist C	− $120,000	+ $336,000 (12% × $2,800,000)	+ $ 216,000
TOTAL	**−$460,000**	**+ $432,000**	**−$ 28,000**

Summary: The production entity is *in the red (unrecouped)* $28,000 (the $460,000 deficit less the $432,000 earnings), and is thus owed nothing.

Grand Summary

Artist A: Unrecouped and not entitled to royalties.
Artist B: Unrecouped and not entitled to royalties.
Artist C: Owed $160,000.
Production entity: Owes Artist C $160,000, but is in the red $28,000 and thus not entitled to royalties.

Owing $160,000 and having no royalties due you is certainly the fuzzy side of the lollipop.

So how do you get out of the box? Well, if you have enough clout, you make the distributor pay the artists' royalties without regard to cross-collateralization. Thus, if you and Artists A and B are deeply un-recouped, but Artist C is recouped, they'd have to pay Artist C's royal-ties. In other words, they can't cross-collateralize any artist's royalties with either your or any other artist's deficits.

If you don't have enough bargaining power for this, then at mini-mum you should require the distributor to pay the artist's royalties and if you're unrecouped, treat these payments as additional advances against your share of royalties. In the above example, that would mean the record company would advance the $160,000 owed to Artist C, and the production entity would then be $188,000 in the red (the $28,000 original deficit plus the $160,000 paid to Artist C). You wouldn't make any money under these circumstances (until you have massive success and eventually recoup), but at least you won't be breaking your kids' piggybanks to pay the artists.

JOINT VENTURES/PROFIT SHARE

A **joint venture,** which is also called a **JV** agreement or a **profit share** agreement, is the same as a single-artist or multi-artist label deal, except the production entity doesn't get a royalty. Instead, the production entity and the distributing record company share profits from the mas-ters. This means they take all of the income that comes in (the gross proceeds from streams, downloads, licensing income, etc.) and put it into a pot. Then they take all the expenses of operations out of that pot, and whatever is leftover gets split between the two entities. Historically, the split was 50/50, but over recent years this has become increasingly difficult to get. Record companies are shying away from joint venture/ profit deals in general, and when they do them, they're trying to pay less than 50%—such as 40%, 30%, sometimes even lower.

By the way, these agreements aren't usually "joint ventures" or "partnerships" in the legal sense. A true partnership or joint venture means one partner can commit both of them to legal obligations. For example, if one partner signs a bank loan for $200,000, both partners can be sued if it isn't paid back. Neither you nor the record company wants this, so the agreements sometimes specifically state they aren't legally partnerships or joint ventures. Thus the name "joint venture" is not technically correct; it just describes a deal where the profits are shared as if a joint venture existed.

Computation of Profits

The economics of a joint venture look like this:

Income Side.   Gross receipts are the monies received by the record company, which is easy to compute if the distributor is independent. However, as we discussed on page 72, all the major distributors are owned by the major record companies. This means you need a different definition of *gross receipts* when the joint-venture distributor is a major. Why? Well, if the same person owns both the distributor and the record company, they can set any price they want between the two of them. To use an absurd example, the distributor might get $100 from streaming and only pay $20 back to the record company, simply to hose you.

The way it's handled is by treating the amount received by the major label's distribution division as the gross, then taking a negotiated distribution fee off that before it goes into the pot. We'll discuss the range of those fees in the next section.

Foreign income from unrelated companies is treated as license income, and the venture usually gets the same royalty paid by foreign distributors to the U.S. company for its entire catalog. In other words, if they get 25% of the monies earned in Lithuania, that would go into the pot as gross receipts and therefore be used for determining profits.

When the foreign distributor is owned by the same company that owns your record company, they establish an **intra-company rate,** meaning a royalty that the foreign distributor pays the U.S. company.

For example, the U.S. company might get a 30% royalty for France (meaning 30% of the French company's receipts). This rate is in place even when there is no joint venture, as it's used by the U.S. company to compute its profits and losses in reporting earnings to the parent company.

Lately, some companies have taken to paying the venture a foreign royalty that is less than the intra-company rate, so there's less money to split with you. For example, the intra-company rate might be 30%, but they only throw 25% into the pot for computing profits. They do this because they get to keep more money that way. There's no logic to this practice; it's just a muscle-move by the company. So you should always try to get the full rate into the pot. Results will vary with your bargaining power.

Note the result of this foreign licensing practice is that a joint venture only shares profits for U.S. sales. On foreign sales, it's simply a sharing of the royalty paid to the U.S. company.

Expenses. From this gross, the joint venture deducts its expenses and other charges. They consist of the following:

1. The first thing deducted is a **distribution fee** for the record company. (There's a gold rule for record labels: If you're getting a percentage, take it out first because that way it's applied to the biggest number.) The distribution fee is a charge to cover the cost of overseeing the distribution of records, meaning the accounting, invoicing, manufacturing, etc., of the venture (note this is for *overseeing*; the actual costs of manufacturing, for example, are charged as well). This will run somewhere in the 15% to 20% range, sometimes even higher, and it includes the distribution fee charged to the company by its distributor. This number will be higher if it includes an overhead/services fee, which we'll discuss in the next section.

   It's often possible to reduce this fee as volume increases, usually on a yearly basis. For example, the fee could be 20% of the first $5 million each year, 19% of the next $5 million, and 18% thereafter. At the beginning of the following year, the fee would start again at 20%.

   The above is what you'll be charged in computing your profits under a joint-venture deal. It may have no relationship to what the record company is actually charged by its distributor. And what, you ask, are the labels actually charged by the distributor? Well . . .

Before I tell you what distribution fee they get charged, let's look at the big picture. Major record labels are judged by their profits and losses, separate from the profits and losses of the company that owns them. For example, the executives at Warner Records get bonuses (or get fired) based on the financial performance of Warner Records, and the executives at Atlantic Records (which is owned by the same people who own Warner Records) get rewarded on the basis of Atlantic's performance. (An element of the executive bonuses at the major labels is the overall company performance, but the biggest chunk is usually the performance of the label for which they're responsible.)

Let's use Atlantic as an example. To figure out Atlantic's profits, you have to know its costs. If Atlantic were a stand-alone company, it would have to make a deal with someone to distribute its records, and that distributor's charges would be an expense for Atlantic. Because Atlantic is owned by Warner Music Group (WMG), it's forced to make a deal with WEA Distribution (also owned by WMG). However, just because they have the same owner, Atlantic doesn't get a free ride. It has to pay a fee to WEA Distribution for handling Atlantic's records.

In one sense, this distribution fee is a fiction, because the money moves from one WMG pocket to another. But it's not a fiction to the executives at Atlantic. The bigger it is, the more it reduces Atlantic's profits (and the executives' bonuses). Same thing on the other side, for the executives at the distribution company.

Typically, the distribution fees charged by a major distributor to an affiliated major label are in the 14% range. In your joint venture, if you've got a lot of clout, you may be able to get the same distribution fee that the label is charged. In other words, if Atlantic pays 14% to WMG (I have no idea if that's correct), you'd only be charged 14% in computing the profits. However, that's only if you've got a lot of bargaining power. In the beginning, you'll pay quite a bit more, as noted above.

2. In addition to the distribution fee, the record company may also charge an **overhead/services fee.** This is for services supplied by the label in addition to distribution, such as sales, marketing, and promotion. The more they supply, the higher this charge will be. It can range anywhere from zero to (more commonly) 4% to 7%. Often this is combined with the distribution fee discussed in point 1, so that there's one percentage that includes both distribution and services/overhead (e.g., 27%).

3. Next deduction is the costs of operation. In addition to the costs you'd normally expect (recording costs, advances, etc.), there are a number of things that aren't charged under royalty deals. These include:
   (a) Advertising and marketing
   (b) Mechanical royalties (we'll discuss these later, on page 215)
   (c) Per-record union payments (for a definition, see page 185)
   (d) Manufacturing and shipping of physical goods
4. Lastly, the record company takes back any payments it made to the production entity, such as reimbursements for promotional and operating expenses of the company. It's a matter of negotiation whether these are charged "off the top" of the venture (meaning deducted from gross receipts as another expense), or whether they're charged solely against the producing entity's share of the profits. It's clearly better for you if it's off the top, because that means both sides bear their respective percentage. In other words, if it's a 50% profit share, you and the company each eat 50% of the cost when it's off the top. If it's taken out of your share, you're bearing 100%.

The amount left after the above calculation is the profit, and the agreed split goes to each party.

Royalty Versus Joint Venture

So how about the key question: Are you better off with a joint venture or with a royalty arrangement? To answer this requires a crystal ball, both as to success, and especially as to foreign income, where you're not sharing in profits. It also depends on how high the royalty rate is, and what percentage of profits you're getting.

As a general rule, if you're extremely successful, certainly in the United States, you're better off with a joint venture. With modest success, you're better off under a royalty arrangement. (If you're a turkey, it doesn't really matter.)

Here's why a profit share is better with success:

As we discussed, you're charged for more costs in a joint venture than you are under a royalty deal, and thus with only modest success, you're behind. However, many of these costs are not "per transaction," meaning they're only paid at the beginning, as opposed to "per-transaction" costs that are incurred for each stream or sale ("transaction") made. (Examples of per-transaction charges are costs of mechanical royalties [the monies paid to songwriters who wrote the songs in the master, to the extent those are paid by the label], union per-record charges [see page 185], and manufacturing and freight for physical goods, which are only paid when a transaction happens. Costs that are not per-transaction are such things as recording costs, artwork, videos, promotion, marketing and advertising, which are unrelated to specific transactions.) Thus, with a great deal of success, the non-per-transaction costs are eaten up by the first dollars that come in, and thereafter the profit per unit is more than a royalty arrangement. Also, your share of profits is likely to be greater than a royalty rate (even after deducting charges that aren't deducted in computing royalties, like distribution/overhead fees).

DISTRIBUTION DEALS

If you are truly a record company in your own right, then this is the deal for you. It gives you the most autonomy and control of your life, as well as the highest profit margin. This is the deal that true independent labels make. Under these deals, you own the masters and artist contracts, so you really can walk away at the end with everything, including both the old and future albums. But of course there's a catch . . .

A **distribution deal** is exactly that—the company agrees to distribute the masters for you, meaning they get your masters into the streaming and download services around the world, manufacture and distribute physical goods, monitor all this, collect the money, and, oh yeah, pay you. For this, they charge a **distribution fee,** which covers their company's overhead, operations, and profit. The range of distribution fees under these deals is about 20% to 25% (unless you're a really huge independent, then you can squeeze it down), with the bulk of the deals around 24% to 25%. So if the company collects $100, they pay you $75 to $80.

In some of these deals, for an extra fee, the distributing company will help with marketing, sales, and promotion. This is called a **services fee,** and it's usually in the range of an extra 5% to 7% on top of the distribution fee. It's often done with a menu, so you need only take what you want. For example, if you want sales, but not promotion, the fee would be less.

Note these figures are higher than the distribution and services fees we discussed in the profit split section above. The reason is that the earlier figures were simply a way to compute profits, so the company was getting the fee plus a share of profits. Here the company pays you everything over and above these fees.

And now for the catch: In these deals, you take on the entire financial risk of signing artists (meaning paying advances, recording costs, artwork, etc.) as well as marketing the records. You also have to pay for your own overhead (staff salaries, rent, lights, computers, pill boxes, etc.), and you have to create accounting statements and pay royalties due to the artists and songwriters. If there are physical goods, you have to front the manufacturing and shipping costs, plus take the risk that the product might not sell and get returned to you (take a look at the discussion of returns on page 84). If there are returns, you not only get no money, but you're also charged for the cost of manufacturing and shipping the CDs. In other words, if your artists fizzle like bad fireworks, you're seriously out of pocket.

So a distribution deal is not for the weak-hearted. But with success, it's by far the best deal for you. Not only do you get most of the income, at the end of the term you own the masters, the artist contracts, and everything else.

These types of deals can be made at the highest level (for example, Hollywood Records [Disney's label] is distributed by Universal under such an arrangement), down to small indie labels who make these deals with independent distributors.

A relatively new animal is the **label services deal,** which is essentially a distribution deal aimed at artists (rather than independent labels, though I'm sure they would handle the right label as well). Under these deals, you own the masters and license them to the label service company, who acts as your virtual record label. Usually there's a 50/50 profit split.

With these arrangements, however, they want the artist to pay for recording, marketing and promotion, and also to take the risk of physical returns. For a known artist, some of the label service companies will front the money for creation of the record, marketing, and promotion, but instead of taking costs off the top like a joint venture (see page 200), they instead take the costs from your share of money.

Lately, label services deals under which they front the costs are getting harder to come by. That's because the label service companies have gotten stung by fronting costs. Also, even if you get them to agree, you may have to repay any unrecouped costs at the end of the deal.

The specifics of label service deals are very customized, so I can't give you any hard and fast rules. But for the right kind of artist, if you're confident of some base level of income, these can be favorable deals.

UPSTREAM DEALS

An **upstream deal** is a cross between an independent distribution deal and a production deal. It works like this:

An independent label goes to an independent distributor that's owned by a major label. It makes a standard distribution deal but also gives the major label a right to **upstream** the artist, meaning the deal miraculously transforms from a distribution deal into a production deal with the major label. (Technically, the upstream deal is made with the major label in the first place. The major label then "supplies" the independent distribution to the indie label. In other words, the pure distribution part of the deal is in a contract with the major label, not a separate contract with the independent distributor.)

When an artist is upstreamed, the distributing label moves the records from the indie distributor to its major distributor. It stops paying the gross income less a distribution fee, and instead pays the independent label a royalty, or, if the indie has enough clout, a percentage of profits. Whether it's a royalty or profit share, the independent gets less money than it would under a distribution deal. That's because the distributing label is now taking a much bigger risk. When it upstreams, it takes over the cost of marketing, promotion, videos, returns, etc. (all of which were the responsibility of the indie label under the distribution deal).

The idea behind upstreaming is that, when an artist's sales get to a certain point, it takes the clout (and money) of a major to move those sales to the mega level. The major labels aren't willing to put out big marketing bucks if they're only getting a distribution fee, so the deal transforms.

The upstream is usually at the discretion of the major label. Sometimes it's automatic, meaning it kicks in when an artist achieves a certain sales level, but this is rare. Upstreaming is rarely at the independent label's discretion, but if you can't get the right to force an upstream, you can sometimes get consent to it happening.

The advantage of doing an upstream deal is basically time. If there were no upstream deal in place, and an artist explodes, the indie would have to run around and make a deal with a major, which takes time and (when you change distributors) can cost you money in the confusion of instructing digital service providers to pay someone else. If an upstream deal is already there, they can immediately shift the project to the bigger system, without loss of momentum.

The disadvantage is that the terms of the upstream deal are preset, so the indie doesn't have the clout of an exploding record to make a better deal when they decide to upstream.

PART III

Songwriting and Music Publishing

15

Copyright Basics

Before you can understand what songwriting and music publishing are all about, you have to understand how copyrights work.

When you deal with something intangible like a copyright (which you can't see, feel, or smell), it's a challenge to nail it down. Copyrights are a tremendous amount of fun—they're squiggly little critters that, every time you think you have a handle on them, take an unexpected turn and nip you in the butt. And many of the concepts have been around since record players had cranks on the side, which makes for some interesting challenges in today's world.

BASIC COPYRIGHT CONCEPTS

When you own a copyright, it's like playing Monopoly and owning all the properties on the board. But unlike Monopoly, you're not limited to the rents printed on the little cards. (Well, actually, there are some preset rents, but for the most part you can charge whatever the traffic will bear.)

Definition of Copyright

The legal definition of a copyright is "a limited duration monopoly." Its purpose (as stated in the U.S. Constitution, no less) is to promote the progress of "useful arts" by giving creators exclusive rights to their works for a while. As you can imagine, if you created something and everybody had the right to use it without paying you, not very many people would go through the trouble of creating anything (including you and me).

What's Copyrightable?

To be copyrightable, the work has to be original (not copied from something else) and of sufficient creativity to constitute a work, which is a pretty low threshold.

There's no specific test to know what's copyrightable; it's decided on a case-by-case basis. For example, the five notes played by the spaceship in *Close Encounters of the Third Kind* are copyrightable because of their originality, even though they're just five notes. We'll talk more about this on page 323, in connection with copyright infringement cases.

How to Get a Copyright

Under U.S. copyright law, as soon as you make a **tangible copy** of something, you have a copyright. **Tangible** means something you can touch, though that has been clarified in the Copyright Act to mean something that can be "perceived, reproduced, or otherwise communicated, either directly or with the aid of a machine or device." Meaning electronic files.

If the work is a musical composition, for example, it can be written down (if you write music notation, which many creative people don't these days), or just recorded. Once this tangible copy exists, you have all the copyright you need.

Many people think you have to register in Washington to get a copyright. Not true. There are some important rights you get from registering, but securing a copyright isn't one of them. (More on this later.)

So it's that simple. If you sing a song in your head, no matter how completely it's composed, you have no copyright. Once you write it down or record it, you have one. If you'd like to take a few minutes right now and copyright something, I'll wait.

WHAT ARE ALL THESE RIGHTS YOU GET?

When you have a copyright, you get the following rights at no extra charge. These rights are **exclusive,** which means that *no one* can do these things without your permission. (For you technical freaks, the rights are listed in Section 106 of the Copyright Act.)

You get the *exclusive* right to:

1. **Reproduce the work.**

   For example, if you write a song, no one can record it, publish it as sheet music, put it in a movie, or otherwise copy it without your permission. (Actually, there are some exceptions, but we'll get to those in a minute.)

2. **Distribute copies of the work.**

   Apart from the right to reproduce your song, you also control a separate right of **distribution.** Notice the difference between making a copy of the work (like recording a song), which is one use of a copyright (it's a reproduction, as we discussed in point 1), and the *distribution* of this copy (streaming to the public, for example), which is another, separate right.

3. **Perform the work publicly.**

   With a song, this means playing it in concert venues, on the radio, on television, through a streaming service (which is also a distribution, as we just discussed), in bars, amusement parks, supermarkets, elevators (you know your career is either soaring or history when you hear your song in an elevator), or anywhere else music is heard publicly. It doesn't matter whether the performance is by live musicians or a DJ playing records; you get to control this right. (If you're wondering how you could ever police this or get paid, stay tuned.)

4. **Make a derivative work.**

   A **derivative work** is a creation based on another work. In the music industry, an example is a parody lyric set to a well-known song (what Weird Al Yankovic does). The original melody is a copyrighted original work, and once you add parody lyrics, it constitutes a new, separate work. This new work is called a *derivative work* because it's "derived" from the original. A more common example is a song with a sample in it, or an original arrangement or remix of a well-known song.

   This concept is even easier to see in other areas. Any film made from a novel is a derivative work (the novel is the original work). The Broadway musical *Rent* is a derivative work based on the opera *La Bohème.* Anyway, you get the idea. (By the way, the original doesn't have to be copyrighted. *La Bohème* is so old that its copyright long ago expired; ditto for all the *Romeo and Juliet*–based movies. But the only parts of the derivative work that are protected are the newly created ones.)

5. **Display the work publicly.**

   Generally, this is the right to put paintings, statues, etc., on public display. In the music area, about the only thing it covers are websites that display lyrics.

EXCEPTIONS TO THE COPYRIGHT MONOPOLY

As I said earlier, the copyright law gives you an absolute monopoly, which means it's your bat and ball, and you don't have to let anyone use it. If you want to write poems and throw them into the sea, so that no human being can ever see them, that's your prerogative. You may be cold and poor in your old age, but you'll have entertained a lot of fish.

However . . .

Compulsory Licenses

There are five major exceptions to this monopoly rule, and they're known as **compulsory licenses.** A compulsory license means that you *must* issue a license to someone who wants to use your work, whether you like it or not. The five compulsory licenses are:

1. **Cable television rebroadcast.**
   Not really relevant to music; it's about cable TV companies re-transmitting over-the-air TV stations.
2. **Public Broadcasting System.**
   The PBS lobbyists did a terrific job of requiring copyright owners to license works to them at cheap rates.
3. **Jukeboxes.**
   It may surprise you to know that, until the 1976 Copyright Act, jukeboxes paid nothing for the right to use music. They were considered "toys" in the 1909 Copyright Act (really). Now they pay set license fees, the details of which have never been relevant to me, so I don't know them.
4. **Digital performance of records.**
   This baby was added in 1995, then modified in 1998, and it requires the owners of recordings to allow performances of masters on digital radio, which also includes non-interactive streaming (radio shows on the Internet). We will talk a little about this on page 312, and we'll hit it harder on page 314.
5. **The use of non-dramatic musical compositions in streaming, digital downloads, and phonorecords.**
   This last one is the most used in the music business, so we'll dis-

cuss it in detail. It's called a **compulsory mechanical license.** And it's recently been pumped up on steroids by something called the **Music Modernization Act,** or **MMA,** which we'll also cover.

COMPULSORY MECHANICAL LICENSES

To understand what the hell I'm talking about, you first need to know about mechanical royalties.

Mechanical Royalties

The term **mechanical royalties** (or **mechanicals** to its friends) developed in the 1909 Copyright Act and referred to payments for devices "serving to mechanically reproduce sound." Even though devices haven't reproduced sound "mechanically" since the 1940s, the name has stuck and the monies paid to copyright owners for the manufacture and distribution of records are still called *mechanical royalties.* The rights to reproduce songs in records are known as **mechanical rights.**

The concept of a *compulsory* license for these mechanical rights grew out of a concern in Congress that the music industry was going to develop into a gigantic monopoly. This desire to keep copyright owners from controlling the world resulted in the compulsory license for records, which accomplishes its mission nicely. Let's take a closer look:

Compulsory Mechanical Licenses

The compulsory copyright license for records is in Section 115 of the Copyright Act. Until 2018, when the **Music Modernization Act (MMA)** was passed, it only dealt with traditional sales of physical product and digital downloads. Because of the MMA, however, it now deals with interactive streaming as well. The streaming compulsory license gets a bit complicated, so let me first give you the parts of mechanical licensing that didn't change under the MMA. Then I'll let you know what your tax dollars have been up to.

Section 115 says that, once a song has been recorded and released to the public, (a) the copyright owner *must* license the song (i.e., they have to issue a compulsory mechanical license) to anyone else that wants to use it in a **phonorecord** (which is a defined term in the Copyright Act, and I'll explain it in a minute); and (b) that license can only charge a specific payment established by the law (more on this later). In other words, if you can't get a **voluntary license** (meaning one where you and the copyright owner agree on a deal), you can invoke the **compulsory license** section of the Copyright Act, and the owner has to let you use the song in phonorecords for a set price.

However, the owner is only required to issue a compulsory mechanical license *if*:

1. The song is a non-dramatic musical work; *and*
2. It has been previously recorded; *and*
3. The previous recording has been distributed publicly in phonorecords; *and*
4. The new recording (called a **cover**, or **cover record**, in the biz) doesn't change the basic melody or fundamental character of the song; *and*
5. The cover recording is only used in phonorecords distributed to the public for private use.

All of these conditions have to exist before you get a compulsory license. If you miss one, you have to beg the publisher for a license, and she can say, "Buzz off."

Let's look at the conditions for the compulsory license:

Non-dramatic Musical Work.   Before you can get a compulsory license, the song must be a non-dramatic musical composition. It's not clear what a "dramatic" musical composition is, but it's probably a song used in an opera or musical—i.e., a song that helps tell a story. No one knows whether or not the term includes a "story song," which tells a story in the lyrics. My guess is that it doesn't, but it's just a guess.

Previously Recorded.   You can't get a compulsory license for the very first recording of a song. The law allows the owner to control who gets it the first time, which is known as a **first use.** Also, even if the song was previously recorded, you can only get a compulsory license if that first recording was authorized by the copyright owner. The fact that someone sneaks off and records the song doesn't trigger the compulsory license.

Public Distribution.   The first recording must have been distributed to the public. This closes a loophole from the prior law. So even if the copyright owner allowed a recording to be made, if it was never released, you can't get a compulsory license for another recording.

Phonorecord Use.   A compulsory license is available only for **phono-records,** which are defined in the copyright law to mean **audio-only** recordings. This definition was the publishers' finest lobbying accomplishment in the 1976 Copyright Act, because it excluded home video devices from the definition of phonorecords (and now excludes video streaming). This means there's no compulsory license for audiovisual works, and, among other things, it means that motion picture companies have to negotiate with every copyright owner for audiovisual streaming of each song. It also means the song owners are free to charge whatever rate they choose. (More on how this is done on page 221.)

No Major Changes.   When you get a compulsory license, you're allowed to arrange the song "to conform it to the style or manner of interpretation of the performance." (This is in section 115(a)(2) of the copyright law, for you detail-oriented folk.) However, you can't change the basic melody or fundamental character of the work. So, for example, you couldn't write new lyrics, or add another melody.

If the above conditions exist, then anyone who wants to use a song in phonorecords or streaming can do it by filing certain notices and paying a set fee called the **statutory rate** (it's called a *statutory rate* because the rate is set by the Copyright Act, and the Copyright Act is a "statute" [meaning a law]). For physical and downloads, the statutory rate is currently the larger of (a) 9.1¢, or (b) 1.75¢ per minute of playing time or a fraction thereof. Thus, if a song runs five minutes or less, the rate is 9.1¢. However, if it's over five minutes (even by a second or two), but not over six minutes, the rate is 10.5¢ (1.75¢ × 6 = 10.5¢). If a song is over six minutes but not more than seven minutes, the rate is 12.25¢ (1.75¢ × 7 = 12.25¢). You get the idea.

Ringtones (which are considered phonorecords under the compulsory mechanical license provisions) have a separate statutory rate, which is currently 24¢. That's obviously much higher than the physical and download 9.1¢ rate, for historical reasons that I could give you, but since ringtones are disappearing, it's not all that interesting and therefore not worth the ink (or worth the electrons, if you're using an e-reader).

Music Modernization Act

In 2018, the MMA created a compulsory mechanical license for streaming. And unlike the compulsory license for physical and downloads, you can get this streaming license even if the master *hasn't* been previously released (i.e., it's a first use and not a cover record). However, you can only get a streaming compulsory license if (a) the recording of the master was authorized by the song owner, and (b) the owner of the sound recording authorized digital distribution.

Huh? If it's already authorized for recording and digital distribution by the owner of the song and the master, why would you need a compulsory license? Don't you have voluntary license?

The answer is actually pretty interesting, and it's rooted in a massive war that happened in the business. But we need a few more concepts under our belt before I can explain it, so hang on until the next chapter (on page 239).

Streaming mechanicals are WAY more complicated. Unlike the pennies in the prior examples, they're a percentage of streaming income, and not a simple calculation. Also, these rights overlap with other rights we haven't yet discussed. So sorry to keep doing this, but please hang on for a few more concepts and we'll hit the streaming mechanicals on page 234.

Foreign Mechanicals

Other than the United States and Canada, most countries of the world use an entirely different copyright royalty system for downloads and physical goods. Mechanicals over there are a percentage of wholesale price, which covers all songs on the record. This means the rate has nothing to do with the length of the composition or even the number of songs. The same amount of mechanicals is paid for an album containing eight compositions as is paid for one with twelve. Also, as we'll discuss later (on page 253), foreign mechanicals are usually paid to a government-mandated agency.

For example, mechanicals for downloads and physical in the United Kingdom are currently 8.5% of PPD (see page 82 for what PPD is), though there are some complexities. If you're curious, or a glutton for pain, take a look at their website, www.prsformusic.com. Finding the details is a little like navigating a Call of Duty battle, but at the time of this writing you go to the home page, click on Writers/Publishers, click on *MCPS* (standing for *Mechanical-Copyright Protection Society*), look under "MCPS Royalty Sources," and knock yourself out.

The rate in the rest of Europe is set by an organization called **BIEM (Bureau International des Sociétés Gérant les Droits**

d'Enregistrement et de Reproduction Mécanique; is that a mouthful, or what?). BIEM (pronounced "beam") is a group of agencies in each territory that collect mechanical royalties for their affiliates. Currently, the BIEM rate is 11% of PPD but they allow some deductions, so the net rate is 8.712% of PPD.

Foreign streaming rates are set by these same organizations, but hang on for a bit.

16

Publishing Companies and Major Income Sources

PUBLISHING OVERVIEW

Now that you're a maven on copyrights, understanding publishing is pretty simple. It works like this:

What Does a Publisher Do?

As a songwriter, you may be interested in business, but your talents are best spent in creating. However, someone needs to take care of business, and that's where the publishing industry came from.

A publisher makes the following speech to a songwriter:

"Sit down, kid. Nice shirt. You got great taste."

The publisher leans forward, rattling the gold chains on his neck. "You're a smart guy, so you'll get this right away. Your strength is writing songs, and mine is taking care of business. So let's make the following deal: You assign the copyright in your songs to me, and I'll get people to use the songs. Then I give 'em licenses, make sure they pay up, and we split the dough. Simple, huh? Now sign this perfectly standard agreement. Wanna cigar?"

Administration

Okay, so I'm being a smart aleck. But these principles are the basis of the publishing business.

The rights the publisher just described—finding users, issuing licenses, collecting money, and paying the writer—are known as **administration rights**. When a publisher makes a publishing deal with a songwriter, it takes on the obligation to do all these things, and thus "administers" the compositions. In exchange, the writer signs over the copyright to the publisher (though, as we'll discuss later, it's now less common for writers to give up 100% of their copyrights, or to give them up forever). The flow of rights looks like this:

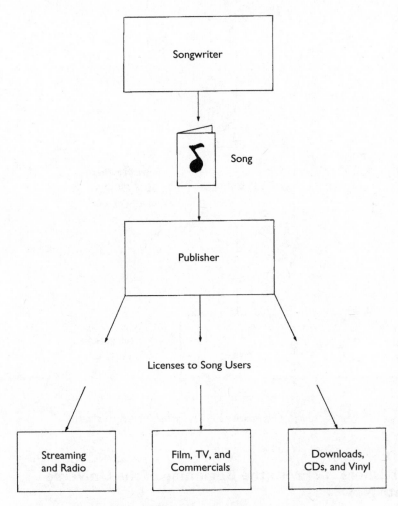

Figure 8. Publishing industry structure.

Traditionally, the publisher split all income 50/50 with the writer (with the exception of performance monies and sometimes sheet music, which we'll discuss later), though publishers today take much less, as we'll discuss. The publisher's piece is for its overhead (office, staff, etc.)

and profit. The share of money kept by the publisher from each dollar is known by a sophisticated industry term: the **publisher's share.** The balance is just as imaginatively called the **writer's share** (see Figure 9).

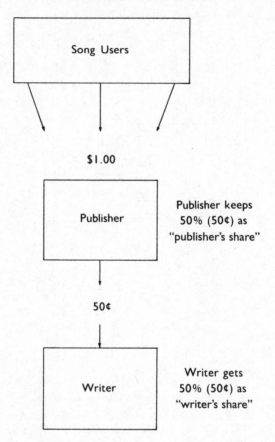

Figure 9. "Publisher's share" and "writer's share."

Publishers . . . From the Beginning of the Universe Until Now

Following the turn of the twentieth century, and well into the 1940s, publishers were the most powerful people in the music industry. (Ever heard of Tin Pan Alley? That's where the publishers' offices were located.) In the early days, most singers didn't write songs, so they (and their record companies) were at the mercy of the publishers, who controlled the major songwriters. Remember, no one can use a song for the first time without the publisher's permission (see page 216), so the publishers decided which artist was blessed with the right to record a major new work. Because of the publishers' power and connections to the labels and artists, it was difficult, if not impossible, for songwriters to exploit their works without a major publisher behind them.

Publishers today are still major players, but their role has changed radically. At one end are "creative" publishers, in the sense that they put their writers together with other writers, help them fine-tune their skills, pitch their songs to artists, etc. If the writer is also an artist, they use their clout to help find them a record deal. At the other end are publishers who are basically banking operations—they compute how much they expect to earn from a given deal, then pay a portion of it to get the rights. From these guys, you can't expect much more than a bet against your future income. And of course there's a rainbow in between.

While all of this is important in the beginning and middle stages of your career, many of the major writers make very skinny deals with the publishers. In other words, they use a publisher to handle the backroom chores of issuing licenses and collecting money, while the writer keeps ownership of their copyrights and the bulk of the money (we'll discuss what those deals look like on page 277). This is because, once a writer is well-known, he or she can get to artists as easily as a publisher can, and maybe easier (artists often call important writers directly, looking for material, or the writer may be a major producer, and the artists they produce are always looking for songs). Also, more and more artists are writing their own songs, so there's no need for a publisher to get songs to them. All they really need is someone to make sure they get paid everything they're owed.

Mechanics of Publishing

A publishing company has a lot fewer moving parts than a record company. (We discussed record company anatomy on page 70.) To be a publisher, you only need the following (and some of these functions can be performed by the same person):

1. An administrator to take care of registering copyrights in the songs, issuing licenses, collecting money, paying writers and co-publishers, etc.
2. A "song plugger" who runs around and convinces people to use their songs, in particular for films, TV, and commercials.

3. A creative staff person, who finds writers, works with them to improve their skills, pairs them up creatively with co-writers, etc. If the publishing company only owns an existing catalog of songs (in other words, it has no writers currently under contract to deliver new songs), you don't even need this person.

Thus, unlike the record business, it only takes a small investment to call yourself a publisher. You don't need a large staff (until you get to be huge), though as the digital world gets more complex, it takes a sophisticated system to keep track of the billions of tiny transactions that generate money these days. So while it's not quite as simple as it used to be, publishers are still much smaller than record companies.

Types of Publishers

For this reason, there are a lot of players in the publishing biz, and it isn't nearly so dominated by the majors as is the record business. There are, to be sure, megaton publishing companies who have world-wide operations and generate hundreds of millions of dollars per year, but there are busloads of others running the gamut from a one-person show to the giants. Here's a broad-strokes view of the different types:

The 900-Pound Gorillas. These are the major companies, such as Universal Music, Sony/ATV/EMI, and Warner/Chappell (all of whom are affiliated with record companies). There are also slightly lighter-weight (500-pound gorillas), such as Kobalt and BMG Rights.

Major Affiliates. There are a number of independent publishing companies, with full staffs of professionals, whose "administration" is handled by a major. The publisher's affiliation with a major may be for the world, or it may be for only certain territories. For instance, a publisher might be affiliated with a major for the United States and have separate deals (with other publishers) for the rest of the world.

Stand-Alones. *Stand-alone* isn't an industry term; I'm using it to mean a company that's not affiliated with a major, and instead does its own administration. In other words, it collects its own money, does its own accountings, etc. It usually licenses territories outside the United States to a major, though it can have offices in certain territories.

Just because the publishing game has a low entry price doesn't mean it's an easy gig. The difference between a good publisher and an unqualified one can mean a lot to your pocketbook. For example, a good publisher knows how much to charge for various licenses and where to look for hidden monies (for example, see page 258, discussing how foreign monies get lost when they're not properly claimed). The bad ones can lose money just by sitting there and not doing what they're supposed to. An inexperienced publisher that's affiliated with a major publisher is a quantum improvement over an unqualified publisher trying to go it alone. However, the major will not have the same incentive to take care of the independent's songs as it will to take care of its own. Also, a major may administer millions of copyrights, so you can get shoved to the back of the shelf. On the other hand, a good independent publisher affiliated with a major can often do better for you than if you signed to the major directly. If the indie publisher has enough clout to become a "squeaky wheel" on your behalf (and remember, the squeaking is on behalf of themselves as well), it can prevent you from getting lost in the shuffle.

SOURCES OF INCOME

As noted, writers get a percentage of the publisher's income. So let's first take a look at the monies a publisher collects, then we'll discuss how you can get the most of it under your publishing deal.

We've already talked a little about mechanicals, which is the third-largest source of income. Coming in at number one are **public performance monies,** with **sync** at number two. What the hell does that mean?

PUBLIC PERFORMANCE ROYALTIES

Remember, when we discussed copyrights, that one of your exclusive rights is the right to perform your composition in public (see page 213)? These rights are known as **performing rights,** or **public performance rights.**

Every time someone performs your song publicly, they need your permission. That includes playing it on the radio, streaming it to a mobile device, performing it on television, in nightclubs, in amusement parks, at live concerts, etc. So does that mean every radio station, nightclub, etc., in the country (of which there are thousands) has to get a separate license for every song they play (of which there are also thousands)? And that every publisher has to issue thousands of licenses to each individual user? The paperwork alone would send them off to buy that trout farm in Idaho.

Well, rest easy. This is taken care of by something called a **blanket license,** which is issued by a **performing rights society.**

Here's how it works:

Performing Rights Societies

In the United States, the major performing rights societies (also called **PROs,** meaning **performing rights organizations**) are **ASCAP** (standing for American Society of Composers, Authors and Publishers), **BMI** (Broadcast Music, Incorporated), **SESAC** (which originally stood for Society of European Stage Authors and Composers but now stands for "SESAC"), and **GMR** (which stands for Global Music Rights). Of the four, ASCAP and BMI are by far the largest, as SESAC only has about 10% of the U.S. performing rights. GMR has even less than SESAC, though they have a lot of major writers.

ASCAP and BMI are *non-profit*, meaning they collect money, pay their expenses, and distribute everything else to the writers and publishers. SESAC and GMR are for-profit, meaning they keep a chunk of the money in excess of expenses, but they say they are able to pay higher rates than ASCAP/BMI for reasons we'll discuss later (on page 230). However, you can only join SESAC and GMR if they invite you (which means their members are established writers, and which also means you'll be joining ASCAP or BMI in the beginning).

Virtually every foreign country has an equivalent PRO for its own territory. Unlike the United States, there's generally only one per territory, and most of those are government-sanctioned, such as SACEM for France, GEMA for Germany, PRS for the United Kingdom, etc.

The PROs go to each publisher and say, "Please give us the right to license performing rights in *all* your songs. We'll then go to the people who want to use them (radio stations, TV stations, concert halls, night clubs, etc.) and make a deal that lets them use *all* the songs of *all* the publishers we represent. For each license, we'll collect the fees, divide them up, and send you a share."

So publishers sign up with (known as "affiliating with") a PRO. If the publisher has a lot of writers, they affiliate with all the PROs. These societies then issue licenses to the users, collect the monies, and pay the publishers. Got it?

Blanket Licenses

The license that the performing rights societies give each music user is called a **blanket license** because it "blankets" (i.e., "covers") all of the compositions they represent. In other words, in exchange for a fee, the user gets the right to perform *all* the compositions controlled by *all* the publishers affiliated with that society. The yearly fee can range from a few hundred dollars for a small nightclub to multimillions of dollars for television networks.

Separate Writer Affiliation

It isn't just publishers who affiliate with these societies. The writers also sign on, and even more important, *the writers are paid 50% of the money (the writer's share) directly by the society.* In other words, the writer's performance earnings are not paid to the publisher; they're sent to the writer. This is designed to protect the writer (which it does nicely) from flaky publishers who might steal their money.

By the way, writers can only affiliate with one society at a time in the United States (most of the other territories only have one, so it's not much of an issue there . . .). Historically, writers had only one society for the world, but there's a recent trend for writers with a lot of international success to divide the world (for example, they might affiliate with ASCAP or BMI in America, and PRS [the PRO in the UK] for the rest of the world).

Allocation of License Proceeds

So here are the societies sitting with squillions of dollars from their licenses. How do they know how much to pay each publisher and writer?

First, the monies are used to pay the operating expenses of the society. At ASCAP and BMI, everything left over is divided among the participants. At SESAC and GMR, they keep a profit before they distribute.

But how, you ask, do the societies know who to pay? Who knows how many times your songs were played in Pennsylvania nightclubs? Baseball stadiums? Dinner theaters? Chuck E. Cheese?

Historically, the distributions were all based on radio and TV airplay, then extrapolated for everything else. But in the digital age, the data pool is far more detailed (and complicated), so they can more accurately allocate the money. (If you're really into 50 Shades of Performance

Allocation, both BMI and ASCAP have details of their calculations on their websites, so go on over and spank yourself to your heart's content.)

Generally, here's how it works:

1. **Radio.**
   Both ASCAP and BMI use media monitoring companies to scour radio stations across the nation, 24/7. They believe they cover about 85% of all the licensed stations, and from that, they extrapolate the other 15%.

2. **Television.**
   Television stations are required to keep **cue sheets,** which are lists of every musical composition broadcast, how long it was played, and how it was used (theme song, background, performed visually, etc.). The cue sheets are then filed with the societies.

   There are specific dollar amounts paid for each type of use (theme, background, etc.). The amount also varies with the size of the broadcast area (local stations pay a lot less than networks), and the size of that program's audience. Both ASCAP and BMI supplement the cue sheet data by digitally monitoring broadcasts, and they also use independent statistics to verify the data.

3. **Streaming.**
   One of the advantages of digital delivery is that the service providers have precise data of what's been played, how often, and to how many people. The disadvantage is that they overwhelm the societies with megatons of data that some poor schlump has to sort out.

4. **Live Events.**
   The societies pay based on domestic concert performances, but it's only for the top three hundred grossing tours as reported in a magazine called *Pollstar.* The PROs distribute money based on **set lists**—lists of the songs played on the tour—which they get from either the venues or the artist's management.

   PROs say they also track sports stadiums and arenas, to pick up the songs that everyone claps along to.

   If you're performing in coffee houses and small venues, these aren't tracked separately, but both BMI and ASCAP have programs for you to submit your materials and get paid something.

5. **Background Music.**
   The fine music you find in airports, grocery stores, and waiting rooms is also logged separately.

In addition to a share of income determined by the above, BMI and ASCAP both pay substantial bonuses to big earners, from a pool of money they set aside for this purpose. I'm sorry I can't give you much guidance on how the bonuses work because (a) the rules change from time to time, (b) the amounts also vary by category (pop, classic rock, classical music, didgeridoos, etc.), and (c) I've never actually needed to understand exactly how they work, so I have no clue.

Both societies pay quarterly (four times per year), and both societies pay about nine months to a year after the calendar quarter in which the monies are received.

Motion Picture Performance Monies

Due to some fancy footwork by the film industry a number of years ago, PROs are not allowed to collect public performance monies for motion pictures shown in theaters in the United States. There is no logical reason for this (showing movies is certainly a public performance); it's just historical and political. However, foreign territories have never bought into this nonsense, and motion picture performance monies over there are significant. The fees are collected by local societies, then paid over to your United States PRO, unless of course you're a direct member of the foreign society.

Foreign film performance monies are a percentage of the box-office receipts, which means they generate a good amount of green (or whatever color the local currency is). How much? Well, the composer of a smash film score can earn hundreds of thousands of dollars in foreign performance monies alone.

Which Society Is the Best?

The best gauge is to look at cross-registered songs, which means a song that's registered with both ASCAP and BMI. This happens when a song is co-written by an ASCAP and a BMI writer. ASCAP collects its share of the song's performance monies and pays the ASCAP writer and publisher, while BMI does the same for its writer and publisher. Since each society collects and pays independently of the other, we get to see who pays more. And the result?

No clear answer. As noted above, the societies change their distribution rules on a regular basis, and the bonuses also affect the results. So the answer shifts around. For mainstream writers, I've been told they're pretty similar. For specific genres of music, however, one tends to do better than the other, but that changes over time (because of changes in the distribution and bonus rules). So unfortunately, I can't give you an accurate scorecard.

The big picture is that it shouldn't matter much if you're an artist with broad appeal, but if you're in a specific genre, you should join the society that will treat you more favorably. That's unfortunately one of those rules that's easier said than done, because that information has to be current, and it's not so simple to dig up. The people with the data are some of the bigger business managers (they can look at their clients' catalogs and compare earnings), or if you've got access to a big a publisher with cross-registered songs, they can give you an even better comparison because they have much more information. Otherwise, lick your index finger, stick it up in the wind, let it blow. And know that you'll be in the position to make a better decision in a few years, when you're big enough to get access to the data you need to make the right choice.

As noted earlier, SESAC and GMR claim they pay better rates than ASCAP or BMI. The only information I have isn't public, so I can't really comment. But it's certainly possible because of how they're set up.

Let me explain.

In the United States, ASCAP and BMI are under what's called a **consent decree,** which is fancy legal jargon for the fact that they're so big and scary that the government puts restrictions on what they can do (if you want a little more technical explanation, it means they consented to a legal judgment that spells out rules they have to follow; if they don't follow those rules, they're violating the United States' anti-trust laws).

One of these consent decree restrictions is that they can't refuse to license anyone. In other words, they have to let everyone perform their songs no matter what. However, they can argue about how much they should get paid for that license. If the PRO and the user can't agree on a price, they go to a judge who sets the rate.

This seriously impacts the PRO's bargaining power. If they can't leverage the user by refusing to license a song, they don't have anywhere near the same clout as if they could.

Enter SESAC and GMR, who are too small to be regulated by the government. Which means they have no consent decrees. Which means they're allowed to say, "We think your offer sucks, so you can't use our music." Accordingly, they should be able to charge more money, and even after taking out their profit, they can in theory pay more to the writers.

The Music Modernization Act that I mentioned earlier has some goodies that make this situation a little better for ASCAP and BMI. Historically, when there was a disputed rate, it was decided by one judge (one for ASCAP and one for BMI) who was appointed for life to hear all the performance rate cases. And some people felt those judges were too tough on the PROs. In addition, when the PROs argued for a higher rate, the evidence they could submit was very limited (for example, the court couldn't consider the rates paid for sound recordings).

Under the MMA, while the PROs still can't refuse to license music, a different judge is now randomly assigned to each case. Also, the MMA allows the rate court to consider *all* the market evidence in determining the rate, including the rates for sound recordings.

These changes should result in higher rates down the road, so stick around. We should find out in the not too distant future.

MORE ABOUT MECHANICAL ROYALTIES

As we discussed on page 215, mechanical royalties are monies paid by a record company for the right to use a song in phonorecords. It's easy to see how this works for CDs and downloads. The publisher issues a license to the record company that says, for each record manufactured and distributed, and each digital copy that's downloaded, the record company will pay a royalty equal to a specified number of pennies (currently 9.1¢, unless the song is over five minutes).

Harry Fox and CMRRA

Two major organizations are delighted to issue mechanical licenses for publishers. One is the **Harry Fox Agency,** which is the largest organization of its kind in the United States, and its Canadian counterpart, **CMRRA,** standing for **Canadian Musical Reproduction Rights Agency.** Basically, these organizations act like a publisher's agent for mechanicals. They issue mechanical licenses for the publisher, police them (i.e., make sure the users pay), and account to the publisher. For their services, Harry Fox currently charges 11.5% of the monies collected, and CMRRA currently charges 6%.

Fox and CMRRA periodically audit record companies and the streaming services on behalf of all their clients, and then allocate the recovered monies among their clients in proportion to their earnings. This is particularly significant for a smaller publisher, as the cost of an audit for low earners is prohibitive. (Today, a typical publishing audit can cost $15,000 to $25,000 or more, and unless the recovery is likely to be several times this amount, it's not economical.)

For more info, check out their websites: www.harryfox.com and www.cmrra.ca.

It may surprise you to know that many midsize publishers (and some larger publishers) use Fox and CMRRA, because the cost of hiring a staff to issue numerous licenses and police them is more expensive than the fees these organizations charge. Recently, however, the trend is for the larger publishers not to use Fox or CMRRA, as technology has made it easier for them to directly license the users.

STREAMING AND DOWNLOADS

If I stream a song to my mobile phone, is that a performance, a mechanical, or both?

What if I download a song to my phone? Is that a mechanical only, or is it also a performance?

Ah, the joys of shoe-horning new technologies into a copyright law that was first written when wax cylinders were the rage.

Here's the debate:

The PROs say that streaming a song is just like listening to it on the radio, which is clearly a performance. Plus they say that a download has to be streamed to a phone or PC in order to deliver it, so that's also a performance.

The Harry Fox folks, who collect mechanical royalties, say that you can't stream music without making a copy on the DSP's computer server, and caching it on a mobile phone. And those are reproductions of the song, meaning you need a mechanical license. Also, downloading a song is just like the sale of a CD, so it's clearly a mechanical right.

Well, they're both sort of right. But underneath all this posturing was really a fight about who got paid to collect it: the PROs, the Fox people, or both?

Interestingly, Europe worked this out before we did (of course, over history, they've worked out a lot of things before we did . . .). In most of Europe, the countries agreed that a download is 25% performance and 75% mechanical, while streaming is considered 75% performance and 25% mechanical. However, the United Kingdom splits 50/50 between performance and download, and in Switzerland and a handful of other countries, they don't recognize any performance right for a download. (So maybe they didn't work it out so well after all . . .)

Anyway, after the predictable wrangling in the United States, everyone's come to an understanding on this issue. Here's today's scorecard in the all-star game of Mechanical vs. Performance:

Permanent Downloads

Let's start with an easy one: permanent downloads, like the ones sold on iTunes.

It's well settled that these downloads are treated just like sales of CDs. That means you get a mechanical royalty only, and it's not a performance.

Non-interactive Audio Streaming

Non-interactive means someone else decides what you hear (as opposed to you choosing the music yourself). It's essentially a radio station that's delivered via streaming to your phone, and not over the air to an antenna.

It's now settled that you only get performance monies (from ASCAP, BMI, etc.) for non-interactive streams. Which is exactly what you'd get if an over-the-air station played your music.

The rates are pretty complex, and they change over time, but in essence they're a percentage of revenue, with minimums per stream (in case the user doesn't have much revenue). For the most current state of play, you can check out the standard ASCAP, BMI, and SESAC non-interactive performance licenses on their websites (www.ascap.com, www.bmi.com, and www.sesac.com). Generally, it's about 5% of the revenue (for all the PROs combined).

Monster streaming companies (Spotify, Apple Music, and the like) don't take these standard, off-the-shelf licenses, in the same way that CBS television doesn't take an off-the-shelf performance license that's geared to local TV stations. Instead, the big guys negotiate their own specific deals with each PRO.

For the technical freaks out there (the rest of you can skip to the interactive streaming section on page 234), there's an important difference between Internet streaming and over-the-air stations. As I mentioned earlier, before you can stream on the Internet, you have to make a copy of the song on your server, and two lawsuits have held that a server copy of a copyrighted song requires a license: *UMG Recordings et al. v. MP3.com, Inc.*, 92 F. Supp 2d 349 (2000), and *Rodgers and Hammerstein Organization et al. v. UMG Recordings, Inc., and the Farm Club*

Online, Inc., 60 U.S. P.Q. 2D [BNA] 1342 (2001). Note this server copy license is *in addition* to the performance license. A performance license lets you stream. The server copy license lets you make a copy. (Take a look back to our discussion of the various rights in a copyright on page 212. One is the right to perform, and the other is the right to duplicate. However, as industry practice, the publishers only require a performance license for non-interactive streaming.)

Over-the-air radio stations also make server copies of recordings for broadcast, but they're allowed to do this without a license under a specific provision of the copyright law (their server copy is called an **ephemeral recording** under Section 112 of the Copyright Act). Technically, this only gives them the right to make a copy of the sound recording, not the song, but if they have a performance license, they're good as a matter of industry practice.

Webcasters who are not over-the-air broadcasters wanted the same rights, and after some back and forth, the industry practice settled down to the same result: non-interactive services only need a performance license.

Interactive Audio Streaming (On-demand Streaming)

Now for some more complicated stuff. Stay with me; this is the biggest part of the business and growing.

As we discussed, interactive streaming lets you call up whatever song you want to hear, whenever you want to hear it. The big players are Spotify, Apple Music, and Amazon Music.

As you may recall, there's a compulsory license for songs used in interactive streaming (see page 215). The rates for this streaming license (and all other compulsory licenses, not just music) are set by the **Copyright Royalty Board.** The Copyright Royalty Board (**CRB** to its pals) is made up of three administrative judges who probably have no sense of humor. These judges take in lots of evidence (shockingly, record companies argue that the rate is too high, and copyright owners say it's too low), then sit around and think about it. When they're done cogitating, they deliver the new rates for compulsory licenses.

By the way, the Music Modernization Act recently changed the standard that the CRB uses to set rates from a limited-evidence process to a "willing buyer/willing seller" standard, which the music industry has wanted for years. "Willing buyer/willing seller" means the rate two people would agree in a free marketplace if they wanted to make a deal, and it allows the CRB to consider all the market data.

In 2018, much to the dismay of the digital service providers, the CRB gave the publishers a gigantic increase over the old rates, with more bumps built into the future years. Some of the DSPs have appealed this decision, and at the time I'm writing this, it's still pending. So these rates may change. But let's take a look at where they are as I write this. I wouldn't use the word "uncomplicated" to describe the rulings . . .

The rates are a set of formulas that cover (a) subscription streaming services; (b) subscription streaming services that are bundled with other services (which we'll discuss in the next section); (c) portable services (meaning you can get the music on a portable device); (d) nonportable services (you can probably figure out what that is); and (e) non-subscription/advertiser-supported services. (Whew.)

But wait, there's more! We have subcategories for the subscription services! There are rates (a) for services that only play when you're connected to the Internet, (b) those that play both when you're connected and when you're not, and (c) limited offering subscriptions, meaning subscriptions that are either (i) noninteractive, or (ii) for only a particular genre, or limited playlists. Can you stand the excitement?

Note this license covers only *mechanicals*, and not performance money (though the rates are reduced by the amounts paid by the DSP for performance money, which I'll discuss below). Also, remember this is only for *songs*, not masters. There is no compulsory rate for interactive streaming of masters (we covered how those are paid on page 144).

In a very simplistic form (and I use the word "simplistic" guardedly), the compulsory license for interactive streaming works like this.

1. First, you look at the rate for the applicable year. Under the CRB ruling, the rate for 2019 is the *greater* of:
   (a) 12.3% of the service's revenue for the period involved, or
   (b) 22% of something called **TCC**, meaning **Total Content Cost.** In other words, the total amount that the service pays out for the right to make interactive streams and limited downloads of sound recordings for that period.

   Under the CRB ruling, the percentages in (a) and (b) will increase over the next few years, as follows:

2019–2022 Interactive Streaming Rates

Royalty Year	2019	2020	2021	2022
Percent of Revenue	12.3%	13.3%	14.2%	15.1%
Percent of TCC	23.1%	24.1%	25.2%	26.2%

[The rates before the 2018 CRB ruling were 10.5% for

(a) above, and 21% to 22% for (b). So you can see there was a huge increase.]

2. Once you have the result of that multiplication game, you subtract the amount that the DSPs have to pay for performance license (generally a little over 5%). Let's call that the **Net Subscription Amount** (a term I just made up).

3. We discussed *per subscriber minimums* (PSMs) on page 144, in the context of streaming masters. This concept is alive and well in the publishing world, thanks at least in part to the CRB's rate ruling. In other words, regardless of what the digital service actually collects, they can't pay out less than a per-subscriber minimum (PSM) multiplied times their total subscribers. This keeps the DSP from dropping its prices too low (or at least it costs the DSP a bigger percentage if they do).

   The PSM under the CRB rate ranges from 15¢ to 50¢ per subscriber per month, depending on the kind of service being licensed (assuming, of course, there are subscribers, which there wouldn't be in an ad-supported service). In determining the number of subscribers for this calculation, they treat a family plan as 1.5 subscribers.

   To be clear, the PSM is not 15¢ to 50¢ per song per month; that would bankrupt the digital service provider. It's a minimum figure that the service has to pay for all the songs used, divided among all the songs and their publishers

4. Okay. So now you've computed the Net Subscription Amount (under 2), and the PSM (under 3). You take the higher of those two figures (let's call it the **Base**, which is another term I just made up), then figure out your share of it. This is done by computing the percentage that your plays for the period involved bears to the total plays for that period, then multiplying that percentage times the Base. So if you had 10% of the total plays, and the Base was $100,000, you'd get $10,000.

   But Wait! There's even more. In computing your percentage of the Base, you get more of the pie if your songs are longer than five minutes. Here's the formula:

   (1) 5:01 to 6:00 minutes: Each play = 1.2 plays
   (2) 6:01 to 7:00 minutes: Each play = 1.4 plays
   (3) 7:01 to 8:00 minutes: Each play = 1.6 plays
   (4) 8:01 to 9:00 minutes: Each play = 1.8 plays
   (5) 9:01 to 10:00 minutes: Each play = 2.0 plays

(6) For playing times of greater than 10 minutes, continue to add .2 for each additional minute or fraction thereof.

Got it?

If you *really* want to understand this in more detail, check out 37 CFR Part 385, which is published in the *Federal Register*, vol. 74, no. 15, p. 4529, as amended by *Federal Register*, vol. 74, no. 27, p. 6832, and further amended in 37 CFR 835, Subpart C. You might want to print a few copies and keep them next to your bed, in case of insomnia.

By the way, outside the United States, there are no compulsory mechanical licenses at all. Instead, in many territories there are "published tariffs" set by the local societies or a government agency that everyone follows.

Stuck in the Middle with . . .

What if you're sort-of an interactive service? For example, you don't get to hear anything you decide to punch up at the moment, but the service lets you skip unlimited numbers of songs? Replay songs? Get a listing of songs before they play? Hear a specific artist more than a few times each hour?

Some DSPs have a mid-tier service that lets you replay songs and listen to a limited number of stations when you're not connected online. The DSPs could take a compulsory license for this, but it would be too expensive, so the deals are negotiated specifically. While the terms aren't public, I understand the rates are somewhere between a performance license rate (a little over 5%) and the above statutory rates for interactive streams.

Video Streaming

You may remember that there's no compulsory license for videos. That means the CRB has no jurisdiction over video streaming services like YouTube and Vevo. Which means the publishers can charge whatever they want.

So this area's been like the Wild West.

Here's what's happenin' down on the ranch, pardner.

For record-company-produced videos, the publishers get a percentage of ad revenues and/or subscription monies. The rates aren't public, but I understand it's somewhere in the 10% range. Sometimes they also get a fraction of a penny as a minimum per-stream payment, or a minimum per-subscriber payment.

For user-generated videos (the UGC we discussed on page 150), the major publishers have licenses with YouTube, and Fox represents some of the indies (but not all of them). Meaning there's no central place for the YouTubes of the world to make a deal for all their music.

As to rates, after some amount of wrangling, the National Music Publishers Association (NMPA)—an industry organization that represents publishers in both lobbying and dealing with users—came to an agreement with YouTube and that deal is the norm (for a while anyway). The Fox Agency can do the license for you, though they act for YouTube (meaning they're not representing you; they were hired by YouTube to help them). YouTube also has an opt-in license, which you can find on its website, meaning you elect to use it ("opt-in") with a few clicks and therefore directly license your music to them. The direct license has the advantage of dealing directly with the DSP (rather than have Fox in the middle).

The terms for UGC video are:

1. If it's a user-created video that includes a commercial recording of the song, the video streaming service pays the publisher 15% of net ad revenues. (Some of the smaller streaming services actually pay the record label, which in turn pays this amount to the publisher.)

2. If it's a new recording of the song (like Uncle Lenny, the musical saw virtuoso of Picayune, Texas), the publisher gets 50% of net ad revenues. The only exception is cases where the uploader gets some of the ad revenue (for example, if Lenny has a YouTube channel and gets a cut of ad money). In that case, YouTube deducts whatever it pays Lenny from the publisher's 50%. However, this deduction is subject to a limit of 15%, meaning the publisher never gets less than 35% of net ad revenue.

   While I understand that YouTube's content identification program does a good job of recognizing commercial sound recordings, I'm told it doesn't pick up live versions of UGC as well. So your publisher has to police this—yet another example of how complicated the world is becoming, and how difficult (and expensive) it is for publishers to make sure they get their share from the river of pennies (more accurately, "fractions of pennies").

Interestingly, as massive as YouTube is, the ad revenue around music, especially UGC, is pretty low. That's because the audience is so wide that it's hard to target ads—nobody pays much to advertise tampons to a sixty-year-old dude. So until this gets more efficient, the ad rates will stay low, and the money from YouTube isn't what it could be.

As you can see, these models are not only complicated, but also require publishers to track usage all over the Internet. And while the big publishers have sophisticated tracking systems, what about the rest of us? Well, the Fox Agency offers these services, as do a number of competitors. For example, Songtrust helps songwriters and publishers track and collect all their publishing income. They are located, not surprisingly, at www.songtrust.com. Other companies in this area are Audiam (www .audiam.com) and AdRev (www.adrev.net), which monetizes YouTube.

MUSIC MODERNIZATION ACT

All right! You've now got enough background to really understand what the Music Modernization Act (MMA) is about. (Well, at least most of it. There's a little more to come later.)

As we discussed, a compulsory license is one that a publisher has to give you, whether they want to or not, as long as you check the right boxes under the Copyright Act. And to get a compulsory *mechanical* license for physical or downloads, one of those boxes is that your master must be the second or later recording of a song (meaning a cover record).

Well, for the first time under the copyright law, the MMA created a compulsory license for the *first use* of a song. But (a) this license is only for streaming, and (b) you can only get this compulsory license if both recording and the song have been licensed for streaming. Meaning you already have a voluntary license to stream the song.

So, as I asked before, why would you need a compulsory if you already have a voluntary license? Well, time to answer that question:

You don't need a compulsory license for streaming when you already have a voluntary license.

Does that mean Congress was insane? (You can take the Fifth Amendment.)

Well, not this time, anyway. They passed the MMA in 2018 to fix a nasty problem that existed in the streaming world.

Here's the background. When streaming was an infant, Spotify and the other services went into uncharted waters with their business model. They quickly discovered that they were dealing with multi-millions of songs, and billions of lines of data. And that a lot of these songs had more than one owner.

To put it mildly, the digital service providers (DSPs) were overwhelmed. For starters, they had no idea who owned a lot of these songs, much less where to reach them. It's simple enough to find the major publishers, but they don't control all the songs. In fact, even on songs where the majors have an interest, they sometimes don't have all the rights (because some of the multiple owners of the songs aren't major publishers, or because the major only controls certain territories of the world, etc.). And even if the DSPs could find the owners, they weren't set up to handle tens of thousands of licenses from obscure publishers around the world.

All this resulted in the DSPs having tens of millions of dollars that they didn't know where to pay. So they did what any red-blooded businessperson would do—they kept it. (In the biz, we call these unallocated monies **pending and unmatched.**)

It didn't take the indie publishers long to wake up, and when they did, they sued the DSPs. Their lawsuits claimed that the DSPs were infringing their copyrights because they didn't have licenses to use their songs. And they were right; the DSPs didn't even know who to ask for a license.

Historically, the tech business and the music biz were not the best of friends. After all, when Napster started, the techies made a lot of money selling computers, access to the Internet to steal songs, CD burners, and the like. And as we discussed earlier, YouTube is still a serious problem for us.

But with the DSPs heading for a crashing loss in court, they suddenly had a stake in finding a solution to this pending and unmatched problem. Meanwhile, the music publishers wanted a system that got everyone accurately paid, so they didn't have to sue and wait years to get their money. In other words, we had one of those rare times when both sides were aligned in their goals, and this kum-ba-ya moment gave birth to the MMA.

With both sides pushing the bill forward, Congress didn't get any of the vicious threats it usually gets from the opposition. So the bill was passed and signed into law relatively quickly. (Don't get used to that . . .)

The MMA solves the pending and unmatched problem by setting up something called the **Mechanical License Collective (MLC).** This new organization, which the DSPs will fund, has the authority to collect all the mechanical rights money from the DSPs. (It doesn't collect performance monies; those go to the PROs.)

To give the MLC the right to collect all this dough, the MMA created the compulsory license we discussed. In essence, this a *blanket license* (see page 226, where we talked about PRO blanket licenses). As long as the DSPs pay the MLC for all their streams, they can stream any song without being guilty of copyright infringement. This neatly solves the problem of DSPs not knowing who to pay, and puts the dough in the hands of an independent party instead of the DSP's bank account.

The MMA also allows the MLC to collect money from *voluntary* licenses negotiated by both sides. In other words, the major publishers can still make their own deals with the DSPs, but the MLC will collect the money centrally and pass it on.

Under this system, publishers will file claims with the MLC for the songs they own, and the MLC will pay out *one hundred percent* of the money it collects—as I noted earlier, the law requires the DSPs to fund the MLC, so there's no deduction of costs or commissions.

But what if no one claims a particular song? That means the MLC doesn't know who to pay. What happens to the money?

Well, the MLC hangs on to it for a period of time, then (if it's still unclaimed) pays the money to everyone who did file claims. Specifically, MLC holds unclaimed monies until January 1 of the second full calendar year after the license availability date, then if nobody shows up to claim it, they pay it out to the people who did claim (other) songs for that period. These unclaimed monies are allocated on the basis of the market share of each publisher who claimed money. So, for example, if you had 10% of the market share in that period, you'd get 10% of the unclaimed money. (This is very similar to black-box monies we'll discuss in subpublishing deals on page 259.)

An interesting aspect of the MMA is that it requires publishers to pay at least 50% of the unclaimed monies to their songwriters, allocated on the basis of each song's earnings. This is similar to the breakage concept we discussed on page 146.

Remember this all started because the DSPs couldn't figure out who to pay? Well, the MMA requires the MLC to set up and maintain a free, publicly available database of all the songs, publishers, and writers. This will truly be a valuable asset. If you've ever tried to track down a song, it's not a fun journey . . .

So now you understand why the weird compulsory license. Without it, there'd be no basis for the DSPs to pay the MLC and be absolved of copyright infringement.

You can bank that in your database.

17

Even More Publishing Income

Now let's take a look at other kinds of publishing income: synchronization, print, foreign monies, and other assorted goodies. And along the way, we'll hit controlled composition clauses. You won't want to miss that one.

SYNCHRONIZATION AND TRANSCRIPTION LICENSES

A **synchronization license** is a license to use music in "timed synchronization" with visual images. It's also called a **sync** (pronounced "sink") license, and sometimes spelled **synch** (also pronounced like a kitchen basin). A classic example is a song in a motion picture, where the song is synchronized with the action on the screen. It also includes television programs, commercials, audiovisual streaming, video games, home video devices, etc. Interestingly, it doesn't include radio commercials (since they're not synchronized with visuals). Radio commercial and other audio licenses (like podcasts) are called **transcription licenses.**

Fees

The fees for synchronization licenses are really all over the board, and they vary with exactly how the song is used, which media you want, how long you want to use it, and the importance of the song. The budget of the production is also a factor—fees for a big budget, major studio film are much more than that of an indie film; an established TV show pays more than a new one, and all of those have more money than a purely Internet webisode.

Also, keep in mind that this chapter is only talking about fees for the *song*. If the master is also being used, there's a separate fee for that, which is almost always an equal amount.

An example of the lowest-end fee would be a ten-second background use of an unknown song in a television show (maybe being played on a jukebox while the actors are talking and ignoring it). A high-end example would be an on-camera, full-length performance of a well-known song in a major studio's high-budget film.

And when we get into the realm of commercials, the fees go even higher.

Here's an idea of the range:

1. **Motion picture:**
   Major Studios. Motion picture sync licenses for a major studio film generally run in the range of $15,000 to $25,000 (for very minor usage of a song that's not particularly well known) to over $100,000. **Main title** usages (meaning over the opening credits) are generally from $75,000 to $400,000, and **end title** usages are less, in the range of $35,000 to $250,000 (why pay as much for a song that plays while everybody's walking out of the theater?). The end title song fees may also be lower if there's more than one song over the credits, which happens commonly these days.

   Of course, if it's an incredibly hot, recent hit song, and the film company is salivating over it, these figures can get very high into six figures.

   For these fees, the film companies want more than just the right to use the song in the movie. They also want **in-context** uses. *In-context* means using the song with the same visual images that accompany it in the film. For example, if your song is played in the film while lovers stroll down a beach looking lovingly at each other, and that same scene is in a commercial for the film, that's an in-context use. The primary in-context uses are for advertising, like I just described, **trailers** (those "previews of coming attractions" that you see online and in your local theater before the movie), clips, and promotions (like excerpts shown on talk shows while the film's stars are interviewed).

   In addition, the studios also want rights to use the song in things like **featurettes** (short films, often showing behind-the-scenes footage that was taken while the film was being made; this is also called a **making-of**), playing the song over

DVD menu selections, and usage in deleted scenes. They'll also ask for **out-of-context** uses, which are, not surprisingly, the opposite of the in-context uses we discussed in the preceding paragraph. In other words, *out-of-context* means using the music differently from the way it's used in the film. For example, playing the song in a television ad while showing another scene from the movie.

The above fees normally include in-context usage and DVD menus (though I wouldn't give DVDs a particularly long life span). But you should get more money for other uses. For example, featurettes are in the range of about $15,000 to $50,000. And you should get a lot more money for *out-of-context* uses, because in essence they're licensing your song into a commercial for the film.

How much more?

If the song is used in the film as well as out-of-context (meaning you're already getting a chunk of money for the film and in-context uses), the out-of-context fee is an additional payment of anywhere from $25,000 to $100,000, though if it's a major song, it can go higher. For licensed songs that are not in the film at all (for example, a song that's licensed only for trailers or ads for the film), the out-of-context fees are higher, anywhere from $25,000 to $200,000 and up, depending on the importance of the song and nature of the use. For out-of-context instrumental background music (called **cues**), it's usually around $20,000. (By the way, we're talking here about cues from a licensed song that wasn't written for the film. If it's a cue from the underscore that was written for the film, we'll cover that in Chapter 30. Spoiler alert: The composer doesn't get any extra money.)

2. **Independent Films:**
For low-budget, independent films, the deals get much more creative. Funny how things always get more creative when someone doesn't have any money.

The fees are of course much lower, at least initially (as we'll discuss), and the price also depends on the kind of indie film involved. Documentaries are the serious bargain basement, since they rarely make much or any money (though with the advent of Netflix, HBO, and other players getting into this space, the documentary budgets are rising). Next step up are true indie films, with unknown directors, actors, etc. At the top are indie films that feature major stars and/or directors who are working as a labor of love. While this last category may be low budget, the publishers are not all that sympathetic—these films can have commercial success. Accordingly, these kinds of films often pay higher fees (sometimes as much as the major film fees discussed above), at least for important music.

If an indie film was made by producers who barely scraped the money together, and they don't even have a **distributor** (meaning a company to put the film in theaters and pay for advertising and marketing), the producers run around to film festivals with the movie tucked under their arm, trying to find someone to adopt their baby. A typical sync deal is a cheap license that only allows them to show the film in festivals, and it's usually limited to a term of one year. For documentaries, the festival fee might be $500 to $2,500, depending on the use and importance of the song, and there's often no deal beyond that. The idea is that the filmmaker looks for a distributor, and if they find one, comes back to the publisher and gets a license for broader rights.

Non-documentaries pay a similar license fee for festivals, but they usually want options at preset amounts for more rights. That way, if they find a deal, you can't hold them up for ransom. In other words, they set the ransom price up front.

For example, an indie film might pay $1,000 for festivals only. Then, if it goes into theatrical release, there's a preset fee of $2,500 to $7,500 (there might be a smaller fee for "art house" releases, and a larger one for a mainstream release). The publisher would then get the same amount again if the film is released on television. And that amount again if it goes into DVD or is made available for video-on-demand streaming (like Netflix, Amazon, etc.). These are called **step deals,** because the money comes in steps.

There might also be **kickers** (additional fees) if the film achieves certain success. One recent deal for a very low-budget film paid amounts equal to the original license fee if the film had worldwide box office gross of $3,000,000, and additional kickers at every $3,000,000 increment, up to a maximum of four times the original fee. Other deals don't have a maximum, so the publisher can make out nicely if the film does well.

3. Television:
Except for the competition and talk shows, which we'll discuss in a minute, most TV licenses are now in perpetuity and include

the rights to all media now or hereafter known. But here's some things you should try to carve out:

a. You shouldn't give out-of-context trailers (see page 244 for what that is), though you'll have to give in-context trailers.

b. Except for in-context trailers, don't let them use clips of your song apart from the show. (This is tougher to get with competition shows.)

c. Exclude theatrical releases, as some TV shows get released in theaters, particularly outside the United States.

How much can you get? Around $10,000 to $50,000 plus, depending on whether they're licensing an obscure song or a well-known hit, and also how prominently it's used. If you're an indie artist looking for exposure—some artists have launched their careers by having music on a big TV show—you might give them a very cheap rate, meaning $1,000 or so. Sometimes it's even less, since they know they "gotcha." On the other hand, if you're a superstar who couldn't care less, you'll carve out their livers.

Unless you're a really major player, you won't get any more money for in-context ads; that's always included in the price. However, if they want out-of-context ads, you can usually get around $1,500 to $5,000 per week for promo uses, which is payable for as long as the promotion runs.

The competition shows (*American Idol, X Factor, The Voice, Dancing with the Stars,* etc.), and talk shows (Fallon, Ellen, Corden, etc.), have a Chinese menu, meaning they only pay for what they actually use. They then take options, for specific amounts if they want more rights. All these deals are done on a **most favored nations (MFN)** basis, meaning they pay the same fee for every song on the show, no matter what. Because these shows use such a huge amount of music, they don't have time to negotiate every deal separately, so the publisher just decides if they're in or out. And because these shows are great promotion for the songs, the publishers are almost always "in."

The exact license fees vary from show to show, but if all rights were exercised, they'd be in the range set out above. However, they start with a small fee (which also varies amongst the shows, but it's several thousand dollars) that allows them to use the song for two to five years, in the United States and Canada only. For that initial fee, they get things like unlimited broadcasts (within the two- to five-year term), **recaps** (a program that features clips from earlier shows in the season), streaming, and in-context usage for advertising and promotion. Some shows are even sophisticated enough to license the lyrics, in case the camera pans past a contestant who's reading the lyrics while singing.

If they want to go beyond those rights, they'll pay additional amounts for things like territories outside the United States and Canada, downloads of the program, and extending their rights to perpetuity. They also have to pay if they **repurpose** the original use, meaning use it apart from the show. For example, taking a clip from a TV show and exploiting it alone online. Payment for this can be a flat fee, or sometimes a rolling fee based on the view count of a video (for example, $X for every 500,000 views). Sometimes there's a revenue share of the gross earnings, anywhere from 15% to 50%. The specifics depend on the usage, stature of the song, etc.

4. **Streaming services (Netflix, Amazon, Hulu, etc.):**
The deals for these services are in line with the motion pictures and television deals we just discussed. However, the performance money is much smaller than you get from television or foreign theaters. So try to get a higher fee.

5. **Commercials:**
For commercials, a reasonably well-known song can get anywhere from $50,000 to well into six figures for a one-year national usage in the United States, on television, radio, and Internet. Really well-known songs in major campaigns can go higher, sometimes over a million for a classic, iconic song.

These figures get scaled down for regional or local usages, and for periods of less than a year.

Internet-only usage is on the rise, and the prices are rapidly going up for the simple reason that these ads reach a lot of people—particularly the younger folks that advertisers want, who rarely watch television these days.

The issue of "territory" on the Internet is interesting, as the net is of course available worldwide. Your license should require the advertiser to **geo-filter,** which means the commercial can only be available to users in the territories you gave them. That works reasonably well, though I'm told it's not that hard for a die-hard to get around it.

A new twist that really scrambles your brain is the "repurposing of commercials for commercial use."

Huh?

Well, for example, you take an incredible Super Bowl commercial, put it on a YouTube channel and run ads around it (ads that run prior to playing the video, which are called **pre-rolls**), banner ads, etc. So you're actually making money running commercials, by running other commercials. I know, weird . . .

At any rate, you should get more money for giving these rights. It's usually an additional flat fee, or a share of the revenue (15% to 50%, depending on the usage and the stature of the song).

6. **Video Games:**

Here we're talking about real video games (like Call of Duty, Grand Theft Auto), and not apps. Apps are on deck, coming up next.

As we discussed in the context of masters (on page 155), video game makers don't think any particular song adds that much value, so the deals are almost all flat fees, and not royalties.

The fee for a video game license can be as low as "nothing," for example, if you want to hammer the song into the heads of teenage gamers while they chase down zombies. Most licenses are in the $8,000 or $10,000 range for lesser-known songs and artists, and around $15,000 to $20,000 for big hits.

These licenses are usually for perpetuity, unless it's an annual sports type game (such as NBA Basketball, which has a new edition each year), in which case the licenses are three to ten years.

The only exception to flat-fee video game licenses is for music-based games, such as Guitar Hero (it'll be back . . .), SingStar, and karaoke games. These licenses allow the manufacturers to sell games with music embedded in them, and also to sell downloads of songs (or packs of songs) that can be added to the game. Because music is essential to these products, the gaming companies are willing to pay a royalty for every game sold. The specifics of these licenses are confidential, so I'm not free to publish them, but the deals are structured as advances against either (a) a penny-rate royalty for each game unit sold and each download, or (b) a percentage royalty, which is set aside for all the music rights, then pro-rated among all the music involved in the sale or download.

If the game company wants to use the song in a commercial for the video game, you can sometimes get an additional $30,000 to several hundred thousand dollars, depending on the importance of the song and how it's used.

7. **Apps:**

By **apps** in this section, I mean the same kinds we talked about with masters on page 153 (in other words, apps that use music, as opposed to apps that simply let you access a music streaming service like Spotify, Apple Music, or iHeartRadio—these latter ones are covered by the streaming section).

The app deals are either a flat fee (the amount varies hugely, depending on how the music is used) or a share of revenue. More and more, publishers are insisting on some kind of sharing.

As a general rule, the record masters and publishers combined try to get 50% of the revenue. The publishers try for half of that, though they sometimes end up with more like 10% to 20% of the *total* revenue (meaning 10% to 20% of 100% of the money, which is 20% to 40% of the master/publishing 50% of the money).

Some apps don't use the masters, and in that case publishers can get up to 50% of the revenue, depending on how important music is to the project. However, the norm is closer to 30%.

As we discussed when we talked about masters, the platform selling the app (e.g., the iTunes or Android store) takes 30% off the top, so these percentages are applied to the money that's left over, which is 100% of what the app developer gets.

App deals are all short-term (one year to eighteen months), so they can renegotiate if the app is a success.

There's a company called Songlily (www.songlily.com) that makes deals with the labels and publishers, then licenses the tracks to developers. The idea is to make the process simpler for everyone, especially developers who have little patience for these kinds of things.

8. **Bundled Services:**

As we discussed on page 155, a bundled service is one that puts together two or more products or services (Two for the Price of One!). There are two flavors of bundles: **mixed service bundles,** and just plain ol' **music bundles.** A *mixed service bundle* is the sale of a music product (like a streaming service) along with a non-music service. For example, you get a music streaming subscription when you buy Amazon Prime. A *music bundle* is the sale of two or more music-only products together, such as a download code when you buy a CD; these are obviously disappearing.

For music bundles, you get your rate for each piece of product, though of course the company will come to you for a discount since they're getting a price that's less than what they'd get if the two pieces of product were sold separately.

For a mixed service bundle, you get the same percentages you get for streaming, computed exactly the same way as the streaming royalties on page 234. The difference is that the percentages are applied to the money left after deducting the price of the non-music element. For example, if you get a streaming subscription when you buy a phone, you'd deduct the price of a phone. But to keep that from being zero, there's a per-subscriber minimum, which for subscription bundles is currently 25¢. (Flip back to page 234 if this is making your eyes spin.)

9. **Ringtones and Ringbacks:**
Ringtones are permanent downloads (see page 155 for what those are), and as we discussed on page 217, the compulsory mechanical royalty for ringtones is 24¢.

As we also discussed, ringbacks aren't downloads. They're stored on the servers of the mobile provider and just played to the caller, so they're considered a stream and paid at those rates (see page 234).

10. **Podcasts:**
Podcasts deals are small, and usually a flat fee. Just like we discussed for masters, a lot of podcasters simply use music and don't bother paying anyone. The publishers are cracking down on this, but it's still happening a lot.

SAMPLES

Congrats! You now know enough for me to tell you about samples. I couldn't have put this section earlier, because you needed to understand both records and publishing first, but now you do, so let's boogie.

Sampling is the art of taking any sound (whether it's a full master recording, or just a drum sound, synthesizer riff, voice, etc.), and making a digital copy, which you then incorporate into your own masterpiece. Unless you've been living in a moon colony for the last few years, you know that every rapper on the planet samples massively from other people's works.

When the technology first developed, everyone thought it was so cool that they basically stole other people's masters without bothering to ask. Turns out folks didn't particularly appreciate that, and after a slew of lawsuits in the 1990s that slammed record labels, everyone now handles sample licensing with white velvet gloves. Indeed, companies won't release a record containing samples without assurances that the samples have been **cleared** (meaning properly licensed), and you as an artist want the same thing. It's you that's left holding the bag if there's a lawsuit.

Clearing samples is a major pain in the butt. You have to get a license from both the owner of the master *and* the owner of the sampled song. But there's nothing in the law that requires anyone to let you use a sample of their work, so a record company or publisher who's been sampled can make you pull it off your record. Or pay the equivalent of a ransom for the ruler of a small kingdom.

And it gets worse. You can't clear a sample until you finish the track—the publisher and record company want to hear exactly how the sample is used before they'll tell you how much they want to charge, or whether they'll let you use it at any price. That puts you in the position of spending money to make a record before you know whether you can use the sample in it. If you're on a tight schedule and/or if it ruins your song to take out the sample, you're toast. Sound like fun?

Suppose you don't actually sample, but just duplicate the track by playing it in the studio. Does that solve your problems? Well, only half. You've just created what we call a **replay.** *Replays* eliminate the need to license the master, but you still need to license the song (unless you qualify for a **fair use,** which we'll discuss on page 325). The problem is there's no bright-line test of whether something's a fair use, so you can't be sure that you're okay. And it will be expensive to prove you're right if the other guy comes after you. And at any rate, as a practical matter, your label won't risk a lawsuit if you include an uncleared sample, meaning they'll insist on your getting a license before they release the master.

So if you use a master, you'll need two licenses. The record company that owns the sampled master, and the publisher of the song in the published master.

If the record company gives you a license, it will want a royalty, generally in the range of 2% to 8%. I know that's a big range, but the amount depends on the specific situation: How extensively is it used? How prominently? Did you sample an important song, or an obscure recording? How desperate do they think you are?

Publishers always insist on owning a piece of the copyright and getting the same share of income. Again, the percentage varies with how significantly the sample is used in your record. If you've lifted an entire melody line, or their track is the bed of your song, they might take 50% or more; for less significant uses, the range is 10% to 30%.

Both the record company and the publisher will often ask for an advance against their share, and the publishers sometimes want nonrecoupable money.

A particularly fun thing happens with multiple samples. I've seen several situations like this: Your song has three samples. Publisher X wants 40%, Publisher Y wants 40%, and Publisher Z wants 30%. If you do some quick math, you'll see that's 110%. So every time you sell a record, you get to write a check out of your own pocket. By the way, don't assume the publishers will be the least bit sympathetic. Their attitude is usually something like "Those other publishers are pigs. But my share is really worth 40%, so go squeeze the other guy."

Even when you get past all these hurdles, the publishers (and some record companies) usually limit the usage of their sample to just your audio records and single-song videos. Also, the publishers will co-administer their portion of the composition (see page 299 for what co-administration is). This means they can stop you from granting a particular license—for example, you couldn't license the song in a film or a commercial without going back to the sample's record company and publisher and getting their consent. So when you sample, you can easily lose control of your own song.

The lesson in all this is that putting a sample in your record is serious business. So think about it carefully. A moment of pleasure can mean a lifetime of pain.

If you're on the *Fast Track,* go to the Bonus Section on page 274. Everyone else, onward . . .

FOREIGN SUBPUBLISHING

Except for the worldwide conglomerates, publishers don't have branch offices in all territories. So how do they collect their money when you have fans in Abu Dhabi?

Well, they do it by making deals with local publishers in each territory to collect on their behalf. The local publisher is called a **subpublisher.**

Foreign Mechanicals

Before we talk about deals with the local publishers, you should know about an unusual creature that lives in most territories outside the United States. This is the *mandatory* mechanical rights collection society. It works like this:

Most countries have a mechanical rights collection organization (mostly government mandated) that licenses *all* musical compositions (regardless of who owns them) used by *any* record company in that territory. It's similar to the Harry Fox Agency (see page 231), except that it's mandatory, and it's exactly what the MLC will be for streaming when it's up and running (see page 240).

As noted on page 218, mechanical licenses are not issued on a per-song basis outside the United States and Canada. Rather, the entire record is licensed for a percentage of the wholesale price, regardless of the number of compositions. This greatly simplifies the process of putting all the monies through one place.

So the local society collects mechanical royalties from the record companies, holds them for as long as they can get away with it (they can earn interest on these monies and keep the interest for themselves), and finally sends the monies to the appropriate publishers. Just like ASCAP and BMI, they deduct their operating expenses before they distribute income, but they also deduct some things we don't have here, like cultural and social deductions and non-music-related investments. And these other deductions can be significant, meaning 10% to 20% or more. Frankly, the societies are a bit on the murky side about all this, and their practices have stirred up concern in the last number of years. The mood of reform is in the air, so we'll see how it plays out.

At any rate, the societies now have all this money left after expenses. How do they know who to pay? Under this system, just like MLC, each local publisher files a claim with the organization, saying it owns a particular song. It can either be a claim for the entire song, or a percentage share if the rights are split among several publishers in that territory. If a claim is contested (and in some territories even if it isn't), the publisher is required to file proof of its claim, such as a copy of the contract with the U.S. publisher.

Foreign Performances

All foreign territories have some sort of performing rights society, usually only one per country, and usually government mandated. These societies pay the *publisher's share* of performance monies to local sub-publishers. They pay the *writer's share* to the writer's PRO (which in turn pays the writer), again keeping these monies out of the publishers' hands (as we discussed on page 227).

If there's no foreign subpublisher, the publisher's share will ultimately wind its way back to the U.S. publisher through the American PRO. However, it takes substantially longer, and it's worth paying the subpublisher a piece so you can get it earlier. Also, the subpublisher has "boots on the ground" in each territory, so they can make sure the songs are properly registered, and also use their relationships to solve any local problems.

How much do subpublishers get paid for all this? Well . . .

Subpublisher Charges

The range of deals for subpublishing allows the subpublisher to retain anywhere from 10% to 50% of the monies earned, with the vast majority of deals being from 15% to 25%. The contracts are actually written the opposite way, stating that the subpublisher collects all monies and remits 75% to 85% of it to the U.S. publisher. The shorthand industry expression of these deals is "75/25" or "85/15," referring to the percentages kept by each party. (Oh, and you don't pronounce the "slash." You just say, "Seventy five, twenty five.")

By the way, I heard of one deal where the local subpublisher kept no percentage whatsoever of the earnings (i.e., they remitted 100%). Can you figure out why anyone would do this? See page 272 for the answer. (You haven't yet learned about part of the answer yet.)

Covers

It's customary for the local publisher to get an increased percentage for **cover records**. As we discussed, a cover record, also called a **cover,** is a recording by an artist other than the original artist, and in this case, it means a recording of a U.S. composition by a local artist. The subpublisher usually gets 40% to 50% of the earnings from cover recordings (meaning it remits 50% to 60%). In other words, they keep more money on covers as an incentive for them to beat the bushes.

When you make a subpublishing deal, be sure to limit the subpublisher's increased percentage to the earnings from the cover recording only. If you don't, you'll decrease your money on the U.S. version when the local publisher's nephew records the song.

By the way, you should try to make sure that all covers have a different title. Since it's usually in the local language, that's not an issue. But sometimes it's in the original language, particularly in an English-speaking territory. If the cover has the same title as the original, it can get difficult to sort through which version earned what in the way of mechanicals and performances, so it's always a good idea to push for this.

Performance Monies

A number of subpublishers want a bigger percentage of performance royalties than they do for other monies. For example, they may keep 25% of all monies except performances, but keep 50% of performances. Why?

Here's their argument:

Assuming the subpublisher gets 25% of all earnings other than performances, for every dollar of earnings it gets 25¢. The 75¢ paid back to the U.S. publisher includes both the publisher's share and the writer's share (as did of course the dollar paid to them in the first place), and thus their percentage applied to the total writer/publisher combination. All cool.

On performances, however, remember that the writer's share is paid to the U.S. performing rights society, and not to the local subpublisher (see page 254). This means that, instead of collecting the full $1 of performance monies, the subpublisher only gets 50¢ (the publisher's share).

Here's a chart:

	Mechanicals	Performances
Total Writer/Publisher Earnings	$1.00	$1.00
Amount Paid to Subpublisher	$1.00	$ .50
		(other $.50 paid to writer directly by society)
Subpublisher's 25% Share	$ .25	$ .125
Percentage of Dollar Earned	25%	12.5%

Accordingly, subpublishers argue, they're really only getting 12.5% of the performance dollar. Thus they should have 50% of performance monies, so they can get 25% of the full performance dollar and be in the same position as they are with other monies. This 50% equals 25¢

(50% of the 50¢ publisher's share of performance monies), or 25% of the total writer/publisher performance dollar.

This reasoning, while clever and not without merit, usually gives way to sheer bargaining power. If the subpublisher has enough bargaining power, they'll pull it off. Otherwise, the U.S. publisher simply says no, or compromises somewhere in between.

Advances

It's customary for subpublishers to pay the U.S. publisher an advance against their earnings. This is basically a banking transaction—if the U.S. publisher's catalog has a track record, the subpublisher pays an advance based on historical earnings. It will vary, of course, with the size of the territory and the size of the catalog. The range of advances is anywhere from zero (for a new artist or a so-so older catalog) to millions of dollars for major catalogs in major territories.

Again, as with all other rules, there are exceptions. For example, if the publisher controls a new artist whose record is doing extremely well in the United States and the local subpublisher is excited, the advance can get driven up, despite the lack of historical earnings.

Advances are also affected by the currency exchange rates. When the dollar is weak, high U.S. dollar advances are relatively easy to come by; the opposite is true, of course, when the dollar gets stronger. In other words, the same number of English pounds equals more or fewer dollars at any given time, depending on the current exchange rate. When it equals more, you can get a larger dollar advance.

A deal with no advance is known as a **collection deal,** meaning the subpublisher merely collects on behalf of the U.S. publisher. Also, if there is no advance, the percentage kept by the subpublisher is lower, usually in the 10% to 15% range.

"At Source"

If your subpublishing deal isn't directly with the publisher in a particular territory (for example, you make a deal with a major U.S. publisher for all of Europe), one of the most important points to have in your subpublishing agreement is a requirement that all monies be computed "**at source**." We touched on this in the context of streaming, on page 93, but since the fun and games were invented by old-time publishing rip-off masters, let's take a closer look.

If your deal is "at source," it means the percentage you get must be based on the earnings in the country *where they are earned*, which is the *source*. For example, if you have an 85/15 deal at source in Germany, and $1 is earned there, you get 85¢. If you don't say "at source," you'll pay 15% to the local subpublisher in Germany, then another percentage to your U.S. publisher when the money comes back to the United States.

An extreme example of why your deal should be "at source" is this scam, which has been around long enough to have a beard like Dumbledore:

A subpublisher in the United Kingdom makes a 75/25 deal with a U.S. publisher for all the territories of Europe. The subpublisher in Germany (owned by the U.K. publisher) collects a dollar, keeps 50¢ as its collection fee, then pays 50¢ to the U.K. publisher. The 50¢ received in the United Kingdom is then split between the U.S. publisher and the U.K. publisher.

Here's a play by play:

Earnings in Germany	$1.00
Less: German Company's 50% Share	– .50
Amount Remitted to UK	$ .50
Less: UK Company's 25% Share	– .125
AMOUNT REMITTED TO U.S. PUBLISHER	**$.375**

It doesn't take a genius to see that the $1 earned at source (in this case, Germany, where the actual earnings were generated) gets dwindled radically before it finds its way into your pocket. And your 75% deal is in reality only 37.5% (you only got 37.5¢ out of the $1 earned in Germany).

This hustle is no longer played in the shadows, but right up front. If you don't say the deal is "at source," the contract will say that the publisher can deduct both the foreign subpublisher's share and its own share before paying you.

If the publisher doesn't own the foreign affiliate, the local publisher's share doesn't go into their pocket, so you don't have the same argument. But you can argue that the U.S. publisher's share has to include the foreign publisher's fee. In other words, if the U.S. publisher gets 25%, it could pay 15% to a local publisher and keep the other 10%, so in effect you're getting 75% "at source." If you can't do that, then you should limit what the subpublishers can charge. For example, put in your contract that they can't deduct more than, say, 10% to 20% before sending the dough back to the United States. The result of this push-pull depends on bargaining power.

When you look through the smoke and mirrors, this is only a matter of dollars: How much do you get, and how much does the publisher keep? But make sure you address this issue directly. Either the deal is "at source" or it's not; say so from the get-go.

Translation/Adaptation Shares

An interesting quirk of subpublishing deals is the **translator** or **adaptor** share. If your song is popular, many territories will want to release a version with lyrics in the language of that territory. This all sounds innocent enough, but it creates some problems:

1. First of all, under local society rules, the local lyricist automatically gets a share of royalties. Most societies require that the lyricist receive about one-sixth of gross (meaning combined writer and publisher shares) for mechanicals, and one-sixth of the writer's share only for performance royalties. The societies pay this share directly to the lyricist, so you don't really have anything to say about it.

2. Subpublishers, naturally, want to take this share completely from your royalties. If you have sufficient bargaining power, you may be able to muscle them into absorbing it out of their percentage. As their percentage decreases, however, so does the likelihood of your making them eat it. So, more commonly, the translator's percentage comes off the top, which means you pay your share of it. In other words, if a dollar comes in and the translator gets 16%, you split 84¢ with the subpublisher. That means, if your deal pays you 60% of the earnings from covers, you're absorbing 60% of the translator's share, and the subpublisher eats the other 40%.

3. Always require that the translation be registered separately with the society (since it will have a foreign title, this isn't so difficult), and also require the publisher to make sure the translator doesn't get paid on the English-language version. This can be done in most territories, but some (notably Germany) insist on paying the translator on the *original* composition no matter what you do (in the case of Germany, however, the translator gets only a piece of mechanicals and not other income).

The upshot is that you should have the absolute right to approve whether the subpublisher can authorize a local translation. Apart from the fact that a translation takes money out of your pocket, you want to be sure you like what they're doing. Make them send you an English translation of the lyrics for approval before they can record. If you don't, your ballad may find itself associated with a number of shady topics, drugs, Republicans, etc.

The Black Box

Remember, as we discussed on page 253, that the societies collect mechanicals for *all* songs, not just those registered. But they only pay out for the songs that are registered. If you recall our discussion of this issue with MLC, you've probably figured out that there may be some songs not claimed by any local publisher. And you're right—there are always unclaimed songs. For example, through sheer inadvertence, a U.S. publisher may not have a subpublishing deal in a particular territory. Or maybe the rights are disputed in the United States, so there are no deals with a foreign publisher.

These unclaimed monies are called **black-box** monies. In some countries (notably Germany, Italy, Spain, France, and Holland), if the funds aren't claimed after a set period of time (usually three years), they're paid to the local publishers. Each publisher gets a portion of them, based on the ratio that its earnings bear to the total earnings of the society, and also based on seniority. So if a publisher earned 100,000 drapkes and the society collected 1,000,000 drapkes, it might receive 100,000/1,000,000, or 10%, of the black-box monies, and perhaps another 3% because it's been around for twenty years. This can be a substantial source of additional revenue, and the local publisher keeps it all because the monies aren't earned by any particular compositions.

If you get into the "major leagues" of publishers, you may be able to get a portion of the black-box money. The usual formula is to take a proportionate amount of the black box, based on the ratio that your songs' earnings bear to the total earnings of that subpublisher. For example, if your songs earned a total of $200,000 for the subpublisher, and its total earnings were $1 million, you would get 20% of the black-box monies, because your $200,000 is 20% of its $1 million total.

In recent years, the societies have begun allowing electronic registration, which enormously simplifies the process, and makes it easier to register compositions around the world. Because of this, most songs are now properly registered, and the amount of money in the black box is dropping. But it's still around.

PRINTED MUSIC

Printed music historically meant paper (remember that?), but today it means much more. The traditional print music market was **sheet music** (printed music of a single song—the kind you stuff inside your piano bench) and **folios** (which are collections of songs, such as *Greatest Hits of the Nineties, The Complete Led Zeppelin, The David Hasselhoff Songbook,* etc.). Collections of songs by a number of different artists are called **mixed folios.** Another type is a **matching folio,** which has all the songs of a particular album (i.e., it "matches" the album). Matching folios are usually printed with the album artwork on the cover and various posed candid shots of the artist inside.

Royalties

The following royalties are what's paid to a publisher for physical (meaning printed on paper) print rights. We'll hit digital print in the next section.

For single-song physical sheet music, the standard royalty is 20% of the marked retail price (currently most single-song sheet music has a $4.95 retail price, so the publisher gets about 99¢).

Royalties on folios are 10% to 12.5% of the marked retail price, and the current marked selling price of most folios is $24.95. A **personality folio** is one that has the picture of the performing artist plastered all over it, such as *Stevie Wonder's Greatest Hits.* (A matching folio [see the previous section for what that is] is also a personality folio.) For a personality folio, there's an additional royalty of 5% of the marked retail selling price for use of the name and likeness of the artist, and it goes to the *artist* (who may or may not be the same person as the songwriter). If the songwriter is also the artist, the publisher may get the extra 5% if their deal with the writer includes name and likeness rights. But you should ask to keep it for yourself in your deal.

Unless the folio represents the selected works of a particular songwriter and only one publisher, it'll have songs written and/or published by a number of different people. Thus, the royalties are pro-rated, in exactly the same way as record royalties are pro-rated. For example, if there are twenty compositions in the folio, and you own ten, you would get $^{10}/_{20}$ (one-half) of the 10% to 12.5% royalty. When you negotiate a pro-ration provision, be sure to insist that the royalty can only be pro-rated on the basis of *copyrighted, royalty-bearing* works in the folio. Otherwise your royalty gets reduced by "Mary Had a Little Lamb" and "The Star-Spangled Banner," even though the printer isn't paying anyone for these songs.

The balance of print music consists of things like instructional music (such as putting your songs in *How to Play the Nose Flute*), marching band arrangements, choir arrangements, dance arrangements, etc. The royalty for these is generally 10% of retail unless it's a folio of lyrics only, in which case the royalty is 5% to 7.5%.

Print rights also include reprints of lyrics in books, magazines, greeting cards, etc. For books, if it's just a snippet of the lyrics, the rate is around 1¢ per unit, with a $200 minimum. For more extensive reprints, or a use that's significant to the story, the per-unit rate can climb to about 4¢, with an advance based on anticipated sales—for major book authors, the advance can go over $100,000.

The fee to use lyrics in films varies with the kind of use. If they're used as the title of the film, it could be in the range of $5,000 to $10,000, sometimes much more for a major song. If the script is based on the lyrics of the song, there can be a really substantial fee and even a profit participation in the film. If the film includes the song as well as the lyrics, the sync license will include the film company's right to use the lyrics in closed captioning and subtitles in other languages.

For paper greeting cards (we'll discuss digital e-cards in a minute), the publishers get the greater of a penny rate (usually 12.5¢ to 15¢) or a percentage of the wholesale price (usually 5% to 8%). If it's a greeting card that actually plays the song, publishers also insist that their royalty can't be less than what's paid for the master.

Reprints of lyrics on clothing run from 8% to 11% of wholesale, depending on whether the goods are sold in high-end stores or through a **mass merchandiser** (meaning a store like Walmart or other places that sell at deeply discounted prices in a no-frills environment). The mass merchandiser's sales are at the lower royalties, around 6% to 8% of wholesale, because the discounted prices mean there's a thinner profit margin.

Advertising uses (such as printing the lyrics in magazines, newspapers, and on billboards) are flat fees, and can run up to $25,000 or more for major uses.

Traditional lyric reprints on inserts in physical albums are customarily free. However, as physical disappears, lyric videos are today's equivalent of lyric reprints. As we'll discuss on page 271, publishers try to get more money for these.

Digital Print Rights

The most direct transition of traditional print to digital media are sites like Musicnotes.com and SheetMusicPlus.com, which sell download-able sheet music. That is truly the equivalent of (and a substitute for) paper sheet music. Also, sites like Tonara and Chromatik have apps for tablets and smartphones that have cool things like ticking metronomes and pages that turn in sync. The cost of these products is about the same as physical print music, which is currently $4.95 per song. To li-cense these rights, publishers get 50% of the income—a big jump from the 20% they get on physical print.

A much broader use in the digital world is posting lyrics online with-out the music. These are places like Genius, LyricFind, and Musix-match. The lyrics are usually available free to users, because the sites have advertising up the yin-yang, though some sites have subscribers.

For allowing sites to reprint the lyrics, publishers get about 50% of the advertising revenue, often with a minimum amount per view, and (if it's subscription based) a minimum amount per subscriber (the PSM concept we discussed on page 144).

A number of lyric sites aren't licensed at all, though the publishers have become more aggressive about shutting them down.

There are also lyric videos, which we'll discuss on page 271.

E-cards, meaning those cutesy-wutesy pictures of snow falling on sleighs while music plays in the background, are another form of digital print. For these, the publisher gets 5% to 8% of the retail price, with a minimum of 10¢ to 15¢ per unit.

Music instruction and notation apps (such as one that scrolls along as you play the song), are another form of digital print rights. The deals range from 15% to 25%, depending on how interactive it is, and whether it's really educational or just entertainment. If the master isn't used, the norm is more like 50%. The publishers know the app would have to pay 60% to both the master and the publisher if they did use the master, so they give a discount to 50% if they don't. That incentiv-izes the app developers to not use the master, and of course makes the publisher more money.

Unlike physical print deals, digital deals are *non-exclusive*, meaning the publisher can license the same rights to multiple users. This is a big shift in the industry. Historically, setting up a printing company, buying the presses, hiring a sales and warehouse force, and taking the inventory risk (which of course doesn't exist with digital) was so ex-pensive that the printers wouldn't put out a particular song catalog unless they had it exclusively. The publishers were fine with this for two reasons: (1) they didn't want to invest in setting up a print company, and (2) by making long-term exclusive deals, the publishers could get a good-sized advance from the print company. Obviously as the physical print world shrinks, so does the potential revenue and therefore the amount of advance they can get.

Term

Licenses for print music are for limited periods of time, usually three to five years. The exceptions are licenses of lyrics for books, movies, and things like that, where they run for the life of copyright.

As we just discussed, these licenses are nonexclusive, except for physical goods. Also with physical, you have to agree to what they do with the stuff at the end of the term. Certainly they can't manufacture any more inventory, but can they continue to sell what they have?

Normally these licenses give the printer a right to sell their existing physical inventory for a period of six to twelve months after the term expires. These sell-off rights are non-exclusive (meaning someone else can sell the same materials at the same time). At the end of the six to twelve months, they have to trash anything left over. For mixed folios (because they're so much more expensive, and also because there are a lot of other writers involved), the printers try not to have any time limit on their sell-off rights, and in fact want the right to keep manufacturing them.

When you make these deals, make sure there's no **stockpiling, dumping,** or **distress sales.** *Stockpiling* is where the printer manufactures eight quadrillion units right before the end of the term, so that they have tons of your inventory to sell after the term. (Your new printer won't like it if the market is already flooded with the same books it's trying to sell.) You stop this by saying the printer can only manufacture enough to meet their reasonably anticipated needs during the term.

Dumping and *distress sales* mean the printer sells your inventory at less than customary wholesale prices. *Way* less. You don't want this because, if they end up with a ton of goods left over, they'll blow it out at whatever rock-bottom price they can get. (Since they have to destroy everything they don't sell, they use the age-old theory that it's better to get something than nothing.) This practice, shall we say, "perturbs" your new printer, who is trying to sell the same stuff at full price. You solve this by saying your materials can be sold only through normal retail channels, at normal wholesale prices.

CONTROLLED COMPOSITION CLAUSES

Congratulations! Two times!

Congratulations Number One: You now know enough to talk about **controlled composition clauses** in record deals. Just like samples, you need to understand both record deals and publishing to get these concepts.

Congratulations Number Two: Most of the provisions in these clauses are rapidly becoming irrelevant. So you don't need to waste nearly the amount of time I did in learning this crap.

The **controlled composition clause** (also known to its buddies as a **controlled comp clause,** although it has no "buddies" except record companies) puts a limit on how much the company has to pay for each controlled composition. It used to be one of the most significant provisions in your recording arrangement. That's because it deals with mechanical royalties, and if you're a songwriter, mechanicals are paid even when your record deal is unrecouped.

The importance of controlled comp clauses is rapidly disappearing for several reasons. In the CD era, these were serious monies, and we fought hard over the controlled comp clause. So the drop in CD sales is a major factor, but there's more to it than that. Under the Copyright Act, digital downloads created under record deals made after June 22, 1995, can't be subject to a controlled comp clause, so those were never an issue. But the most important change is that streaming mechanicals are paid by the DSPs (not your record company), so the record companies no longer care how much you get.

As a result, the companies don't fight a lot about controlled comp clauses. So if you don't win any other points in your deal, you should be able to score here.

Still, there's a controlled comp clause in every record deal, and CDs are still a portion of the record biz, and I had to learn this junk, so why shouldn't you at least get a taste of it? (I'm not really feeling the sympathy here . . .)

Okay, enough snark. There are parts of the controlled comp clause that go beyond mechanicals, to include things like audiovisual works, websites, use of lyrics, advertising and promotion, and other things that are still very relevant. So you still gotta pay some attention.

A **controlled composition** is a song that's written, owned, or controlled by the artist (in whole or in part). However, it's usually defined more broadly than that, and includes:

1. Any song in which the artist has an income or other interest. This means that, even if the artist doesn't own or control the

song, if he or she wrote it or otherwise gets a piece of its earnings, it's a *controlled composition*.

2. The definition also often includes compositions owned or controlled by the *producer* of the recordings. You really have little, if any, control over a producer's publishing, and thus you should try hard to knock this provision out. It's hard to get rid of this, except at superstar levels, but do your best.

Companies limit mechanical royalties on CDs in two ways:

1. Rate per Song
   You may remember that the statutory rate in the United States is now 9.1¢ per song. Up until the 1976 Copyright Act, the statutory had been 2¢ for many years. The ink was hardly dry on the 1976 Act, which raised the rate to 2.75¢, when the record companies hit on the idea that they should require their artists to license controlled compositions at 75% of the statutory rate. (Controlled composition clauses existed before the 1976 Copyright Act, but they didn't reduce the rate below statutory.)

   Companies still try for these 75% and 50% rates with most new artists, though it's gotten easier to push this up as the CD sales fall. Even the biggest superstars have some form of controlled composition clause, although the "limit" is 100% of the minimum statutory rate.

2. Rate per Album/EP/Single
   There is also a limit of ten or eleven times the single-song rate for each album, five times for an EP, and two times for a single.

These issues are much more complex than they seem. So let's take a deeper dive.

MAXIMUM RATE PER SONG

Because the maximum album rate is a multiple of the single-song rate, let's first look at what they do to you on each song. Here's the skinny:

The first argument is to make sure you get 100% of statutory, rather than their standard, off-the-shelf "75% of statutory." As I said, this is getting considerably easier, but if you get a stickler at the label, try to get the percentage over 75%—anywhere over 75% would be nice. If you can't, one compromise is to ask for an escalation on later albums. For example, you might have a 75% rate on albums 1 and 2, an 85% (or 87.5%) rate on albums 3 and 4, and 100% after that. Or another possibility is an escalation based on sales (some companies will include download and streaming equivalents, but some will look only at physical sales). For example, you might get 75% for the first 250,000 (or 500,000) album equivalents, 85% for the next 250,000 (or 500,000), and 100% thereafter.

Some labels offer an incentive for you to sign with their sister publishing company by increasing the mechanical rate to 100% if you give your songs to sis, or by waiving the 360 participation in publishing income if you sign with their affiliated publisher (see page 102 for what a 360 participation is).

Minimum Statutory Rate. The limit per composition is based on the *minimum* statutory rate. This means that all compositions are treated as if they are five minutes or less in duration, regardless of their actual playing time—in other words, there is no additional payment for lengthy compositions as there would be under a compulsory license. For example, the current statutory rate for a seven-minute song is 12.25¢ (see page 217 for why), but under these provisions, you're only paid 9.1¢ if you get 100% of statutory, or 6.82¢ (75% of 9.1¢) if you have a 75% rate.

Changes in Statutory Rate. As we discussed, the statutory rate can be changed by the Copyright Royalty Board (see page 234). But controlled composition clauses set a rate that doesn't change. Thus, even if you get a full statutory rate in your deal, it's normally locked to the statutory rate on a particular date, and there's no increase if the statutory rate later escalates. This is tough to change, even for superstars.

The companies lock in to the statutory rate in effect on one of these three dates: (a) the date of recording; (b) the date the master is delivered to the company; or (c) the date of first release of the master.

The general thinking (and historically this has been correct) is that the latest possible date is best for you—the statutory rate has never gone down, and thus the longer you wait, the more likely it may go up. However, the rate for physical and downloads has stayed the same since 2006, and I wouldn't expect an increase anytime soon.

Free Goods, Real and Imagined. The controlled composition clause will say that you get no mechanicals on free goods (see page 83 for what free goods are). Nothing wrong with that; the company isn't getting paid for them, so they don't pay mechanicals. Some companies also frame this as a discount of the PPD, rather than free goods. In other words, if they take 10% of the PPD to incentivize dealers to buy them, then 10% of the sales would be deemed "free" and not bear mechanicals. (There are also reduced mechanicals for the deeper discounts of mid-price and budget, which we'll discuss separately.)

Multiple Uses.   Controlled composition clauses say that if a particular song is used more than once on the same record, you only get paid as if it were used once.

Short Uses.   The companies don't want to pay for uses under ninety seconds, for **intros** (a little snippet before another song), **interludes** (a short piece between songs), or **outros** (which means either [a] a little snippet after a song, or [b] a belly-button that sticks out).

Reduced Rates.   The company typically asks for a 75% rate for anything other than sales through normal retail channels, and things like mid-price and budget (see pages 158–159 for what those are). Note, if you have a 75% of statutory rate on top-line product, you'll get a reduced percentage of that already reduced rate. For example, if you had a 75% rate on top-line, and a 75% rate on mid-price records, you'd only get 56.25% (75% of your 75% rate).

Public Domain Arrangements.   If a song is an arrangement of a public domain composition, the record company doesn't want to pay you for it. Your argument is that songs like "Scarborough Fair" were extremely successful public domain songs, and if you're brilliant enough to have this concept, you should be paid. (Sorry to use an old song, but I can't think of anything more current.) The typical compromise is that you get a proportionate royalty for public domain material, in the same ratio that the performing rights organization (see page 226 for what those are) pays for the composition involved. In other words, if ASCAP pays you 50% of normal performance monies for the song, you get 50% of the mechanical rate. Everyone routinely accepts this, and a lot of forms will say this at the outset to save time.

Non-controlled Songs.   This is a particularly nasty piece of business. The rate limits may be imposed not just on controlled compositions, but on *every* composition in the album. Most companies don't do this, but there's still a few out there. If you're using **outside songs** (meaning songs that aren't controlled compositions), this may be impossible to deliver—the owner will tell you to get lost. Remember, you can't force an owner to license you for a first use, and even if the song was used before, the owner doesn't have to take less than the full statutory rate (they can tell you either to drop the song or get a compulsory license at the full statutory rate). The only way to pay less for outside songs is to either threaten ("We'll drop your song if you don't reduce the rate") or grovel ("Please, I'm just a poor little singer"). But if you're dealing with major songwriters, unless your records generate truckloads of money, the publisher will tell you to blow it out your kazoo.

The real problem is not whether you can deliver the outside song at a reduced rate, because the record companies know there's a lot of times when you can't. The real problem is how the company punishes you when you don't. Essentially, if they have to pay more than your contractual limit because of outside songs, the company carves the excess out of your hide (meaning it reduces the mechanicals going to you, and if that's not enough, it goes hunting for more).

Canada

There's no compulsory mechanical rate in Canada. Instead there's a contractual agreement between the Canadian Recording Industry Association and a number of major publishers setting the "industry royalty rate." Currently it's 8.3¢ for the first five minutes, plus 1.66¢ for each additional minute or fraction thereof (all in Canadian pennies).

So now you're a master of the single-song limit. You're ready to conquer:

MAXIMUM RATE PER ALBUM, EPS, AND SINGLES

The maximum-per-album concept also applies to EPs and singles, but for simplicity, I'm only talking about albums here. EPs and singles are exactly the same computations, except that the limit is usually five times the single-song rate for EPs, and two times for singles.

Standard Clause.   All controlled composition clauses impose a limit on the total mechanicals for each album, which is called a **cap.**

It's usually ten times 75% of the minimum statutory rate (or ten times the full rate if your per-song rate isn't reduced). This is known as **a ten times rate,** meaning you get ten times the single-song rate. Note this is *an added restriction,* which is independent of the per-song limit. In other words, you must deliver each song at the specified single-song rate, no matter what the total album limit, but you can't exceed the total album limit no matter what you pay for each individual song. This is to keep you from delivering, for example, fourteen songs at a 75% rate, which totals more than the company is willing to pay, even though you haven't exceeded your per-song limit.

As noted, the album limits are based on a multiple of the *minimum* statutory rate (the rate for songs five minutes and under), as we discussed on page 266.

Nowadays, it's not uncommon for albums to have anywhere from eleven to fourteen songs. So you should always try for more than a ten-times limit. It's really only a CD issue, and since they're dying, it's been a lot easier to get eleven or twelve, occasionally a little more.

Wherever you end up, it's pretty easy to slide right over the limit. Lemme show you what happens when you do.

Just for consistency in the examples, I'm going to assume that you have a maximum album rate of ten times 100% of statutory, or 91¢. Under the standard clause, if you deliver more than ten songs, the excess reduces the mechanical royalties on songs you control. For example, if you deliver twelve songs that are all controlled, the ten-times cap means you only get 91¢ for all the songs. In other words, each song earns 91¢ divided by twelve, or 7.58¢ per song (instead of 9.1¢ per song, which is what you'd get if there were no cap).

Special Packages/Bonus Tracks. While this is fading along with CD sales, some artists do special packages exclusively for certain retailers (like Target or Walmart). In exchange for this exclusive product, the retailer gives the product a push (puts it in their brochure, better placement in the store, etc.).

To make these packages "special," they always have more songs than the normal album (usually two or three "bonus" tracks). The problem is that the folks who wrote those extra songs have this nasty habit of wanting to be paid mechanicals for them, and you have a limit on mechanicals that's much lower.

Normally this is worked out at the time, but with enough clout, you can get something in your deal. Of course, as the writer, you want to be paid in full for the extra songs, but second place is that the company can't reduce your mechanicals on the original (not bonus) album because of the extras. For example, if you had ten times full stat for the normal album, and they add two tracks, maybe you don't get paid on the extra tracks, but you won't be reduced by third parties who do get paid on them.

If your clause doesn't cover special packages, be sure to raise these issues as soon as there's talk of extra tracks. If not, the controlled composition clause will clip your ponytail into a buzz cut.

Multiple Albums.   While these are mostly dead except for box sets (as we discussed on page 120), most controlled composition clauses don't distinguish between normal albums and multiple albums. If you don't raise the issue, you'll have a ten-song mechanical limit on a multiple album that has twenty or more songs. As noted earlier, all the economics of a box set are negotiated separately, so you won't likely get much in your normal deal for this. Just be sure mechanicals are part of the discussion when you do a box set, because these are mostly physical product, where this clause is alive and well.

Videos

Every controlled composition clause requires you to license your songs for use in videos. There are two aspects:

1. **Single-song videos.**
   Single-song videos that play on YouTube, Vevo, etc., are considered promotional, because they're free to the consumer and help drive your career. So every controlled comp clause requires you to let the company put these out. If they didn't require it, you could hold them up for ransom by saying they can't do a video without paying you a large fee to use the song that's in it.

   While it's customary to give them a single-song video license, you should get paid by the DSPs. As we discussed, they have to pay under a compulsory license (or under a deal with your publisher) to stream your videos. The record companies of course have no problem with you getting paid by the DSPs since it doesn't cost them anything.

   The exception is that the company will want a free license to stream your videos on the label website.

The only real issue concerning single-song videos is whether you give your label a free sync license to put the song in the video in the first place (see page 242 for what a sync license is). That's separate from the right to stream; it's a fee to duplicate your music into the video, as opposed to a fee for streaming the video, which is a distribution license. Currently, the custom is to give a free sync license under your controlled comp clause, since you're getting paid for the streaming.

The other issue swirling around these days concerns **lyric videos.** Those are videos that show the lyrics on-screen while the song is playing. Most publishers want an additional royalty for lyric videos, arguing that it involves a separate right to re-print the lyrics (which it does). The labels fight back fiercely. Your controlled comp usually says they get lyrics for free, and results vary with clout. More often than not, you won't get anything extra for the lyric video, but if there is an additional fee, it's a couple of percentage points in addition to the normal rate.

2. **Everything Besides Single-Song Videos.**

This would be things like concert videos, TV appearances, compilations of single-song videos, and porcelain unicorns (just kidding about the last one). It doesn't matter that everything be-sides streaming is drying up like a forgotten potted fern. These rates still make their way into your controlled comp clause.

For DVDs and video downloads, independent publishers (those not subject to a controlled composition clause, who can charge what the market will bear) usually get in the range of 8¢ to 15¢ per song, though some get a percentage of PPD (8% to 10% or so). Also, there's almost always a 10,000–15,000 unit guarantee, meaning, for example, if you got 12¢ per unit and a 10,000 unit guarantee, you would get a $1,200 advance (12¢ × 10,000 units). In addition, they often get something called a **fixing fee,** which is a nonrecoupable payment for *fixing* the song in the video (basically, a sync license). These fees range from $250 to $500 per song.

You won't get market rate for these uses, but you should be able to get paid for video downloads and DVDs. The common compromise is around 8¢ per song if it's a penny rate, or 8% if it's a percentage of PPD. You virtually never get a fixing fee.

Other Freebies

The other freebies that the label will want under your controlled comp clause are the right to use your song in advertising and promoting your record and on their website.

Producers

When you hire a producer who is also a writer, you'll discover that the major producers don't want to be bound by your controlled composition clause and will insist on a full rate for their songs, no matter what. If you have enough clout, or if the producer doesn't, you can get them to go along with your controlled comp clause completely. Even if the producer has moderate clout, if your clause is reasonably favorable, you can sometimes get them to sign off. But a number of the major producers insist on a full rate with no cap on the number of songs. For example, if you have a ten times cap, but twelve songs on the album, you'll only be paid $^{10}\!/_{12}$ of the full rate. If the producer insists on a 100% mechanical rate for their writing, you'll have to eat the difference between that and the $^{10}\!/_{12}$ rate you're getting for those songs.

However you end up, even if you give the producer a full rate, be sure they agree to be bound by the other terms of your controlled comp clause (videos, marketing, etc.).

Postscript

Now that you've read it (I didn't want to prejudice you before you did), I can tell you that controlled composition clauses are among the most complicated critters in the music business (you probably figured that out on your own, huh?). This section is packed full of weird concepts, so it may take a few times through to get the flavor. Don't feel bad if you miss some of it the first few times—it took me years to get a decent handle on this stuff.

And now you can feel even better that it's disappearing.

Answer to question on page 254:

While it was a stupid business deal, the subpublisher's thinking was that (a) it would have a certain amount of prestige from having landed a major catalog (which prestige immediately vanished when everyone found out what an idiotic deal they made); (b) even though the subpublisher kept no piece, it collected the monies and held them for a period of six months, which meant the company could earn interest on them (this was back in the days when interest actually meant something); and (c) the publisher got a bump on its share of black box monies, which were very meaningful in those days and not customarily shared with the original publisher.

If you find someone ready to make a deal like this, give me a call because I still have that land in Florida for sale.

Bonus Section!

HOW TO SET UP A PUBLISHING COMPANY

I am now about to save you an enormous amount of time and frustration in setting up a publishing company. The tips I'm giving you here, revealed in print for the first time, were gained by yours truly through a series of hard knocks that will become obvious as you see the proper way to do it.

The Absolute First Thing to Do

Before you do anything, and I mean before you do *anything,* you positively must take this first step: *Affiliate your company with ASCAP* or *BMI* (or if you're an established writer, *SESAC* or *GMR*). You have to do this first because the PROs won't let you use a name that's the same as (or similar to) the name of an existing company. That's for the very good reason that they don't want to accidentally pay the wrong party. So you don't want to have label copy, copyright registrations, and everything else in the name of a company that can't collect performance royalties.

You can affiliate and secure your name by completing an application and giving the PRO three name choices, ranked in order. That way, at least one of the names should clear. If you're also a songwriter and haven't yet affiliated, you should affiliate as a writer with one of the societies at the same time (they won't let you affiliate with more than one as a writer). You'll have to affiliate as a publisher with the same society that you affiliate with as a songwriter because the societies insist on having a song's publisher affiliated with the same society as the song's writer. For the same reason, if you're going to be a "real" publisher (meaning you're going to publish other people's songs, as opposed to only your own), you'll need to have several companies, one for each PRO.

The publishing company affiliation forms are pretty straightforward;

they ask you who owns the company, your address, and similar exciting questions. You also need to give them information about all the songs in your catalog (writers, publishers, foreign deals, recordings, etc.), so they can put the info into their system and make sure you're properly credited (read "paid"). You can get affiliation applications by contacting ASCAP, BMI, SESAC, or GMR at:

ASCAP, www.ascap.com
BMI, www.bmi.com
SESAC (only by invitation), www.sesac.com
GMR (only by invitation), www.globalmusicrights.com

Here's a tip in picking a name. The more common your name, the less likely you're going to get it. So steer clear of names like "Hit Music," "Smash Tunes," and similar choices that, because they're obnoxiously obvious, won't clear. Names using just initials, such as "J.B. Music," also seem to have a hard time clearing (so save that concept for your license plates). For some reason, many of my clients name publishing companies after their streets or their dogs or their children, and these seem to clear routinely (assuming your kid's name isn't "Smash").

Also, get started early—it can take about five weeks to get an approval.

Setting Up Business

If you're doing business as a corporation, LLC, or other entity, and using the registered entity name for your publishing company, you can skip the next step. But if you're an individual doing business under a publishing company name, or if you're an entity using a different name for the publishing company, then you have to file what in California is known as a "fictitious business-name statement." This is a document that's filed with a county recorder and also published, and it has its counterpart in most states. It tells the world that you're doing business under a name that isn't your own, and makes it legal to do so. At least in California, you need this statement to open a bank account and, even more important, to cash checks made out to that name. You can imagine the screaming phone call I got as a young lawyer when I learned this lesson.

Copyright Registration

Next, register the songs with the Copyright Office in the name of your publishing company (see page 337). If the songs were previously copyrighted in your name, you need to file an assignment transferring them to the publisher's name.

By the way, if you're thinking of using an LLC, corporation, or other legal entity, be sure you get tax advice first. There are some serious tax consequences to holding copyrights in these entities, and you should be sure it's cool for you.

PRO Registration

To the extent you didn't do it when you originally affiliated, you need to register all your songs with the performing rights society. That authorizes them to license those particular songs, collect the money, and pay you. Once you have an account set up, you can register the songs online, and it's pretty self-explanatory.

After that, you're in business. You can issue licenses to record companies and other users, as well as make foreign subpublishing agreements, print deals, and so forth. However, there's no particular need to rush into these deals, nor will anybody be interested, until you have a record released, or some other exploitation, like a film or TV show using your songs. In fact, if you don't have something like this going, the societies won't even let you affiliate, and frankly there's not much point in doing any of this. You'll just be all dressed up with no place to go.

18

Songwriter, Co-Publishing, and Administration Deals

Okay. You now understand where publishing money comes from. Let's look at how you can get the most of it when you make a deal for your songs.

There are two primary deal types: a **songwriter agreement** (also called a **co-publishing agreement**) and an **administration** (or **co-administration**) **deal.**

Let's start with a songwriter agreement, which means a deal between you, as a creative songwriter, and a publisher who's going to handle your business. What's that look like?

SONGWRITER AGREEMENTS

The first issue, of course, is what percentage of the earnings do you get? The most common starting deals are 75%, but if you've got enough heat and bargaining power, you can get up to 90% (rarely more, unless you're the most mega of stars). In addition to clout, the higher percentages also depend on whether you want the biggest possible advance— the smaller the advance you take, the easier to get a larger piece of the earnings.

Historically, a "songwriter agreement" meant a contract that gave the publisher 100% ownership of the copyright, and in exchange the writer got 50% of the income. This is where the terms **writer's share** and **publisher's share** that we previously discussed each came to mean 50% of the income. If a writer got more than 50%, they were (under the industry terms of those days) getting the writer's share plus a piece of the publisher's share. And because they had a share of publishing, these deals were called **co-publishing agreements.** In fact, there were sometimes two contracts: one for the 50% writer's share, and the second for a share of the publishing income.

Nowadays, everyone just simplifies things in one contract for a larger percentage. These deals are called **songwriter's agreements,** but because they include a piece of the historical "publisher's share," they're also referred to as **co-publishing agreements.**

Some of these deals try to charge an **administration fee,** also called an **admin** fee, which is usually 10% of the money. The admin fee comes off the top, before deducting expenses, and it's really just a way of changing your split while trying to make you feel like you got more. For example, if you have a 75% split, and they take a 10% administration fee off the top, that leaves 90%. So your 75% of 90% only leaves you 67.5%. The major companies, who do their own administration, will generally knock out the administration fee and just state the real percentage, but you have to be precise when you negotiate splits or you could be rudely surprised. For example, say "75/25, with no admin fee." If you're dealing with an independent company that licenses another publisher to do their administration, you'll generally have to live with that third-party fee coming off the top. In this case, find out in advance how much the administrator charges; you need to know, because it directly affects what goes into your pocket (as you just saw). Sometimes, if you have a *lot* of clout, you can make the independent publisher take the administration fee out of their share and not charge you with any of it. But this is *very* hard to pull off.

WHAT'S IN THE POT?

Songwriter contracts define the pot of income that your percentage applies to. So you want to make sure there's as much money as possible in that pot.

Here's what to look for:

"At Source."   You want your deal to be "at source." As we discussed on page 93, that means your percentage applies to the earnings in each territory, without reduction for the local subpublisher's share. Fight hard for this.

You should almost always be able to get paid "at source" for **affiliated subpublishers** (meaning subpublishers who are owned or controlled by your publisher), and when you make a deal with a major publisher, that covers the biggest earning territories in the world. But when you're dealing with an independent publisher, they're licensing their songs to third-party subpublishers. That means you can't get "at source" because your publisher is being charged by someone else before the money comes back to them. If you have a massive amount of clout, you might make your publisher eat some or all of the the subpublisher's fee, but this is incredibly rare.

If you can't get paid "at source," you should make sure that your publisher's deals with their subpublishers are all "at source." That at least insures that your publisher's income (in which you share) is the largest possible amount because there can't be any deductions besides the subpublishers' fees. And speaking of those fees, your deal should limit what the subpublishers can charge to, say, 15% to 25% for third-party subpublishers, and maybe 10% to 20% for subpublishers owned by your publisher.

Performance monies.   As we discussed on page 226, the performing rights societies pay songwriters directly (instead of paying the publisher, which is what happens with every other type of income). In other words, you get 50% of the performance money (the writer's share) directly from your PRO, and your publisher only collects the other 50% (the publisher's share).

For this reason, publishers want to pay you a smaller percentage of performance monies. For example, if you have a 75/25 deal, they'll want to pay you only 50% of performance monies. They make exactly the same argument we discussed on page 255 in the subpublishing context: you get the writer's share directly from the PRO (which is 50% of the total income), plus 50% of the 50% publisher's share (25% of 100% of the performance money), which gives you a total of 75% of the income. You might want to take a quick look back at that section and the chart, which lays it all out.

It's always worth pushing back on this, and with substantial clout you may do a bit better. But in the beginning, and even mid-level stages, expect to take a reduced piece of the publisher's performance money.

Another issue concerning performing rights money is something called **direct licensing.** Recall that your deal with the PRO gives them the right to license your songs as part of their blanket license (see page 227). Under the consent decree we discussed on page 230, however, all the rights you give your PRO have to be *non-exclusive*, which means you're free to bypass the PRO and directly issue performance licenses to any user you'd like (in other words, you can issue a *direct license*). For example, you could directly license a nightclub or a local TV station to play your music. And because your publisher has the exclusive right to do all your licensing, the publisher could issue a direct license of your songs to a user.

This right hadn't really been used much, but a few years ago, there were rumblings that publishers might issue direct performance licenses to the DSPs for streaming rights (rather than use the PROs to issue those licenses). In other words, they might tell Spotify that they didn't need a BMI license for your songs because the publisher would give them a performance license directly. If they did this, all the performance money (writer's and publisher's shares) would be paid to the publisher, so the writer would no longer get any streaming performance money from the PRO. Instead, the streaming performance money would go into the pot with all the other money that the publisher collects, and the publisher would pay you the agreed percentage.

While direct licensing has gone quiet for the moment, those of us who represent writers made very loud noises about the idea that a publisher could collect the writer's share of performance monies. For starters, it would take you longer to get your money: the publisher would get it when the PRO would have otherwise paid you, but the publisher wouldn't fork it over to you until the next accounting period. Far more serious, however, is that it would also mean the publisher could use this money to recoup your advance—remember, they can't do that now because the money doesn't go through their hands. And if you weren't careful in your contract language, they could even pay you a reduced split on the writer's performance monies (50% instead of the 75% you get on all other income). So for this reason, you need to limit the reduced percentage of performance monies to situations where the writer is paid directly by the PRO.

And on top of all this, direct licensing could kill the PROs by diverting a massive amount of their income to the publishers.

In response to our squawking, the publishers all said they would pay writers outside recoupment even if the contract didn't say so. In fact, they even discussed using the PROs to administer and collect these monies (and pay writers), which would make sure that happened. However, I would put in your contract that, if a society no longer pays writers directly, or if a publisher directly licenses performance rights, the publisher has to pay out the writer's share even if the writer is unrecouped. Your argument is that the publisher never expected to have these monies for recoupment anyway.

Speaking of recoupment from a writer's performance monies, there are some new developments in this area as well. Historically, the societies were so protective of a writer being paid directly by the PRO that they wouldn't honor an assignment of performance royalties by the writer. This, however, has been eroding for some time. The first change was that the societies agreed to honor an assignment of performance monies to a publisher who paid an advance to the writer, and they also agreed to honor an assignment of royalties to a bank that loaned money to the writer. But those assignments were limited to the amount of the advance or loan. Today the PROs will sometimes (reluctantly) honor an overall assignment of monies, but they require a lot of paperwork to make sure the writer really understands what they're doing and that it's really what the writer wants.

"Catch-All." Some contracts, though thankfully this seems to be disappearing, say the songwriter gets a percentage of the publisher's receipts from a list of revenue, like "mechanical, performance, print, and sync" or words to similar effect. The problem is that the language is sometimes a limited list of income sources, which means that the publisher could be collecting monies that it doesn't share with the writer. This is definitely something to avoid (if you're a songwriter), and it's easily solved by adding a "catch-all," which is language to the effect of "all other income not stated herein." Or just by defining "gross receipts" that go into the pot as "all income relating to exploitations of your songs."

Share of Advances. Most contracts also say you don't share in advances that the publisher gets. Most of the time, this is fine—if the publisher gets an advance for its entire catalog of songs (of which you're only a part), you really have no right to share in that advance until your song has earnings that are used toward recoupment. There's no way to know whose songs will earn back the advance, and so there's no reasonable way to allocate a portion of the advance to any particular song until royalties are earned.

What you can share, however, is an advance paid specifically for your composition. For example, your song's lyrics are licensed for a book, and the publisher gets an advance against a royalty for that use (see page 261). Since this advance or guarantee is only for your song's earnings (and doesn't have to be repaid if there's no earnings), you should get your share when the advance/guarantee is paid to the publisher. So add language saying you *do* share in advances and guarantees that are specifically for your composition.

We discussed the concept of **breakage** (unrecouped advances, nonrecoupable money, equity from investments) on page 147 in connection with record companies. This concept also applies to publishers, so you should ask for a share of that in your deal. Most of the companies do it as a matter of policy even if it's not in your deal, but it's cheap insurance to put in that provision.

Print Income.   As we discussed on page 260, physical printed music consists primarily of single-song sheet music and multi-song folio books. Not surprisingly, the physical market is shrinking as the digital revolution takes hold. (We discussed digital print rights on page 262.)

All but one of the major publishers now treat print income the same as all other income, because none of them are in the print manufacturing and distribution business; in other words, they license print rights just like any other rights and you get your agreed percentage of it. The holdout publisher has old contracts with major writers from its golden era that would get an increase in royalties if they switched over to the new system, so they hang on to the old one (which is pennies for single-song sheet music, and royalties based on wholesale for other print uses). If you're dealing with them, try to get a percentage of publishing on top of those royalties to make up the difference.

As we discussed on page 260, publishers can get a higher royalty for use of your name and likeness in a personality folio. If you have enough clout, you can ask that the full bump in royalty come to you, or at least a chunk of it. The argument is that this is for your name and likeness, and the publisher shouldn't share in it. Their argument is that they do have the right to your name and likeness in connection with print music.

No Playing Footsie.   If the publishing company is affiliated with your record company, you want to make sure they don't issue "sweetheart" licenses (i.e., licenses at less than customary rates) to their own record company. In other words, you don't want them playing footsie with their sister companies at your expense. Another example would be where their parent company also owns a film studio, and you don't want them to license your songs into one of their films for a smaller sync fee than what's fair in the marketplace. So add a provision saying that licenses to their affiliated companies must be on an arm's-length, customary basis.

CHARGES AGAINST ROYALTIES

Okay, so now we have this nice fat pot of money. Let's look at what the publisher takes out before they pay you:

"Off the Top" Charges

The publisher will take the following "off the top," meaning it's deducted before they apply your percentage. In other words, they bear their percentage share of these costs.

"Off the top" costs are typically (1) subpublishing fees (see page 254), unless your deal is "at source," in which case there shouldn't be any; (2) **collection costs,** which means (a) monies deducted by collection agencies, such as Harry Fox fees or CMRRA (see page 231) and (b) the cost of chasing deadbeats who don't pay; (3) costs of sample clearances (see page 251), (4) **demos** (we'll discuss them in a minute); and (5) the cost of filing copyright claims. Most forms also include their right to deduct the cost of a **lead sheet** (pronounced *leed* sheet), which means sheet music with a transcription of the lyrics and treble clef melody notes that used to be required by the copyright office. However, since the copyright office started taking physical recordings instead of lead sheets years ago, no one's actually created a lead sheet for decades. In other words, they're a piece of historical litter that still clutters up songwriter contracts.

Under collection costs, some publishers have adopted the practice of deducting an **equivalency fee** or similar words. It came about like this:

As we discussed, if a publisher uses the Fox Agency to collect mechanicals (see page 231 for what the Fox Agency is), Fox will charge 11.5%. The major publishers don't really use Fox anymore, but instead want to charge an amount equal to what Fox would have charged. In other words, they want to take 11.5% off the top before splitting mechanical royalties with you, and this deduction is called an *equivalency fee* because it's "equivalent" to what Fox would have charged. Their argument is that they're doing Fox's job, and since you'd have to pay Fox, why not pay them?

When physical and download were massive, this was a big deal. Mechanicals were a major, and often the main, source of income. Physical of course is now less of an issue, but it looked like the publishers were going to take an equivalency fee on streaming mechanicals, which would have been a *huge* deal. If you ask, they will limit the equivalency fee to physical goods. But it's worth pushing back altogether—your argument is that their percentage of the overall deal is payment for these services. And if you still strike out, at least say that they can't charge an equivalency fee for licenses to their sister record companies. If you have even moderate clout, you should be able to get that.

Another cost to watch is the **demo** cost. A *demo* is an informal recording that's made solely for the purposes of pitching a song to artists, film companies, etc. It's either recorded by the songwriter (if you can sing without causing dogs to howl), or an unknown singer, accompanied by one or two instruments (which, since the advent of synthesizers, can sound like the London Symphony Orchestra).

Often a publisher pays the costs to create a **demo** of your song or, in some deals, they pay you $600 or so for you to make one on your own. First, you want to approve the costs of any demo before they spend it. That's not hard to get. Once approved, the publishers try to charge 50% to 100% of the demo charges off the top. As your bargaining power increases, the amount they can charge decreases to as low as zero.

Not So "Off the Top" Charges

In addition to the above, there are a number of costs that *don't* come off the top. That sounds pretty good until I tell you these charges come *only out of your share* (in other words, you eat 100% of them).

There are two major areas:

First, they will recoup your advances from your share of monies. That's perfectly reasonable; advances are just a prepayment of your money.

Second, they'll deduct all their costs regarding any **infringement claims** against you. We'll talk about infringement claims in more detail later (on page 320), but basically it means someone claims you ripped off their copyright. Under every contract, you're responsible for delivering a song that doesn't get your publisher sued, so if they get hit, it's on you. That means you'll be charged for legal fees, courts costs, etc., as well as any money the other person might recover.

In addition to these two areas, most deals have language saying the publisher can charge you with "any other expenses" in connection with your songs, other than the ones they listed as "off the top" (the costs we discussed in the prior section). That's *really* broad, but not always so easy to change in the agreement. Try your best to spell out what they can charge, but you'll likely have to live with this broad language and hope their good faith will keep them from abusing it.

COPYRIGHT OWNERSHIP

Under these deals, who owns copyrights of your song? Not surprisingly, the choices are:

1. You.
2. The publisher.
3. Both of you.
4. Neither of you (actually, I just threw that in to see if you're paying attention).

Historically, publishers owned 100% of the copyright, but today it's not unusual for the writer to own some or even all of the copyright.

For newer writers, the most common arrangement is for the publisher to own the songs but give them back at some point after the deal is over (as we'll discuss later). With more clout, the writer and publisher can co-own the songs 50/50, again with all rights going back to the writer at some point after the term. And with still more clout (or maybe with a little less clout, if you're not looking for much of an advance), the writer might own 100% of the copyright and just give a publisher the right to exploit the song for a period of time.

A deal where the publisher has no ownership is called an **administration agreement,** and we'll discuss those on page 300.

However, even under administration agreements, the publishers all want a nominal copyright ownership (a few percentage points) during the term of the deal. That's because the publishers aren't eligible for PRO awards if they have no ownership, and publishers love lining their walls with plaques to impress you.

SINGLE-SONG CONTRACTS

A single song contract is a deal for only one song. Are you impressed that I'm willing to share this kind of industry secret with you?

The advance for a single-song agreement is usually not very significant. It ranges anywhere from nothing to $250 or $500, if we're talking about unknown songwriters and no unusual circumstances (such as a major artist who's committed to record the song, which of course changes the whole ball game).

Major songwriters rarely sign single-song agreements other than for films (which are another story entirely, as we'll discuss in Chapter 29).

If they own their own publishing, they keep the song, and if they don't, they're probably under a term songwriter agreement, which by coincidence is our next topic.

TERM SONGWRITER AGREEMENTS

A **term songwriter agreement** is just like a record deal except that, instead of making records, you agree to give the publisher all the songs you write during the term.

Term

The term of songwriter agreements (the period during which you have to sign over everything you write) was historically tied to delivery and release of songs by a major label. In other words, your term might be the longer of one year, or until you have delivered three songs and those songs have been released. It's called a **minimum delivery and release requirement,** abbreviated **MDRC.**

But boy, have times changed.

In the past, a "major label release" meant the record would get some kind of marketing push. Because it was so expensive for the label to manufacture and ship physical product, they had a strong incentive to spend marketing dollars if they wanted to get their money back. But when streaming appeared, especially when it was a minor part of the biz, publishing companies suddenly got worried that artists would just throw product on a streaming service to satisfy the release requirements under their songwriting deal. For example, if you were an artist and songwriter, and your record label hated your record, you'd tell them to just post it on Spotify and do nothing else. That would burn off the songwriter's delivery requirements and let you slip out the back door with an unearned advance in your pocket.

Out of this worry, the publishers majorly tightened up the release requirement. Specifically, they required that a song wouldn't count as "released" under the publishing deal unless (a) it was released on a major label, and (b) it was released in CD format (on the theory that the label had to spend money to manufacture and ship CDs). In other words, the digital release of a song on an indie label could generate millions of dollars, but wouldn't satisfy the MDRC requirement under the contract. And since you had to deliver and release a certain number of songs, you could never get out of the deal.

As CDs faded, and became massively dwarfed by streaming revenue, the publishers came under more and more pressure from those of us representing artists to "get real." They finally waved a white flag and now make deals so simple that I had to chuck the carefully crafted delivery section I sweated over just for you. I hope you're feeling guilty . . .

Anyway, nowadays, songwriting deals are for specific periods, such as one to three years. The publisher then gets from two to three additional options, each for the same length of time. Some publishers require a minimum number of songs per period (usually three or so per year), which is called a **Minimum Delivery Requirement (MDR).** These clauses require you to deliver 100% of a song for it to count, but in today's world, with multiple writers on every song, that's virtually impossible. So instead they aggregate your fractional ownership until it equals one song. For example, if you write 25% of four songs, that counts as delivery of one song.

Some publishers still require that the songs don't count unless they're released. But they've dropped the CD requirement (really big of them) and they will also say it counts if it's released not just on a "major label," but also by a major-distributed independent, or by a nationally recognized indie. And some publishers will even drop those requirements if the song generates a certain dollar amount.

In all these contracts, the term of your deal is extended until your advances are recouped. So even if you delivered all the required songs, you could still be stuck in that period of the agreement. For example, suppose you have a two-year deal that requires you to deliver three songs per year, and they give you a $100,000 advance. If you deliver all six songs but only earn $80,000 over the first two years, you are $20,000 unrecouped. In this case, the term is extended until you earn the next $20,000, at which point it comes to an end.

That's all lovely. Except for the part about your being stuck there forever if the creative muse flies over your house on her way to Uncle Morey's.

Under a deal with a delivery requirement and extension of the term for recoupment, notice that two things could happen:

1. You delivered (and released if required) all the songs, but you're unrecouped and stuck there; or
2. You didn't deliver all the songs (or you delivered them but they weren't released), but you're recouped and stuck there.

Let's not let either of those happen. Here's how:

1. For the first situation (the term is extended because you're unrecouped), put in a provision that says you have the right to repay the unrecouped advance at any time during the extension, at which point the term is over.

   If the publisher agrees to this, they'll want back more than 100% of the unrecouped advance. They commonly want 125% of the balance, meaning that if you're $10,000 unrecouped, you'd have to pay them $12,500. Their reasoning is that, if you'd actually earned the $10,000 to recoup, they'd have made a profit on top of that (remember the recoupment is only out of your share, so they'd be getting money on top of the $10,000 if you'd earned the royalties).

   Sometimes you can get this percentage down to 110% or so. This is easier to pull off if you have a higher percentage under the deal. For example, if you have a 90/10 deal, you might pay back 110%, but if you have a 75/25 deal, you'll have to pay 125%. That sounds weird, but it's because, if they kept the rights under a 75/25 deal, they'd make more money than if they'd kept the rights under a 90/10 deal. So they're losing more money to let you out of a 75/25 deal early, and therefore you have to pay more to get free.

   In determining the unrecouped balance you have to pay back, you should ask the publisher to include **pipeline** earnings. *Pipeline* monies are those received by the publisher but not yet accounted to you. For example, suppose you get a statement on March 31 for the period ending the prior December 31, and it shows you are $5,000 unrecouped. If the publisher got $2,000 in February, that money came after the close of the December 31 accounting period and therefore isn't due to you until after the close of the June 30 accounting period. However, the publisher has it in the bank, so it's in the *pipeline* on its way to you. If your contract says they have to count pipeline income when they compute your payback obligation, you'd only have to pay $3,000 (instead of $5,000) to get back the songs.

Here's another approach to the situation where you've delivered all the songs, but the term is extended because you're unrecouped. You can often get a publisher to agree you can "call the option." What this means is that you can give the publisher a notice that says they have to either (a) exercise their option, in which case you're into the next period of the deal, and your unrecouped balance is deducted from your advance for that new period, or (b) give up the option, meaning the term continues until recoupment or repayment, but then it's over because they can no longer hold you beyond that term (in other words, they lose their option).

2. For the second situation (you're recouped but haven't delivered or released everything), try to add a provision that says, if you're recouped, the term ends at the end of the agreed years even if you're short on songs. For example, suppose you had a two-year deal and agreed to deliver six songs but you only gave them four. However, those four were smashes and you're more than recouped. Under this provision, the term would be over at the end of two years. Your argument is that, even if you're short on the number of songs, they've made enough money to recoup and the publisher is doing just dandy. So they shouldn't get any more songs without moving the term forward (and paying you more advances). This provision is not so easy to come by, but worth giving it a try.

Speaking of advances . . .

Advances

Term songwriter agreements almost always require the publisher to pay advances to the songwriter. Historically, publishers paid monthly advances to "true songwriters" (meaning songwriters who don't come with access to someone who uses their songs). In other words, they're not an artist who records their own songs, a writer/producer who can get songs to the artists they produce, or someone who writes regularly with well-known performers, etc.

It's possible to get this kind of deal for a true songwriter in Nashville, but it's not so easy in the pop world. If you do get such a deal, new writers signing to a major publisher might get an advance in the range of $18,000 to $100,000 per year, and less if you sign to a smaller publisher. The advances are paid monthly, quarterly, or sometimes even annually at the beginning of a contract year. (Don't get discouraged if you're a true songwriter—there's always a need for good talent. And there are true songwriters who make multimillions writing hits for other people.)

If you're an established true songwriter, the advances are based on a historical analysis of your earnings—meaning they guess your future potential based on your past—plus whatever additional gouge factor you can leverage. Some superstar writers get hundreds of thousands of dollars per year, and a few are even into seven figures.

The trend these days, however, is away from paying advances the way I just outlined. More commonly, there's an agreed total for the contract period, and you get a percentage of that up front, and with balance on delivery of songs (or release, if that's part of the commitment). For example, if there is a two-year term and a requirement for six songs, you might get 50% on signing, 20% a year later, and 5% on delivery (or release) of each of the songs. Or sometimes you can get the balance of the advance at certain income levels (for example, if you've recouped 50% of your advance). You should try for both of these, and get the money on the earliest to occur of them.

If you have a lot of clout, you can front-load the deal even more, meaning you could get the bulk, or even all, of the advance on signing.

Advances for subsequent periods should increase, and the most common practice is to use a formula (similar to the formula for record advances we discussed on page 99).

Here's a recent deal for an artist/writer where the advance for the second term was ⅔ of the earnings during the first term, less the unrecouped balance, with a floor and ceiling:

Formula: ⅔ of the year's earnings, less any unrecouped balance, but not less than the floor or more than the ceiling.

	Floor	Ceiling
First period	$100,000	(Not applicable)
Second period	$125,000	$350,000
Third period	$150,000	$450,000

Under this deal, if the writer earns $75,000 during the first period, meaning only $75,000 of the $100,000 is recouped (and she is thus $25,000 unrecouped), the advance for the second period would be $25,000, computed like this: ⅔ of the $75,000 earnings ($50,000), less the unrecouped balance ($25,000), equals $25,000. However, there's a floor of $125,000, so she gets a $125,000 advance (because the formula result is lower than the floor). If the earnings are $180,000 (meaning the writer is recouped), there's no deficit to be deducted from the ⅔ of earnings formula, and she gets ⅔ of the $180,000 earned, or $120,000, but because of the floor, it's $125,000. If she earns $600,000 in the year, she'd $350,000 for the second period, because ⅔ of $600,000 ($400,000) exceeds the maximum ($350,000).

Under some deals, the unrecouped balance is deducted from the *floor*. Using the above example, suppose the writer only earns $15,000 in the first period, and is therefore $60,000 unrecouped. In this case, the floor would be reduced from $100,000 to $40,000 (by deducting the $60,000 deficit from the $100,000 floor). When you have this kind of deal, you want to ask for something called a **subfloor.** That means you get a minimum number, no matter how badly you're unrecouped. (We discussed subfloors under record deals, on page 101, and the concept is exactly the same.) So, for example, if the subfloor was $75,000, then even if the writer was $60,000 unrecouped, instead of the advance being reduced to $40,000 as in our example above, she'd get $75,000.

If you're a new writer with a bidding frenzy, you can get deals that used to be reserved for writers with a sales history. For example, when a writer is the fox with a pack of hounds snapping at their tail, you can get offers of $250,000 to $500,000 per contract period, and sometimes even more. With that much heat, the deal might even be an administration deal (which we'll discuss on page 300).

Record Deal Tie-ins

As noted on page 123, some companies try to grab your publishing when they sign you to a record deal. If there's any possible way to resist this, I strongly urge you to lash yourself to the mast and hang on. If you're dealing with an independent record company, many times their publishing company isn't a real publisher, but rather just another way to make money from you. That's less of an issue with the majors, because their publishing companies are first-rate, but it's always better for you to be free in the marketplace.

POP QUIZ

Now that you have carefully digested all of the above, here's a pop quiz: What is a major source of money that a publisher can't (normally) use to recoup its advances? (Answer on page 304.)

If you're on the *Fast Track,* go to Chapter 19 on page 305.
Everyone else, boogie on.

CO-WRITES (SONGS WRITTEN BY TWO OR MORE WRITERS)

When you write a song with other people, those folks are called **co-writers** or **collaborators.** Virtually all songs in the pop and urban space are co-written these days,

While historically it was a problem, today most songwriter contracts only require you to deliver a song "to the extent written" by you. However, be sure that language is in the definition of what you're giving the publisher. If it doesn't say that, you're promising to deliver the other writers' shares as well, which you obviously can't do. This isn't really a practical problem—the publisher can't expect you to give them a horse you don't own—but make sure your contract says this.

How Are Songs Divided?

Historically, 50% of a song went to the writer of the music, and 50% to the lyricist. No muss, no fuss. So if one person wrote all of the melody, and one person wrote all the lyrics, they each got 50% of the song. If two people equally wrote the lyrics, and one person wrote the melody, then the lyricists each got 25% of the song, and the melody writer got 50%. You get the idea.

Over the past years, this has gotten majorly fuzzed up. The reason is that rap, hip-hop, pop, EDM, and similar music are as dependent on the **track** as they are on the melody and lyrics. The *track* is the background rhythm and instrumentation, on which the melody and lyrics are laid (the lyrics and melody are referred to as the **topline**). Also, the track itself may not come from one place, because there are **beat writers** who only create beats that become part of it.

At any rate, because tracks are so essential to a song, the folks creating the tracks also get pieces of the copyright and royalties. How much? Well, there's no hard-and-fast rule about how much of a song goes to the track. It's negotiated by the parties at the time, depending on their sense of who contributed what to the song, and (frankly) the muscle of the people involved. I've seen deals where the track gets one-third, with the melody and lyrics each getting one-third, and I've also seen deals for important producers where the track gets half the song. Sometimes, if the track contribution is minimal, and the person creating it doesn't have much bargaining power, it gets little or nothing. For example, some beat writers sell their beats for flat fees (a few thousand dollars, or even less), and get no share of the song.

There's an added twist when tracks contain **samples** (as we discussed on page 250, that means the track incorporates somebody else's material). In this case, the sample owner gets a piece of the writing and publishing, and that obviously has to come out of someone's share. Logically, since the person who created the track added in the sample, you'd assume that the sample's share of publishing should come completely from the track's share. However, the track owner argues that it should come out of everybody's earnings, on the theory that everyone benefits from the use of the sample. (The same issue comes up if the melody or lyric writer "borrows" from someone else.) Results vary in direct proportion to bargaining power.

In pop music, it's most common to split songs equally among the writers, regardless of who did what. So if there are three writers, they each get a third; if there are four, each gets a fourth; and so on. There are of course exceptions, like situations where a writer contributed very little (maybe just added a few words, or changed a few notes), in which case they'll only get a small piece.

So sit down, slug it out, and have the survivor call me.

CREATIVE CONTROL

Contractual Approvals

You want as much creative control as you can get over what's done with your songs. Ask the publisher to get your approval before it can do things like:

1. **Make changes in the music.**
   The publisher will normally say that's fine as long as they don't have to ask about simple changes merely to conform to the mood or style of a particular artist.
2. **Make changes in the English lyrics.**
   Again, this approval usually excludes minor changes for gender, mood, or style.
3. **Add foreign lyrics.**
   If you have enough clout, you may be able to approve translations. This is much harder to come by, but it's worth fighting for. Remember, it's also a financial issue—translations reduce your royalties (see page 258).

4. **Make changes in the title (in English).**

   Usually no sweat—just ask for this and you'll get it.

5. **Grant sync licenses.**

   If you have some bargaining power, you may be able to approve all motion picture synchronization licenses. (These are defined on page 242.) If you have a lot of bargaining power, you might also get approval of television sync licensing, but this is much harder to do. The reason is that publishers often have to give a yes or no answer to TV studios within twenty-four hours, and they don't want to lose the opportunity because you're off sipping piña coladas on your yacht. One compromise is to get approval of television licenses with the exception of a few things that the publisher can do without you, such as music-centric programs (like *The Voice* or *Dancing with the Stars*), current programs like *Saturday Night Live* or *Entertainment Tonight*, or live, on-camera performances of the song.

   If you can't get this, another compromise is to say the song can't be licensed for NC-17 or X-rated films, or for a scene in a film involving illicit drugs, sex, violence, or anything else that rings your particular bell.

6. **Use the song in commercials and print ads.**

   At best, you should have the right to approve any usage of your song in commercials and print ads (meaning online, newspapers, magazines, etc.). Note: Even if you have approval of all sync licenses, you don't automatically have approval of commercials. The reason is that not all commercials need a sync license. The TV and online video ads need a sync license, but not radio commercials (because radio recordings aren't made under sync licenses, as we discussed on page 242; there are no visuals to sync with), and neither does the use of your lyrics in ads. So ask for approval of all commercials.

   If you don't have enough clout to approve all commercials, you can compromise by requiring your consent to certain categories, such as alcohol, tobacco, firearms, political candidates, and my personal favorite, sexual hygiene products.

7. **Licensing samples of your song (see page 250 for what sampling is).**

   This isn't usually hard to get. It's serious use of your music and involves a creative decision of whether or not you're comfortable with your song being incorporated into someone else's work (which you may think sucks).

8. **License grand rights.**

   Grand rights are the rights to put your song into a musical play, motion picture, or TV show if the song is integrated into the story, such as an onscreen performance, a dance number, or other use that furthers the story. By the way, the PROs (ASCAP, BMI, etc.) can only license **small performance rights,** meaning concerts, radio, TV, and similar uses outside of a dramatic context. So to get grand rights, a user has to go to your publisher.

REVERSION OF COPYRIGHT

Smile whenever you hear the words **reversion of copyright,** because this will always be good for you (unless you're a publisher, in which case you can scowl). This is different from the termination of copyrights under the copyright law, which we'll discuss later, on page 331, because reversion is a *contractual* provision that's specifically negotiated. It means the publisher must give you back your song at some point in the future.

Conditions of Reversion

What should trigger reassignment? Ideally nothing, meaning you get back your songs, no matter what, at some point down the line. That's our next section. But if you can't get that, here's some things you should try for.

First, be sure you get back all the songs that haven't been exploited. The test of whether a song is exploited used to be "commercially recorded and released," meaning you got back all the songs that hadn't been released. But since release means nothing anymore, the test these days is usually based on the song having no earnings. Better for you than "no earnings" is "minimal earnings," say under $2,000. In other words, if the song has earned less than $2,000, you get it back.

Be sure to require that the earnings have to happen within some time frame. Otherwise the publisher can keep each song for the life of copyright, telling you every week that big money is just around the corner. The usual period is two years after the end of the deal, though it's often extended if you're unrecouped. If that's the case, be sure to get the right to buy the songs back by repaying the unrecouped portion of the advance. Just as we discussed on page 100, in connection with extending the term of your songwriter agreement because you're unrecouped, the publisher will want more than 100% of the advance. Try to keep it down to 110% of the advance, 125% tops.

Reversion of copyright for non-exploitation is something you should *always* ask for. You may not always get it, but you should *always* ask for it. Is it clear I mean *always*? Did I say *always*?

Automatic Reversion

When you move into the major leagues, or if you're in a bidding war, you can ask for a reassignment of all compositions, whether or not they're exploited. And even if you're just getting started, you should ask for this. Owning your songs can really be valuable.

How soon can you get them back? Time frames in general run from five to fifteen years after the close of the exclusive term, with the majority in the seven-to-twelve-year range. This is virtually always tied to recoupment—for example, the publisher will reassign the songs to you ten years after the term, but if you're unrecouped, the period is extended until you recoup. Actually it's a little longer than recoupment; the contracts say they'll reassign the songs at the end of an accounting period for which you get a statement that shows you're recouped. As you'll see, accounting statements come 90 days after the close of a period, so even if you recoup a few days into a six-month accounting period, you won't get the songs back until 90 days after the end of that six-month period. The period of time after the term that the publisher keeps the songs is called a **retention period.**

If your reversion is tied to recoupment, be sure you ask for the right to repay the unrecouped balance, in which case you get the songs back upon repayment, rather than waiting until you actually recoup. If they give you the right to repay, then for the reasons we've discussed, publishers want 110% to 125% of the unrecouped balance. And as we covered on page 288 in connection with the term, you should include pipeline earnings in computing how much you have to pay them.

If you have really major clout, you can sometimes put a cap on the extension for non-recoupment. For example, the songs might come back seven years after the end of the term, extended until recoupment or repayment, but in any event they come back after ten years even if you're still unrecouped.

By the way, this reversion isn't truly "automatic." The contracts say you only get the rights after you give the publisher a written notice with words to the effect of "I want my songs back."

Collection Periods

After you get your songs back, the publisher will want to collect monies earned while they owned the song. In other words, if $100 was earned from streaming during the term, but it isn't paid to the publisher until six months after the term, the publisher gets to collect and keep their share of that. This is customary, but you should limit how long they can wait around for the money to come in. The norm is for them to collect money that's paid within one to two years after the term, and the period during which they can collect the money is cleverly called a **collection period**. Sometimes this period is longer for international, since the monies take a while to get back to our shores. For example, there might be a twelve-month collection period for the United States, and an eighteen-month period for the rest of the world. Of course, you want to keep the collection period as short as possible.

Partial Reversion

A step down from full reversion is to get a **partial reversion,** meaning that you get back the administration rights to your share of the song, but the publisher keeps the administration of their share. You may also get back copyright ownership of your share of the song.

For example, if you have a 75/25 deal, a partial reversion would give you back the administration rights to your 75% share, but the publisher would keep administration of their 25%. This is called **co-administration,** which we'll cover in more detail on page 299, but basically it means you each license your share of the song separately to the users. It also means that anyone who wants to use the song needs permission from both of you.

ADMINISTRATION AGREEMENTS

An **administration agreement,** also called an **admin agreement,** gives the publisher no copyright ownership or long-term retention period, but instead just gives them the right to administer your songs for a specific period of time. When the term is over, all rights come back to you, either immediately or after a short retention period (a year or two). When they do come back, there will be a collection period for monies earned during the term and any retention period. (We discussed retention periods on page 296, and collection periods on page 297.)

Administration agreements are the most typical deal for established writers who own their own publishing. These deals are less common for new to moderate level artists, but doable if there's heat or you don't care about much of (or any) advance.

Admin agreements are also done between major publishers and smaller publishers that don't have a staff. Under these deals, the major administers the smaller publisher's catalog in all or part of the world. Administration agreements for less than the world are the **subpublishing agreements** we discussed on page 254.

Generally these deals are for a short period of time (typically three to five years, usually with extensions if you're unrecouped). And because the publisher gets only a small piece, and only for a limited time, these deals have smaller advances (or no advance at all). However, if you're a superstar writer, or a small publishing company generating steady income, you can get substantial advances. And you can sometimes put a cap on how long the deal can be extended if you're unrecouped. For example, the deal might be five years, extended until recoupment, but in no event longer than seven years.

Administrator's Share

Under an administration deal, the administrator takes an **administration fee,** reimburses itself for any direct expenses, and pays the balance to you. If you control the songs of other writers, the administrator customarily (but not always) takes care of paying them. These monies are of course deducted before paying you.

Administration fees customarily range from 10% to 25% of the gross dollars, though superstars may be able to pay a little less. The deals are actually written the opposite way, meaning that a 10% admin deal would say that you get 90% of the monies.

Cover Records/Co-Writes

Similar to what we discussed in subpublishing deals (see page 254), many admin deals give the publisher an incentive to (a) go out and get **covers,** and (b) set up **co-writes.** A *cover* in this context is a recording by an artist that the publisher makes happen, such as a record or a sync license for a movie, TV show, etc. *Co-writes,* as you probably guessed, are songs you write with another writer. One of the major things that creative publishers do these days is to introduce you to other writers who will unlock the creative magic.

If they deliver a cover, or set up a co-write that generates songs, they usually want an increased percentage of earnings by the cover or co-written song. For example, if the administrator has a 15% administration fee, it might increase to a 25% fee for income from cover recordings and the co-written songs. They may also want a longer period of time to administer covers and co-writes.

You want to limit their increased percentage to covers that are actually procured by the publisher (called a **procured cover**). In other words, a situation where the publisher actively pitched the song and came home with a cover, as opposed to some random artist calling up and asking for it. This clause isn't as easy to get as you think, because the publisher doesn't want to argue about who actually made it happen. They will also say that, if they raise your stature to the point that everyone wants your songs and starts hounding them, they shouldn't be penalized just because you're now famous and people are calling them. But with enough clout, you can pull off a requirement that it has to be *procured*.

Giving a larger percentage of cover income isn't quite as simple as it looks. That's because, if the cover isn't the first recording of a work, you can't always tell which version of the song is generating the money. It's easy enough for mechanical royalties and streaming—the royalty statements list each specific recording. But when it comes to nondigital performances (like radio and television, which are still big money sources), the songs are only listed by title, and there's no way to know which version was played on the radio (the original or the cover?).

The best solution is to give the cover record a different title, even if it just means adding a parenthetical under the song title, like ("stupid version"). If that doesn't happen, you can argue that the publisher should only get an increased percentage on mechanicals and digital, which you can sometimes pull off. If not, there needs to be an allocation between the cover version's earnings and the original's. There's no hard and fast way to do this, so (if you can get this concept at all) we usually have language saying there will be a "reasonable allocation" between the cover version and the original.

CO-ADMINISTRATION AGREEMENTS

In today's world, it's normal to have about three thousand writers for each song (well, maybe a few less . . .). And it's rare that all the writers are signed to the same publishing company. So if a number of different publishers own the same song, how does that work? What happens when several people own the same house?

The answer is what we call a **co-administration agreement,** which basically says everyone each takes care of their share. In other words, if I have 25% of the song and you have 75%, and someone wants to use the song in a commercial, they get a license from me for 25%, and a license from you for 75%. It also means:

1. The user pays 25% of the money to me and 75% to you.
2. If you decide you don't want to give a license, that the deal is dead.

How could you do that to me?

Of course, I could also do it to you.

Oh, and give yourself 100 points if you realized that neither of us can stop a compulsory license. See page 214 for what a compulsory license is.

Now I'll let you in on an industry secret: nobody actually writes up or signs co-admin agreements. That's because there are so many co-written songs that it's just not worth the trouble. Instead, there's usually an email exchange agreeing on what percentage of the song that the various writers and publishers have. Then everyone relies on their rights as co-owners under the copyright law (which we'll discuss in the next chapter), and industry custom (which is what I just described: all of us have to agree to issue a license, and if we do, each of us gets paid our share directly by the user). The only sort-of exception is that co-administration rights can be covered by provisions in another agreement, such as a producer deal where the producer is also a writer, or the agreement for a guest artist who also co-writes.

Accountings

Publishers typically account and pay within sixty to ninety days after the close of each semiannual calendar period (June 30 and December 31). Some superstar songwriters get **quarterly accountings** (meaning March 31, June 30, September 30, and December 31). Historically, this has been rare unless you have massive clout, but as I write this, some of the companies are talking about moving to a quarterly system overall. Stay tuned.

The other issues concerning accountings, such as the right to audit, the period to object to a statement, etc., are the same as record deals, which we discussed on page 164.

Writing Teams

If you're in a band that writes together, or if you write with a partner on a continual basis, and a publisher is signing all of you, there are some special points you need to cover in your deal.

If you don't regularly write with the same people, or if you do, but (a) you and the other people are signing to different publishers, or (b) you're each signing a separate deal with the same publisher, you can skip to the quiz on page 303.

For those of you still here . . . Hi.

Just to make the discussion simpler, I'm only going to talk about a writing team of two people. But the same principles apply to bands or other clusters of souls who regularly write together.

The writing team issues are:

Advances.   Sorry to report, but the advances don't double for a writing team. The reason is pretty simple—even though there are two of you, you're each only writing one-half of a song, and so the total output is the same as the publisher would get from one person writing 100% of the song.

Cross-Collateralization.   If the publisher hands the two of you one contract for you both to sign, listen up. You should try to have a separate account for your earnings and advances, and ask that your two accounts are *not* cross-collateralized (see page 88 for a discussion of cross-collateralization). This isn't necessary if you always split the songs 50/50 and get equal advances—your earnings are going to be identical, as are your advances. And it's not necessary if you're sure this will be true for the life of the deal (even after that night when your partner drives her Toyota over your foot). If you're not 100% positive, ask for separate, non-collateralized accounts, and read on.

The downside of separating your accounts is that it may reduce the total advance. That's because the publisher might not be able to get the advance back from the total earnings. Observe:

1. One or both of you may occasionally write songs by yourself, which means one of you could earn more than the other. For example, if you write a smash on your own, you would recoup

your advances, while your partner's account is still unrecouped. This is good from your point of view, but the publisher is giving up the chance to get back the total advance, and therefore will be less willing to take a risk.

2. You might stop writing in the same ratio that you get advances (e.g., you may take the advances 50/50, but on some songs you split the earnings 60/40 or 75/25). This means the advances are recouped unevenly (see the example below).

3. You may break up as a team completely, and each start writing on your own. In that case, you absolutely don't want the other person's advances charged to your account. And you don't want your earnings used to recoup the other writer's advances.

Let's look at an example. Suppose you and your co-writer, Louise, are each getting $10,000 a year under a songwriting agreement. At the end of year one, you've written a number of songs on a 50/50 basis that earned a total of $5,000. So each of you was credited with $2,500 in royalties. This means you're each $7,500 unrecouped.

Now you write a song by yourself, which earns $20,000 in royalties. If your accounts are not cross-collateralized, the $20,000 earnings will recoup your $7,500 deficit, and the publisher pays you $12,500. *If your accounts are cross-collateralized, the publisher will deduct not only your $7,500 deficit but also Louise's $7,500 deficit.* Thus, out of the $20,000 your song earned, you'd only get $5,000 ($20,000 less your $7,500 deficit and less your partner's $7,500 deficit). Since you didn't get the other $7,500 advance (your co-writer did), you will not be a happy camper. So separate your accounts. I'd hate to read about Louise floating up in the East River.

On the other hand, if you really need the extra advance that comes from combining your accounts, you may decide to let the publisher cross-collateralize your and Louise's earnings and advances. If you do, and if one of you earns more than the percentage of the advance you received, you and your partner will have to work it out between yourselves. For example, using the numbers in the prior paragraph, you should have been paid $12,500, but you only got $5,000 because the other $7,500 was used to recoup Louise's advance. Also, Louise is now recouped, so she'll get paid future monies that she shouldn't have received because she would have still been unrecouped if it weren't for your song. So the bottom line is that, to make things right, Louise has to pay you $7,500.

This adjustment can be done by Louise writing you a check, but more commonly it's done by adjusting income from other places, like future earnings from other songs, or even records, merch, touring, etc. Your business manager can do the math for you.

Separate Obligations.   Another problem with signing one agreement is that you have to be sure your obligations are separate. Otherwise you'll be responsible for a breach of contract by the other guy. For example, if Louise wrongfully terminates her agreement and walks out on the publisher, and the publisher sues her, you don't want them to seize your royalties as a way to pay for their damages and/or legal fees.

NOW LOOK WHERE YOU ARE!

Here you are, only partway through the book and you already know enough to answer the final homework assignment I gave after my nine-week music business class at USC Law School. Very impressive!

Try your hand at this (okay, I updated the questions but kept the principles; hope you can tell I updated it . . .).

You're a rapper who's signed to Universal Publishing as a songwriter. You're the featured artist on a master with JJ, a producer. JJ used a track created by Bull, who's signed to Warner Music as a songwriter. Bull's track had two master samples he borrowed from James Brown.

The Squirrel Brothers, who are two writers signed to Kobalt Publishing, wrote the lyrics. You and your producer JJ wrote the topline melody.

At the last minute, Kendrick Lamar came in to write and perform a guest rap.

You give your record to Republic Records, and it's blowing up.

Each time the track is streamed, downloaded, or sold, who gets paid? (Ignore any recoupment.) Clue: There are eleven, possibly twelve, parties, but you won't know one of them if you're not on the Expert Track.

Answers:

Here's who gets paid.
For the master:

1. You.
2. Kendrick.
3. JJ, the producer.

4. Possibly Bull, if he didn't sell his track outright.
5. The label that owns James Brown's masters (for the sample).
6. AFM and SAG-AFTRA, the unions (you wouldn't know this if you weren't on the Expert Track; see page 186 if you're curious).

The folks paid for the song are:

1. Your publisher (Universal).
2. JJ's publisher (Sony/ATV).
3. Bull's publisher (Warner Music).
4. The Squirrel Brothers' publishers (Kobalt).
5. Kendrick's publisher.
6. James Brown's publisher (for the sample).

Answer to quiz on page 291:

The writer's share of performance monies (see page 279 for why).

If you're on the *Fast Track,* and if you're in a group,
go to Part IV (Chapter 22) on page 357.
If you're on the *Fast Track,* and you're not in a
group, go to Chapter 23 on page 369.
Everyone else, read on . . .

19

Advanced Copyright Concepts

WHO OWNS THE COPYRIGHT?

Copyright ownership is pretty easy to figure out if you sit down with your zither and knock out a smash by yourself. You, of course, are the owner, since you created it. But we lawyers wouldn't have much fun if it were all that simple, so let me show you how we've managed to fuzz it up over the years.

How About Two People Writing a Song Together?

Suppose you and your cousin Louie write a brilliant work together. Who owns it?

As you probably guessed, the two of you do. But . . .

Who Controls the Song?   Suppose you want to put the song on your next album, and Louie wants to save it until he gets a record deal. Can he stop you?

The ever-scintillating Section 201(a) of the Copyright Act spells this out pretty clearly. It says that you and Louie have created a **joint work** (keep the puns to yourself; it means a work created "jointly" by the efforts of two or more people).

When you have a joint work, either of the authors/owners can deal *non-exclusively* with the *entire* composition, subject to the obligation to pay the other person his or her share of the proceeds. That means you can give all the non-exclusive licenses you want to record companies, film companies, etc., subject to paying Louie for his share of the song. And Louie can do the same. (This is only true in the United States, by the way; not in other countries. Over there a user needs a license from both owners to use the song.)

What Exactly Do You Own?   How about this one: You and Louie sit down to write a song. You write only the music, and Louie writes only the lyrics. Suppose you don't like Louie's lyrics, so you take back your music and ask somebody else to write new lyrics. Can you do that and cut out Louie?

My mentor Payson Wolff once told me that creating a joint work is like adding water to a ball of clay and squishing it. My partner Bruce Ramer uses the analogy of scrambling the white and the yolk of the egg. So as you may be starting to guess, the law isn't what you'd intuitively think. It says that, even if two people create separate, distinct parts of a work, they each own an interest in the *whole copyright*, not just their own contribution. That means Louie owns half the music and half the lyrics, and so do you. So you can't just pick up and leave each other. Even if you add new lyrics, Louie still has a percentage of the song.

Does this sound like an absurd result? To some extent, yes; but if you get into dividing up works where the contributions aren't so easily defined as music and lyrics (which is most of the time), the alternative is even more impossible. Think, for example, about all the elements that go into making a film. What part is the screenwriter's? The director's? The producer's? The wardrobe designer's? Or what about a song where three people work on the lyrics, while two work on both music and lyrics?

What Makes a Joint Work "Joint"?   By now you're beginning to see that this is more complicated than it first appears. But we're just getting warmed up.

Try this one:

A songwriting team consists of one person who lives in California, and another who lives in New York. The California writer, totally on her own, writes a piece of music and emails it to her friend in New York. A few days later, the guy in New York sits down and writes the lyrics. Is this a joint work? When they work totally separately, did these two people create the song together?

The law says, to have a joint work, you only need an author who *intends*, at the time of creation, to merge his or her work with someone else's. In other words, when the musician wrote the music in California, did she intend to have lyrics written for it? That's certainly the case in our example, even though the lyricist and melody writer never physically got together. (It's almost always true that a lyricist intends to merge the words with music, since he or she probably has little call for poetry readings.) So, to have a joint work, you don't need to be in the same room (or on the same planet), and you don't even have to know each other. As long as there's an intent to merge the work at the time of creation, it's a joint work whenever the rest of it comes together.

If you wanna see this principle carried to extremes, get a load of this: In the 1940s, a guy named Ernie Barnett wrote the melody of a song, and his wife, Maybelle, wrote the lyrics. They sold it to a publisher who thought Maybelle's lyrics were pretty awful (a lot of "moon" and "June," I'll bet). So the publisher tossed out Maybelle's words and had a new set of lyrics written by a total stranger, George Norton. The result was a song called "Melancholy Baby."

Based on these facts, a court held that "Melancholy Baby" was a "joint work," and that George was one of the joint creators. Even though Ol' George came along after the song was supposedly finished, he was still a joint author because, when Ernie wrote the melody, he intended to merge lyrics with it. The fact that the lyrics were ultimately written by someone Ernie never met was irrelevant. Moreover, the new lyricist had an interest in the music (although the case didn't deal with that issue). Nice coconuts, eh?

For the legal freaks, the case is *Shapiro Bernstein v. Vogel*, 161 F.2nd 406 (1947).

WORKS FOR HIRE

When Teddy Kennedy was at Harvard, he hired someone to take an exam for him. As you can imagine, it caused a pretty big stink. But guess what . . . The copyright law is one place where this is perfectly legal.

It's done with a **work for hire** (technically called a **work made for hire** in the copyright statute, but the industry shorthand is *work for hire*). A work for hire happens when you hire someone else to create it for you. If you follow the technical formalities, the employer actually becomes the author of the work insofar as the copyright law is concerned. And when I say "the author," I really mean *THE* author. It's as if the person you hired doesn't even exist (in the eyes of the copyright law), and indeed their name doesn't even have to be on the copyright registration form.

I suspect (but I really don't know and would hate to disillusion myself by researching it) that the "work for hire" concept was developed to cover such things as fabric companies that print copyrighted designs on their cloth. They wanted to be sure that the company (not the back-room dork who actually designed the pattern) was the owner of the copyright. Seems reasonable enough.

But for showbiz . . .

Works for Hire in the Entertainment Industry

Here's an example of works for hire in the entertainment world. Suppose you are Walt Disney Pictures and you hire someone to write the theme for *Snow White*. (I picked the example of a motion picture for a particular reason, as you'll see on page 309.) In this situation, Walt Disney Pictures (the corporation) becomes the author of the work, and the person hired to write it disappears. Does this mean the writer won't get his or her name listed as the writer of the song (in the film, on the charts, etc.)? Usually not; the real creator customarily gets credit. (But sometimes, for example with jingles written for radio or television commercials, a creator doesn't.) Also, the amount of money that the real creator gets isn't usually affected by this type of arrangement—most of the time they're paid exactly the same money, whether or not the work is "for hire." However, a number of important rights are drastically different in works for hire (as you'll see later, on page 312). So whenever you're creating a work for hire, be alert to the consequences—they're not good for you.

Technical Definition

Under the copyright law, a work for hire can be created in only one of two ways. They're set out in Section 101 of the Copyright Act and are a bit technical. (You can skip to the "Duration of Copyright" section on page 310 if technical things make you squirmy. But try it first.)

The two ways to get a work for hire are:

1. The work is made by an **employee** within the **scope of employment.** An example of this is the fabric designer I mentioned before.

   The test of whether there is "employment" is not the one used for the income tax laws, or in fact for any other type of laws. The law says that the employer must actually be "directing, or supervising the creation of the work, in a very specific way." (The major case in this area is *Community for Creative Non-Violence v. Reid*, 490 U.S. 730 [1989], in which the Supreme Court held that a Vietnam memorial sculpture was not a "work for hire" because the people who paid to have it created didn't exercise control over the details of the work, didn't supply the tools, had no ongoing employment relationship, etc.).

Normally (although not always) a songwriter is given a lot of latitude in his or her creation, so it would fail the employment test. I suppose, if a songwriter is given very specific instructions, and is supervised during the process, he or she might be considered an employee under the copyright laws. But that's very rare. The most common works for hire in the music area are those that fall under this next provision.

2. If a copyright is not created by an employee within the scope of employment, it can only be a work for hire if it meets *all* of the following criteria:

   The work must be (1) **commissioned** (meaning created at the request of someone, not a previously created work); (2) created under a written agreement that specifies it's a work for hire; and (3) created for use in one of the following:

   (a) **A motion picture or other audiovisual work.** This is the most common area where songs are treated as works for hire. It includes musical scores, a title song written for a film, etc. Remember, these songs do not have to be written by employees. They just need to be under a written agreement that says (1) they're works for hire, and (2) they're commissioned for use in an audiovisual work (meaning created for that work; not a pre-existing song that's added to the work).

   (b) **A collective work.** A *collective work* is a collection of individual works, *each of which is independently capable of copyright*. Examples are an anthology of short stories; a magazine with a number of copyrightable articles; an encyclopedia; etc.

   (c) **A compilation.** A *compilation* is a work made by compiling a bunch of things, and thus it includes collective works (where the parts are separately copyrightable). However, it also includes works where the compiled materials are not separately copyrightable, such as a reference index to the Bible.

   (d) **A translation of a foreign work.** *¿Qué pasa?*

   (e) **A supplementary work,** which is a work supplementing another work (clever definitions, these copyright guys, eh?). These are things like the introduction to a book.

For a brief period in 1999, master recordings were added to the categories listed above (in other words, the Copyright Act said they could be works for hire). However, the artist community went ballistic, and after a battle royale, Congress reversed itself and took out "masters." Nonetheless, record companies take the position that an album is a "collective work" and therefore think they have the right to treat masters as works for hire anyway. We'll talk about this in more detail on page 355.

Before we can discuss the consequences of something being a work for hire, you need a few more concepts. So, plug it into your memory bank (or put a Post-it or electronic bookmark on this page if your memory is like mine), and we'll come back to it.

DURATION OF COPYRIGHT

Remember that a copyright is a *limited duration* monopoly? The next logical question is, "How long?"

History

Prior to 1978, the United States had this bizarre copyright concept that was adopted in 1909 and not changed for almost seventy years. I tell you about it because (1) it's still relevant for older copyrights; and (2) I had to learn it, so why shouldn't you listen to it?

The main thing to know about these old copyrights is that they used to last for a period of twenty-eight years from publication of the work. (I could spend an entire chapter on what *publication* means, but I'd like you to finish my book awake, so I'll skip it. Basically, it means "distributed to the public.") These copyrights were then renewable for an additional twenty-eight years, so the maximum copyright protection was fifty-six years.

In 1976, Congress did a major, seventy-thousand-mile overhaul of the copyright laws. It was so extensive that the 1976 Copyright Act wasn't effective until January 1, 1978, because Congress wanted to give everyone a year to study it.

This new law dumped the twenty-eight plus twenty-eight nonsense. Instead, it said that the duration of copyright for works created after January 1, 1978, was the life of the author plus fifty years (which was already how the lives of copyrights were measured in a lot of other countries). Congress also extended the old fifty-six-year terms (for works created before January 1, 1978) by nineteen years, for a total of seventy-five years.

In 1998, the congressional folk got together again to talk about copyright. In memory of Congressman and Croonster Sonny Bono, they slapped on another twenty years (known as the Sonny Bono Copyright Term Extension Act, or as I like to think of it, "I Got You Twenty, Babe"). This act extended the copyright term for pre-1978 songs (if they were still under copyright) to a total of ninety-five years, and gave the 1978 and later copyrights a term equal to the life of the author plus seventy years.

When a copyright expires, the work goes into the **public domain** (also called **p.d.**), which means anyone can use it for free.

So new copyrights last for life of the author plus seventy years. Simple, right? Well, how about:

1. A work written by two people. Whose life do you use to measure the copyright duration?
2. A work written under a phony name (called a **pseudonymous** work)? Or something created anonymously? How do you know whose life to check on?
3. Works for hire. Remember, the author is the employer, who could be a corporation. And some of those suckers live forever.

Rest comfortably, dear friends, because all of these have been handled. They work like this:

1. In the case of a joint work, the copyright lasts until seventy years after the death of the last survivor. So write all your songs with your five-year-old daughter.
2. Anonymous (no name) or pseudonymous (phony name) works last the sooner of ninety-five years from publication, or one hundred twenty years from creation. **Creation** means the first time it's fixed in tangible form (written down or recorded). **Publication,** as I said, is a tricky little devil, but for our purposes just assume it means distribution to the public.
3. Works for hire are the same as anonymous.

RIGHT OF TERMINATION

One of the best goodies that creators got in the 1976 Copyright Law is the **right of termination.**

The termination provisions say that, even if you make a bonehead deal, the copyright law will give you a second shot—thirty-five years later. In other words, thirty-five years after a transfer, you can get your copyright back.

By the way, this termination is only for the U.S. copyright. You're stuck with whatever deal you made for the rest of the world. As it happens, the United States is the only country where you get a do-over.

The exact mechanics get a bit technical, so I've stuck them back on page 331, in a section for the die-hards.

Termination of Works for Hire—Not So Fast, Charlie . . .

Now you know enough to understand the consequences of something being a work for hire (see page 307 for what that is). With works for hire, there are *no* termination rights, because there was no transfer in the first place, and therefore no transfer to terminate. Remember, the creator never existed in the eyes of the copyright law—the person or company commissioning the work owns it as if they had created it themselves. So with works for hire, there's no copyright coming back to you and your kiddies. Bummer.

Be very aware of this consequence when you create a work for hire.

PUBLIC PERFORMANCE OF MASTERS

In most developed countries outside the United States, the *artist* and *record company* are paid a royalty every time a recording is played on the radio. (Note, we're talking here about record company and artist payments from the public performance of *masters*, which is very different from royalties that are paid to a *songwriter and publisher* for the public performance of *musical compositions,* which was always done in the United States.)

Even though artists and record companies have been paid for the performance of masters in other territories from the beginning, the United States didn't recognize this right until 1995. In fact, as we'll discuss later, when Congress created a sound recording copyright in 1972 to stop piracy, it went out of its way to say there was no public performance royalty. And when they finally did get around to a performance royalty in 1995, Congress limited it to *digital* performance of the masters. So unlike other countries, there's no performance money for use of the masters in over-the-air radio broadcasting (also called **terrestrial radio.**) We'll discuss this in more detail on page 314.

In foreign territories, the master performance monies can be really significant. That sounds like good news, except that U.S. artists aren't usually entitled to collect them. The reason is pretty simple: since the United States doesn't pay foreign artists when their masters are performed in the U.S., foreign countries don't pay U.S. artists when their masters are performed over there. In part, this comes from a sense of fairness, and to keep a balance of monies going in and out of the territory. But it's also a way to make more money available to the local artists. (If U.S. artists aren't taking money for the performance of masters, there's more left over for the locals. However, in some territories the record companies collect these monies if the artist can't.)

In recent years, it's been possible for Americans to get paid for some countries, but only if you jump through the proper hoops. Those hoops vary from place to place, and a key player in this obstacle course is something called the **Rome Convention** (an international treaty dealing with intellectual property). If your country signed the Rome Convention, you get performance monies from all the other countries that signed it. Most of the countries that signed it are in Europe and Scandinavia, though Japan and Australia also came to the party. Guess which country didn't sign it? Right . . . the U.S. of A.

Still, you can get some foreign monies. Portugal, Romania, Hungary, Russia, and Spain pay everybody. Germany pays if the record is released in a Rome Convention country within thirty days of its initial release in a non–Rome Convention territory, which (because of streaming) means most every record these days.

You can also get paid if you're signed to a label that's based in a Rome Convention country.

Another way to be eligible for payment is to record (or partially record) your masters in a Rome Convention country. (By the way, Canada is a party to the Rome Convention and they have great recording studios. . . .) The place where you render your services is the key to whether you're entitled to foreign performance money. For example, if you record your vocals in Canada, you're golden. If all the musicians record in Canada, but you sing in Wyoming, you're toast (though Wyoming is lovely this time of year).

Okay, let's take a look at what Congress did for us Americans.

U.S. Digital Performances of Masters

In 1995, Congress amended Section 106 of the Copyright Act with something called the **Digital Performance Right in Sound Recordings Act of 1995.** Those folks in Washington sure know how to put a sexy title on something, huh?

Section 106 says you get paid for performances of your master if all of the following apply:

1. It must be a *digital* public performance, meaning a digital transmission rather than over-the-air AM and FM radio.

   In the last few years, many radio stations have converted their over-the-air signals to digital (HD radio), which is a digital signal. So it sounds like you'll get performance monies when they play your masters over the air, right? Well. . .

   Turns out the broadcasters have a lot of friends in Congress. In a nice little lobbying move, they managed to exclude digital over-the-air broadcasts from the definition of digital performances.

   The only exception is when a radio station **simulcasts** its signal over the Internet (meaning it streams the signal at the same time that it broadcasts over the air). In that case, you get paid for the streaming portion (but not the over-the-air part). With the world moving to streaming, however, this means more money coming your way.

2. You only get paid for the digital performance of *audio-only* sound recordings (meaning the artist doesn't get paid for performances of a master in films, TV shows, or commercials).

So, to break it down, the only digital performances that fall under Section 106 are audio-only digital transmissions that don't go over the air. This includes satellite radio services (like Sirius XM), digital cable and satellite television audio music channels (e.g., Music Choice), noninteractive webcasters (both retransmissions of FCC-licensed radio stations on the Internet and originally programmed "Internet-only" services), services that stream to commercial businesses (grocery store music), streaming to mobile devices, and other assorted digital weirdos.

If a broadcast qualifies for a performance royalty under this criteria, you get paid one of two ways:

1. In 1998, Congress followed up their 1995 extravaganza with the **Digital Millennium Copyright Act** (also known as the

DMCA). This baby set up a *compulsory* license for *non-interactive* streaming of masters. That means, under certain conditions (which we'll discuss in a second), the owner of a sound recording *must* allow a user to transmit it. If the broadcast qualifies for the compulsory license, you get the fees laid out by the Copyright Royalty Board (which I'll give you in a second).

If the use doesn't qualify for the compulsory license . . .

2. Remember, as we discussed on page 214, that a copyright owner can stop someone from using their work without permission unless they can get a compulsory license. Because the DMCA compulsory license we just discussed is limited to non-interactive uses, an *interactive* digital service provider (DSP) such as Spotify, Apple Music, and Amazon has to get a **voluntary license** from the owner of the sound recording. Otherwise they're out of business.

That's the big picture. Now let's take a look at the compulsory and voluntary licenses in more depth.

Non-Interactive Compulsory Licenses. How does a broadcaster qualify for a compulsory license? The rules are found in the riveting Section 114 of the Copyright Act, where there's a whole slug of requirements that boil down to making you act like a non-interactive radio station. For example, you can't announce your playlist in advance, there are limits on how many songs of a particular artist you can play in any three-hour period, there is a limit on the number of songs from a particular album in a three-hour period, and stuff like that.

If a broadcaster qualifies for a compulsory license, it pays statutory license fees (meaning rates set by the statute) to an outfit called **Sound-Exchange.** SoundExchange is a nonprofit organization whose board is made up of record company people, artists, and artist representatives. Essentially, it acts like ASCAP and BMI, meaning it collects fees from all the users, deducts its costs, and pays the balance to its members. Except, of course, that it's dealing with the performances of masters instead of songs.

SoundExchange collects substantial monies. In 2018, it collected over $950,000,000 (a double-digit increase over 2017), and it expects to go over $1 billion in 2019. SoundExchange divvies up the dough as follows: 50% to the record companies, 45% to the featured artists, and

5% to a fund controlled by the American Federation of Musicians (for non-featured musicians) and AFTRA (for nonfeatured vocalists) (see page 61 for who AFM and AFTRA are). The artist monies go to you directly, not through your label, so they can't be used to recoup any advances or costs. Thank your representatives in Congress.

The rates are incredibly complex. They vary with whether you're a **commercial webcaster** (an FCC-licensed station or other webcaster that puts its signal on the Net), an **educational webcaster** (like a college radio station), or a **non-commercial webcaster** (a charity, NPR, and the like). Also, within the commercial category, there's a distinction between subscription-based webcasters and ad-supported (free to the user) webcasters.

Got all that? Good, because there's more.

At the higher end, there are **SDARS,** which sounds like a lung disease epidemic but in fact means **satellite digital audio radio services** (the only one is Sirius XM); **BES,** meaning **business establishment services,** who pump music into restaurants, hotels, and tropical fish stores; **CABSAT,** standing for **cable/satellite services,** who deliver music over cable or satellite to your TV or set-top box; and **PES,** which means **pre-existing subscription services** that were in existence prior to July 31, 1998, like Sirius XM and Music Choice. Because the older subscription services have been around a while (and because they have strong lobbyists and lawyers), they get a senior citizen discount and pay about half of what others pay for the same service. Because this includes the massive Sirius XM, the record companies aren't exactly thrilled . . .

The rates are fractions of pennies for each performance, and if you really want to know the details (though I can't imagine why), head over to SoundExchange's website (www.soundexchange.com), click on "Service Provider," then click on the tab to the left that says "Rates" (I'm sure the exact clicks get changed now and then, but I'm guessing you can figure that out). When you've had your fill, be sure to "Like" them on their Facebook page.

Other than National Public Radio, there's a minimum per year for each service of $500 per channel or station, with a cap ranging from $50,000 per year to as high as $100,000 per year for the CABSAT/SDARS/PES folks. BES folks have a minimum of $20,000 per year. These minimums are advances against the per-performance fees.

Voluntary Licenses. If a performance doesn't fall within the statutory license (primarily this means performances on interactive services), then as we noted, the record company charges whatever the traffic will bear. In other words, this is a voluntary license between the record company (the owner of the master) and the DSPs. Note: unlike the compulsory license, all the money goes to the record company. That means artists are paid through their record deals, and the money is available for recoupment.

Under these voluntary license deals, the DSPs pay a percentage of their revenue to the labels, as we discussed on page 144.

To Interact or Not to Interact?

There are some legally interesting in-between types of services that are arguably interactive and arguably non-interactive. For example, Pandora lets you tell them what kind of music you like, then they customize a stream for you. You can also tell them whether or not you like each song, and the more feedback you give them, the better they get at pleasing you with their choices (at least in theory). So you sort of control the content, but not exactly—you can't tell them to play a specific song at a specific time. But you can shape what's coming at you.

The record companies argued that this made these services interactive, and therefore they had to get a voluntary license (which is much more expensive than a non-interactive license). The services had a very different opinion, saying they were non-interactive and therefore entitled to a compulsory license. This led the major record companies to sue a company called Launchcast (which had a service similar to Pandora's) for copyright infringement.

All the record companies settled this case except Sony, who took it to trial in New York. The trial court ruled in favor of Launchcast, saying their service wasn't interactive, and Launchcast won the appeal as well. So for now, these services are non-interactive.

However, some of the DSPs offer a mid-tier service (priced in between non-interactive and interactive), which has more interactivity, such as the ability to repeat songs, hear some material offline, maybe see the songs in advance, etc.). They can't get a compulsory license when they offer these features, so they have to go to the record labels and get a voluntary license. These deals look just like the interactive services deals; meaning they pay the labels a percentage of their revenue in the mid 50% range. This percentage, however, is applied to the lower fee charged for the mid-tier services (as opposed to the full interactive subscription fee for customers that get the fully interactive service).

Video Streaming

There's no compulsory license for video streaming, whether it's interactive or not. So the companies charge whatever they can get. We covered the rates that publishers and master owners get earlier (on pages 238 and 150). But these deals are worse than the deals for audio streaming.

Really?

Yeah, really.

Why?

It's not a pretty picture.

The DMCA and Its Not-So-Safe Harbor

The most important issue in video streaming is the **safe harbor** rule of the DMCA (see page 314 for what the DMCA is).

To understand what this is about, think back to the list of rights you get when you own a copyright. One of these is the right to *distribute* your work. In other words, if someone creates an infringing work, and someone else distributes it to the public, you can go after both of them (one sleazo infringed the duplication right, while the other one infringed the distribution right).

Under the DMCA (section 512 of the Copyright Act), there's an exception to this distribution liability. Specifically, a digital service provider isn't liable for distribution of infringing material if it didn't create it, post it, or know it was infringing. In other words, if one of the users puts up an infringing video, the DSP can't be sued for copyright infringement (you can only sue the dork who put up the video). The reasoning is that so much content goes through the DSP's pipes that they can't be responsible for every bozo who posts something. However, if the copyright owner gives the DSP a notice that says it's distributing infringing material, the DSP has to take it down. If it keeps distributing after the notice, then the owner can sue them for copyright infringement.

That all sounded reasonable enough when it came into being, but then YouTube showed up. Suddenly hundreds of millions of videos were being uploaded, and a lot of those infringed somebody's rights (for example, fans routinely put up an entire album, including the cover artwork). So a record company or publisher sends them a notice that says, "Knock it off," and they stop. Easy, right? Well . . .

What actually happens is what we in the industry call "Whack-A-Mole," named after the arcade game where a mole pops up, you bop it on the head with a mallet, and another mole pops up nearby. In other words, as soon as YouTube takes down a particular post, hundreds of identical others appear. So the copyright owners send out hundreds more notices. YouTube takes those down, and thousands more appear. Out go thousands of notices. Rinse and repeat.

Meaning, no matter how many notices you send, the lemmings keep coming.

Viacom sued YouTube over this, claiming that videos on YouTube were using a massive amount of Viacom television content (which they were). Viacom's claim was that (a) YouTube was chock full of infringing material (it was and still is); (b) YouTube knew it was infringing; and (c) YouTube could stop it if they wanted to. YouTube basically said, "Under the law, we don't have to stop it, and we don't want to."

After some legal wrangling, the courts agreed with YouTube. But the appeals and fighting continued hot and heavy. Finally, the case was settled. (There's a reported appellate decision, *Viacom International v. YouTube*, No. 10-3270, 2012 WL 113085 [2d Cir. Apr. 5, 2012] for the technical freaks, but there was a lot of action before and after that decision in the lower courts. If you're interested, google "Viacom vs. YouTube" and you can get a lot of information. There's some irony in that, since Google owns YouTube.)

Anyway, to date, no one has found a way to stop this practice, so the industry decided to just give a license to YouTube, on the theory that it's better to get something rather than nothing (which is what they were getting from sending take-down notices).

The music biz is not happy. YouTube streams more music than all the other sites put together, offers a fully interactive service on mobile (where most of the music consumption happens these days), and because they're advertiser based, they pay way less money than the subscription services (as we discussed on page 142). If the labels and publishers had the legal right to stop YouTube, they could stop or limit its ability to give away what the subscription services are charging for. But since they can't stop them (so far), they don't have that much leverage in the negotiations.

YouTube did start a paid subscription service, and made essentially the same deal that the subscription DSPs made. But at least as of this writing, it's dwarfed by the other services. And seriously dwarfed by the free YouTube music streams.

A late-breaking (at the time I'm writing this) development is that the European Parliament voted to do away with the safe harbor in Europe. That's really big—if YouTube can't stream in Europe without making a deal, they'll be forced to give better terms worldwide. The Parliament's vote is in essence an instruction to members of the European Union, telling them to get rid of the safe harbor in their country. However, the various countries aren't required to do this for two years, and meanwhile the tech folks are lobbying their silicon off in an effort to stop it.

WHAT HAPPENS WHEN SOMEONE RIPS OFF YOUR COPYRIGHT?

When someone uses a part of your song without permission, they **infringe** your copyright. And there have been a lot of high-profile copyright infringement cases in the music area over the last few years, the most notable being the "Stairway to Heaven" case, *Skidmore v. Led Zeppelin*, 905 F.3d 1116 (9th Cir. 2018), and the "Blurred Lines" decision, *Williams v. Gaye,* 895 F.3d 1106 (9th Cir. 2018). The "Blurred Lines" case is finished (the Gaye estate won), and Zeppelin is still ongoing at the time of this writing. Basically, as with every other copyright infringement lawsuit, they turned on the same issue: *Did you steal my song?*

If you think someone ripped off your song, you can sue them for it. But there are quite a few hurdles you have to jump over before you can back a truck up to their house and fill it with money, lamps, and rugs.

Here's the story:

1. First, before you can file suit, you have to either:
   a. Be the copyright owner, or
   b. Have an exclusive license of the rights that are being infringed, or
   c. Be what's called a **beneficial owner,** which means you sold someone your copyright in exchange for royalties, or
   d. Be a nutcase, but have $400 and know where the courthouse is. (Unfortunately, my clients have seen a number of these.)
2. Assuming you're one of those, you then have to **register** the copyright with the Copyright Office (more about that on page 337) before you can file the suit. Registration is also important because you can only sue for things that happened within the three years before you filed your lawsuit. So the later you register, the longer you have to wait before you can sue.

   To be more specific, you can only file suit for copyright damages *within three years after the infringement.* So if they stopped using the infringing materials more than three years ago, you can't sue them. If the infringement is continuing (for example, they're still streaming records with your song), you can file suit more than three years after the first infringement, but you only can recover damages based on monies earned in the three years before filing.

Some courts have held that the three years don't start until you either knew or should have known about the infringement (a concept called **delayed discovery**). In other words, if you never knew about the infringement, or couldn't reasonably have known about it, you can get damages all the way back to the first infringement, even if it was twenty years earlier. However, there's a cloud over this sunshine. The Supreme Court seemed to say (but not 100% clearly) that three years from the first infringement was absolute, even if you didn't and couldn't have known about it. [The case is *Petrella vs. Metro-Goldwyn-Mayer, Inc.,* 134 S.Ct. 1962 (2014)]. Because this opinion wasn't 100% clear, however, some lower courts still use the delayed discovery rule. To date it hasn't been decided by an appellate court, so feel free to give it a whirl.

There is also a recent case concerning registration that affects all this, but I've stuck it back on page 338 because it's a bit more technical.

3. Okay. You've registered and filed, what do you have to do to win?

4. The first thing you have to prove is that the thief actually copied your work. Since most infringers don't say "Yeah, I copied your song" (though some do, as you'll see), you have to prove they did. Maybe someone saw them copying your song. Or maybe they recorded their writing sessions and those recordings show that they were thinking of your song at the time.

This, of course, almost never happens. Usually you have to prove they copied you by showing the court that your work and theirs have a **striking similarity.** *Striking similarity* is a legal term that means the two songs are so much alike that it can only be explained by copying.

And of course this also rarely happens (though it can). Most thieves are smart enough to change the work a bit. Now what?

Even if there's no striking similarity between your song and theirs, you're not dead yet. You can still win if you prove that

(a) there is **substantial similarity** (this is a lower standard than "*striking* similarity") between your work and theirs, *and* (b) the infringer had **access** to your work.

There's no bright line for what *substantial similarity* means, and because each case is unique, there's not much guidance. The courts say it means more than "insubstantial" (duh), and more than "insignificant." If what was taken was really minimal (but of course attorneys have to use fancier words than that, so it's called **de minimis**), there's no infringement. If it was substantially similar and not de minimis, it's an infringement.

Access is a legal term that means they had a way to hear your song and rip it off. For example, someone gave your song to an artist, hoping they'd record it, and that artist later wrote a song that was substantially similar to yours.

In the early days of the Internet, some courts assumed there was access if your song was posted on the Web, even if you only had twelve hits. But that's been cut way back. With billions of postings on YouTube, the access test now requires that your song be very widely known (for example, in the top 50 on a credible record chart), or that it was in a genre that the thief listened to a lot, or in a section of the Internet where the thief went repeatedly. Things like that.

By the way, you don't need to prove there was access if you can show *striking* similarity (the test we first discussed) between your song and theirs. That's because of a concept called **presumed access,** which means a court will "presume" the thief had access to your song if the two works are *strikingly* similar. However, if they're only *substantially* similar, you need to show access.

But wait, there's more.

5. Okay, you've shown access and substantial similarity. Do you win?

    Maybe . . .

    Even if there's substantial similarity and access, there's no infringement if the infringer can prove they independently created their song. In other words, if someone writes a substantially similar song all on their own, without hearing your song, there's no copyright infringement—no matter how close the two songs are.

A particularly interesting case in this area involved George Harrison, who was found guilty of copying the song "He's So Fine" in his song "My Sweet Lord." George claimed he created "My Sweet Lord" without even thinking about "He's So Fine," and what's unusual about this case is that the court actually believed him.

But he still lost.

This case created a principle we call **unconscious copying.** That means he copied without being aware of it, because the song was very well-known and somewhere buried in his brain. (For the legal folks, the citation is *Bright Tunes Music Corp. v. Harrisongs Music, Ltd.*, 420 F. Supp. 177, 1976.)

6. Okay, you proved that this scumbag had access and didn't create his work on his own. Now you're a ways down the track. How far?

The next test is whether or not the material he copied is protected by copyright. In other words, you have to prove what he copied from your song was **original** to you. This means two things: (1) you created the material yourself (rather than copying it from someone else), and (2) what you wrote has some degree of creativity. For example, regarding (1), if you borrowed your melody from Mozart note for note, you didn't create anything, and the thief is free to use that melody. Or regarding (2), if your lyrics were "I love you with all my heart. You mean everything to me," they'd not only be boring, but also so commonplace that they don't have enough creativity to be copyrightable. (For the legal freaks, the primary case in this area is *Feist Publications, Inc. v. Rural Tel. Serv. Co.*, 499 U.S. 340, 345, 111 S. Ct. 1282, 1287, 113 L. Ed. 2d 358 [1991]).

A significant case about originality is the Rentmeester case, where a photographer took the original picture of Michael Jordan in his famous jumpman pose. That's the one where he's leaping in the air with his legs split and his arm extended holding a basketball (I'd be happy to print it here, but I don't want to get sued for copyright infringement. Google it.).

Nike liked what he did and licensed copies of the photo from Rentmeester for very limited use. Then they decided they wanted to use the image in a major way, but instead of paying the photographer for more rights to use the picture, they decided to stage their own photo of Michael Jordan in the same pose.

Mr. Rentmeester was not pleased. So he sued Nike, claiming they'd infringed the copyright in his photo by duplicating the pose.

And Mr. Rentmeester was even less pleased when the court tossed out his case, saying that he couldn't claim copyright infringement.

I don't know anything about ballet, but apparently Jordan's pose was inspired by a dance move known as a *grand jeté* (sounds more like a jacuzzi part to me, but hey). At any rate, grand jetés existed long before Rentmeester did. Also, the Nike photo was in a different location, meaning it had a different background and a different hoop. So even though Nike admitted copying the concept, the court (the law court, not a basketball court) decided there was no infringement because none of Rentmeester's original elements were used. (This case also illustrates the principle that you can't copyright an idea, just the expression of that idea.)

So the score is Nike 1, Rentmeester 0. (If you want to relive his sorrow, the case is *Rentmeester v. Nike, Inc.*, 883 F.3d 1111 [2018].)

The fact that the dance move preexisted the Rentmeester photo leads us nicely into another aspect of copyright infringement known as **prior art.** That means, as the name implies, that you can't claim you created something that existed before you created your work. This is an especially important element in music cases, as there are only twelve notes in a scale and they've been used a lot. In other words, if the thief copied a phrase in your song that's the same as a phrase used in forty songs that existed way before yours (prior art), you can't claim enough originality to sustain an infringement suit.

Another aspect of this issue is whether the infringed materials were just following a well-worn path of prior art. In other words, if the infringed material has to naturally flow from the genre or idea of the material, it's not protectable. For example, in the film area, if you make a space movie, it's not protectable just to have space ships, aliens, ray-gun battles, and things like that. And in music, there are standard blues chord progressions that you pretty much have to use (if you want to write the blues, anyway). Or if your song is a waltz, it has to be in ¾ time.

7. So let's say you're through those hoops. You've shown that the material they stole from you is original and protected. What's next?

Wheel out the operating table, because the court will now

dissect your work. If your song has some original elements and some that aren't original, they're going to toss out everything that isn't original. That's because you can only sue over stuff that's protected by copyright, meaning, original material created by you. For example, if you wrote new lyrics to the tune of "Old MacDonald," you couldn't sue over the melody, just over your new lyrics. Or if you wrote something using the standard blues progression, you can't sue over that chord structure, just your words and melody.

This dissecting is done very clinically. Experts make up charts of both songs, play recordings of your song and compare them to recordings of the other song, and then argue about what it all means. When they're done yelling, the court decides which parts are protected and which aren't. They then compare your protected parts against the thief's work to see if there is *substantial similarity* between the two (the test I mentioned earlier). If there is, we're on to the next hurdle. If not, you're off the track.

8. Well . . . you've shown that they copied protected material from you, and that their work is substantially similar to your protected work, and it's not de minimis. Are we there yet? Are we there yet?

No, honey, but I'll let you know when we are and I'll buy you an ice cream.

The tests above are all reasonably cut-and-dried. The way that the experts lay out the songs on a table and look at the words, notes, chord progressions, prior art, etc. is an **objective** test, based on the bones of the two works. Sort of like taking two pieces of paper with similar writing, putting one on top of the other, and holding them up to the light to see how much alike they are. Once you get past that, you arrive at the next test, which is a **subjective** one. In essence, that means, "Does it sound like an infringement?" Even if it looks very close on the objective scale, would someone listening to it think it came from your work?

If the answer is yes, do you win? Probably, but . . .

9. Even if the works sound alike and you prove they stole a protectable part of your work, the infringer may argue that his use was something called **fair use.** And if that's true, you lose.

Fair use is a complicated and pretty interesting area of the law that says you're allowed to use protectable parts of someone's work for certain purposes without permission (and without paying them). In other words, if you meet the legal tests, so that you've made a "fair use" of the work, there's no copyright infringement.

The fair use criteria are in Section 107 of the Copyright Act, but they're only a general description (as you'll see). The reality is that every fair use case is very fact-specific. Which of course makes lawyers happy, because we get to argue about which foot will fit into the Cinderella slipper.

So here's what the Copyright Act says:

A fair use is not a copyright infringement if it's "for purposes such as criticism, comment, news reporting, teaching (including multiple copies for classroom use), scholarship, or research." It then lists things you should consider in deciding whether you went over the line into infringement territory. However, it says the factors determining fair use *include* the things on their list, which means you can look at other stuff as well. (See what I mean about it being a "general description"?)

Anyway, here's the list in Section 107. To determine if there's a fair use, you need to look at:

(1) the purpose and character of the use, including whether it's a commercial use or nonprofit educational purposes. It's okay if there's some commercial aspect involved, but the more there is, the stricter the test.

(2) the nature of the copyrighted work (the one that's been copied). The courts have distinguished between creative works (songs, novels, paintings, etc.) and factual works, such as nonfiction books and directories. Creative works have more protection, as you'd expect.

(3) the amount and substantiality of the portion used in relation to the copyrighted work as a whole. The general principle is that the more that's used, the less likely it's fair use. However, there's an argument that using even a small portion that is the "heart" of a work could go over the line.

(4) the effect of the use upon the potential market for or value of the copyrighted work. The question here is whether the new work would be a substitute for the original in the marketplace and therefore financially hurt the original. For example, a *Saturday Night Live* parody sketch of a movie isn't going to hurt the market for the movie; in fact, it most likely helps. But a parody song that uses most of the elements of the original song might in fact be a substitute for the original.

As I said, fair use is always going to be very fact specific, meaning it's hard to know with certainty whether you've got one. An easy example would be a professor at a nonprofit college who copies a few paragraphs from a book into a classroom handout (clearly a fair use) versus someone who copies an entire book and sells it to the students (clearly not). In between, things get hazy.

A major issue that's come out of the courts in determining fair use is whether the use is **transformative.** This concept started with a music case that went all the way to the Supreme Court, over 2Live Crew using the lyrics of "Pretty Woman" in a rap song. The background is that they tried to license the song, got turned down, then went ahead anyway. So the owners of the song sued them for infringement. To the industry's surprise, the Supreme Court held there was no infringement because the new use parodied the original song by satirizing the idea of what was "pretty," and used the song in an entirely different setting. The case is *Campbell v. Acuff-Rose Music,* 510 U.S. 569 (1994).

Since then, there have been a number of cases on transformation, including some fun things like superimposing Leslie Nielsen's head on the pregnant body of Demi Moore (that was held to be transformative and a fair use). If you want to see an assortment of goodies to better understand the concept, Google "transformative use copyright cases."

To make this even more fun, the courts in various parts of the country have a difference of opinion. Two of the circuit courts held that using copyrighted material to create another work is transformative and fair use, but one circuit said it's an infringement because it's just another derivative work (see page 213 for what "derivative work" means).

Unless and until the Supreme Court weighs in, we'll continue to live in Fuzzy-Land.

Okay, honey, we're there. What flavor ice cream do you want?

I Won! . . . Now What?

If you prove someone infringed your copyright, what do you get? Some of this is peculiar to the copyright (and also trademark) world. Here's how it works:

1. **You get the fair market value of the use they made.**
   For example, if they rip off your song in a commercial, and that use of the song is worth $25,000 in a marketplace deal, you can get $25,000.

2. **You can recover the infringer's profits.**

If the sleazeball made a profit using your work, you can recover his profits, which may be more than the fair market value of the usage. (If you pick this remedy, you don't also get fair market value.)

3. **You can get an injunction.**

That means the court **enjoins** (stops the infringer from using) the infringing work. If they continue to use it anyway, they're subject to substantial fines, and sometimes even jail.

4. **You can recover statutory damages.**

Statutory damages are a real copyright original. This is where you can't prove actual damages—for example, your infringer was not only a thief, but also a bungling businessman, and he lost money with your rip-off. Or maybe his profits are so well hidden that you can't find them. In this case, if you registered the copyright before the infringement commenced, the court can give you anywhere from $750 to $30,000 for a single infringement (this is per act of infringement, not the number of copies actually made; for example, putting out 100,000 CDs with your song is still only one act of infringement). The judge can raise this to $150,000 if it's a willful (intentional) infringement, and can lower it to $200 for an "innocent" infringement.

5. **The court can order destruction or seizure.**

The court can grab, or make the scumball destroy, all the infringing copies. This is also not a common remedy outside the copyright area.

6. **If the infringement is willful, there are criminal penalties.**

An interesting bit of history is that the Marx Brothers stole some poor schlub's copyright for a radio show and were convicted of criminal copyright infringement.

7. **You can get your costs.**

You can get back your court costs and, to a limited extent, you can recover your **attorney's fees.** The latter is unusual, because you usually don't get attorney's fees even if you win a lawsuit.

If you're on the *Advanced Overview Track* and are in a group, go to Part IV (Chapter 21) on page 343.
If you're on the *Advanced Overview Track* and you're not in a group, go to Part V (Chapter 22) on page 357.
Experts, keep rollin'.

20

Even More Advanced Copyright Concepts

SOUND RECORDING COPYRIGHTS

It may surprise you to know that, prior to 1972, the United States had no copyright protection for a sound recording itself. I'm now talking about the physical, master *sound recording* (not the musical composition). And pirates were making a lot of money by duplicating sound recordings and not paying anyone.

This smelled like thievery (which it was), but there was no federal copyright in the sound recording to stop them from duplicating. The companies did pretty well by suing pirates under the copyright laws of individual states—there was no federal law, so they had to go to the states (and these state laws have interestingly become important in the last few years; more about that in a minute).

In 1972, Congress enacted a full-fledged, legitimate copyright law provision dealing with piracy (which is now Section 114 of the Copyright Act). It prohibits the unauthorized duplication or dubbing of a sound recording that was created on or after February 15, 1972, by creating a copyright in the actual recording. (This is in addition to a separate copyright in the musical composition.) It is imaginatively called a **sound recording copyright.**

One of the most interesting aspects of this sound recording copyright is what it did *not* protect. While it's clear you can no longer duplicate records without consent, the sound recording copyright doesn't prohibit a "sound-alike" recording, no matter how closely you duplicate the original. In other words, nothing in the sound recording copyright stops you from hiring a singer to imitate the original artist, or hiring a band that sounds just like the original recording, regardless of how close you come. Of course, you still need to license the song, and you have to disclose that the recording isn't the original. If you didn't label your record as an imitation, you'd run afoul of various trademark and unfair practices laws, which deal with the proper labeling of goods (and thus stop you from defrauding the public into thinking they're getting the original when they're not). These are the same laws that stop you from calling a cereal Grape Nuts if it's not made by Post, even if it has exactly the same ingredients.

Not So Happy Together

So the sound recording copyright is good for masters created after February 15, 1972, but there's no federal sound recording copyright for pre-'72 masters. Recently, that little quirk came back to life like some monster in an old horror movie. And the villains this time?

The digital streaming services (our old friends, the DSPs).

Remember, as we discussed on page 144, the DSPs pay out each month on the basis of how many plays you get compared to the total number of plays on their service. Well, these oldies had a fair amount of play, so they should've gotten some of the money. But the DSPs said they didn't have to pay for them because there was no sound recording copyright. Accordingly, they allocated a share of their revenue to the old masters (based on their number of plays), carved that chunk out of what they paid everyone else, and stuck it in their pockets.

As you can imagine, the recordings of the Beatles and a lot of other classic artists get a helluva lot of play on these services, so they were not pleased. This led to a number of lawsuits over this issue, essentially using the state law claims that were used to shut down pirates before the sound recording copyright existed.

The biggest case was headed by the RIAA (an industry group that represents the major labels), and there was also a **class action** led by the Turtles (*class action* means that a lawsuit on behalf of everyone similarly situated, which in this case meant everyone who owned pre-1972 masters and wasn't suing on their own).

The result was mixed—some states said there was protection, while others said there was no performance right in the sound recordings. Most of the cases were settled, though some are ongoing. Anyway, all this shook up the streaming services enough to support a section of the **Music Modernization Act** (see page 239) called the **Classics Protection and Access Act.** The Classics Protection section says it's *not* creating a copyright for the pre-1972 masters, but instead gives the owner of a pre-'72 master the same rights to collect money that owners of post-'72 masters have. In essence, for interactive services, this means the labels now license pre-1972 masters to the DSPs on the same terms as post-'72 masters. For non-interactive uses, the Classics Act says the pre-1972 masters are subject to the same compulsory licenses as the new stuff, meaning they get paid by SoundExchange at the same rate as post-'72 masters.

Interestingly, unlike federal copyrights, state law copyrights have no expiration; so in theory the old stuff could have been subject to payment longer than the new recordings (like . . . forever). Under the MMA, however, there is now a limit on how long you can get paid for pre-1972 recordings. Specifically, it's 95 years from first publication (meaning release to the public), but there are some extensions of this 95 years for older masters. If a master was first published before 1923, you get until December 31, 2021. If it was first published between 1923 and 1946, you get five years beyond the 95 years. If it was first published between 1947 and 1956, you get an extra 15 years on top of the 95.

The party's over for all pre-1972 masters on February 15, 2067 (95 years after the effective date of the 1972 sound recording act).

HOW TO TERMINATE A COPYRIGHT TRANSFER IN YOUR SPARE TIME, FOR FUN AND PROFIT

As noted on page 312, the 1976 Copyright Act lets you undo any deal (for songs created on or after January 1, 1978) thirty-five years later (we'll talk about the pre-1978 songs later, on page 333). So if you sell your song to a publisher and have a lifetime of regret, you can get it back after thirty-five years by merely sending a notice (remember, this is only for the United States; you're still stuck for the rest of the world).

Here's how to do it.

You can give a notice of termination no less than two years, nor more than ten years, before its effective date, and that effective date has to be within five years after the end of the thirty-five-year period. To be more precise, if the grant of the work covers publication, which it almost always does, the right to terminate is effective on the sooner of forty years from the grant, or thirty-five years from publication. This protects you even if the work is never published.

This is easier to understand if we use some actual years. For example, if a copyright was transferred and published in 2000:

Year of Publication: **2000**

Years in Which Termination Can Be Effective (From 35 to 40 Years After Publication): **2035 to 2040**

First Year That Notice Can Be Sent (10 Years Before First Possible Effective Date): **2025**

Last Year That Notice Can Be Sent (2 Years Before Last Possible Effective Date): **2038**

If you really want to know the details, take a look at Sections 203 and 304 of the Copyright Act, which you can find online.

The Sonny Bono Copyright Term Extension Act, which we discussed on page 311, added some frills to this. They are:

1. Previously, only a living author, surviving spouse, or surviving children or grandchildren could exercise the right of termination. Now, if none of them are alive, the author's estate can do the honors.
2. There's a second bite at termination rights for pre-1978 copyrights, which I'll go over in a minute.

Remember, as we discussed previously, this termination only applies to U.S. rights. If you sold off your copyright in foreign territories, *Quel dommage.*

Attempts to Avoid Termination

As much as the publishers would love to avoid termination, Uncle Sam says no. The copyright law says that nothing you do with the termination rights is valid until you actually have the rights back—in other words, you can't sign them over to anyone until you actually have them in your fist. The only exception is that you can make a deal with the guy whose rights are about to be terminated after you've sent the notice. In other words, if you send a notice to the publisher saying the termination is effective three years from now, you can make a new deal with that publisher during the three years before the rights come back, and that's enforceable. This gives the current publisher a head start, because they can make a deal (and pay you for the rights) before anyone else can.

EXTENSION RIGHTS

Extension Recapture

So Congress took care of folks who wrote songs after 1978, by giving them the right to get out of a stupid deal after thirty-five years. But what about the oldsters who made stupid deals?

There's a transitional quirk thrown into the 1976 Copyright Act that takes care of the pre-1978 copyrights. (If you weren't writing prior to 1978, or aren't the heir of such a writer, you can skip to the next section on terminating sound recording copyrights. This isn't mandatory; feel free to read this for your general education, but I don't suggest driving or operating heavy machinery afterward.)

As we touched on earlier, pre-1978 copyrights lasted for a period of fifty-six years (the twenty-eight plus twenty-eight we discussed on page 310). The 1976 act extended that to a period of seventy-five years, meaning it added nineteen years to the fifty-six years that already existed. And as we discussed, this has now been extended to ninety-five years.

In 1976, in addition to extending the life of the copyrights to seventy-five years, your congresspeople gave the author (or his or her heirs) the right to take back the new nineteen years. The recapture procedure is similar to that for termination rights of post-1978 copyrights (the right to terminate after thirty-five years, which we discussed in the prior section). It's done by giving a notice no sooner than two years, and no more than ten years, before the beginning of the nineteen years (i.e., no more than two years, or later than ten years, before the end of the fifty-sixth year).

For example, if a song was first published in 1972, the fifty-six years expire in 2028. So, beginning in 2018 (ten years before the end of the fifty-six years), and ending 2026 (two years before), you can give a notice to be effective in 2026. After the effective date of the notice, the nineteen years added to the copyright (the extension from 2026 to 2045) belong to the author, or his or her heirs. As with the termination rights, this is only for the United States. The rest of the world has still gone bye-bye.

Just like the thirty-five-year termination, Congress gave the original publishers a nice perk. The law says that, before the extended term actually comes into effect, but after giving a termination notice, the person who got the original grant can make a new deal for the added nineteen years. So the original publisher has the ability to buy the rights at least two years before any outsider, and therefore has an advantage in getting them. Unless the publisher has really been a jerk during the first fifty-six years (which is no small "unless"), it can usually keep the copyrights.

Now enter the Sonny Bono Copyright Term Extension Act of 1998, which added twenty years to the copyright term and made the extension period thirty-nine years after the original fifty-six years (in other words, a total of ninety-five years). They also threw in (at no extra charge) an added bonus: If your right to recapture came up before October 27, 1998, and you forgot to send the termination notice, you get another bite. At any time within five years after expiration of the first seventy-five years (the old fifty-six, plus the nineteen you blew), you can get back the newly added twenty years.

What Exactly Did I Just Get Back?

So you've sent your notices, waited until the magic date to get your rights back, and are ready to rumble. What exactly did you just get handed? Can you now do anything you want with those rights?

Well, it's not exactly simple . . .

A provision of the termination/extension law rights says that the original publisher can no longer license any new works, but they can continue exploiting derivative works created while they owned the song (see page 213 for a definition of *derivative works*). And for a while, this derivative work exception looked like it was going to be a loophole you could drive a truck through. The opening act was a U.S. Supreme Court case involving the appropriately titled song "Who's Sorry Now." (If you want to look it up, it's *Mills Music v. Snyder*, 105 SCT 638 [1985].) In this case, the publisher (Mills Music) acquired the rights to "Who's Sorry Now" from Ted Snyder and two other writers. Snyder went to that Great Songbook in the Sky, and in 1978, his heirs exercised their right to terminate the last nineteen years. (So much for the idea that the initial publisher can hang on to the songs.)

After termination, Mills Music argued that all of the *records* it had licensed were derivative works, and therefore it had the right to collect mechanical royalties for sales of these records after termination. As you can imagine, Mr. Snyder's heirs took a contrary view. They felt these rights should come back to them, so they could then license the record companies (and get all the money). The decision flipped back and forth until it came to the U.S. Supreme Court (known to its friends as "the Supremes"). In a closely divided decision (five of the nine justices in favor, four opposing), the Supreme Court found that indeed the records were derivative works, and that the money from them went to Mills Music, the terminated publisher. Mr. Snyder's heirs had the right to money from future recordings, but not the existing ones. Sorry, all you little Snyders.

After *Mills Music*, two other cases dealt with the scope of a publisher's right to hang on to derivative works. The first was *Woods v. Bourne Co.*, 603 F.2d 978 (2d Cir. 1995), where the terminated publisher argued that every piece of printed music was based on the original lead sheet, and therefore the right to put out sheet music forever belonged to the old publisher (see page 283 for what a lead sheet is). The court kicked the publishers' butts on that one, holding that new versions of printed music weren't derivative works and therefore belonged to the new publisher.

Next came *Fred Ahlert Music Corp. v. Warner/Chappell Music, Inc.*, 155 F.3rd 17 (2d Cir. 1998), where the court made the derivative work exception even narrower by saying that the reissue of a master recording with a different catalog number was not a derivative work, even though it was the same recording. Accordingly, the new publisher of the song could issue the mechanical license (and get the dough).

So, as you can see, the sentiment in the later cases is to expand the rights of the person getting back their copyrights. Stay tuned to this channel; as the older copyrights tick on and terminations become more prevalent, there may be some more interesting law.

Sound Recording Copyright Terminations

The right to terminate transfers of sound recordings, which started coming up in 2013 (thirty-five years after the 1978 act), is a fascinating area. What's happening is that artists are sending termination notices to record companies, and the companies are fighting back.

Since the earliest days, record contracts have all had language that says the sound recordings are "works for hire," and remember there's no termination right for works for hire. (Take a look back at page 307 if you want a refresher on "works for hire"). To be a work for hire, however, you need more than just that language. As we discussed previously the work has to fall into one of several specific categories (see page 308).

One of the "work for hire" categories is a "collective work," and the record companies argue that masters are contributions to a collective work (an album) and are therefore works for hire. They also throw in any other arguments they may have in each specific situation (for example, the form or timing of the notice might have been defective).

In virtually every instance of which I'm aware, the companies and artists have come to an agreement to settle the claims. The companies offer better terms under the deal (higher royalty, advances, etc.), and the artist generally goes along. In part, this is because a fight would be incredibly expensive, and it's also because the stakes for the record labels are very high. If they get a court decision that says masters aren't works for hire, it could cost them all their old masters. So they will fight to the death. On the artist side, however, they're only fighting about a few masters that many times don't earn enough in the United States to justify the expense of litigation (remember terminations are only for the U.S.). Also looming in the background is the idea that neither side necessarily wants a court result—if it favors the company, the artist is stuck with an old deal, and if it favors the artist, the companies lose massively on their catalog. So they compromise.

There was recently a class action filed on behalf of artists over this very issue. A class action means that it covers everyone who's similarly situated, so it's more economical to have an expensive fight. This could bring the issue to a head, but at the time of this writing, it's way too soon to tell.

THE COPYRIGHT NOTICE

The copyright notice (other than for sound recordings) is a © followed by the year of copyright (the year that the work was first fixed in tangible form). The symbol for sound recordings is ℗. Look for these on your CDs, assuming you still have any.

Copyright notices are much less significant under the 1976 Copyright Act than they were under the old law, because the consequences of leaving it off, or making a mistake in it, are no longer very serious. (Under the old law, you could lose your copyright.) It's not worth getting into all the niceties, but nowadays a notice basically just protects you from someone saying they had no idea the materials were copyrighted—in other words, they can't say they were an "innocent infringer." (You don't get a free pass if you're an innocent infringer, but it could affect how much you have to pay if you get nailed.)

For songs, the copyright notice is primarily significant for printed music. That's because you need only put a notice on "visibly perceptible copies" of something. Since you can't "see" a song by looking at a digital file or CD, there's no need to have a copyright notice for the song.

So why do you see copyright notices on CDs? Good question! The reasons are:

(a) sometimes the lyrics are printed inside, and since they are "visually perceptible," you need a copyright notice;
(b) there is a copyright in the album cover artwork; and
(c) there is the sound recording copyright notice.

REGISTRATION AND DEPOSIT

The Myth

It's a myth that you get a copyright by registering your work with the Copyright Office. As we discussed, you get a copyright by fixing the work in tangible form.

However, registering a copyright with the Copyright Office gives you certain legal remedies you don't otherwise have, so you should always do it if you're going to commercially exploit your work. But the failure to register doesn't affect the validity of your copyright. So if you're a beginning songwriter, it's probably not worth the money until someone bites.

The old trick of mailing a copy of the work to yourself actually accomplishes something. It's sometimes called a "poor man's copyright," but that's not true. Remember, you already have the copyright by putting it in tangible form. The only thing you get from mailing it to yourself is a clearly established date on which you created your work. So if someone rips it off at a later date, you can prove your work was created before theirs.

If you're going to do this, send it by certified mail and don't get excited and open it when it arrives; store it in a safe place, and let a judge open it if someone ever gets cute.

Having a date-stamped digital file accomplishes the same thing, though I'm told (anecdotally, not reliably) that digital dates may be manipulated. If that's true, then this evidence isn't as strong as a letter.

If you've posted your song to a website, that's pretty reliable info, but you have to be sure the site keeps track of the date, and of course that the site is still in business when you have an issue.

Why Register? Let me count the ways . . .

If your work is going to be commercially exploited (released on records, used in a film, a commercial, etc.), you should register with the Copyright Office. If you don't, you lose the following goodies:

1. You can't collect compulsory license royalties (see page 215).
2. As we discussed earlier, you can't file an infringement action unless you've first registered the copyright. That means you can't recover damages or stop someone from using your song until you've registered. You're allowed to wait and register just before you file the lawsuit, but it's a better idea to take care of it as soon as you know there's going to be a recording (because of numbers 3, 4, and 5 below).
3. A recent Supreme Court case held that you must have a registration in your hand before you can file your lawsuit. (For Supreme Court stalkers, the case is *Fourth Estate Public Benefit Corporation vs. Wall-Street.com*, 138 S.Ct. 720 [2018]).

   Before that case, some of the lower courts said it was enough for you to have *filed* the registration, but now it actually has to be *issued* (meaning the Copyright Office has officially accepted it in their records) before you can sue. And waiting for the government to grind your registration through its gears can mean a delay of up to nine months after filing. Which means a delay before you can file your lawsuit. So today it's an even better idea to get going early if you've got a record coming out.
4. If you don't register within five years after first publication of the work, you lose the **legal presumption** that everything in the registration is valid. This mumbo jumbo basically means that if you do register within the five years, a court will assume that everything in your registration is correct, and the infringer has the burden of proving it's not. If you don't, you have to prove it's correct.
5. You can't recover attorney's fees, nor can you get **statutory damages** (see page 328), unless you registered before the infringement happened.

You can get the forms you need to register (and in fact register electronically) at www.copyright.gov, unless that's now become an Amazon subsidiary.

Deposit

A separate requirement from registration is the obligation to deposit copies of "the best edition" of your work within three months after publication. If you don't, there's no loss of copyright, but there are penalties and fines. The purpose of this is to keep the Library of Congress overflowing with tons of crap that nobody has ever heard of, and the system works quite well. You can deposit CDs or sheet music for songs, or if your work is unpublished, or published only in electronic form, you can deposit electronically.

MORAL RIGHTS

In a number of countries outside the United States, there's a legal concept known as **moral rights,** or by the snooty term **droit moral** (which in French means "moral rights," and in Czech means "no parking"). The concept (among others) is that an author can stop any mutilation of his or her work, even though they may have parted with it long ago. For example, the creator of a painting (even though it's been sold four or five times) could stop someone from cutting it into smaller paintings, drawing mustaches on it, etc. Similarly, the author of a musical work can stop substantial changes in the music or lyrics. And you also get the right to stop someone from falsely attributing your work to someone else.

The United States has never recognized a moral rights concept for music (even though it is required to do it under something called the Berne Convention, which is a multi-nation treaty designed to protect creative works). The best we've done is a limited moral right for paintings and fine art. Accordingly, to the extent you want any protection, you gotta put it in your songwriter/publisher contract, as we discussed on page 293. And, in virtually every contract, you'll be asked to waive (meaning give up) your moral rights, which you'll have to do.

If you're in a group, keep straight ahead.
If not a group, go to What's in a Name, on page 357.
If you're bored, take a nice walk around the block.

PART IV

Group Issues

21

Groups

If you're a member of a group, everything in this book applies to you. But you also get a whole set of treats that don't concern individual artists. Let's take a look at them.

GROUP PROVISIONS IN RECORD DEALS

There's a whole section in group record deals that isn't in a solo artist's contract. It spells out what happens if the group breaks up, or if one individual (a prima donna or the only rational member, depending on your side of the fence) decides he or she no longer wants to play with the others.

Key Members

Most agreements will say that a breach of the record deal by one member of the group is treated as a breach by all members of the group. In other words, if one member refuses to record with the others, the whole group is in breach. This is not such an unreasonable position if we're talking about the lead singer or main songwriter or key instrumentalist, but it's not so hot if we're talking about a percussionist who neither sings, writes, nor knows what state he lives in.

To handle our percussionist friend, we who represent artists gave birth to the concept of a **key member.** Under this system, a few folks in the group are listed in the contract as *key members,* and if a key member leaves the group or otherwise breaches the agreement, the record company can treat that as a breach by the whole group and exercise its various options (which we'll discuss in a minute). If anyone else screws up, it can't.

This is something you have to ask for—no company uses a key member concept in its form agreements. Also, as you might imagine, working this out has been known to rankle bands—the people who aren't named as key members can get their noses out of joint. It also puts the lawyer/manager in the position of dealing with who's key and who isn't, which can sometimes make non-key members feel like their representatives are "playing favorites." However, as you'll see, it isn't always so great to be a key member.

The Company's Rights to Leaving Members

What can the company do if a member (key or not) leaves the group?

1. All companies provide that, if a member leaves a group, the company has the option to get his or her services as a solo artist (and as a member of any other group). This is reasonable enough—without it, you could get out of your record deal just by leaving the band.

    Even when you have a key member concept, however, the company will want the right to pick up *all* leaving members, key and non-key alike. I like to argue that the company has no business (or usually interest in) keeping the services of non-key members, such as our percussionist. (This is also how you sell the percussionist on not being a key member—if he decides to leave the group, he can split from the record company and make his own deal, while a key member can't. But if the company insists on the right to pick him up as a soloist, even if he's not a key member, it scraps this argument.)

2. The company gets the option to keep the members who *don't* leave the group (assuming, of course, there's not a total breakup).

3. The company has the option to terminate the members who didn't leave, since the group is no longer the one they signed. Note this means, if they don't exercise their option for the leaving member, that the deal is over. So make sure that only a key member's leaving can trigger this right.

4. There's a relatively new concept that some companies are using, regarding band reunions. It says that, if 75% or more of the band gets back together within five years after the deal was terminated for any one or more of the members, the company gets to reinstate the deal for the band. This is to keep you from breaking up to get out of the deal, then having a miraculous primal therapy session that gets you back together the next week. From your point of view, keep the period as short as possible.

By the way, if they've picked anyone up as a soloist before your reunion, those deals stay in effect even if they reinstate the overall band deal.

Leaving Member Deals

The person leaving the group is cleverly called a **leaving member.** The terms of a leaving member's solo agreement are spelled out in the group's deal and are almost always less favorable than the deal for the group. The record company's position, which is understandable, is that the soloist is an unknown quantity, whereas the group was the reason for making the deal. Success is by no means assured—there are many cases of soloists who have left groups to fall flat on their faces (as well as those who have been more successful than the groups they came from). If the group is important enough, the soloist's royalty may be close to or the same as the group's, but the advance is almost always substantially less, and the commitment is usually for one album at most (sometimes only demos). As your bargaining power increases, so does your ability to negotiate these clauses, particularly if a member of a group has been emerging as the star, or had an earlier solo career.

As a practical matter, no matter how funky the leaving member provisions are, the company is often willing to negotiate better terms when the breakup happens.

TRIVIA QUIZ

Name the lead singers who have had solo careers after leaving the following groups:

1. The Police
2. White Stripes
3. Destiny's Child

Name the groups from which the following soloists came:

1. Justin Timberlake
2. Neil Young (*not* Crosby, Stills, Nash & Young)
3. Eminem

(Answers on page 356.)

Deficits

What happens to the group's deficit (unrecouped balance) when a soloist sets out on his or her own? Suppose a group breaks up and is $500,000 unrecouped. The company then picks up one member as a soloist, who streams in the billions. Can the company take his or her solo royalties to recoup the group's $500,000 deficit? Conversely, if the group was recouped but the soloist is a flop, can the company use the group's royalties to recoup the soloist's deficit?

Many companies, at least in their first draft contract, take the right to do both these things. If you ask, however, they will sometimes agree that only a pro-rata share of the group's deficit can be charged to the soloist, though this is harder for key members. For example, if there are five members of the group, only one-fifth of the deficit ($100,000 of the $500,000 in the above example) can be carried over to a solo deal. Conversely, if you ask, they'll also agree only to charge the soloist's pro-rata share of *group* royalties with the *soloist*'s deficit. Companies will sometimes agree not to charge the soloist's share of group royalties with a deficit under the solo agreement, but this takes more bargaining power.

You should provide that, if the group continues to record without the soloist, no *future* group deficits can be charged to the soloist's account or to the soloist's share of group royalties. It's not uncommon for a successful group, after a key member leaves, to record several dud records, which then eat up all the old, successful record royalties. If these flops also eat up the ex-member's royalties on the successful records, he or she will be, shall we say, perturbed.

For example, suppose Harvey leaves the group after making four successful albums. Because the group did well, it's fully recouped, and Harvey retires to that dream house in Elk's End, expecting to live on his future royalties from these four albums. The group, without Harvey, then goes into the studio and runs up $1,000,000 trying to make the next *Sgt. Pepper's Lonely Hearts Club Band*, which streams three hundred times. If you don't change the form, the company will take Harvey's royalties from the four successful albums and use them to get back the $1,000,000 it spent on the flop. Harvey will not be pleased.

Most companies will agree not to charge future costs against a person who has left, because the leaving member doesn't participate in the future records' royalties and thus shouldn't bear the costs. But you gotta ask.

INTERNAL GROUP DEALS

Why You Need an Internal Contract

Suppose there are two plumbers in Bugtussle, Kentucky (there really is such a place; Google it if you don't believe me. And I'm pretty sure they have at least one plumber . . .). If these plumbers decide to go into business together, they know enough to have a lawyer write them a partnership agreement. Or at least go to Legalzoom.com and get a form. On the other hand, groups earning tens of millions of dollars sometimes never get around to formalizing their relationship. And, every once in a while, this neglect bites them in the butt.

The time to make an agreement among yourselves is *now*, when everybody is all friendly and kissy-face. When you're fighting with each other, particularly if there's a lot of money on the table, you may find yourself killing the goose that lays the golden eggs, as well as supporting the Retirement Fund for Entertainment Lawyers.

One of my early experiences as a music lawyer was trying to solve the problems of a major group who'd never formalized their relationship. One of the two founding members got pumped up by a relative, who told him he was the real star of the group (even though he didn't sing or write). So he tried to stop the other guy from using the group name. Because they were set up as a corporation, with equal votes, they got so deadlocked that they couldn't agree to pay the phone bill. We had to go to court and ask the judge to appoint a neutral third director to break the tie. The court chose a crusty ex-judge, who wore a three-piece suit with a watch chain. He'd done this for many bitterly fighting corporations and was supposed to be the tiebreaker that finally let the corporation move forward. Well, His Honor lasted about three months, saying, "I've never in my days seen anything as nasty as this," before disappearing into the sunset and leaving behind a large bill.

The upshot was that the litigation lasted more than nine years, and it cost the parties more than a million bucks in legal fees. The group was killed early in the process, and the fellow who started the fight ended up broke. All of which could have been avoided with a simple agreement and a few hours of planning.

So pay attention and take care of it now. I know, nobody likes to talk about negative stuff (like breakups) when everything is working well. But, believe me, when everything is going well is *exactly* the time to discuss it, because you can do it in a friendly way. It's like insurance— you may never need it, but you'll sure be glad you have it if you do. So find a third party (like a lawyer) to blame for raising the issue, so you don't have to take the heat. (I routinely say that I'm the jerk insisting on this, so you can be a good guy.) Or show everyone this page and highlight this paragraph.

But enough fatherly advice. Here's what you should do. (I'm referring to folks as "partners" in this discussion, though there may be a different legal structure, as we'll see later.)

The Most Important Asset

Can you guess what your most important asset is?

Apart from your good looks, charm, and talent, your most important asset is the group name. So, whatever else you do, by all means figure out what to do with your group name if there's a fight. In fact, if you only deal with your name in a written agreement, I will be happy (but not ecstatic; to get me there, you have to deal with everything).

You have to think through everything about the group name, such as what happens if:

1. The lead singer and songwriter leave the group.
2. The drummer who doesn't write music or sing leaves the group.
3. Three out of five members leave to form another group.
4. The group breaks up and everybody goes back to Waxahachie.

Obviously, there are about ten thousand other possibilities, but all of them can be covered with a few general rules. You can of course do anything you want, but the most common solutions run along these lines:

1. No one can use the name if the group breaks up, regardless of how many of you are still performing together (short of all of you, of course).
2. A majority of the group members performing together can use the name. For example, if there are five people in a group that breaks up, any three of them together can use the name.
3. Only the lead singer, Sylvia, can use the name, regardless of who she's performing with.
4. Only George, the songwriter who founded the group and thought of the name, can use it, regardless of who he's performing with.
5. George and Sylvia can use the name as long as they perform together, but if they don't, no one can use it.

If one or two people really created the unique sound of the group, I've always thought they should have the right to use the name. That's because the others alone wouldn't truly represent the group to the public. On the other hand, many groups operate on a "majority rule" principle, regardless of that spirit. And I'm sure we can both name successful touring groups who've replaced the lead singer over time. So anything you can imagine is okay as long as everyone agrees and it has some rational basis that a judge can understand. Just do *something*.

What happens if you don't do anything? As you can gather from my previous horror story, the law is not very helpful. In fact, there is very little law on the subject (surprising as that sounds). That's because most disputes are settled privately, even though they may start as lawsuits. The cases that have gone the distance turn on the question of whether the performing members are deceiving the public. The argument is that one or more key people are the "essence" of the group, and anyone using the name without them defrauds the public. And that gets decided by a judge whose favorite singer is probably Wayne Newton.

If you think this sounds messy and expensive to resolve, you're right. So solve it yourself. *Now!*

Percentages

The next important thing to decide is everybody's percentages. It may surprise you to learn that there are many bands who, despite laughing, giggling, and slapping high-fives onstage, are in fact owned or controlled by one or two people, and everybody else is merely a hired hand. Being a hired hand doesn't necessarily mean you're on a salary—you can be a hired hand and get both a salary and a percentage of the profits. It does, however, mean you serve at the will and pleasure of the employer, which actually makes for a rather pleasant band atmosphere—somehow the knowledge that you could be out on the street tomorrow keeps people's attitudes a lot healthier than if they think they have a lifetime gig. (Hiring people usually isn't practical for new artists, because you don't have the money to pay them much of a salary, if you have any money at all. So most of the time with new bands, everyone works for a percentage of the future pie.)

Assuming you're all going to be partners, how should the profits be shared? Again, there are no rules. You can do it any way that makes you happy. The simplest way, of course, is to split things equally—if there are five of you, everyone gets one-fifth, or 20%. This is common in new bands, but it can become a source of irritation if some members work harder or contribute more than others (such as handling all the media interviews). Another approach I've seen (with a band that was built on a core of two people who were together for a number of years before the others joined) gave the two founders a bigger percentage than the others. And frankly, even when everyone has been together from the beginning, there may be one or two key members who deserve more than the others.

By the way, nothing says you have to use the same percentage for all areas. Sometimes bands split evenly on concert monies (on the theory that everyone is out there sweating together) but have different splits for records, merchandising, television performances, etc.

Control

Just as ownership doesn't need to be equal, neither does control of the band's decisions. Normally you vote in proportion to your percentage of profits, but this isn't carved in stone. So even if your percentages are equal, one or two key members may control the vote—for example, they may have two votes where everybody else has one. Or it can be set up so that the group can't act without one of the key members agreeing, regardless of how many people want to do it. The possibilities are endless, but they need to be thought out carefully. For example, try not to have an even number of votes, because this allows a **deadlock** (meaning an equally divided vote where nothing can be done). If you have an even number of votes, you could have a third party like your manager break the tie, but it's way better to do it inside the group.

Songwriting/Publishing

Another common issue is how to handle publishing. Does everyone own the songs (or shares of songs) that they create? Meaning that every time you write a song, you agree on the percentage everyone contributed, and each writer owns that percentage of the song? Or are all the songs split evenly, maybe owned by a group entity, regardless of who wrote them? I've certainly seen both, but the majority tend to have the creators own their share of the songs individually. Over time, with big success, it can also become a source of resentment if someone is getting substantial money from songs they didn't write.

Outside Activities

Can any of you do something outside the group? For example, can you have a solo career, or a side project with another band? Or individually endorse a product (say a drum set if you're a drummer)? And if so, do the earnings from that belong to the individual, or does the band share in it?

Most of the time, unless someone joins the band who already has a solo career, side projects require the band to agree, and things get worked out case by case. If there's an agreement up front to allow outside projects, the agreement will say that the band has to be the **first priority,** meaning the soloist can't take on something that would interfere with the band's schedule of recording, touring, publicity, etc. That of course means first priority for your time (you can't schedule an outside activity while you're supposed to be on tour with the band), but it also means there can't be any other kind of interference (for example, you couldn't endorse Coke as a soloist if the band is sponsored by Pepsi).

Other Issues

Here are the other major issues in a partnership agreement:

Firing. What kind of vote does it take to fire a member? Majority? Unanimous of everyone else? (Unanimous of everyone doesn't work, since the guy being fired usually votes the other way.)

Hiring. What kind of vote is required to take in a new partner? Or to hire a lawyer, agent, or manager? Majority? Unanimous? When my son Danny was twelve, we came back from vacation to discover that his band had hired a manager and keyboard player without even asking him. It ultimately broke up the band. Yours could be next.

Quitting. Is everyone free to quit at will? Note this only concerns leaving the other band members. You're not free to quit under your record deal, and if you're in the middle of a tour, you're not free to walk out on the concert promoters without getting the teeth sued out of your mouth.

There's no way to force someone to continue working with a group, but you can penalize them if they don't. For example, you can stop him or her from working as a musical artist after quitting, require the member to pay his or her solo earnings to the partnership (meaning the other group members get a piece), and require him or her to pay for any damages caused by their leaving. On the other hand, I've always been in favor of letting people go if they're unhappy, as long as they don't walk out in the middle of a tour or otherwise leave some third party hanging. Why force someone to stick around and make both your lives miserable?

Incurring Expenses.   What kind of vote do you need for the group to spend money? It's common to say that some extraordinary issues, like borrowing money or spending over a certain dollar amount, take a bigger percentage vote than day-to-day expenses.

Contributions.   What kind of vote do you need to make partners contribute to the partnership (translation: put in money)? For example, if the group needs dough to buy equipment, cover unexpected expenses, etc.?

Amendment of Partnership Agreement.   What kind of vote does it take to change the terms of the partnership deal? For example, can a majority vote reduce your percentage? Or does it take your consent?

Death or Disability.   What happens in the event of your death or disability? Your partners don't usually want your surviving spouse or parents voting on partnership matters (not likely they'll get onstage and sing). For this reason, there's normally a buyout (see the next section), and you're treated as if you'd quit the partnership or were terminated.

Ex-partners.   If you quit or are terminated as a partner, do you keep your same percentage level for past activities (almost always "yes")? Do you get a percentage of future activities (almost always "no")? Do you get bought out of your share of assets of the group, and if so, at what price and over what period of time?

Buyouts

Here's a buyout provision used by one of my clients for leaving partners:

Price.   The price of the buyout equals the leaving partner's percentage of all "hard" assets owned by the partnership. "Hard" assets means things you can touch (sound equipment, instruments, cash, etc.), as opposed to "intangibles" (such as the group name, recording contracts, etc.). For example, if the hard assets are worth $100,000, and the partner had a 25% interest, his or her share of the assets would be worth $25,000. This is usually done on a "value" as opposed to "cost" basis, because used equipment is generally worth less than the cost. It can also be done on something called "book value," which is an accounting concept meaning the "value" on the books of the partnership. *Book value* is typically the original cost minus some scheduled factor of depreciation that's worked out by your accountant. Of these three methods, book value is likely to be the lowest, although it's possible the real value could be less. Cost is the least accurate measure of anything.

I specifically provide that there is no value given to any intangible rights. First, I think they're very difficult to value, if not impossible, and it's expensive to hire an appraiser to give an opinion. Second, and directly tied in, is the fact that the value may be very different after someone leaves the group. For example, if the lead singer/songwriter goes, the group name and record deal may be worthless. Conversely, a new lead singer might join and make things a lot more successful than they were before. Also, I think the leaving member's contingent payout (discussed in the Contingent Payout section below) compensates for the intangibles—in essence, that's a form of valuing them.

You should know that not everyone agrees with this approach to intangibles. There are certainly situations where a name is worth a lot of money after the group has broken up. For example, the Beatles, the Doors, and Led Zeppelin still generate tons of dough from the use of their names in merchandising, and it's not illogical to give an ex-member some reduced piece of materials created after the member has left. (Note, if the band breaks up, everyone continues to own their shares of the name.) Despite all that, and despite the fact that it could arguably create an unfair result, I still like my way. You can't know in advance what a particular member will really contribute to the value of the name, or how much value will be added or lost after that member leaves. And figuring it out after the fact makes lawyers rich. So in this client's deal, we say there is no value given to the intangibles.

Cash Payout. In the partnership deal for this band, the value of hard assets is paid out over a period of two years, at the rate of 25% each six months. Thus, in our $25,000 example, $6,250 would be paid six months after termination, $6,250 paid twelve months after, and so forth. Because the total isn't paid up front, the leaving partner usually gets interest on the unpaid balance.

The reason for structuring a payout over time is to protect the remaining members from having to come up with a big chunk of cash (which they may not have). Also, it's not uncommon to provide that the terminated partner can look only to the assets of the partnership for his or her buyout payments. That means the other individual partners aren't personally responsible if the partnership tanks and has no money to pay.

Contingent Payout.   The leaving member(s) get their continuing percentage from activities of the partnership in which they participated. This means royalties from records they played on, monies from merchandise using their names or likeness, concerts and TV shows in which they performed, etc. (Remember, there are special record contract provisions about leaving members, which may affect their continuing royalties. See page 344.) In this deal, the leaving members don't get any portion of group earnings from performances and other activities that happen after they leave.

Legal Ethics

You should be aware of a common ethical problem that groups have. As we discussed on page 57, a lawyer who represents a group and draws up a partnership agreement has a built-in **conflict of interest.** A conflict of interest, called in shorthand a **conflict,** means the lawyer represents two clients whose interests are adverse to each other. So if a lawyer represents the partnership, he or she can't take sides and represent any one of you against any other of you. However, this is exactly what making a partnership agreement requires, because the various members' best interests aren't the same. For example, extra chunks of money going to Sylvia have to come from the others, whose best interests are to keep them. Same with voting percentages. (A manager, business manager, or agent who counsels you about group matters also has the same conflict, though lawyers are subject to strict ethical codes that don't apply to others.)

This situation, of course, happens every day, so those of us in the industry are used to dealing with it. And all ethical lawyers will advise you of its existence. You can do one of two things:

1. Each member can get independent counsel (which may or may not be affordable) to negotiate the agreement among yourselves.

This also takes a long time and can be destructive if anyone decides to be a hero. However, it's the best way to do it.

2. Far more commonly, the lawyer explains all the issues to you openly, and then lets you decide among yourselves how you want to resolve them. In this case, the lawyer doesn't represent any of you, but rather just acts as a "secretary," writing down whatever agreement you reach on your own. If you use this route, your lawyer will ask you to sign a conflict waiver, which says he or she has explained the conflict to you, and you're going ahead anyway.

Corporation versus Partnership

Once you've decided all these issues, how do you set yourself up? The choices are a partnership, LLC, or corporation, and the major differences (as we discussed on page 189) are the tax-planning aspects, the liability limitations, and the fact that corporations are more expensive to set up and run. By *liability limitations,* I mean that corporations limit the assets that can be grabbed by someone suing you. In a corporation, if you handle things properly, they can only get the assets of the corporation. With a partnership, however, they can grab both the partnership's assets *and* the personal assets of *every partner* (that means you). While these are nice benefits of corporations, they're offset by the increased cost of setting up and running the suckers, so it's marginal in your early stages. Also, as we noted earlier, a corporation doesn't protect you from record company liability (because of the inducement letter we discussed on page 190), nor does it protect you from copyright infringement liability (as we discussed on page 188).

A limited liability company, or **LLC,** is basically a partnership, but it provides the limited liability of a corporation (though it has the same exceptions to liability we just discussed for corporations, meaning it doesn't shield you from claims by your record company or copyright infringement claims). Because an LLC is as cheap and easy to use as a partnership, it's the vehicle du jour for many groups.

The mechanical difference between a partnership or LLC and a corporation is that, if you want a partnership or LLC, you need one agreement, and if you want a corporation, you need two agreements. Specifically, for a partnership you need a written partnership agreement, and for an LLC, you need a **member agreement** (the owners of the LLC are called **members**). For a corporation, you need: (1) a shareholder agreement (meaning an agreement among the shareholders of a corporation), and (2) employment agreements between yourselves and the corporation or the LLC.

To sum up, if you don't have a written agreement, most states have laws that spell out what happens—generally everybody owns everything equally and has an equal vote—which may not be what you want. So I highly recommend that you do your own agreement. As we just discussed, there are complicated issues to solve, and you'll be *way* better off doing it yourself rather than leaving it to the ding-a-lings in your state capitol.

Answers to quiz on page 345:

Groups:

1. The Police—Sting
2. White Stripes—Jack White
3. Destiny's Child—Beyoncé

Soloists:

1. Justin Timberlake—NSYNC
2. Neil Young—Buffalo Springfield
3. Eminem—D 12

22

What's in a Name?

RIGHTS IN A NAME

A number of years back, a band named Green Jellö changed its name to Green Jelly to avoid a dispute with the owners of the Jell-O trademark. While the group ultimately got some good publicity from all the flap, having a name that steps on somebody else's toes can be a serious problem.

The most common problems don't come from naming your band after snack foods, but rather from another group that used the name before you did. And this is equally important if you're an individual, especially if you're not using your real name. Or sometimes even if you are using your birth name (No, I'm not *that* Paul McCartney . . .)

So when it comes to your name, there are two legal things to deal with:

1. Before you start, you have to make sure nobody is already using your name; and
2. Once you're clear, you have to take some steps to keep other people from ripping it off.

Check It Out

You should figure out if someone else is using your name as soon as possible, ideally before you use it. If you use someone else's name just on Facebook, SoundCloud, Bandcamp, FanBridge, or some similar site, you might get a snippy letter, but you can usually work it out (see page 360 for how things get worked out). Things get way more serious when you release music or start touring over a wide geographic area. And changing a name once you've built up a following is not a happy event.

If you're about to sign a record deal and someone can stop your label from putting out your music, it could cost the label a lot of money. And if it does, the record company will turn to you with a handful of "gimme"—every record deal makes you guarantee that they can use your name without any legal hassles, which means you have to pay for the mess if there is one.

After being stung by a few of these situations, most record companies now check the names of new artists before they release music. Their goal is to determine (a) if someone is currently using the name, and whether they started using it before you did, or (b) whether someone used it awhile ago and still has some recordings available or is planning a reunion. Unfortunately, there's no way to ever be 100% sure, but here's what the record companies do, and you can also check these sources on your own:

1. **The Internet** is a great way to do your preliminary searches.
    a. Try looking up your name on a search engine, like Google or Bing, to see what comes up. Also try social networking sites, like Facebook, SoundCloud, Twitter, Bandcamp, FanBridge, or Last.FM. Look for YouTube videos and also check some of the music websites like Spotify, Apple Music, Amazon, Discogs.com, Billboard.com, Allmusic.com, and Artistdirect.com. However, this is only a starting point: Finding your name doesn't mean the other band or person is still around using the name (bands break up regularly, in case you didn't notice, and artists retire to paint landscapes in Farmersville). Just as important, not finding your name doesn't mean it's clear.
    b. Look for your name at *www.whois.com*, which is a registry for websites. Just start entering some website addresses in your browser, and use variations, like yourname.com or yournameband.com or yournamemusic.com, and so forth. This could not only lead you to another band with your name, but also let you know whether you can get a domain name registration for your website.
    c. It's a good idea to lock up your domain names before you become popular. If you don't, the pirates will swoop down as soon as your name means something. More about this on page 364.
2. The U.S. Patent & Trademark Office has a website where you can search federal trademark applications and registrations.

Go to http://www.uspto.gov/trademarks-application-process /search-trademark-database. Searching there can get awkward (what government procedures aren't?), but this can be a good jumping-off point.

3. California and many other states have a website that lets you check public records for corporations and limited liability companies that might have names similar to yours (in California, it's http://kepler.sos.ca.gov/). Because so many groups hang out in California, it's not a bad idea to take a quick look there even if you're in another state.

4. The U.S. Copyright Office also has a searchable catalog for copyright registrations from 1978 to the present. This can be another source for locating names of groups. Go to the following link: http://cocatalog.loc.gov/cgi-bin/Pwebrecon.cgi?DB =local&PAGE=First. When you get there, search under "Title." However, if your name is a common word, this could be a waste of time because you'll come up with a lot of irrelevant information.

5. If the record companies don't find anything in the above sources, they order a **comprehensive trademark/service mark search** to look for registrations, as well as other listings of the name and anything similar. It currently costs about $400 for a preliminary search, and about another $1,200 to $2,200 for an in-depth one, which is cheap insurance in the long run. There's an even more extensive search known as a Music Media search, which is offered by CompuMark, whose address is listed below. That's an excellent search if the bucks are available. (Whichever search your label uses, it's recoupable from your royalties.)

These comprehensive searches are conducted by independent search companies and by lawyers who specialize in trademarks. (If you use an independent search firm, it's a good idea to have the report reviewed by a trademark attorney who can advise you whether anything you found might be a problem.) Here are a few searchers:

CompuMark (800) 692-8833, www.compumark.com.
Corporation Service Company (800) 927-9800, www.cscglobal .com/global/web/csc/trademark-search.html.
CT Corsearch (800) 732-7241, www.corsearch.com.
Fross, Zelnick, Lehrman & Zissu [a law firm with a lot of music experience] (212) 813-5900, email: fzlz@frosszelnick.com.

As noted above, searches can never be 100% foolproof (for example, there may be a local band that hasn't registered a service mark but has been performing under your name for years). But it's the best you can do.

IMPORTANT NOTE: When your record company does a search, *they're doing it to protect themselves, not you.* Also, their goal is to sell music, so their search will focus on recordings and music group names. But if you plan to use your name in another product category—like T-shirts, headphones, perfumes, hamster earmuffs—they're not likely to search those areas. The record company might consider it safe to use your name for their purposes, but not all the uses you may want. And if they screw up the search and something goes wrong, it's your rear end that's on the line.

If your search turns up a group or person using your name, or using a name that's similar to yours, you have to deal with it. (If you find a name that's similar, you'll need a legal opinion as to whether or not it's too close—the test is whether the public is likely to confuse the two of you.) Most of the time you can contact the other group and work out a deal. If you find them and discover that they broke up or abandoned the name, they may have lost their rights and you don't need to worry about them. But you need a legal opinion on this. Also, some of these groups never give up dreaming, so even if the band name looks dead, if it's the same as yours, it pays to still look into it more deeply. For example, you might find they're on the eve of a reunion.

If they're still using the name, and if they're willing to change it, they'll want to get paid. The most common deal is the payment of a lump sum in exchange for their drifting into the sunset (usually in the range of a few thousand dollars to maybe $20,000 or so, though it can get into six figures if they smell blood). But whatever you do, be sure you buy out all rights. Sometimes the other artist wants to license the name to you and keep ownership of the mark. Don't do this. For one thing, you'll be building up goodwill for a name you don't own, and in addition, you'll have to live with this license for your entire career. Which means they're always in your professional life.

If you do make a deal, you'll need a knowledgeable lawyer to draw it up because this is a very tricky area. *Never* try to handle this kind of deal by yourself.

By the way, making a deal doesn't assure you of total peace. For example, you might buy out the New York dude, only to later find some other guy was using the name in Seattle, and that he started before the one in New York. Or there might be a girl in Dusseldorf who was using it before any of them. In that case, you're back to square one (actually, square *eins* in Dusseldorf), minus several thousand bucks.

Occasionally, the other folks in this situation think they've got you by the squeezable parts, and they hold out for enormous sums of money. When you get one of these, or if you come across someone who simply won't sell the name, you have to change yours. Sometimes you can keep part of the name by adding something to it, but you need to add something distinctive that clearly separates you from the others. For example, if you were using the name Silver and found that it was taken, you might call yourself Denver Silver. (I always think of that great scene in the movie *Spinal Tap* where they talk about having been called the Originals, only to find another group had that name, so they called themselves the New Originals.) But this procedure is tricky, and you'll need legal help.

Protecting Your Name

Okay, you checked things out and you look clear for takeoff. How do you make sure some yo-yo can't grab your name as you fly down the road to stardom?

The way to protect yourself is by getting a **service mark,** which is similar to a **trademark**—a trademark is a name used for *goods* (like Heinz ketchup, Kleenex tissues, etc.) and a service mark is a name used for *services* (like Delta Air Lines, Tommy's Dry Cleaners, Chloe's Colon Cleansing, etc.). In the United States, you get rights in a mark by actually using the name. To get federal protection, you have to use your name in **interstate commerce** (meaning commerce between two states). That's simple to do these days: just put your music and other materials on the Internet. Or send an email blast to your fans in more than one state.

In addition to using your name in interstate commerce, you also need to have the name associated with you in the mind of the public. The legal name for this association is **goodwill,** meaning people feel good vibes when they hear the name because it makes them think of you ("goodwill" is what people in 1900 called "good vibes"). In other words, if your name makes the public scratch its head or think of their Uncle Clarence, you don't have much. But if your name makes them think of your gigs, your recordings, your merch, or whatever other weird stuff you do, then your name has turned into a **trademark with goodwill.** And when that happens, it's yours and no one else's. Congratulations!

Once you've established a trademark with goodwill, you can even stop names that are different from yours but are similar enough to confuse the public. That's because the public might think it's you or a spin-off group. There's a famous case from the 1920s where Charlie Chaplin stopped someone from using the name "Charles Aplin," and there's an even more fun case where the Dallas Cowboy Cheerleaders stopped the porno film *Debbie Does Dallas* from calling its star an "X Dallas Cheerleader." (For you research freaks, the case cites are *Chaplin v. Amador*, 93 Cal. App. 358 [1928]; and *Dallas Cowboy Cheerleaders, Inc., v. Pussycat Cinema, Ltd.*, 604 F.2d 200 [2d Cir. 1979].)

In the United States (though not everywhere, as we'll discuss shortly), your rights come from *using* the name, *not* from registering it. (There's one exception to the requirement that you actually use a name, called an **Intent to Use,** but hang on; we'll get to that on page 363). **Registration** means filing a public notice in the U.S. Patent & Trademark Office that tells the world you claim a particular name, and you get some major rights if no one opposes you and the Feds okay your registration. More about this in the next section.

Another important area in trademark is something called **dilution.** Historically, you only got trademark protection in the specific area where you did business. In other words, if you were a phone company named Presto, you probably couldn't stop a massage parlor from using that name, since people wouldn't think their massages were coming from your phone repairmen. Nowadays, there's a law that says using a famous name in another area *dilutes* the value of the original trademark, and it may be possible to stop the massage parlor. So, for example, even though the Beatles don't have a record label under that name, you couldn't get away with a company called Beatles Records.

REGISTRATION

At some point in your career you want to file a **registration** of your service mark. *Registration* tells the world that you're using a particular name and that the name has goodwill attached to it (or more accurately, it tells everyone in the United States; foreign protection is a different story, as we'll discuss on page 364). Registration also establishes a date on which you were using the name, and creates a **legal presumption** that you own it. A *legal presumption* means that the other user has the burden of proving you *don't* own it; without the presumption, you have to prove you *do* own it. Also, in addition to this basket of legal goodies, a registration makes sure that your name shows up in any search that somebody else does (see point 5 on page 359). Plus you get to use the symbol ® with your name on the items you've registered for, which is ultra-cool, don't you think?

You can get federal applications from the incredibly sexy website of the U.S. Patent & Trademark Office, at www.uspto.gov. You can also call them at (800) 786-9199, or email them at usptoinfo@uspto.gov. While I hate to tell you this, you can file an application online. I *really* don't recommend it; this area is very tricky and technical. I strongly suggest that anything having to do with these rights be run through a trademark lawyer—even with my experience in music law, I wouldn't do it myself.

If you're a group, or if you're thinking of having a company hold your service mark (rather than you holding it personally), it's really important to get that nailed down before you file an application. The application has to be in the name of the owner of the mark (meaning the one who controls the use of it), and if you use the wrong applicant, your application is worth less than a broken guitar pick. So if there's any disagreement over ownership, get it sorted out before you file.

Do You Have a Reservation? There is one major exception to the requirement that you use a mark to get rights. You can register an **Intent to Use** before you actually use a name, *if* you have a genuine intent to use the name in the not-too-distant future. If you're the first one to file an Intent to Use, then even if someone else uses the name before you do (but after you file), you can stop them after your registration is issued.

You can turn the *Intent to Use* into a real, live registration application by filing evidence that you've actually started using the name. The evidence only needs to be something that shows you've used your name in interstate commerce, such as making your music available on the Internet, or sending out a multistate email blast.

If you don't file this evidence within three years after the government okays your application, then your application is declared invalid, turns into a frog, and you have to start all over.

After filing your application, it can take a year or more to get the registration. And that's if everything goes smoothly (your tax dollars at work). First, the guys in the federal Patent & Trademark Office check around to see if someone already has a registered mark that they think is too close to yours. If they do, your application gets bounced, and you can start squabbling with them. If you get past these guys, the Patent Office publishes your name in the *U.S. Official Gazette* (so if you haven't made it anywhere else, at least you can happen there). This is so that anybody who reads the *Gazette* (don't you and all your friends?) can object to registering your name because it's too close to theirs.

Once you're registered, you have to continue using the name in order to keep up your rights. In fact, there's a legal presumption that you've abandoned the name if you haven't used it for three years. (*Presumption* means that you have to prove you didn't abandon it, as opposed to the other guy having to prove you did.) However, if you use a name continuously for five years after your registration is issued, you can file something called an **Affidavit of Incontestability,** which is fancy talk for saying that no one can ever come along and claim they had the name before you did (actually, they can still give you a hard time, but it's really tough for them).

Foreign Registration.   Many countries of the world have a registration system similar to the United States, but I doubt you could stay awake through a discussion of different territories' intricacies (and in fact, I don't really know them because I fell asleep during the lecture). Foreign registrations are only meaningful when you're having success on an international scale, but at that point you should start registering in other countries. At a minimum, you should register in major territories such as Australia, Canada, Japan, and something called an **EUTM registration,** which is a single registration that covers all twenty-eight countries of the European Union, including the United Kingdom—at least until they leave the EU, which might have happened by the time you read this. If they've actually Brexited, you'll have to file in the United Kingdom also.

Unlike the United States, many territories (notably the EU and Japan) have a **first to file** rule, which means that someone who's never used the name could file ahead of you in a particular territory and stop you from performing there. Since only a moron would rip off the name of a dud group, this isn't usually important until you're having some success. But when you do, start registering pretty quickly. Filing outside the United States is expensive, so focus on places where you'll be making the most dough (or whatever "dough" is called in Turkistan).

Domain Name Registration.   As noted earlier, once you're committed to a name, it's a good idea to check if anyone else owns that domain name (see the discussion of using www.whois.com on page 358). Be sure to check ".net" and ".org" as well as ".com," not to mention things like ".biz" and ".porn." If the name is clear, it's usually worth the money to register it as a domain name, so you can set up a website at some point in your career. You may also want to register on the major social media sites (Facebook, Instagram, Twitter, YouTube, SoundCloud, Tumblr, etc.).

All these "dot whatevers" (.com, .net, .porn, etc.) are called **top-level domains (TLDs)**. (The full name of each website (like www.your name.xxx) is called a **URL** [meaning **Universal Resource Locator**]). There are now so many TLDs that it's cost-prohibitive to buy up your name in every one of them (there really is a .porn, and there are tons of others that you can find by Googling "TLD list." Some pretty weird stuff in there, like .boo, .plumbing, .rehab, and so forth). Because the TLDs are endless, the best you can do is grab the ones you think are most important to what you're doing, and when you're really famous, steel yourself against the inevitable pirates who will grab some of the others. Most artists let the pirates do their thing as long as it doesn't create confusion with your fans (meaning the pirate site doesn't look like it comes from you). If they go over the line, you can look into stopping them, but that's not cheap.

In any event, owning a URL is nothing like a federal trademark registration, and doesn't give you any trademark rights. It's more like a telephone number—useful to have, but without the other protections, not much more than a locator.

Logos. Some artists come up with a distinctive logo. That gives you another level of identification with your fans, even beyond your name (for example, the Rolling Stones' lips with the tongue sticking out). If you want to use a logo, all the same rules about searching and registering your name as a trademark also apply to registering your logo. And you have to register the logo separately from the name (meaning more expense).

In addition, the artwork in your logo (if it's original enough) is protected under the copyright laws, which means you want to get a copyright registration for it as well.

If you didn't do the logo artwork yourself, then the artist who created it would own the copyright. You can argue it's a work for hire (see page 307 for what that means), but as we discussed earlier, that's very difficult without a written agreement. So always get the artist to sign a written transfer of the copyright to you. And do this even if your best friend created your logo—friendships have a way of fraying when there's a lot of money involved. I strongly recommend you get a lawyer to help you with this one, because it's a tricky area.

By the way, if you take an image for your logo from a website that rents or sells images (called **stock images**), be sure to read their terms and conditions carefully. Most stock images are for limited uses in ads or artwork, and they specifically prohibit using the images as a logo. Even some big companies get into trouble over this. However, there are online logo vendors that run contests for logo creation, where you can get all the rights you need. But you still have to read carefully to be certain you're getting all rights, and even when you do, you have to make sure that your logo doesn't infringe somebody else's.

So, to recap: Names are a very complicated legal area, requiring careful analysis of your specific facts. If you have any problems with your name, no matter how small you think they are, you MUST get a lawyer. Do not ignore the problem—it will only lie there sleeping until you're successful, at which point it will wake up and chomp a large gash out of your rear end.

PART V

Touring

23

Personal Appearances—Touring

Now let's see what happens when you hit the road, to get up close and personal with your fans.

ROLES OF TEAM MEMBERS

Here's what your team does when you tour:

Personal Manager

Your personal manager is the chief executive officer of your touring life. He or she ensures that your agent is bringing you the best touring options (read "hounding the agent on a regular basis"); helps you decide which tour is right for your career; works with the agent to make the best possible deals for you; and mechanically makes the tour happen. More specifically, he or she coordinates and supervises:

1. Booking the tour (in conjunction with your agent) by making deals with the **promoters** (the people who hire you, rent the hall, advertise the event, etc.; see page 375 for more about promoters).
2. Overseeing rehearsals, hiring band members, watching the finances.
3. Hiring the crew and making sure they do their jobs.
4. Transporting people and equipment, booking flights, hotels, trucks, buses, etc.
5. Collecting money on the road.
6. Coordinating advertising, marketing, and radio and Internet promotions, both in advance and while you're in each city.
7. Handling day-of-show activities, such as interviews, meet-and-greets, etc.

8. Putting out whatever fires crop up (such as missing equipment, improper advertising, dates that aren't selling well, lapses in security, etc.).
9. Dealing with illness, cancellations, or other assorted disasters. This is a really tough part of the job, because the manager and agent have to reschedule the dates and sometimes refund money to fans. And by the way, no one gets paid for any of this, since you're losing money.

With bigger artists, a lot of these jobs are delegated to a tour manager and/or tour accountant. But the personal manager is ultimately responsible, and the buck stops with him or her.

Agent

The agent, in conjunction with your manager, books the tour. He or she makes the deals with the promoters (which includes picking promoters that will produce the show professionally and not disappear with your money). At the early stages of your career, they'll be pounding promoters to book you. At the later stages, they'll be pounded by promoters to book you.

Agents also put together **packages,** meaning shows with two or more artists playing together. When done right, this grows your audience. And even if you're established, it can expose you to different audiences who wouldn't have come if you weren't touring with that troupe of dancing donkeys.

In addition, agents, along with your manager, help with the promoter's marketing of the tour. Over the last number of years, tickets are going on sale earlier and earlier, sometimes as much as a year ahead of the concert date. And because people know they can buy a ticket later from a ticket broker, there's not the rush of sellout of tickets that used to happen in the past. So marketing the tour, and sustaining it over the period while tickets are on sale, is critical. And because the agents handle so many tours, they have a lot of experience in this area. For example, they might get your promoter's marketing plan and compare it to marketing plans of other artists they represent. In other words, the agents have so much knowledge that the promoters can't jive them by skimping on the marketing plan.

Your agent and personal manager also help you with the following decisions about your tour:

Itinerary. Your **itinerary** is (a) your tour routing (which cities and in what order) and (b) which venues you play in each city. If you're the opening act for a major tour, setting the itinerary means you show up when you're told. If you're headlining, the itinerary is critical. Proper routing can save or lose you a bundle of money. While it may seem obvious, the tour has to be planned so you don't end up going from New York to Oregon to Florida in a four-day period. However, concert venues are not available at all times (not just because they're booked by other artists, but because they have basketball games, hockey games, tractor pulls, etc.), and the juggling act of matching routing with availability is a truly artistic maneuver.

Image. How does the tour work with your image? This is twofold:

1. If you're an opening act, is the headliner compatible with your audience? If you're a heavy metal band, for example, you probably shouldn't open for the Osmond Family Reunion tour.
2. What venues are you playing? It says one thing if you play a brand-new 5,000-seat amphitheater in a high-end neighborhood, and it says something else if you play an older, 3,500-capacity hall with no seats, on the funkier side of town. In other words, you want to be in a venue consistent with your image, and in the right part of the city for your fans.

Skating Through the "Radio Promotion" Jungle. Ever notice how many radio stations either "present" a concert, or else have concert tie-ins, ticket giveaways, live reports, etc.? That's because radio exposure is a critical element of selling tickets. These promotions never happen by chance; they're always carefully planned. Apart from just picking the right station, it has to be done in a way that doesn't upset the other stations in the market (who might promptly drop your record). For that reason, it's almost always coordinated with the radio promotion people at your record label.

When to Put the Tickets on Sale. Simple answer: when you're hot. If you've got a lot going on, you want your tickets out there, even if the dates are far away.

Pricing of Tickets. Although your first reaction may be to "grab all the gusto you can" by charging the highest ticket prices the market will bear, this decision isn't so black-and-white. Many managers and agents are squarely within this camp, and their thinking is persuasive: Nobody knows how long things will last, make hay while the sun shines, get 'em while you're hot, etc. On the other hand, many respected managers and agents take a different view, feeling that a lower-priced ticket draws more people (particularly younger people, who can't afford expensive tickets), creates a bigger buzz, and in the long run is a better career-building move. Also, even when they're very successful, some bands keep a low ticket price as a way to say that they're putting their fans ahead of their business. (Keep in mind, when you're setting prices, that ticketing charges [like Ticketmaster] get slapped on top, and these can be as much as 40% of the price.)

This pricing debate is also related to where you are in your career—if you're an established artist, you needn't worry as much about building for the long term.

Most popular artists straddle the pricing issue at the same event: They **scale** their tickets (*scale* is an industry term for setting ticket prices) to charge more for up-front seats, and less for the back of the house, so that all kinds of fans can afford to come. And by charging more for up-front tickets, they also take a bite out of the scalper business (which of course means the artists make money rather than have the scalpers grab it).

Speaking of secondhand tickets, sites like StubHub!, SeatGeek, Vividseats, ScoreBig, eBay, Craigslist, Razorgator, and TicketsNow have become important sources for tickets. This is known as the **secondary market,** meaning a place where tickets are resold after their first sale. Ticket brokers (the ones you see advertising hot tickets at outrageous prices) are also players in the secondary market, but the Internet ticket sites have kicked them back quite a bit.

Over the last few years, some artists have taken a number of their tickets and put them through a secondary player like StubHub! or a **platinum ticketing service** run by the promoter for the *initial* sale (as opposed to the second sale after someone already bought it). The theory is that the true value of prime tickets isn't the face value, but rather what someone is willing to pay in the secondary market. This practice is known as **competitive pricing** or **dynamic ticketing,** which is similar to airlines, where computer algorithms set prices based on demand. Why shouldn't the artist have those monies, rather than some yahoo who takes no risk in producing the show, going on the road, etc.?

Pre-sales.   The ticket scalpers have developed sophisticated **bots** (automated computer programs) that rush in to buy tickets ahead of everyone else. They also jam the system so that real fans get frustrated and give up before they get their tickets (which then drives them to the secondary market, where tickets harvested by the bots are for sale). In response to this, some artists use a **verified fan** program, to assure that real fans get access to the seats. The basic idea of these programs is that, if you show that you're a real fan, you get a code that puts you ahead in line to buy tickets. The specifics vary, but for example you might need to show that you're a fan club member, or that you bought merchandise, or watched music videos, or posted on social media, etc. This idea of getting tickets to fans ahead of the public sale is called **pre-sale.**

Another pre-sale practice is for credit card companies (like American Express and Citi cards) to offer a certain number of tickets to their cardholders in advance of the public sale. This seems to work best with heritage artists, whose fans are older (and have credit cards). In exchange for access to the tickets, the credit card company puts up money for advertising, and sometimes pays a "bounty" for each ticket they sell (meaning money on top of the ticket price).

Pre-sales are also done through fan clubs if you have one (see page 416), and if you're doing this, the number of tickets you sell through your fan club is built into the promoter deal. There are also pre-sales by the venue itself, by local organizations who use them as fund-raisers or perks, and by gas stations (just kidding about the last one).

With very hot tickets, it's a management decision about how many tickets should go through a pre-sale program. Some managers think it should be minimal, so that the public has a shot at the bulk of tickets, but others think it's okay to pre-sell the entire venue on the theory that a "sellout is a sellout." On the conservative side you might see 20% of the venue allocated for "pre-sale," leaving the rest open to the public. On the aggressive side, you might see 90% of the venue sold in "pre-sale," meaning the remaining 10% will sell out to the public in minutes. Feel free to chime in on the debate.

Deposits. Agents are also responsible for collecting **deposits,** which are monies paid by the promoters prior to your show. In order to hold you for a particular date, the promoters historically paid 50% of your fee about thirty days ahead of the performance. It's a way of ensuring that you don't get stiffed (at least completely). For example, if your deal is $10,000 for a show, the promoter would pay $5,000 in advance. As we'll discuss in the promoter deal section on page 375, there are two mega-promoters these days (LiveNation and AEG), who buy a lot of the big tours. Because they're solid financially (and because they're big gorillas), they want to pay a much smaller deposit (10% or so), and they only want to pay it three to five days before the date. Other promoters, with a track record and solid history, such as casinos for example, still pay 50% or so when the dates are confirmed, or at least before the tickets go on sale.

If you're dealing with a new promoter, or a new festival, the agent may want a personal guarantee by the owners of the promoter—new promotion companies have a way of going bankrupt if the event doesn't go well, and the artist (and agent and manager) get stiffed. With these newbies, the deposit is often more than 50%, and I've even seen deposits of 100%. This is also true for international dates in shady places, and for **private shows** (meaning shows that aren't open to the public, such as a corporate event for employees only, or some rich guy's birthday party).

Deposits are held by the agent and paid to you when you perform the gig (after deducting their commission).

You *never* want to put your tickets on sale without a deposit. If the promoter goes wonky and disappears with your money, you'll have to cancel the show, and the fans will get mad at you for flaking out after they bought their tickets.

Business Manager

Your business manager is in charge of all financial aspects of the tour. This job begins way before the tour starts, by forecasting (a fancy accounting word for predicting) the income and expenses, and projecting how much you're going to make or lose. If you're a new band, this information helps you go to the record company and beat them up for tour support (see page 180). At all levels, it helps avoid unhappy surprises.

When the tour gets going, all your road personnel (the people who set up the equipment, supervise your crew, etc.) are on payroll, and the business manager is in charge of getting everyone paid. He or she also makes sure your performance fees are collected from the promoters (which is physically done by a tour manager or tour accountant, if you have one) and that all bills (travel, hotels, food, etc.) are paid. They handle withholding taxes (both by states and foreign countries) and file tax returns in all those places. It's also the business manager's responsibility to make sure the tour doesn't run over budget without an alarm being sounded in advance, while there's still a chance to fix it.

The business manager, through a tour accountant if the tour is big enough, also double-checks everyone's math while the tour is happening. This not only means catching innocent errors, but also making sure that promoters don't pad the expenses to make a few extra dollars (more about that later).

Tour Manager

If you have a tour manager (and if not, your personal manager should be doing this job), he or she is responsible for everything running smoothly on the road. They make sure that your hotel reservations are in fact there, that your airline tickets are confirmed, that the bus is where it's supposed to be, that you're on the bus when you're supposed to be, etc. It's the tour manager who's responsible for collecting the money after each show, reviewing the promoter's accounting on the night of the show (called **settling the box office** or the **settlement**), and depositing the dough in the right place. (As you move up the ladder, you'll have a tour accountant doing the money part of the job.)

Promoter

Promoters are the people in each market who hire you for the evening and are responsible for marketing your show and maximizing your ticket sales. They can be "local" (meaning they work only in one city or area), regional (several states), national (covering the entire United States), or international. (National promoters also book regionally as well as nationally.) Promoters rent the hall (which means they owe rent even if nobody shows up), pay for marketing the concert, and supervise the overall running of the show.

Promoters actually have a tough time. If they lose, they can lose big, but as acts get more successful, the artists squeeze the deals and limit the promoter's upside (as discussed below). The result is a friendly game of "hide the pickle" that promoters routinely play in stating their expenses. But I'm getting ahead of myself, because we're going to talk about this later (on page 385).

Two companies, Live Nation and AEG, are international promoters, who purchase entire tours. In other words, they make a deal to promote every date. These deals have their own complexities, which we'll discuss when we get to promoter deals on page 385.

Over the last few years, **venues** (meaning the owners of the physical buildings—the amphitheaters, arenas, etc.) have begun buying shows themselves. Deals for these are imaginatively called **venue deals.** As we discussed above, promoters traditionally rent the buildings from the owners, then turn around and make the deals with the artists. Under venue deals, the building owners contract directly with the artists, in effect acting as promoters themselves. In fact, they're directly competing with the promoters who rent from them.

Sometimes the venues will pay artists more than promoters pay. This is partly because they've eliminated the middleman, but more importantly, it's because they have income from parking, food, beverage sales, and other areas that promoters don't share.

Another alternative is what you might call "invisible venues" (not an industry term). By "invisible" I mean you can do an entire tour in these places and none of your friends will ever know about it. I'm talking about state and county fairs (it may surprise you to hear that fairs pay big money for artists, because it brings people in to see their prize cows and spend money throwing darts at balloons), casinos (same idea of luring in spenders), and **performing arts centers.** *Performing arts centers* are small theaters (1,200 to 4,000 seats) that put on all kinds of entertainment for their local community. These are things like dramatic and musical theater, classical symphonies, family shows, well-known speakers, and touring musical artists.

For the right kind of act (usually an older demographic, country, Christian, etc.), these invisible shows can be very profitable.

MARKETING

The biggest change in the concert business over the last few years is in the way concerts are marketed. Traditionally, it was all about advertising in newspapers, on radio, and (for really big tours) on TV. These days, most of the marketing happens over the Internet, as do most of the ticket sales (at the time of this writing, more than 85% of all tickets are sold over the Internet). Accordingly, your visibility and presence on the Web (streaming numbers, YouTube views, your website, social media, blogs, email blasts, tweets, etc.) go a long way toward bringing warm bodies into your shows.

As discussed previously, credit card companies are sometimes involved in marketing, in exchange for the ability to sell tickets to their card members before the public sale.

PERSONAL APPEARANCE DEALS

It's difficult to make much money touring until you're a major star. In the traditional music biz, you couldn't put a lot of tushies into concert seats until you'd sold a lot of records. Until then, you were touring to create a buzz, get a record deal, sell records, and then tour profitably. Now it's about streaming hits, which not only drive ticket sales, but also give you a road map to your fans—the streaming companies will tell you where the listens are coming from. However, there are (and always have been) artists who have low streaming numbers (low sales and airplay in the old days) but who pack concert halls. Conversely, some artists stream in the hundreds of millions but can't fill a high school auditorium.

Some bands can tour locally and regionally, build a base of 500 to 1,000 people per night, sometimes even fill 3,500-seat theaters, all without a record deal. This seems to work best for DJs, rockers, jam bands, and digital stars (like YouTube phenoms) who can build a huge audience that wants to see them in person. We talked before (on page 15) about the ways new artists can build a buzz through direct contact with their fans, and if it works, it spreads by word of mouth (like through people who go, *Hey, dude, check this out!*, then email the artist's SoundCloud link to all their friends). Performers like this can make money and develop a cult following, which can lead to a healthy touring career and a record deal (if they want one).

In the beginning, unless you're one of these phenoms, you'll most likely lose money on touring. You'll also get stuck opening for another act, in uncomfortable dressing rooms, with food left over from last night's headliner. And you'll be regularly humiliated, playing to half-empty concert halls, since the audience is coming later to see someone else. Also, the people who show up early will be buying beer, talking loudly during your ballads, and chanting the headliner's name if they don't like your show. Otherwise, it's a blast.

Ready to sign up? Let's look at the anatomy of personal appearance deals:

New Artists

You first goal as a new artist is to play as a headliner in clubs (meaning venues of 100 to 1,500 people or so). In the very beginning, a lot of clubs will only take you if you buy a certain number of tickets to your show, which you then have to re-sell (or eat). If you can't sell enough tickets to cover yourself, then a good way to build a buzz is by playing local clubs that have themed nights of cool music from unknown acts (for example, in Los Angeles, a club called Bardot has "School Night" each week, which is a lineup of developing bands). Assuming the club has enough credibility, there'll be a built-in audience, and hopefully tastemakers will show up and blog about you, or at least be a loud-mouth to their friends.

If you're signed to a record label, you might get a gig as the opening act on a big tour. How you get to be the opening act on a major tour is very political. If your record is only doing so-so, and there are several other groups in your position, then it depends on the clout of your manager and agent—it's that simple and cold. If you're streaming well, have a hot video, or are generating big numbers on social media, you'll have an edge in the political process. But it's still political. The exception is where you're really exploding out of the box. In this case, the headliners may be clamoring for you. For example, a well-known headliner may not be selling tickets very well and wants a hot new opening act to bring in younger people.

If you can build enough of a profile to get yourself booked at a **festival** (meaning all-day or multi-day events, like Coachella, Bonnaroo, etc.), that's another way to push your career forward. In the beginning, you could end up playing at eleven in the morning to about a hundred hungover people, which is marginal of course. But at least you can say you were on that festival, and try to parlay that into booking another festival or getting a support slot on a tour. And if your performance sets off an Internet buzz, it can truly move the needle. Of course, everyone's vying for these festival slots, so getting one takes serious momentum, usually coupled with an aggressive manager or agent. And politics.

Fees

If your record is beginning to make some noise, or you've got a local following, you can get fees in the range of $250 to $1,500 per night, either from clubs or opening slots. If you're really big in the local/regional scene (like we discussed above for jam bands), and can draw 1,000 or so people per show, you can get $5,000 to $10,000 or even more per night. And if you're big enough to get an opening slot on a big tour, you can get even more (see the numbers in the mid-level artist section below).

Splits/Guarantees

Some clubs will pay you no front money, but will give you a **split** of the **gate** (meaning a share of the money charged for admission). The splits run from 20% to 60%, depending on your stature, and also depending on the number of other acts on the bill. For example, if there are three acts, you might divide up 60% of the gate. If your band is the biggest **draw** (meaning you draw in the biggest crowds), you can ask for more than an equal share. Sometimes you can even get 100% of the gross after the promoter gets back his or her expenses for the evening (advertising, sound, lights, etc.), and with a lot of clout, you can get 100% of *all* the gross (the promoter makes money selling beer to your fans). This is most common when the promoter is also the club owner and is happy to break even on the door charge just to get thirsty mouths into the seats.

As to the accuracy of the club's count, you'll have to rely on the club's reputation or else have Bruno, your three-hundred-pound roadie, stand at the door and check.

If you're really hot locally, you might get a minimum guarantee of $100 to $250 or so against your share of the gate. Or maybe just take a higher fee, of say $500 to $800 per night (with no share of the gate). (I'm basing the numbers in this section on the club scene in Los Angeles, because it's the one where I have the best info. These are also based on a ticket price of about $10 to $12. I'm told the basic pattern holds true for most major cities.)

Expenses

The *minimum* cost of putting yourself on the road is the money to rent a van you can use to carry equipment and sleep in, plus three meals a day at McDonald's. And you'd better get along really well with each other, or else expect some violent crimes.

The next step up (three or four to a room in cheap motels, slightly better meals, and maybe someone to help move the equipment) gets a lot more expensive, as you can see. But if you watch it carefully, you can get by cheap enough to play the independent circuit and make a few bucks.

If you're headlining larger clubs, or if you're the opening act on a bigger act's tour, the minimum cost of putting a four-piece band on the road can run around $10,000 per week, broken down roughly as $1,000 for crew, $2,000 for food and hotels, $2,500 for equipment and personnel costs, and $4,500 for insurance, commissions to managers and agents, equipment repairs, etc. With travel, setup, etc., you can't really do more than five shows per week, and you don't need to be a math genius to see that you're going to lose money. Five nights at even $1,500 per night is only $7,500, which is $2,500 per week less than it costs you to be there. And the longer you stay out the more you're going to lose.

So where does this lost money come from? (See page 180 if you don't remember the answer.)

Midlevel Artists

Let's assume you're past the new-artist level, with a lot of social media, and you're streaming in the hundreds of thousands or low millions. You now have the option, in addition to opening for a major artist or playing clubs, of headlining small venues.

At this point, you should at least be able to break even, and you may be able to take home a nice profit. If you're going out as an opening act on a big tour, you should be able to make about $5,000 to $50,000 per night, depending on the stature of the headliner, size of the venues and ticket pricing, and your heat. Most of these opening act deals are in the $20,000 to $30,000 range.

If you're headlining small venues (1,500 to 2,500 seaters), you are likely in the $5,000 to $25,000 range, depending on your stature, the size of the venue, pricing, etc. If you can headline small **amphitheaters** (meaning venues of about 5,000 seats), you can get anywhere from $20,000 to $100,000 or more per night, depending on the ticket pricing.

As we touched on earlier, many artists like to keep their tickets cheap (in the range of $20 to $35 per ticket), for their credibility and/or the fact that nobody will come if they raise their prices. If this is you, because of what it costs to be on the road, you'll break even or make a small profit. However, if you're able and willing to charge $40 plus per ticket, you can make a decent profit. And if you can get a $50 to $60 or higher ticket price, you could get $250,000 or more per night! Note also, because your expenses are fixed, the first $10 to $15 per ticket covers them. Thus, almost every dollar of increase (which isn't exactly true because the promoter, manager, and agent take a part, as we'll discuss in more detail in a minute) goes directly to your bottom line (meaning into your pocket).

At midlevel you can also get into **splits,** which is usually 85% of the profits. (We'll discuss splits in detail under superstars, so I won't ruin the surprise.) The only difference is that the guarantees against splits at this level are of course lower than the superstars' guarantees (midlevel artist guarantees are in the range of $7,500 to $25,000 per show, or more if you raise your ticket price).

Heritage Acts

Heritage acts are classic artists of the 1960s, '70s, '80s, '90s, etc. that once filled **arenas** (12,000+ seaters), but no longer draw such big crowds. They've settled into a comfortable touring groove that keeps them on the road for most of the year and makes them a good living. Other than the obvious superstars from these eras (Paul McCartney, Stones, Springsteen, etc.), their deals fall somewhere between the high end of the midlevel deals and the superstar deals of the next section. They play amphitheaters, festivals, fairs, performing arts centers, and casinos, and generally stick to comfy places with plush seats because most of their fans are older (despite what the band may think). The plus side of an older audience is that they have more money, so they can pay more for a ticket—after all, it's not just a show, it's a trip back to their youth (well, musically, anyway).

A lot of the heritage dates are something called a **soft ticket,** which means that people come for reasons besides the show. For example, casinos give free tickets to their high-rollers; performing arts centers have season subscribers; and fairs draw people who may catch the show after a day of deep-fried Twinkies and pig races. (**Hard tickets** mean just the opposite; it's a show where people only come to see your performance, such as an arena.)

Because heritage acts spend a lot of time on the road, they hit the same markets frequently. So they often package themselves in a double-header with another heritage act to keep people from saying, "I think I'll pass because I saw them last year."

Superstar Touring

Now we get into some real fun. And some real money. If you pay close attention, I'll tell you how to put a lot more bucks in your pocket. If you choose not to listen, don't get mad when your agent, personal manager, and other team members have more money than you at the end of the tour.

Splits

First let's look at the money you can earn. Here's how the deals work when you're a superstar: Instead of being paid flat fees, you get a **guarantee** against a percentage of the **net profits** or **gross** of the show. (As with the new and midlevel deals, your share is called a **split**. These deals are also known as **versus** deals, because you get a guarantee **versus** a percentage, whichever is higher.)

Guarantees work exactly the same way as an advance against your record royalties; if you don't make any profits, you still keep the guarantee. If you do make profits, the promoter deducts the guarantee and pays you the excess.

These numbers are not chopped liver. Major artists in arenas (meaning venues of 12,000 to 20,000) get guarantees in the range of $100,000 to $500,000 plus per night, sometimes as high as $1,000,000 or more. Also, major artists can often sell multiple nights in the same venue, which can be a substantial savings of costs—you don't have to move the equipment, yourself, or your crew every night, and you can get a better rental rate for the concert hall when you're a "long-term" tenant.

The usual split is from **85/15** to **90/10,** meaning the artist gets 85% (or 90%) of the net profits of the show, and the promoter gets 15% or 10%. Superstars sometimes push promoters even further (e.g., 92.5/7.5, or even 95/5), but that takes a *lot* of clout and it only kicks in after the promoter has gotten back all their money. For example, there might be a 90/10 split until the promoter breaks even, 92.5/7.5 to a certain level above break-even, then 95/5 after that. (There are also deals based on *gross,* which we'll discuss on page 386.)

Let me give you an example: If a date has gross ticket sales of $250,000 and the promoter's expenses are $150,000, there's $100,000 in net profits ($250,000 income less $150,000 expenses). In a 90/10 deal, 90% of this, or $90,000, goes to the artist. If the artist got a $60,000 guarantee, that's deducted from the artist's share, so the artist gets an additional $30,000 (the $90,000 share of profits less the $60,000 guarantee). Here's a cheat sheet:

Gross Ticket Sales	$250,000
Less: Promoter Expenses	−$150,000
Net Profits	$100,000
Times: 90%	×90%
Artist Share:	$90,000
Less: Guarantee	−$60,000
PAYABLE ON NIGHT OF SHOW	**$30,000**

The sensitivity of profits to ticket pricing, which we covered in the previous section for midlevel artists, is even more dramatic when you get to the superstar level. As we discussed, once you've covered expenses, almost all of the price increase goes directly into your pocket. And stars who attract older audiences normally charge in the range of $75 to $175 per ticket, with some superstars charging as high as $400 per ticket (occasionally even more). Which means these artists can walk away with truckloads of money.

We previously discussed charging higher prices for better seats, but now let's take a deeper dive into it. There are normally two, but sometimes up to four, levels of pricing at each concert, from **P1** (meaning **Price 1,** the most expensive), down to **P4** in the nosebleed section. The gray areas between these sections (for example, the last row of P1 and the first row of P2) are called **flex,** and there's a new trend in ticketing called **flexing the house**—which means you vary the ticket prices based on demand. For example, if the front orchestra is selling well, the promoter may expand P1 pricing to include more of the middle/back orchestra. If demand dies down, those seats drop to a P2 price.

Also, as we discussed on page 372, some artists put their tickets through a **platinum ticketing** platform, which is another way to price tickets based on demand.

Computation of Net Profits

Let's look at some of the finer points in computing **net profits.** *Net profits* are defined as "gross receipts less the promoter's expenses." The calculation looks like this:

Gross Receipts. *Gross receipts* means gross monies from ticket sales, less selling costs (such as ticket fees, credit card charges), taxes, and facilities charges. That's pretty straightforward, but your team should go to great lengths to make sure you get an accurate accounting. For example, some of my clients have their tour accountant "count the house" (meaning they actually count the number of seats and people in them) and/or (especially in dates where there are no seats) stand at the door with clickers and count the number of people who come in (in response to which one promoter opened three other entrance doors without telling us).

Also included in gross receipts are the monies from **VIP Ticketing,** which I'll talk about in the next section.

Sometimes **sponsorship** money is also included, which is discussed in the section after VIP Ticketing.

Expenses.   From the gross, the promoter deducts every expense he or she can possibly think of. The major ones are:

1. Advertising. It's obvious when you think about it, but not until then, that the more important an artist you are, the less advertising money the promoter has to spend. One or two announcements of a major show usually does it. So watch this expense.

    On the other hand, major stars don't want the promoter to underspend. That sounds weird at first—in a profits deal, 85% to 90% of the advertising is charged to you—but the reason is that advertising can be a cross-promotion for a current record, and it also helps make sure your tour is perceived as an "event."

    Some of the larger promoters own their own advertising agencies, and the ad agency charges 15% on top of the advertising monies paid to Internet sites, radio stations, etc. For example, if the promoter spends $10,000 on radio ads, their ad agency would charge an extra $1,500 (15%), for a total of $11,500 in computing your profits. The promoters argue that if they used an unaffiliated advertising agency, they'd have to pay this 15% (which is true), so why should you get a break? You say that the promoter owns this agency, so the money is only moving from one of the promoter's pockets to another. If you have enough clout, most or all of the 15% disappears.

2. Rent for the facility
3. Personnel (box office, cleanup, ushers, ticket takers, doormen, etc.)
4. Rental of equipment (PA [public address system], lights, pianos, etc.)
5. Insurance

6. Security
7. Stage crew
8. Ground transportation for the artist and entourage
9. Catering for artist and crew
10. Public performance license for the music (see page 227 for what this is)
11. Medical
12. Elvis impersonators (just seeing if you're paying attention)

Over the years, as promoters' profit margins got more and more squeezed, they developed systematic ways of "adding" to the expenses. Crasser promoters have been known simply to create phony invoices for various items. A more sophisticated example is where the promoter advertises so much on the local radio station that they get a rebate at the end of the year. In other words, if they spend $100,000 for ads on a radio station, the station gives them back $5,000 at year end. This doesn't show up on each individual invoice, and thus the shows are charged for the full amount.

Another example is a rebate that promoters get from Ticketmaster and certain venues, which they also don't share.

The interesting part is that everyone knows what the promoters are doing, and so there is this little "waltz of the toreadors" while your agent negotiates how much the promoter can steal from you (using much more civilized terms, of course). Because everyone knows what expenses really are, there are accepted amounts of stealing, and it's bad form for (a) the promoter to steal more than is customary; or (b) the artist to "catch" the promoter and not allow the accepted level. So in this bizarre netherland, everyone reaches a happy compromise.

Promoter Profit Deals

In a **promoter profit deal,** a promoter's profit is added as an expense, which has the effect of delaying your split of proceeds until the promoter gets a negotiated amount of money.

This is easier to understand using numbers. For example, if the gross from a particular show is $100,000 and the expenses are $60,000, the net profits would be $40,000 ($100,000 minus $60,000). If your deal is 90/10, you would get 90% of $40,000, or $36,000. However, if the promoter's deal allows them to add a profit of $10,000 as an expense, the net profits would only be $30,000, because the expenses are now $70,000 (the $60,000 actual expenses plus the promoter's $10,000 profit). Thus you would get only 90% of $30,000, or $27,000, instead of $36,000. (In other words, you got $9,000 less because you're paying 90% of the $10,000 profit.)

Deals that add a promoter profit are also called **split point deals.** That's because adding their profit raises the *point* at which you *split* the net. Using the above example, if there were no promoter profit, you would split the monies after $60,000 of gross income (when the gross equals the expenses). In a split point deal, you wouldn't start sharing until the gross equals $70,000 (expenses plus a $10,000 promoter profit), so $70,000 becomes the split point.

As your bargaining power increases, the promoter's ability to add a profit disappears.

Splits Based on Gross

Some superstar acts get a percentage of gross income. (In these deals, the expenses are of course irrelevant.) The range is 65% to 70% of gross, and the artist can get even more when the ticket prices are high. Remember, the expenses are fixed, so that as gross income (i.e., the ticket price) goes up, expenses become a smaller percentage of the gross. Which means the artist can get a bigger piece of it. For example, if the expenses were $50,000 and the gross was $100,000, the expenses are 50% of the gross. But if the gross was $200,000, the $50,000 expenses would only be 25%. So the higher the ticket price, the bigger the artist's share of gross.

Actually, these deals are not based strictly on "gross," but on something bizarrely called **net gross.** *Net gross* means the promoter's gross income, less surcharges (amounts the building adds to the ticket price and keeps for itself), ticket fees, credit card fees, parking (if parking is part of the ticket price), and taxes.

VIP TICKETING

Another profit center for big tours is **VIP Ticketing.** These are P1 tickets (the most expensive tickets) packaged with a value bonus. The bonus can range from a basket of goodies (signed photo, signed poster, special T-shirt not otherwise available, custom spatulas, etc.), to a special area in the venue with drinks and maybe food, up to a meet-and-greet with the artist before or after the show. Some VIP packages let you into the venue early to watch a **sound check** (essentially a rehearsal where the artist does a few songs onstage to make sure the sound is right in the arena), sometimes followed by a question-and-answer session with the artist from the stage.

If you're doing a national tour with one promoter (more about that later, on page 390), VIP Ticketing is usually built into the overall deal. If not, there are companies that specialize in VIP Ticketing, including some merchandising companies, who will handle this for you. These folks put together the packages, sell the tickets, make arrangements with the venues, manage the fans when they get there, etc. The VIP Ticketing companies charge 10% to 25% for this, which includes all the costs (the merchandise, customer service fees, building rentals, etc.).

SPONSORSHIP

Major tours can do deals with sponsors, who pay money to be associated with the tour as a marketing move. The terms of the deals vary massively, depending on your stature, the length of the tour, and the rights you're giving the sponsor. For example, is it just a tour sponsorship, or are you also doing a commercial? Are they the only sponsor? If not, are they the main sponsor, or are they an "also presents"?

I've seen deals from as little as $10,000 for a baby band, to well into seven figures for major stars. I know that's not particularly helpful, but it's a little like trying to answer the question, "How much is a car?"

The major deal sponsorship points are:

1. How many dates are they sponsoring?
2. In what territories?
3. What is the exclusivity? For example, if your sponsor is a soft drink, what products do you have to avoid endorsing besides soft drinks? It's almost always bottled water and flavored waters, but it could be liquor. And sometimes the soft drink company owns other companies that make random things like computers, so they don't want you endorsing those either.
4. Are you doing a commercial? If so, in what media, and in what territories? And how long can they run it?
5. Can they use your music in their ads? If so, who's paying the record company and publisher for the rights?
6. Do they get free tickets? Free tickets actually cost you money on a hot tour, because you won't get the price of the tickets from a

fan. Whether or not the sponsor gets freebies, they will want the right to buy tickets before the public gets them. If you agree to that, how many tickets do they get, and in what sections?

7. Will you do a "meet and greet" with the sponsor's guests? If so, how many guests, how many shows, and in which markets?

8. How will the sponsor's name be positioned on tickets, and in tour ads?

9. How will the sponsor's banners be positioned in the venues?

I'm only scratching the surface here, because these deals get pretty complex, but you get the idea.

HALL FEES

Over the last few years, agents have become responsible for negotiating hall fees. A **hall fee** is the amount charged by the building for selling merchandise (T-shirts, posters, etc.), and it's a percentage of the gross sales. We'll hit this in detail in the next chapter (on page 403), so hang loose 'til then.

RIDERS

The actual contracts for each appearance are customarily handled by the agency. At lower levels, they're merely AFM printed forms, though most agents have standard forms they attach to this. As you hit midlevel to superstar, they're the same printed forms with an attached **rider** (an addendum that *rides* on top of another contract). Your attorney (together with your manager and agent) puts the rider together for you, and it's the guts of the deal. The contract itself is only one or two pages, listing the specific terms (dates, guarantee, hall size, splits, etc.). Riders can run thirty pages or more.

Here are the major points covered in your rider:

Expenses.   If your deal involves a split of profits, the promoter's expenses should be listed separately, with *maximum* amounts for each category. (Sometimes this list is in the contract itself.) In other words, the rider says you can only be charged for the actual expense, or the maximum in the contract, whichever is *less.* The rider should also spell out your right to verify expenses by auditing invoices, checks, etc.

Free Tickets. You should get a certain number of free tickets for yourself (called **comps,** an abbreviation of *complimentary*) to each performance (usually fifty to one hundred, though that varies with the size of the venue). You also want to limit the number of free tickets that the promoter can give away without your consent (usually twenty-five or so). Also, as noted above, if you have a tour sponsor, you may have to give and/or sell tickets to them, and the rider covers this as well. Keep this in mind with respect to freebies: if you had put these tickets on sale, 85% to 90% of the money from those sales would have been yours. So go easy on the comps.

Free tickets are usually a minimal item, and not a big deal. However, some artists may not do so well in certain cities, so the promoter might give away as many tickets as humanly possible to make the house look full. This is called **papering the house,** and it's done very quietly. (If you find a lot of police officers, firefighters, city councilors, and similar folks boogying and/or holding their ears in your audience, there's a good chance you've been papered.)

I use an interesting clause that says the promoter's free tickets can't be in the first ten rows. Can you guess why? (Answer on page 397.)

Billing. *Billing* means the way your name is listed (how you will be *billed*) in ads, publicity, billboards, tickets, the venue marquee, and anywhere else that credits show up. You of course want 100% headline billing, and you should have the right to approve the presence and size of anybody else's name along with yours.

Recording. The rider should have strict prohibitions against the promoter recording your performance in any way, whether audio and/or visual. A poor-quality (or even worse, a good-quality) bootleg recording is a serious rip-off of your professional life, not to mention a possible violation of your record deal. I put in extraordinarily tough language, including high damages for a violation.

With the advent of smartphones, however, it's impossible to keep audience members from photographing or recording shows (unless you hire storm troopers to goosestep through the auditorium). However, you should print on your tickets that they can't use professional equipment or commercially exploit what they record.

Merchandising. Your merchandiser will require you to include specific language giving them the exclusive right to sell merchandise at your concert. (Merchandising is discussed in Chapter 24.)

Interviews/Promos.   Be sure the promoter can't commit you to any interviews or local promotions or sponsors without your consent.

Catering.   I have so much fun reading the catering requirements of riders that I've made it a hobby. Many riders have three or more pages listing food and drink that the promoter has to provide for the artist and the crew. They range from mundane foods for the crew to true exotica for the headliner. (I always get a kick out of artists who require organic, GMO-free antioxidants, together with six cases of beer.) Here are some of the better items, actually lifted from various riders over the years:

    Turkey (white meat only; never rolled or pressed)
    Gourmet-grade coffee—no canteen type
    Lactaid nonfat milk
    Shelled red pistachios
    M&Ms, with the brown ones removed

Technical.   You need to have very specific technical specifications for your show, such as the size of stage, what equipment the promoter has to supply, power requirements, security needs, dressing room facilities, sound check (meaning the time you can come into the actual venue and set the levels of your sound equipment), etc. Sometimes this is in a separate tech rider.

Legal.   Riders have a lot of legal sections regarding cancellation, bad weather, riots, mechanics of payment, insurance, lawyer jokes, etc.

I'LL TAKE THE WHOLE THING...

Many artists sell their entire tour to a single promoter. These deals look very similar to single-night deals, except of course they cover all the dates. The major economic difference is that all the dates are *cross-collateralized* (we discussed this concept in record deals on page 88). For tours, it means the promoter gets back their losses on turkeys from successful shows. This of course isn't good for you as an artist—without cross-collateralization, you'd get paid on the good dates, and the promoters would eat the bad ones. On the other hand, you can usually get a larger overall guarantee in these deals because the promoter is hedging their risk.

Sometimes you can get a limited cross-collateralization. For example, the six major market dates might be crossed with each other; the eight secondary market dates are crossed with each other; etc.

These deals are easier logistically because you only have to deal with one promoter, and you only have to do one contract for the entire tour, as opposed to separate negotiations for each date. But since you're dealing with a huge promoter, and gargantuans tend to flex their muscles, they can push back harder than individual promoters.

As discussed on page 386, when you're doing one of these deals, the issue of VIP Ticketing comes up. The national promoter wants these rights as part of the package, and their guarantee is priced higher because it includes VIP package income as well as straight concert revenue.

The major promoters have divisions that do VIP Ticketing, who of course they want to use. If the promoter allows you to use an independent VIP Ticketing company, it will want the income put into gross (which means they can use it to recoup their guarantee). You can sometimes make a deal to keep all the VIP income yourself, but it'll mean less of a guarantee.

The national promoters also want to share in any tour sponsorship income. Their argument is that it's an element of the tour and therefore the money should go in the pot. But this is negotiable. Some deals include sponsorship if the promoter finds the sponsor (for which they'll want a 20% fee off the top, before putting the money into gross). With enough clout, and if their advance offer wasn't based on getting sponsorship money, you can keep at least a portion of the sponsorship income outside the pot. If the sponsorship deal includes a commercial endorsing their product that doesn't mention the tour, you should keep all of that money yourself.

There's some controversy over what these one-promoter tour deals mean for the agents. Some people argue that, since you only have to make one deal (instead of the usual multiple deals for a tour with different promoters), maybe you don't need an agent. On the other hand, someone needs to supervise the national promoter, and agents have a lot of experience working with them. For example, you need to make sure the promoter is properly marketing your tour, that you're getting an honest ticket count, that the promoter is making the best deals with the venues (in fact, some of these promoters own the venues, so you have to be especially careful how they deal with themselves), etc. So arguably these big promoters need even more supervision—you're dealing with one powerful source, rather than a number of smaller players.

Good, bad, or ugly, these deals are becoming the norm for major acts. However, when the promoters consolidated into big chunks, more little seedlings began winding their way through the cracks. In other words, alternatives to the big players are starting to grow up as real forces in the marketplace. Specifically, these are the "invisible venues" we discussed on page 376, meaning fairs, casinos, and performing arts centers.

MULTI-SHOW DEALS

A new creature that's developed over the last few years is the idea of making multi-show deals that aren't tied to specific gigs. Under these contracts, you agree to perform a set number of shows, but the dates and locations are worked out in the future. For example, a promoter signs up you for fifty shows over the course of the next year or two, at times and places to be mutually agreed.

Generally, these deals pay up to half the money when you sign, and sometimes you can also get nonrecoupable money as a bonus.

Multi-show deals are *exclusive*, meaning you can't perform live for anyone else during the term of the deal. Because of this, they're very close in concept to a record deal, where only one company has the rights to your services. However, there are some things you can usually carve out of the exclusivity. At a minimum, you should have the right to do non-public gigs (for corporations, in connection with a sponsorship deal, for some rich dude's wedding, etc.), as well as charity concerts, radio concerts (see page 177), and TV appearances.

So how did these multi-show deals come about? And why would you want one?

From the promoter's point of view, they want to tie you up because they're betting you'll get hotter. If they're right, they not only get a bargain price for your shows, but they also keep you from playing for their competitors. It's not a coincidence that the biggest players in the multi-show game are Live Nation and AEG, who both control venues they need to keep filled.

From your point of view, you can get substantial guaranteed money (multimillions, if you're really hot), and you can get a good chunk of the dough up front. So if you need or just want a big check, these are the deals for you. In addition, the promoters say that they'll put more juice behind you if you're exclusively tied to them. For example, they'll market you in all the venues they control, push you on their ticketing sites, etc.

Multi-show deals come in two flavors: **guarantee deals** and **earn-outs.**

A **guarantee deal** means there's an amount of money guaranteed for a set number of concerts. This is exactly like the deals we just described for a specific tour, except that it doesn't specify which shows you'll be playing. For example, you might get a $1 million guarantee for 20 shows on mutually agreed dates over the next year, meaning $50,000 per night. Of that money, you might get $500,000 on signing, and the balance as the shows are played.

Note that you'll have expenses when you play these shows (travel, sound, lights, band, hotels, etc.), so you want to make sure there's enough money left to cover each date's expenses, ideally with some profit on top. Otherwise, if you've gotten your entire profit up front, you'll be on the road making zero. Or writing a check to cover expenses. Which means you won't be so anxious to head out . . .

You're probably thinking, hey, no sweat, I'll just do 20 dates, and if the promoter bets wrong and loses money, too bad. Well, that's *mostly* true under a guarantee deal. I say "mostly" because it's not always the case; if the promoter hasn't earned back the guarantee at the end of 20 shows, they want the right to tack on more dates (the norm is 10% to 20% of the total dates, meaning 2 to 4 additional dates in our 20-show example). You of course don't get paid for those, because you're still paying off your guarantee. But after those shows, even if you're still in the hole, you can walk.

Because the promoter is risking that you might walk out and leave them with a loss, guarantee deals are not easy to come by. And for the same reason, if you can do a guarantee deal, it will pay you less money than an earnout deal.

Speaking of earnouts . . .

The far more common multi-show deal is an **earnout,** which means the term of the deal continues until you earn back the money, regardless of the number of shows. Using our example of $1 million over 20 dates, in an earnout deal, the 20 shows are really just a minimum—the term of the deal is extended until you've played enough dates for the promoter to get back their money. And if your career does a belly flop, that could be a *LONG* time. During which you might be working for zero because you've already gotten all the dough.

The lesson is that, in an earnout deal, always try for a right to end the deal by repaying the unrecouped money. If the promoter agrees to repayment, you'll only have this right after you've played the minimum number of shows (to keep you from walking out early if you get incredibly hot halfway through the deal). For example, if you play 20 shows and earn back only $900,000 of the $1 million, you could pay them $100,000 and be done. You won't likely have the money to write a check, but your next promoter could. Or more commonly, when you get near the end of the deal, you renegotiate with your promoter to extend the term and get more money. Which furthers the promoter's original goal of keeping you in their orbit.

LINING YOUR POCKETS WITH MORE GOLD

And now to my promised method of making you more money. Let me first say a couple of words about money in general.

More Income versus Cutting Expenses

It's more expensive to put another dollar of income in your pocket than it is to put a dollar of cost savings in your pocket. This may sound a bit weird, so let me explain.

For every dollar of income you make, you have to pay your manager, agent, and perhaps business manager and/or lawyer (if they're on a percentage) out of it. This will leave, for example, only about 65¢ to 75¢ to go into your pocket. On the other hand, for every dollar of expense you save, the whole dollar goes in your pocket because you've already paid the professionals on the money that would have been used to pay the expense. (Of course, if your professionals are paid a percentage of your net income instead of your gross, it doesn't save money, but I still want you to cut costs for your and their sakes.)

Let's look at an example: Suppose your tour grosses $1,000,000, and your professional team's fees total 35% ($350,000). This means that you have $650,000 after commissions, out of which you have to pay $400,000 in expenses. Thus, your net after everything is $250,000 (I'm ignoring income taxes).

Had you earned another $100,000 on the tour, 35% would have gone off the top to your professional team, leaving you $65,000. Since your expenses are already covered, the full $65,000 would be in your pocket. Thus, your net after everything is $315,000 ($250,000 plus the $65,000). On the other hand, if you didn't earn another $100,000, but instead saved $100,000 in expenses, the picture looks quite different: Instead of deducting $400,000 in expenses, you'd deduct only $300,000, and your net after everything would be $350,000. You thus keep the full $100,000 by cutting expenses, *which is almost 60% more than the $65,000 you would put in your pocket by earning another $100,000.*

Here's a chart:

	Example	EARN $100,000 more income	SAVE $100,000 expenses
Earnings	$1,000,000	$1,100,000	$1,000,000
Less Commissions (35%)	−$350,000	−$385,000	−$350,000
Subtotal	$650,000	$715,000	$650,000
Less Expenses:	−$400,000	−$400,000	−$300,000
NET	**$250,000**	**$315,000** ($65,000 more in your pocket)	**$350,000** ($100,000 more in your pocket)

If you add another zero or two to these numbers, they get even more impressive.

What to Do

How do you pull off this minor miracle? It's pretty simple, but you may not like the answer:

Spend less.

Here are the biggest areas of abuse:

Salaries. Watch carefully how much you're paying your band and crew, and really think about how many of them you need. This is primarily your manager or tour manager's area of expertise, and you obviously don't want to scrimp on essential personnel. But you don't always need to carry as many people as you think, or to pay them as much as they demand. And it's not just salaries—for every extra person, it's also hotels, transportation, food, etc.

Be extra careful with friends and relatives. Hiring "pals" with little or nothing to do is not only wasteful, it's demoralizing to the people who really work. And you have the added expenses for hotels, food, etc.

Stage, Sound, and Lights. Your stage, sound, and lighting systems have to be up to your level; anything less cheats your audiences. On the other hand, these expenses can eat up a large chunk of your profits. And the costs aren't just the obvious ones of building fancier sets. Larger staging also means you need to hire more trucks to haul the stuff around, hire more folks to drive those trucks, and hire more crew to load it, unload it, set it up, and tear it down. Not to mention transporting, housing, and feeding those extra mouths. So plan your staging smartly.

Remember, your fans are there to see you perform, and if you need an array of animals and rocket ships to keep their attention, either something is wrong with your show or you're being insecure and hiding behind the hoopla. (You're better than that—you wouldn't be where you are if you weren't.) Of course you should always do something innovative and spectacular, but be practical as well.

Start-up costs.   It's expensive to get ready for a big tour. There are equipment costs, like building a stage, designing and renting sound systems, lighting rigs, and video screens (all of these together are called the tour's **production,** meaning what it takes to put on ["produce"] the show). On top of production, you have the cost of rehearsing the band and dancers, which means paying and housing them (and some crew) for a number of weeks, as well as renting halls to rehearse in. You can save a good amount of money by rehearsing the band and dancers in a small venue, then waiting until just before the tour to move into a big hall with the full stage, sound, lights, and videos.

Travel.   You can save a lot by traveling light. This means two things:

1. Almost nothing I know of (except non-income-producing real estate and owning a restaurant) eats money like chartering (or heaven forbid, owning) your own jet. When you reach a certain level, particularly if you're a paparazzi magnet, it makes economic sense (or at least not a significant difference) to begin chartering planes. But for the most part, flying commercial is feasible and substantially less expensive. I know it's more inconvenient—the hassles of the public in the airport and on the plane, delayed flights, missing planes, etc.—but every major celebrity and political figure has at one time or another flown commercial, and all survived the experience. Remember, it's *your* money.

2. Try not to **hub.** *Hubbing* means you base yourself in a central location (say, Dallas–Fort Worth) while you play venues within a short flight from that city (other parts of Texas, Oklahoma, and

Arkansas). When you stay in one place like this, you double your mileage—every day you not only fly to the gig, but you have to fly back. And most artists like to hub out of expensive cities, which increases your hotel/lodging bills.

Catering.   Some artists are particularly notorious for having lavish spreads backstage, much of which is never eaten by them (or even touched by human hands). Or, worse yet, it's eaten by the hangers-on who show up to see what they can scam. (I said that to make you mad; but it's true.) Because these goodies are supplied by the promoter as part of your deal, it feels like the promoter is paying for them. But in truth, 90% of this expense is yours. Remember, as you get into the major leagues, you make only a portion of your money from the guarantee. A nice chunk of it comes from the profit split, which is usually 90/10 (see page 382 for a description of profit splits). Thus, every dollar spent on food for scavengers is 90¢ less you put in your pocket. So ditch the imported caviar and order in from Burger King.

Just Watch It.   The above isn't exhaustive; there are many other ways to cut expenses (and I'm always surprised that people find even more innovative ways to spend money). I know the road is a hassle and you want to be comfortable. There's nothing wrong with that. But be mindful of your expenses and keep them down. You'll be glad you did when you get home and count your take.

Answer to question on page 389:

Nothing is as much fun as playing your heart out to a standing, screaming audience, only to have a bunch of coat-and-tie zombies sitting in the first ten rows looking at their smartphones.

PART VI

Merchandising

24

Tour Merchandising

So now you're famous, and kids can't wait to plaster your face and logo on their backs, fronts, caps, bedroom walls, etc. And bootleggers can't wait to rip you off by illegally making your merchandise (more about bootleggers later).

Selling products (T-shirts, posters, hoodies, hats, etc.) that use your name, logo, or likeness is called **merchandising** (also called **merch**).

As the world swings to streaming, merch is taking on an interesting importance. With CD sales drying up like a Serengeti water hole, if your fans want something tangible with your vibes in it, they're limited to vinyl (a "new technology" to youngsters) and merchandise. Since most people don't wear vinyl albums, merch is one of the few ways they can impress their friends by showing they're a fan of yours.

And apart from the money, every T-shirt is a walking billboard for you.

There are three flavors of merch rights:

1. **Tour merchandising.** This is the stuff sold at concert venues, for prices you'd never pay anywhere else, so you can prove you were there.
2. **Retail merchandising.** This is basically the same stuff (without tour names or dates), but it's sold at the mall or in other brick-and-mortar stores and through those retailers' websites.
3. **D2C** (meaning **Direct to Consumer**), which is also called **E-Commerce** or **Internet Sales.** These are online sales through your Web store, and they're also called **direct sales** because you deliver the goods directly into the consumer's hands, rather than going through a retail store.

Merchandisers will also run your **fan club,** if you want one. More about that in the next chapter (on page 416).

Of the three categories, tour merchandise is by far the more significant moneymaker (assuming, of course, that you're touring; otherwise, it doesn't mean much). While retail and D2C merchandising may be more visible, they don't create the same sales frenzy as concerts do, for the obvious reasons—people are all pumped up by the show, they want a souvenir, they want to wear something that lets their friends know, "I was at the show, and you weren't," etc.

So let's discuss tour merchandising first, then we'll deal with retail and D2C in the next chapter.

TOUR MERCHANDISERS

Tour merch can be a good source of dough. In the beginning, you can handle it yourself by printing some T-shirts and selling them at your shows. However, as you start to sell more tickets, and get to bigger clubs, it takes a lot more effort to handle the sales. For example, you'll need (a) more space to carry the stuff around, (b) someone without sticky fingers to do the selling and keep track of it, and (c) a lot of administrative help, such as paying sales taxes, dealing with border crossings and customs issues, etc. At that point, it makes sense to get a merchandising company to take care of all this.

When you make a merch deal, you license the right to use your name and likeness to someone cleverly called a **merchandiser.** A *merchandiser*, very much like a record company, manufactures the goods, oversees the sales at your concerts, and pays you for each sale.

ROYALTIES

Most tour merchandising royalties are based on sharing the net profits from your merch sales, though it's sometimes possible (at the superstar levels) to get a royalty based on the gross sales price of some items (more about that in a minute). The computation of net profits is pretty much what it sounds like: the merchandiser throws the gross selling price of all your merch into a pot, then deducts the cost of manufacturing, credit card fees, freight, sales taxes, VAT, hall fees (more about VAT and hall fees in a minute), etc.

The range of artist royalties for touring merchandise in the United States and Canada is about 75% to 80% of profits, and there are higher splits for superstars. It's not uncommon to escalate your royalties based on sales, which can either be on a per-night basis, or a cumulative basis for the entire tour.

In the superstar world, you can sometimes get a royalty based on **gross sales,** as opposed to the net, which means the merchandiser doesn't deduct the costs (well, actually, they deduct a few, as we'll discuss in the next paragraph). But this kind of deal is getting harder and harder to come by. Of course, a royalty based on gross sales will be lower than a royalty computed on net profits, because the base is so much higher. The range is 30% to 40% for the United States, and Canada is often a few percentage points less.

The *gross sales* to which your royalty percentage applies is a term of art. It means the selling price to the public, less only taxes (sales tax, value-added tax, excise, and similar taxes), and credit card fees. **Value-added tax,** or **VAT** to its pals, is something we don't have (yet) in the United States, but it's common in other countries. VAT is a tax on goods at each stage of creation, based on the "value added" at that point. For example, there's a tax on the lumber mill as it cuts down a tree and turns it into lumber (adding value); a tax on the furniture manufacturer when it turns the lumber into furniture (more value added); a tax when the upholsterer does its thing, etc. The tax gets bigger at each stage, but through a system of crediting back (which I have never needed to fully understand, so I don't) each guy gets a credit for the tax paid by the previous guy. But it pumps up the price to the consumer.

If you do get a deal based on gross sales, which as I said is rarer and rarer, the merchandiser will not want to pay a gross royalty on tour programs or **specialty items** (meaning "expensive items"). That's because the cost of creating those goods is so high that they can't afford to fork over a big piece of the gross price. For example, tour programs require someone to create the artwork, write the text, clear the rights to the photos, and print them up. Also, major artists sometimes have **designer goods,** such as a custom-made $100 plus sweatshirt, or a $500 plus leather jacket. Because a designer is paid a fee (or royalty) on these goods, your royalty is lower, usually around 75% of net profits.

HALL FEES

As artists pushed royalties higher, the merchandisers started building limits on **hall fees** into their contracts. What's a hall fee?

Your merchandiser doesn't usually hire people to sell products in each of the venues. Instead, they make a deal with the **hall** (meaning the building where you're playing) to supply the personnel, display racks, etc. It works like this:

The merchandiser pulls up its truck early on the day of the show, checks in a certain quantity of merchandise to the hall personnel, and at the end of the evening gets back the remaining merchandise plus payment for what's been sold or otherwise disappeared. From the money that's turned over, the venue keeps a percentage, and this is the *hall fee*. It covers the cost of hiring the people to actually sell the crap plus the venue's profit. Hall fees often include a charge (usually 1% of gross) for bootleg security (more about that in a minute). (By the way, not all venues actually supply the merchandise personnel themselves. There are a couple of companies that contract with venues to supply the vendors. In that case, the independent company gets a percentage of the hall fee from the venue.)

Your agent negotiates the hall fee percentage with the venue, though your merchandiser may help. A standard hall fee is from 25% to 30% of the gross monies collected for the merchandise (minus tax), and superstars can sometimes knock it down even lower. So if you sold $10,000 of merchandise after deducting taxes, the hall would keep 25% to 30% ($2,500 to $3,000) and pay the balance to the merchandiser. These are U.S. numbers. You can sometimes get lower fees (around 18% to 20%) in foreign markets. You can also negotiate a lower fee (10%) for "non-apparel" items like CDs, vinyl, or program sales.

If you go over the hall fee limit, the excess comes out of your royalties. For example, a merchandise deal might say that you have a royalty of 80% of profits, and that the hall fee can't exceed 30%. Under this deal, if your hall fee for a particular date was 35% (i.e., 5% more than the allowed 30%), the extra 5% would come out of your royalty. Note this doesn't mean you go from 80% of profits to 75% of profits. It means you get 80% of *profits* less 5% of *gross sales*. That 5% of gross is much bigger than 5% of net, so you're getting less than 75% of profits. In other words, this is a big deal point.

It's to your advantage to push the hall fee down in your deals with the venues, because you get most of the savings. In the above example, if you got the hall fee down to 25% (i.e., you saved 5% below the 30% maximum), that 5% savings reduces expenses. So if your deal is that you get 80% of net profits, 80% of those savings slide over to your side of the table.

The buildings like to stick a 5% credit card fee on top of the hall fee. In a net profit deal, this is one more expense that comes out before you split. In a royalty deal, the merchandiser will charge the full 5% against your royalties. Because you're paying most (or all) of this fee, try to get the building to lower it to the amount actually charged by the credit card company (which is less than 5%). That's not always easy to get.

Hall fees are negotiated by the artist's agent (at the same time they make the overall deal for the guarantee, splits, etc.). Ironically, the agent doesn't get paid for this—the agent's commission is based on the artist's earnings from the performance only, and not from merchandising. So the agent is in the position of negotiating a part of the deal that gives him or her no benefit. However, their incentive goes way up when the artist glares daggers at them, so they've gotten quite good at muscling down the hall percentages.

ADVANCES

As you learned from record and publishing deals, where there are royalties, there are advances. And merchandising is just such a place. Unfortunately, they're not nearly as favorable as record and publishing advances, because they're almost always **returnable.** In other words, unlike the nonreturnable advances you get from record companies and publishers, which you keep whether earned or not, you might have to pay back some or all of the merch advance (we'll get into payback mechanics in a minute). Also, you might have to pay them interest on top of the advance, meaning you'd pay back more than you got.

In other words, merchandising advances are very much like loans.

Tour merchandising advances are usually paid over the course of a tour. For example, if your merchandising advance is $100,000, you might get $50,000 when you sign the deal, $25,000 a third of the way through the tour, and the balance when you've done two-thirds of the dates. As your bargaining power goes up, you can get more of the advance sooner.

A lot of artists use their merch advance to pay for the **start-up costs** of a tour. *Start-up costs* are the monies you buzz through before you go on the road, for example to buy equipment, rent a rehearsal hall, hire your crew, build a set, put together sound and lights, hire dancers, jugglers, and mimes, etc.

The size of the advance is based on a projection of your merch profits times your royalty rate. It'll therefore be bigger for larger tours—the more bodies you play for, the more merchandise you can sell. Advances will also be higher if the deal includes retail and D2C merchandising (which we'll discuss in the next chapter).

Because they are so deal-specific, it's hard to give you any hard-and-fast numbers. The broad range is anywhere from nothing to $25,000 or $50,000 for a developing act, to several million for a superstar.

Because the advances are returnable, and because the term gets extended if you don't earn it back (see our next topic), a number of artists opt to get a better royalty rate and take less of an advance, or no advance at all. This is particularly true for bigger artists who don't need the money. If you're with a good merch company, you can often make a lot more money this way.

TERM

The term of most merchandising agreements is 18 to 24 months, though it's occasionally longer if you're going on a massive tour. However, if the advance isn't recouped after that time, the term is automatically extended until the date of recoupment. Which means the deal could go on forever if your career crashes, or if you stop touring because you're disabled or bored.

When you're negotiating a tour merch deal, try to get the right to repay the advance and terminate the deal during these extensions. That keeps you from having a perpetual merchandiser. For example, if you have a two-year deal with an extension until recoupment, and at the end of two years you've recouped all but $10,000 of a $500,000 advance, it means you've done pretty well. However, if you don't have the right to repay, the term would continue until you recoup. Thus, the merchandiser could automatically get your next tour for no advance. If you have the right to repay, however, you can write them a check for $10,000 (which should be more than covered by the advance you'll get for your next tour) and move on. Or more commonly, you rattle your sabre by threatening to repay the advance, which brings the merchandiser to the negotiating table and gets them to give you an additional advance to make a new deal. (This payback right can only be good for you. If the unrecouped amount is really big, it means something is seriously wrong and you won't leave because no one else wants you; if it's a small amount, you want the ability to pay them off or renegotiate the deal for the next tour. For this very reason, this provision is also getting harder to come by.)

ADVANCE REPAYMENT

As noted above, unlike record and publishing deals, tour merchandise contracts require repayment of the advance, generally with interest. This is triggered by things like:

1. The tour doesn't start on time.
2. You're disabled or otherwise unable to perform all or part of the tour. This is based on the same theory as the tour not starting on time, and also protects them from the possibility that you might not tour for years, after which the public has forgotten you exist.
3. You don't play an agreed number of dates. The merchandiser bases their advance on a forecast of the number of concerts and the size of the venues. If you decide to chuck the stadiums and play clubs, they won't be happy. Or if you cancel dates because tickets aren't selling, they won't be much happier (of course, neither will you).
4. If the advance isn't recouped at the end of the agreed term (for example, 12 to 18 months), the company can demand repayment instead of just extending the term. As a practical matter, if you don't have the money, they can't really get it, but they'll grumble. And if you do have the money, they can get quite serious about wanting it back.

When you negotiate these provisions, make sure you don't have to pay back more than the unrecouped balance. A lot of deals talk about paying back "the advance," which could mean the total amount paid, regardless of what's recouped. So be sure your deal isn't one of those.

EXCLUSIVITY

Tour merchandise deals are of course exclusive, as the merchandiser doesn't want anyone else selling stuff with your name on it. The usual restriction says you can't sell your merchandise within two miles of a concert site, within forty-eight hours prior to the show.

Be sure you exclude retail sales from this restriction (otherwise, you'll be in breach of both your concert merch agreement and your retail sales agreements). You should also exclude any record company promotions (such as T-shirt or poster giveaways to promote your album) and any merchandise that your record company has the right to make (see page 178).

If you have a tour sponsor or you do a commercial, the sponsor sometimes wants to give away or sell merchandise. For example, they might run a contest where the prize is a special T-shirt that has your picture and their product logo on it. In this situation, you have to specifically deal with this in your merchandising agreement—and your merchandiser isn't going to like it very much. So be extremely careful in giving these rights to a sponsor. The usual compromise is to limit the amount of merchandise the sponsor can give away in a specific city for a number of days before your concert, which is in both your and the merchandiser's interests—if the sponsor gives all your fans a T-shirt just before the show, your concert sales won't be so hot.

CREATIVE CONTROL

Each of the three merch areas (Tour, Retail, and D2C) appeals to slightly different fans. And a good merchandiser will guide you to create distinct artwork and products for each outlet.

Now, speaking of creating products:

You should have the right to approve the design, artwork, photos, drawings, layout, etc., used in all merchandise, as well as the quality of the goods themselves. For the most part, merchandising companies give you creative approval without much of a fight (in stark contrast to the wrestling match you have with your record company over these same issues).

If you want to use photos as part of your merchandise, you'll often have to go to the photographer to get the rights. The same might be true of a graphic artist who created unique artwork for your album cover, or who designed a special font, etc. The reason is that, when record companies hire photographers and graphic artists, they pay only for the minimal rights they need to use the material in connection with your records. That means those creators keep all the other rights. Which means you don't have the right to put their work on your merchandise.

So you have to go to the photographer/graphic artist and say, "How much?" The answer is usually a flat fee that varies with exactly what kind of rights you want, and also the stature of the photographer/ graphic artist who created the work. *Very* rarely, and only for the most superstar of photographers, a photograher might get a royalty.

It's essential that you clear the merchandising rights *before* you use the materials, or else the photographer/graphic artist will have you in a squeezy-squeezy and demand a seriously huge amount of money. By asking early, if you find out the rights aren't available at a reasonable price, you can use something else.

If you have a federally registered service mark for your name (see page 359 for what that is), you need to approve the merchandise quality in order to preserve your mark's legal status. In this case, you should also make sure the merchandiser puts your TM symbol on the goods. Even if you haven't registered your mark, however, you should still insist on approving quality to make sure your image isn't tacked on to a piece of mild cheddar.

Your merchandiser will pay the cost of creating artwork for your merch (called **origination costs**), but this cost is treated as an advance, and therefore comes out of your share of net profits, or out of your royalty. If you have some clout, you may be able to treat origination costs as an expense that's deducted in computing net profits, meaning you only pay a portion of it. But there's usually a cap on what they'll pay on this basis, and anything over the cap comes 100% out of your money. For this reason, you should have approval over what they spend, at least for amounts that go over the cap.

If they agree to deduct origination costs off the top, it will only be for tour merch only; they'll charge the entire cost against your royalties for D2C and retail.

Especially if all the origination costs are charged to you, you should own all the artwork and be able to use it after the term of your merch deal. And even if it's off the top, you should try to get these rights. If you have some clout, you can pull it off.

SELL-OFF RIGHTS

At the end of the term, the merchandiser wants the right to sell off any remaining merchandise, usually for a period of six months. They should have no right to *manufacture* after the term, only to sell whatever is on hand. The merchandiser will ask for the right to sell it through wholesale (meaning retail) outlets and D2C, which is reasonable since there won't be any more concerts. You get a royalty for these sales, which is the same as if they were sold under a retail or D2C deal (we'll talk about those on pages 413 and 415).

The sell-off period should be non-exclusive, because your new merchandiser will be getting into the market at the same time.

You can add a provision that gives you the right to buy the inventory at cost plus 10% to 15% at the end of the term, in which case there would be no sell-off rights. You would then give the goods to your new merchandiser, and in fact you'll get your new merchandiser to put up the money to buy it. Of course, you'll only do this if you're confident you can sell the stuff.

Assuming you're not going to buy the goods, and the merchandiser has a sell-off period, here are some other things to ask for (which are very similar to the sell-off rights under print music deals on page 263):

1. Your contract should say the merchandiser can't **stockpile** goods. This means it can't manufacture a ton of goods right before the end, so that it has a lot of leftovers to sell. Specifically, get language that restricts their manufacturing to "only such quantity of goods as is necessary to meet reasonably anticipated sales requirements."

2. Your merchandiser can't do **distress sales,** meaning they can't sell your goods at super-low prices just to get rid of them. (This practice is also called **dumping.**) Otherwise you'll be adorning a lot of 99¢ Store shoppers and swap-meet fans. It also perturbs your new merchandiser, who's trying to sell your stuff at full price. However, this has become extremely hard to get over the years, as merchandisers' profits have been squeezed, and their tolerance for dining on leftover goods has been stretched to the regurgitation point.

3. At the end of the sell-off period, they should again offer you the remaining merchandise at their cost plus 5% to 15%. If you decide not to buy it, they should have to destroy it, or else donate it to a charity.

BOOTLEGGERS

Merchandisers want the right, and you should encourage them, to chase **bootleggers.** The term *bootlegger* was coined in the 1890s, because people illegally sold booze to Native Americans by smuggling bottles onto the reservations in the legs of their tall boots. During Prohibition, it came to mean anyone who illegally sold booze.

The modern-day equivalent of these fine citizens are people who, without any authority, manufacture merchandise with your name and/ or likeness on it and sell it outside the venues. Legitimate merchandisers are always inside the facility; bootleggers are the guys who hit you on the street or in the parking lot. (One of their tricks is to hire college students for $100 or so per night, so the vendors look wholesome, clean-cut, and somewhat innocent, while the manufacturers stay out of sight.) Not only are these people costing you money because you don't get paid for the merchandise, but their goods are usually of inferior quality. And guess who gets the complaint letters when some Tuscaloosa fan's T-shirt shrinks to fit her Barbie doll?

The legitimate merchandisers have been relatively successful in dealing with these pieces of slime, and have found that in some cases they are large, sophisticated operations (one even owned its own T-shirt factory). Through means I'm not free to tell you, the merchandisers have been able to track the bootleggers down and get the courts to stop them. (The laws abroad aren't always so hospitable, by the way.)

The merchandisers will ask you to pay part of the money to chase the pirates, but if you have some clout, they'll front it and charge it back to you, either out of any money recovered from the bootlegger and/or from your other royalties.

You can also do your part in this game of hide-and-seek. Use your social media to post pictures of official merchandise, and let your fans know that the pirated stuff is really shoddy. Also, educate them that they shouldn't buy anything outside the venue.

25

Retail, Direct to Consumer (D2C) Merchandising, and Fan Clubs

RETAIL MERCHANDISING

Retail merchandising means, as the name implies, selling merchandise through retail stores (Hot Topic, Zumiez, Urban Outfitters, Walmart, H&M, Zara, Gucci, etc.) and their websites. It can be a significant way for an artist to make money.

Don't take it personally, but not all artists have retail sales appeal. You have to be pretty high-profile before stores will give your merch any of their floor space, because if a pair of yoga pants will sell better than you, you're out. But when you get big enough to be loved by the mall stores and mass-market stores (Walmart, Target, Gap, Taco Bell—maybe not the last one), you can get into six- or seven-figure retail merch money.

So how do you get your goods from the oven to a retail rack? You make a deal with a retail merchandise company, who creates the products and sells them to the retail stores. Unlike tour deals, you don't get a share of profits in these deals, but rather you get a royalty percentage of the wholesale sales price (the same way record royalties are computed). So, for example, if you have a 20% royalty, and there's a $10 wholesale price, you get $2.00 per unit, regardless of the cost of the goods, shipping, and all the other costs.

The merch company's job is to get your stuff into as many stores as possible. Sometimes that means selling directly to the stores, and sometimes they sell via sales reps (people who don't work for the company but make a business out of representing companies and going to the stores and saying, "You gotta have this T-shirt!").

For certain types of goods, the merchandiser licenses your merch rights to other companies who specialize in a particular niche. In other words, they (a) give another company the right to make a product with your approved photo, imagery, likeness or logo, (b) get paid by that company for the merch they sell, and (c) split the money with you. This is called a **sublicense,** because the merch company licenses the rights from you, then under that license (*sub* that license, meaning "under it" like a submarine) re-licenses those rights to someone else. Many of these deals are in small areas (such as stickers, belt buckles, patches, trading cards, condoms, etc.), but some can be really big, such as liquor or slot machines.

The merchandisers keep a percentage of the sublicensing income, ranging generally from 15% to 25%. In other words, they make a deal with a company to manufacture and sell bumper stickers with your name, then pay you 75% to 85% of the royalties and advances they get from the sticker company. In exchange for their percentage, they negotiate and sign the license agreement, then police it (meaning they make sure the merch quality is there, that the sublicensee does their job, and that you and your merchandiser get paid).

As you move further into the superstar realm, you may want to make some of these deals directly. However, entering into a lot of small licensing agreements is best described as a "pain in the butt for little money," so paying this percentage is usually worth it. It's more worthwhile to do it yourself for the really big deals (like liquor or slot machines), but if the merchandiser delivers you a major opportunity, and uses their expertise to maximize it, they bring value to the table.

By the way, a lot of these deals can be on the tacky side. And since they don't generate much money, a lot of artists don't do them at all. No reason to risk damaging your cachet for peanuts. So make sure you have approval of all sublicenses.

Now . . . I got this snow globe opportunity for you that's gonna be *huge*. Picture a little statue of yourself inside this glass ball with gold glitter . . .

ROYALTIES

The royalties for retail merch that's sold by your merchandiser (things like T-shirts, sweatshirts, hats, posters, buttons, cards, belt buckles, etc.) are generally in the following range. When your merchandiser sublicenses, it will get a royalty from the licensee in this range (and you'll get your percentage of that, as we just discussed).

1. **United States retail sales:** 20% to 30% of the wholesale price for top-line/specialty retailers, depending on bargaining power.

For the midlevel stores (JCPenney, etc.) you'll get 75% of these rates (15% to 22.5%), and for mass-marketers (Kmart, Walmart, Target) you'll get 50% (10% to 15%). The reason for lower royalties is simple: Stores that push out tons of merchandise have a lot of clout, and they beat up the merchandise distributor to give them lower prices (which means there's less profit for the merchandiser, so they can't afford to pay a full royalty). It's just like that great schoolyard tradition: He who gets beaten up by the bully turns around and beats up the next-smaller person.

2. **Foreign sales:** Roughly 80% of the U.S. rates.

OTHER DEAL POINTS

Other than the royalty calculations, when you make a retail merchandise deal, most of the considerations are exactly the same as tour merchandising deals, such as:

1. Approval of the merchandise items
2. Approval of your likeness
3. Approval of the designs and layout
4. Restrictions on sell-off rights
5. Right to purchase merchandise at the end

In addition, there are a couple of points peculiar to retail:

Approval of Sublicenses.   As we discussed, you want the right to approve all agreements that your merchandiser makes with sublicensees (see page 413).

Cross-collateralization.   If your retail agreement is with the same company that has your tour merchandise (which it almost always is), you have to deal with whether the advance under the tour agreement is cross-collateralized with the retail deal (and vice versa). (For a discussion of cross-collateralization, see page 88.) Cross-collateralization is never good for you, but it usually means you get a bigger advance because the merchandiser is spreading their risk. So allow cross-collateralizing only if they offer you a humongous amount of money that you can't get any other way.

DIRECT TO CONSUMER (D2C)
(E-COMMERCE/INTERNET SALES)

As we discussed, **D2C** (also known as **E-Commerce** and **Internet Sales**) means selling merch through your official Web store (on your website) and via links to your social media. D2C started with wearable goods (T-shirts, hats, etc.) but has grown to include things like concert tickets, VIP experiences (see page 386 for what those are), and fan clubs. If you're big enough, D2C sales can exceed tour or retail earnings, but to make that happen, you need a good merch partner to set up and execute all this.

In the beginning, you can do your own D2C by manufacturing your own merchandise, then hiring someone to take the online orders, collect the money, and ship the goods. There are companies who do this for a percentage. As you move up, however, your volume will get too big for this kind of operation, and you'll need a merchandising company to take it over. In part this is because you need someone to handle the larger volume, but even more importantly, it's to get their expertise in designing and marketing product for D2C. For example, a good merchandiser knows how to analyze fan data to design merchandise that can maximize your sales.

When you license your D2C rights to a merchandiser, the U.S. royalty rates are in the range of 25% to 35% (foreign royalties are about 80% of those). Note this is higher than the 20% to 30% royalty we discussed for retail merchandise in the last section, and even more important, your D2C royalty rate is applied to the *retail* (selling) price of the goods (less sales tax, shipping, credit card fees, and the like), as opposed to retail merchandise royalties which are applied to the *wholesale* price. Since the retail price is obviously higher than wholesale, you can quickly see that you're getting much more money per unit on D2C than you are on retail (a higher percentage applied against a higher price). Merchandisers can afford to do this because they're the actual retailer who's selling directly to the public—meaning there's no store taking a profit in between the merchandiser and the fan. In fact, in D2C, there's no wholesale price at all—just the price to the consumer. So the merchandiser gets more money, and you get a bigger piece.

Another plus for D2C is that, when your merch is sold by a retailer or on tour, you have no idea who bought it. With D2C, when a fan buys something on your Web store, you know their name, email, and address. Meaning you have a way to talk to them in the future. Meaning you can keep them engaged with your career by feeding them information. Meaning you can pitch them to buy more merchandise, tickets, VIP packages, etc.

To your fans, the Web store looks like it's run by you because the merchandiser invisibly handles the back end (taking orders, collecting money, shipping, etc.). This is very cool, but it also means that it's your image on the front line with your audience. Fans who spend money on your Web store are likely your most die-hard fans, and you don't want to upset them if something goes wrong and it's not fixed right away. If someone orders a kiddy T-shirt and gets a bumper sticker that says "Up Yours," it's not the merchandise company's name that'll be in the angry tweets. So it's critical to have a solid company running the machinery behind the curtain.

We talked about bootleggers at concerts, and I suspect you won't be shocked to hear they're even more alive and well online. These sleazes sell phony goods on the auction sites, as well as a few places that specialize in knockoff goods. So be sure your D2C merchandiser has the resources to fight these scuzzbags.

In addition to these unique D2C issues, all the merchandising points we previously covered (artwork, approvals, sell-off, etc.) apply to D2C as well.

FAN CLUBS

Fan clubs are still around, but they're far less meaningful than they were in the past. And they're dwindling.

Here's why.

The purpose of fan clubs is to develop a community of your most loyal fans, so you can talk directly to them. In the dark days before the Internet, the only way to communicate with your fans was to go on radio or TV, or do interviews in magazines and newspaper. So fan clubs started as a way to create an "insider" experience for the most loyal fans. These fans sent in their dues by mail, got back a membership card to impress their friends, and also got exclusive content during the year (a newsletter, photos, information about the artist that wasn't yet public, etc.). And the artist made money on the fan club because of the membership fees.

Today, artists are constantly talking to their fans over social media, and every major event is immediately spread all over the Web. So the fan club experience of directly communicating with your peeps is so . . . 1980s. The only stuff a fan club can really offer is things like early access to tickets, or maybe streaming a record ahead of release, or a chance to win an exclusive experience with the artist. And even then, to make a fan club really viable, artists have to commit some serious time to creating exclusive content for the club. Most artists no longer bother to do that, since their fans are already getting real-time communication every time the artist goes to the grocery store.

For these reasons, I'm told only about 15% of artists have a fan club these days, and a good number of those are free to join. The reason a lot of artists stopped asking for membership fees is that they decided it's more important to build a database of fans than it is to charge dues. The ones who still require members to pay fees are usually major live performers who incentivize fans to join by giving them early access to tickets.

Even if fan club membership is free, you can still make money through the club by selling tickets or merchandise, especially if it's stuff you can only get if you're a member. If you're selling merchandise, your share is the D2C royalty we just discussed. For tickets, as we discussed on page 373, artists can get the right to sell a certain number of tickets through their fan club, and most merchandisers are set up to handle the ticket sales for you (just like D2C merch, it looks like the fan club is selling the tickets, but it's really the merchandiser in the back room doing the heavy lifting). Their deal is to add a fee per ticket (usually a few bucks) on top of the face value, which compensates them for handling the sales.

CAUTION

Before you tackle the rest of the book, be sure you have a pretty good understanding of record and publishing basics in Chapters 7, 8, 15, 16, and 18. If you skipped ahead and don't already know this stuff, I suggest you go back. Even if you're reading straight through, you might want to review those chapters quickly. The areas we're about to discuss are a bit complex and you need a solid grasp of the basics before attempting them.

Keep your arms and legs inside the car at all times.

If you're on the *Fast Track* or *Advanced Overview* and
you're interested in Classical Music,
go to Chapter 26 on page 421.
If Classical music puts you to sleep, saunter
on over to Motion Picture Music
in Chapter 27 on page 429.
If you answered "None of the above," *Fast Track* to the
Conclusion on page 489.

PART VII

Classical Music

26

Classical Music

I shall now tap my baton on the music stand to politely engage your attention, as we move into the world of classical music. Please do not applaud between movements, and speak only in quiet, mellifluous tones for the duration of this chapter.

The major labels, and a few larger independent classical labels, still do deals on the same basis as all other kinds of music, meaning the structure of a royalty, advance, etc., that we've already discussed. In particular, **crossover** artists like Andrea Bocelli (*crossover* meaning their appeal extends beyond the classical market to other genres) have deals that are virtually identical to the contracts we've discussed for pop artists.

But these deals are the exception. And Why, you ask? To use a refined term, the economics of classical music "suck." For example, the cost of recording a full orchestra can run $150,000 to $400,000, and typical album sales (at the time of this writing, CD and download sales are still the mainstay) are in the 5,000 to 15,000 unit range *worldwide* (remember, the sales levels in the earlier chapters for pop artists are only for the United States). In fact, a "big seller" classical album is 50,000 worldwide. Meanwhile, CDs and downloads are both declining rapidly, while streaming is just starting to kick in.

By the way, the recording costs I just gave you are typical for studio albums in the United States, where it's particularly expensive to record classical. That's because the AFM sets minimums for recording the musicians that make it far more expensive to record here than in Europe (at least other than the United Kingdom), where the unions aren't as involved in recording. However, live albums have recently gotten much cheaper in the United States, due to a new AFM union agreement that swapped a lower upfront fee (about 20% of the union fees for a studio album) for a big piece of the income. Specifically, if the orchestra owns the recording and enters into a distribution deal, the union gets 55% of the recordings' gross receipts.

But even with the union's concession, if you do the math, and throw in some marketing dollars, a traditional classical music recording can't make any money. Moreover, as CDs and downloads disappear, and the traditional classical music consumers go further into their golden years, things are looking even less rosy.

And in case that's not bad enough, classical is also disadvantaged in the streaming age. That's because streaming revenue is divided based on the number of plays, and a twenty-minute classical piece counts as one play. Perhaps this will change in the future, but as yet there are no signs of it. If we move to a per-user calculation (see page 145), that would likely make a difference. Also, as we discussed on page 217, publishers get more for streaming long songs, but most classical music is in the public domain, and this formula doesn't apply to masters. So for the moment, classical is a like a neglected cousin.

Because of all this, classical record deals have changed to a world where the label is more of a collaborator and distributor than a financier. In other words, the labels pay little or nothing for the albums, but rather just agree to distribute and market them. Meaning the artist has to find their own funding (more about that in a minute), deliver a finished album, and then license the rights to the label for distribution (usually for a limited term of ten years or so). In exchange, the labels often don't even pay royalties; they just give the artist a flat fee of a few thousand dollars, which is less than the recording costs. And if that's not funky enough for you, the labels sometimes make the artist buy a minimum number of units (in the range of 500 to 1,500) to offset their risk.

If there is a royalty, it's in the range of 20% to 30%, which sounds high, except that it's computed very differently from the artist royalties for mainstream folks. Instead of the royalty being a percentage of PPD (see page 82 for what that means), it's a percentage of the record company's receipts, meaning what they get from the distributor (in other words, the PPD minus a distribution fee).

More and more, this structure is becoming the norm even in cases where the label pays the recording costs.

So if the labels aren't paying recording costs, and the sales can never recoup recording costs, how do classical albums ever get made? The most common answer may surprise you:

Rich Donors.

The major orchestras are all nonprofit organizations, who are supported by charitable donations. And they use some of that money to record albums.

But why? Who puts money into a deal where they can't ever make it back? Are they idiots?

No, they're not stupid (well, there's this one oboe player . . .)

Orchestras know they can't make money from the albums, but they see records as marketing tools that build the orchestra's profile by showcasing them as recording artists.

So that's most of the biz these days—loss leaders. And indeed, because it's only a marketing tool, a number of orchestras (for example, the London Symphony Orchestra, the San Francisco Symphony Orchestra, and the Seattle Symphony Orchestra) simply make distribution deals (similar to what we discussed on page 202, with a distribution fee of about 15%). In these cases, they do their own manufacturing, marketing, and promotion, and brand it as their own label. Or sometimes they'll do a hybrid deal, where the orchestra pays the recording costs, but the label pays for physical manufacturing, and shares marketing and promotion, in which case there's a 50/50 profit split.

Now let's cleanse our palate with an amuse-bouche—the other terms of a classical record contract.

TERM AND PRODUCT

Because classical artists don't generally compose the material they record, and because their recordings are in essence "live performances," they can make records much faster than pop artists. Also, since the compositions already exist, the recordings can be planned very far in advance, which is not practical in the pop world. So for both of these reasons, classical artists can record several albums per year.

Historically, classical deals would commit the company and artist to record two or three albums per year, and the term of the deal would be for several years, firm. However, as the classical market shriveled, and costs continued to rise, multi-album commitments dropped off radically and are rare these days unless you're a *very* significant artist. Instead, similar to pop deals, the record company commits to one album at a time, with options for more. And nowadays, the companies don't even want more than one album per year. They don't think the market can handle more than that without cannibalizing an earlier release.

Historically, classical deals had the same exclusivity provisions as pop deals, but as the labels commit to less and less, the artists push back on the exclusivity. Ideally, there's no exclusivity for anything other than audio-only records. But even if the exclusivity is broader, they will (if you ask) carve out broadcasts and simulcasts. Catch-up streaming (meaning a stream of an earlier broadcast, usually on the broadcaster's site) can sometimes get carved out, but often the companies won't do this up front, so the artist and label just work it out on a case-by-case basis.

ROYALTIES

If you have a royalty deal (as opposed to the distribution license we already discussed), you won't be surprised to hear that royalties in the classical world are also lower. The good news, however, is that you're paid on every record sold, meaning the company eats all of the recording costs. In other words, the only thing recouped is the advance you put in your pocket. As you've seen, this is a radical difference from the pop world, where the company will recoup anything that crawls. (Remember, in this section, we're talking about a traditional classical deal, not crossover artists. Crossover artist deals recoup recording costs just like pop artists.)

How much lower are classical royalties? A typical deal is in the range of 7.5% to 10% (See page 92 for the range of pop music royalties). However, classical artists' royalties aren't "all-in" (see page 96), which means you aren't responsible for a producer, and thus you keep all the royalties (though you often have to share them, as noted in the next paragraph).

Classical albums are frequently an amalgamation of several artists. For example, Yo-Yo Ma plays with the Boston Pops, and Gustavo Dudamel conducts. Since important guest soloists like Yo-Yo get a royalty, and so do major conductors and very successful orchestras, the royalties are spread around. In fact, it's sometimes difficult to tell whose album it is. For the one I just described, is it a Yo-Yo, Boston Pops, or Gustavo album?

Just like guest artist recordings on the pop side (see page 152 for what those are), the royalties are allocated among the participants in an agreed proportion. While there's no hard-and-fast rule, a principal soloist might get 4% to 8%, a conductor 3% to 5% (if there's a conductor royalty; the conductor often gets a flat fee and no royalty), a guest soloist 2% to 3% (if not a flat fee), and a well-known orchestra 2% to 4%.

ADVANCES

As noted above, a typical classical release sells far less units than a typical pop release (or at least far less than what the pop company hopes to sell). So because of this, advances even for the superstars are much smaller, typically in the range of $5,000 to $10,000 per album. If an artist has "marquee value," meaning that his or her name is recognizable (e.g., Yo-Yo Ma, Plácido Domingo, John Williams, etc.), the advance is generally from $15,000 to $50,000.

The size of an advance also depends on:

1. The extent you participate in the recording. If you're only guesting, for example, your advance will be lower than if you're the principal soloist.
2. The expense of the recording. If you're the principal piano soloist on a recording, for example, you'll get a lower advance for an orchestral recording (which is expensive) than you will for a recording of piano solo works (where they just set up a microphone and drop a few bucks in your brandy snifter).
3. And lastly, your advance depends on that common denominator of all business: clout.

MECHANICAL ROYALTIES

Much of classical music is in the public domain, which means there's no mechanical royalties paid for the music (see page 311 for an explanation of public domain, and page 215 for a discussion of mechanical royalties). However, some of the compositions may be more recent, or even contemporary, and the record company has to pay mechanicals to the publishers of these works. Also, as we discussed, arrangements of public domain works are copyrightable if they have enough originality, and these also bear mechanical royalties.

When a company has to pay mechanical royalties, there is usually a reduction of your royalty. You're typically charged about half of the burden, although this is negotiable, and it's not always as simple as I've just stated. For example, sometimes the contract just says that your royalty rate goes down a point or two if the company has to pay mechanicals. By an amazing coincidence, this also results in your eating about half of the mechanicals.

As we move to a streaming world, where the digital service providers pay the mechanicals rather than the company, you should be sure that your label doesn't reduce you for mechanicals they don't pay.

MARKETING TIE-INS

Because of the limited sales potential of classical recordings, the companies look for alternative ways to market their albums. And marketing is particularly important for big artists who make expensive recordings. The reason isn't just the higher investment—it's because most classical compositions have been recorded many times before, by many other artists, so there's a need to convince buyers that this new recording is a "must-have."

One of the most powerful marketing tools is for you to appear in a public television special, or perform a concert tour, open a car dealership, etc. If you have some clout, you can get the label to commit money to these ventures. For example, you might get tour support (which we discussed on page 180). Or they might help pay for a PBS special. But while TV shows definitely help sell records, they're very expensive—public television only pays $50,000 to $100,000 for their programs, and the costs can easily run $500,000 to $700,000 or more. You might get some money back from artsy places like NHK in Japan, or Arte in Germany, but not enough to cover the costs of recording the video. So this is only feasible for high-profile orchestras that can self-finance (alone or with the label's help), or individual artists whose labels will pick up the costs to drive visibility and album sales. But as the market shrinks, record company contributions are shriveling with it.

If you're on the *Fast Track,* and you're interested in Motion Picture Music, go to Chapter 27 on page 429.
Otherwise, *Fast Track* to the Conclusion on page 489.

PART VIII

Motion Picture Music

27

Overview of Motion Picture Music

Congratulations! You are now in graduate school. To understand music in films, you need a complete knowledge of the music business (records, copyrights, and publishing), as well as a knowledge of the film business. I couldn't have put this chapter earlier, because you wouldn't have been ready for it. But now you are, so let's go.

INTRODUCTION

I have seen music screw up more motion pictures than bad directors. This is because music is a stepchild in movies. Its budget is small in comparison to the budget of the film, and as you'll see, putting music in films is really complicated. It's normally left until the last minute, at which point there's a massive panic and very little time to get it together. Often this is for a good reason—it may not be possible to record the music until the studio knows exactly what the picture looks like— but many times it's simply a matter of neglect. As music supervisors became more important in the industry (more about them later), this seems to have changed (a little). However, there are always panicked emergencies, no matter what.

ONE SONG—EIGHT DEALS

One of the main difficulties is that film people, by and large, don't fully understand music (not that they should—their expertise is in making films). And it doesn't help that film music is a twisted tangle of Gordian knots. For example, for every song going into a film, there are always deals to be made with at least three, and often up to eight, different folk:

1. The performer (singer/instrumentalist)
2. The record company to whom the performer is signed
3. The record producer
4. The songwriter
5. The publisher to whom the songwriter is signed
6. The owner of a master recording that's being licensed into the film or sampled in a song
7. The publisher who owns a song that's been sampled
8. The record company putting out the soundtrack album

If you have several songwriters signed to different publishers, several performers signed to different record companies, and a number of samples, you can get up to fifteen or twenty deals for just one song.

Now if any of these balls drop while you're juggling, or if any of the rights under one agreement don't match those required by another, the song may have to be trashed. And film producers on a tight delivery schedule with a multimillion-dollar film at stake don't like to be told that a song is holding up their picture (would you?).

For all these reasons, the music supervisors/business affairs/lawyers/studio executives in charge of film music have extraordinarily difficult jobs. If they deliver the music and pull off a minor miracle by balancing all the competing interests, it was expected and they're lucky to get a thanks. However, if something goes wrong and the film producer can't use the song, they're the villains. Wanna sign up?

So clearing music for films is (as we say in Texas) like being a one-legged man in an ass-kicking contest. But it's fun and satisfying when it works, and if you're strong of heart, come along and I'll show you this side of the business.

THE RIGHTS INVOLVED

Film music rights fall into two categories:

Acquisition of rights for the picture.   These are deals to put music in the film, meaning deals with:

1. Performing artists
2. Songwriters, composers, publishers
3. Record producers
4. Record companies, for the right to (a) use existing masters or

samples, and (b) allow one of their exclusive recording artists to create something new for the film.

Licenses of rights from the picture company to others.   Once the film company acquires the music rights, it makes deals to license that music to other people. Specifically:

1. A deal with a record company to release a soundtrack album
2. Licensing film clips for music videos
3. Possibly a publishing administration deal
4. Possibly a co-promotion deal (something that promotes both the film and a product; see page 435 for what those are).

Okay, that's a map of the landscape. Let's go visit the hot spots.

28

Performer Deals

OVERVIEW

The deal for an artist to record a song for a film has two distinct parts. One is to use the recording in the picture itself (which is pretty straight-forward), and the other is to use the recording on a soundtrack album and/or single (which can be horrendous).

PERFORMANCE IN THE FILM
(NO RECORD RIGHTS)

The deal for an artist to record a song for a picture is usually a flat fee. No muss, no fuss, no complications. Well, maybe one gigantic complication . . .

Remember, as we discussed on page 166, most record deals say that the record company owns all "recordings" made during the term, and that language is broad enough to include films. Also, the definition of "records" in every record deal includes electronic transmissions (un-derstandably, since the world has moved to streaming), which means streaming the film also falls under their exclusivity. So performing a song in a film requires the record company's consent, and your label becomes a cozy partner in these deals (meaning they'll be wanting a nice chunk of the fee). Often they'll want all of the fee (particularly if you aren't recouped), but will graciously apply half of that fee against your account. However, this is negotiable—meaning you might get some of the fee paid through to you.

Since you can't make this deal without the record company's con-sent, you have to involve them as soon as a proposal comes up. So, before you even start negotiating, **you must clear the deal with your record company.** In case you didn't hear me, *BEFORE you start nego-tiating, you must clear the deal with your record company.*

And in addition to the record company, if you're writing the song, your publisher will have to license the rights to use it in the film. So you also need them on board at the beginning.

Today, the major film companies have been stung enough to make sure the artist's record company and publisher have blessed the deal. But minor and independent film companies may not be so careful, and in the rush of the moment, anyone can slip in a puddle of oops. In addition, there are sometimes missed signals and miscommunications on both sides. For example, a director may have a relationship with an artist, and they get each other all excited and pledge their eternal love without realizing other folks need to come to the party. Or a manager might think he's cleared the rights with the record company, and indeed he has (sort of). For example, he may have discussed it with the company, and the company said it "sounds okay." That seems pretty good, but the record company may have only meant their approval was subject to working out a deal to compensate them, while the manager believed he had approval without qualification. So the moral is: Have the film company talk directly to the record company.

Of course, if your record deal has a built-in exclusion for soundtracks (see page 170), you don't have to worry about this. But most of the time you don't. And even if you have an exclusion, you may not want to use it for this film. (If the record company agrees to a particular soundtrack, you might want to save the exclusion for a time when they don't.) Or you may have already used the exclusion—the exclusion may only allow one cut every album cycle or so, and there may be a second film you want to do. Or the film company may require more rights than your exclusion allows. So be sure everyone knows what everyone else is doing.

And even if you have that exclusion in your record deal, your publisher will have to be involved if you write the song.

Fees

The artist's fee for the film can range anywhere from union scale (see page 87 for what that is) up to $400,000 plus for a major artist. The norm is about $5,000 to $10,000 for a minor artist, escalating to somewhere around $15,000 to $25,000 for a midlevel artist. Superstars tend to be in the $100,000 to $200,000 range, with some occasionally going higher if the film company is hot for them and the star is playing hard to get. Title songs (songs played over the opening or closing credits) pay better than background music. If the artist is also giving the film company soundtrack record rights and songwriting services, big names can get $200,000 to $400,000 plus.

Featured instrumentalists (for example, a solo violinist playing over the titles) get fees in the range of $10,000 to $20,000 for lesser-knowns, and sometimes as high as $100,000 for big names.

Sometimes films use specialty vocalists the same way that featured instrumentalists are used—sort of like being a "vocal instrumental." Usually it's someone well-known in their particular genre, like opera, Native American chanting, fraternity songs, etc. These folks usually get a fee of about $10,000 or so per track, though it can go higher if they're well-known and their vocal increases awareness of the film.

If your fee is at the high end of this range, all or a portion of it will often be treated as an advance against your royalties (we'll discuss soundtrack record royalties in a minute).

All-in Deals

Some artists prefer to negotiate an **all-in** fee deal with the film company, which is the same concept as the recording fund we discussed in connection with record deals. For example, for a total of $75,000, they'll record and deliver a completed track. In this case, the artist pays the recording costs out of the $75,000 and keeps the difference as a fee.

Unless the fee is extraordinarily high, and the artist produces himself or herself, I generally don't like this. Directors are fussy about what goes into their films, and you don't want to be in the position of having to re-record it several times at your expense. Also, if the artist isn't the producer of the recording, you have to pay out a producer's fee, which can be an unknown variable. I much prefer just having the artist show up, sing, and leave.

On the other hand, if you're fully self-contained (like an EDM artist who produces yourself and can do the track on your laptop), your costs are minimal and most of the fee goes straight into your pocket. In this case, to the extent you can treat most of the fee as "recording costs," your label won't share in that part of it (Shhh . . . don't tell them).

Rights Granted

If the film company wants to use your song in advertising and marketing the film, the first question of course is whether you want that to happen. Your record company will also have an opinion on this, depending on what else they're promoting at the time. For example, if you have a big song out at the same time, they may not want another of your songs in ads for the film. On the other hand, where the film looks to be massive, so that having your song associated with it will help both the song and your career, you'd definitely want them to use your song in advertising and marketing. Always great to have someone spend millions of dollars to pump your music into people's ears.

Assuming everyone's cool with it, you don't want to give the film company any more than the right to use your master (a) in the film, (b) in the marketing of the film (if that's part of the deal), (c) on the soundtrack album, and (d) on a single. This means you're excluding things like licenses for commercials, licenses for other films, etc. You and your record company should control these other rights, although they're often restricted (as we'll discuss in a minute).

Unless you have very little bargaining power and are up against an obnoxious film company (or unless you're dealing with an animated film, where they dig in no matter who you are), none of this should be a serious problem. If you keep all these rights, the usual film studio restriction is that you can't issue a synchronization license for the master (meaning you can't license the master to another film or television show, or a commercial) for a number of years, if not forever. The theory is that they don't want someone else getting the goodwill of a song closely identified with their picture.

The other kicker is that some film companies require the right to use your recording in sequels and remakes of the film, as well as ancillary uses such as theme park shows and attractions, movie-related merchandise, and studio tours. You almost always have to give up these rights, but sometimes you can get an additional fee for the use. Either it's a set fee per use, which the film company pays according to a schedule in the contract, or sometimes, with a lot of clout, you can leave it to be negotiated in good faith at the time of the use (with the provision that you can't stop them from using it; you just get to argue about the size of the fee).

Another issue is **co-promotions.** That's where the film company ties into an advertiser (such as McDonald's, Burger King, Le Sex Shoppe, etc.). These folks do things like give away plastic cups and toys to promote the movie, hang posters in their stores, hype the film in their advertising, write the film's name on their men's room walls, etc. As part of this package, the film company will want to use your master in radio and TV commercials that promote both the advertiser and the film, and that's a source of negotiation. You may well object to having your voice on a commercial for something besides the film—certainly without getting paid, and maybe altogether if it's inconsistent with your image. Also, if you're a superstar, the right to use your voice in a commercial is a serious exploitation of your persona.

This is usually resolved by bludgeoning you into submission, since the film companies fight hard for these rights—co-promotions can mean millions in advertising for the film. If you have a lot of clout, you may be able to get a pre-negotiated additional payment, or even prohibit some or all co-promotions without your consent (which means you can make a deal later, if you're willing to allow it, but otherwise they can't do it). Another compromise is to limit how the song is used in the co-promotion (for example, it can only be used to promote the film itself, not to promote the product). You may also be able to get category restrictions for co-promotions, though they usually give you things that wouldn't likely sponsor the film anyway, like tobacco or firearms. Or if you have an existing sponsor relationship—for example, Pepsi won't be happy if you endorse them and the film company uses your recording in a co-promotion with Coke. Alcohol may be an issue if the film wants to go after that demographic, since liquor folks pay big bucks for co-promotions, but if you have a personal concern about being associated with liquor, they'll usually respect that.

You also want to be careful about credit on the soundtrack album cover, and in particular CD stickers (obviously a dwindling issue, but still around). Particularly if you're a major artist, your label (and you, too) won't want your name used more prominently to sell the product. Most record labels only allow your name to be listed as long as at least three or four other artists on the album are listed, and they'll say that your name can't be larger or more prominent than any others. They may also require the listing to be in alphabetical order, to keep you from being the main piece of bait on the hook.

Credit

The other major negotiating point is credit. Unless you have the main title song (which I'll talk about in a minute), you won't have much to say about credit. Just make sure your credit is no less prominent than any other artist's, both as to size and placement in the film. In reality, this means you'll be included in the **crawl,** which are those credits resembling an eye chart that roll by at the end of the film after everyone's left the theater. (Everyone except me, that is, because I always stay to see who did the music. Half the time I can't read it because it goes by too fast.)

If you do the **main title song** (meaning the song at the beginning of the picture, as opposed to the **end title song,** which is, not surprisingly, the song played over the credits at the end), you can sometimes negotiate a credit in the **main titles.** *Main titles* are where the director, writer, and stars are credited, and are usually, but not always, at the beginning of the picture. If they're at the end, they're the first credits after the picture finishes.

Whether or not you get main-title placement, a title song performer should be able to get a **single card** credit (meaning no other credit is on the screen at the same time as yours), or at least a card shared only with the songwriter.

You should also ask for your credit to be the same size as the director's, writer's, and (film) producer's credit.

RECORD RIGHTS TO FILM PERFORMANCES

When we move into soundtrack records, things get more complicated. *Way* more complicated.

First, as with your performance in the film, your record company has to sign off. You're their exclusive artist, and if the soundtrack album isn't on their label, they have to agree you can go somewhere else.

Assuming you get your record company to go along, then you not only need to negotiate a deal for the use of your recording in the film (which involves the same issues we discussed in the prior section), but also for the use of your recording on the soundtrack album. There are seven (count 'em, Seven!) aspects to soundtrack album deals:

1. What's your royalty? Is it all-in (if you've forgotten what that means, we'll discuss it in a second) or net to you?
2. Is your royalty paid to you (rarely) or to your record company?
3. What can the company distributing the soundtrack album recoup against your royalty?
4. Once the soundtrack distributor recoups, and royalties are payable to you, what can your record company recoup against that royalty?
5. Exactly what record rights does the film company get?
6. If your label doesn't distribute the soundtrack album, can your label use the master? And if so, how can they use it?
7. Who's responsible for what in connection with music videos?

Let's take these in order:

Royalty

Artists' royalties on soundtrack albums generally hover in the range of 12% to 14%, **all-in** (i.e., including the producer, mixer, guest artists, and any other royalty participants), and if you're a new artist, it's sometimes even lower. If you get a **net royalty,** meaning the record company pays everyone else and you get to keep everything they pay you, it will of course be lower (at a minimum, they have to pay a producer, but they could be obligated to pay a royalty to a guest artist, mixer, etc.).

Animated films like to pay even less (animation pays less for pretty much everything, by the way, since the star is often a singing weasel).

If you're midlevel and up, your royalty will almost always be lower than you would get in the marketplace because the film company takes part of the royalties. Also, this royalty is pro-rata (see page 162), which means you only get a small piece of the royalty on albums (because you'll only have one or two cuts out of the ten or more on the album). In the streaming era, this is becoming less and less relevant, since you get the full amount on single-song streams and full album sales and downloads are swirling down the drain. But those are still around, so let's go over it.

If all the artists on the album are at about the same level, the 12% to 14% pro-rata is pretty fair. However, if you're the only star on the record (such as an album whose other cuts are minor artists, or if you're the only song on an album of **underscore** [meaning the orchestral score], or if you're the only superstar among a bunch of low and midlevel artists), you should definitely get more. In these cases, you're justified in asking for a much higher royalty, say in the 16% to 18% range— sometimes more if you've really got clout. You might also ask for a **floor,** meaning that no matter how many tracks are on the album, your pro-rata royalty will be no less than say $\frac{1}{10}$ (or $\frac{1}{11}$, or $\frac{1}{12}$, depending on your bargaining power) of the total royalty. For example, if you had a 10% royalty and a floor of $\frac{1}{10}$, you'd get 1% on the album even if there were fourteen masters. Still another technique is to get a non-pro-rated royalty, of say 1% to 1.5% on the entire album. The companies will kick and scream, but if you have enough clout, you can pull it off. It's getting easier because this concept is only relevant for CD sales and full-album downloads, which are dying.

It's also possible to get escalations based on sales of the album.

An exception to all this is where the soundtrack album is the same label to whom you're signed. In that case, you should get no less than the royalty you have under your record deal.

For a featured instrumentalist or a featured vocalist (which we discussed on page 434), royalties are in the range of 9% to 10%, pro-rated based on the number of album cuts, and further pro-rated if you're performing with another royalty artist (for example, if you sing with an orchestra that gets a royalty).

The Record Company Piece

Record companies want to collect all the royalties you get from soundtrack recordings. They normally keep 50%, as a cost of waiving your exclusivity and allowing your recording to be released on somebody else's label. If you have an enormous amount of bargaining power, you may be able to beat them down below 50%, but it's getting tougher to pull this off. However, if your company happens to be distributing the soundtrack album, you should ask for 100% of the royalty, because you're not being released from any exclusivity.

The companies normally treat your share of royalties exactly the same as all other royalties under your deal. That means they use your share to recoup your deficit, or else pay it to you on your next accounting statement if you're recouped. Sometimes you can get half or all of your share paid to you even if you're unrecouped. The ability to do this varies directly with your bargaining power.

If you get an advance against your royalties, the record company will also want a piece of that.

Recoupment

Unlike record deals, where everything is recoupable, in films you can often knock out a good portion (sometimes even all) of the costs. Let's look at them individually:

Recording Costs. You can sometimes make all or a portion of the recording costs nonrecoupable. You do this is by arguing that the costs of recording are really costs of the film, which they'd have to spend even if there wasn't an album, and therefore it's not fair to charge these costs against your royalties. If you're a superstar, you can pull it off; if you're not, you'll end up with anywhere from 50% to 100% of the costs being recoupable.

Artist's Performance Fee. Another question is whether any of your fee to record for the film is recoupable from your royalties. Again, you can take the position that this is a fee to perform for the film, not on records, and so they shouldn't recoup it. If you have some bargaining power, you can pull this off; otherwise, a part of it may be recoupable. (As a negotiating ploy, if you want to increase your fee and are getting nowhere, try making a portion of the increase recoupable. But use this as a last resort.)

Sometimes soundtrack albums are financed by a record company that pays for the music and gets the right to put out the album (we'll discuss these deals in Chapter 33). The monies paid by the record company are advances against the soundtrack album royalties, and because the film performers' fees come out of these advances, all or a portion of the fee is often treated as an advance against the artist's royalties.

Conversion Costs.   As good as all this news sounds, there are costs recouped under film deals that aren't chargeable under record deals. They're not charged under record deals for a simple reason: They don't exist in record deals.

These babies are known as **conversion costs,** a name I take credit for inventing. (I'm really a pretty modest guy, but every once in a while something gets the better of me.) *Conversion costs* are the costs of converting a film recording to a master that can be used in a record. For example, the recording for the film might only be thirty seconds, but you need a three-minute version for the record. The conversion costs are the costs to do this, and they include the kind of costs you'd expect, such as remixing, editing, overdubbing additional instruments (called **sweetening**), and sometimes even totally re-recording the song. But they also include something you haven't seen before, called:

Re-use Fees.   Whenever you take a recording made for one medium (in this case, a motion picture) and use it in another (like records), the union charges you a fee. These fees are called **re-use fees** or **new-use fees** because they are charges to re-use an existing recording in a different way (a new use). (Re-use fees are also payable when you go the other way around—taking a recording made for records and using it in a film—and in other situations like going from television to records, records to television, records to commercials, etc.) The reasoning is that, when you use an existing recording, you don't have to hire the singers and musicians you would have needed to re-record the song. Since you're putting union members out of work, the unions allow you to do this only if you pay them an amount listed on a schedule (which is close to union scale for the missed sessions).

The re-use fees charged for a particular recording are directly proportionate to the number of performers on the track. Thus, a three-piece band is cheap, and the Los Angeles Philharmonic Orchestra is not. Indeed, for a fully instrumental, orchestral soundtrack album, the re-use fees can run $90,000 or more.

Conversion costs are almost always recoupable from your royalties.

Re-recording Restriction. Just like your record deal, soundtrack deals include a re-recording restriction (see page 170). The period is usually five years, but the date can be from recording, from release of the picture, or from release of an album or single. If the date is measured from anything except the date of recording, be sure the restriction period someday expires. For example, if it's measured from release, and the track is never released, it goes on forever.

Also, even during the restriction, try to exclude live streams, festival broadcasts, TV appearances, and the like.

Singles. Another point of contention is the question of whether there will be a single, and if so, who can put out a single with your performances on it. (We touched on this on page 171.)

The "whether" question depends on scheduling. A single is most helpful to the film if it's a hit right when the film opens. But if you're promoting your own singles around that time, your record company won't want a competing single out there fighting for attention.

Assuming there's going to be a single, the next question is, which company will put it out? Historically, the artist's label always kept singles rights, because they wanted to coordinate it with their other marketing efforts around you. Then singles got to be unprofitable because, as we discussed, it can be expensive to promote a single, and single sales dwindled. However, in those days a successful single drove sales of albums, and since the soundtrack distributing company got the profits from the album, it had an incentive to spend money on singles. So the artist's labels quit being so precious and let the soundtrack album companies handle the singles.

Then the streaming age arrived, album profits fell off a cliff, and a "soundtrack album" became primarily a "playlist" on the streaming services. Moreover, most consumers don't stream the entire album; they just listen to the tracks they like. Meaning everything is basically a single. Now what?

Well, it was clear that physical and downloads would be handled by the soundtrack album company, but if those were the only rights they had, they couldn't make enough money to justify their expenses. So the practice now is that all rights (including streaming) are controlled by the soundtrack album distributor, but they pay a large chunk of the money, maybe even 50% of the profits, to the artist's label.

Can Your Record Company Use the Master?

As noted earlier, one nice goodie you can sometimes get is the right to use the recording on your own albums. Because of declining album sales, this has become much less of an issue, but for the time being, it's still around.

If the film company allows you to use the master on your own album, they'll limit it to one album, or maybe one studio album plus one Greatest Hits. They'll also say you can't put it on your record for a period of somewhere between six months (if you've really got clout) to two years, with the norm being around one year. The period before you can release the master on your record is called a **holdback.** The clock may start at release of the picture, release of the soundtrack album, or release of your recording as a single. Whatever you do, make sure the date someday arrives. For example, if you measure your period from release of the soundtrack album, and the album is never released, you could never use it. If you ask, the film company will usually agree to an outside date after which you can use it no matter what.

Sometimes your record company wants to put the cut on your own album at the same time as the soundtrack album is out (in other words, there's no holdback). The film company (and especially the record company with the soundtrack album) won't like this at all. But if you're important enough, and it's the only way they can get you, they may go along.

When you use the track on your own record, you'll of course get the royalty under your own deal, which is likely higher. However, you're responsible for paying the producer and any other royalty participants.

In recent years, with rare exceptions (like *La La Land,* or *A Star is Born,* for example), soundtrack album sales have been abysmal, so there's been a trend for many pictures not to have a soundtrack album at all. In that case, the only records with the soundtrack cut are the artist's own, and there's obviously no holdback in these situations. When there's no soundtrack album, your label and the film company may nonetheless work together to promote your song as a single.

The film company may ask for a piece of your royalty if you use it on your record, and my response is to tell them to stuff it. So far, they've generally stuffed it, though they may work out a deal with your record label.

Music Videos

If there's going to be a music video, the record and film company usually share the cost 50/50, and the film company customarily supplies footage from the film (at no cost) to be included in the video.

In the beginning, film companies turned these videos into long previews of the movies. This worked terrifically until the TV broadcasters figured out they were giving away free advertising for the film, at which point the practice came to an abrupt halt. So now there's limited footage from the film in a music video, and in fact there's usually a second version without any film footage.

You should ask for some creative approvals of videos, but this is really hard because the film company (rightly) sees this as marketing for the film. You can usually pull off consultation rights (meaning they talk to you about it, but don't need your approval).

29

Film Songwriter Deals

TERMINOLOGY

Let's now look at film songwriter deals. By songwriter deals, I mean deals for *songs* (both music and lyrics, or sometimes instrumental only) written for the film, as opposed to what's known as the **score** or **underscore,** which is background music underneath dialogue, action, etc. (We'll deal with underscore in Chapter 30.) Also, this chapter deals with *creating* a song for the film, as opposed to licensing an existing song (not written for the film). (Licensing songs is covered in Chapter 31.)

DEAL POINTS

When you write a song for a film, you typically get a fee plus songwriter royalties. If you're a songwriter of even moderate stature, you may be also able to keep a piece of the publishing.

Fees

The range of songwriting fees is anywhere from zero to $100,000 plus for established writers. There are occasionally deals even higher in the stratosphere, but they're rare. Zero is even rarer, but it can happen with a low-budget film that has no music budget and, instead of paying, lets the songwriter keep all the publishing (see page 229, where we talked about the fact that songs in films can earn substantial performance monies in foreign territories, as well as on television here).

The majority of deals fall in the range of $25,000 to $50,000 for major studio films. Whether or not the writer gets a part of the publishing also affects the size of the fee.

If you're a big-name songwriter, you can sometimes get additional monies (called **kickers**) based on the success of the film. For example, you might get more dough if the film does $100 million U.S. box-office gross; another kicker at $150 million, etc. There can also be kickers based on streaming numbers and/or singles-chart performance.

By the way, a film company will never obligate itself to use a song. The most it will do is agree to pay the fee, which is known as **pay or play** because it can either use your song (play) or pay you to go away. This is similar to the pay-or-play provisions in record deals, which we discussed on page 111.

If your song isn't used, you should ask them to assign back any interest in the copyright they may have gotten. You may or may not get this, since they've paid you the full fee.

Step Deals

Songwriter deals are sometimes done on a **step** basis, meaning the deal is done over a series of "steps." The steps are:

1. The writer creates the song and gives the company an informal demo recording. They only get a small amount of money for this, or sometimes nothing other than the costs to record the demo.
2. If the film company doesn't like the demo, it either passes or goes to step two, which requires the writer to rewrite the song for a small additional fee (or maybe no more money). If the company then likes it, it's a firm deal; if not, the deal is off.
3. Once the film company is happy, it goes forward on a pre-negotiated deal to use the song. At this point the deal is the same as the songwriter deals we just discussed, although I like to ask for more money because we've covered their downside.

All of this is a fancy way of saying the writer does it **on spec** (meaning "on speculation"). In other words, he or she writes the song without a commitment from the film company to pay a full fee. It may be completely on spec, meaning no writer's fee up front, or the film studio may pay a small fee (usually in the range of $2,500 to $5,000, sometimes as high as one-half the normal fee) for writing the song. If the studio likes the song and wants to go forward, it pays the rest of the full fee.

If you're a major songwriter, you should do very little on spec, because you don't want to spend your time working on a project that will pay you half or less of your normal fee. Also, rejection is not good for your self-image, unless you get your full fee. (It's not great even then, but at least you didn't totally waste your time.)

If you're doing a step deal, try to get your song back if they don't accept the demo. The studio will only be out a few bucks, and they shouldn't get ownership rights. They, of course, argue that they paid for the demos, and may have even given you a small fee, so they should own everything. Still, with some clout, you should be able to get the song back. However, if you use the song elsewhere, the studio will require you take out any specific melody from the underscore, or any reference to the title, characters, or plot of the film.

Another way to get your song back (you didn't hear it here . . .) is to simply not sign anything until the demo is accepted and the deal is firm.

Rights Granted

Music written for films is always treated as a work for hire (see page 307), so your contract will have the magic language that makes it so. The film companies insist on this because, if it's not a work for hire, you (or your heirs) could terminate the copyright assignment after thirty-five years. (As we discussed on page 312, there's no termination right for works for hire.) If you were able to terminate, you might stop them from exploiting their film, or you might demand a percentage of the gross national product to let them continue.

With respect to usage, the film company wants the right to use your song not only in the film, but also in **sequels** (films that start where the last one left off), **prequels** (films that take place in time before the film for which the song is licensed), and **spinoffs** (films with the same characters in different adventures), advertising, trailers, co-promotions (page 435), and out-of-context uses (page 244). If you have a *lot* of clout you can sometimes prohibit some or all co-promotions, or at least limit how the song is used in the co-promotion (page 442 for limitation on masters; you can get the same things for the song).

Over the last several years, film companies have radically expanded this list of things they can do with your song, all without paying you: studio tours, theme parks, live entertainment (like Broadway shows, ice shows, etc.), storyteller and sing-along records, a TV series based on the film, film-themed video games, merchandising, DVD menus, outtakes (scenes deleted from the film), making-ofs (behind-the-scenes footage of filming), toaster ovens (just seeing if you're paying attention), and whatever else they can throw in the soup.

You usually have to give up these rights, but with some clout, you can get more money for them—either by increasing your original fee, or getting additional monies if the song is used in one of these categories. If they agree to pay more, it'll either be a pre-negotiated amount listed in the contract, or a requirement for them to pay you a "customary fee" that you can argue about later. Go for the customary fee if you can; any fees they list today could be really low by the time you actually get there.

Songwriter Royalties

Traditional film deals require you to transfer the entire copyright ownership to the film studio, and you get 50% of the song's earnings. As we discussed on page 221, these monies are called the "writer's share," and the film studio's remaining 50% is called the "publisher's share." Under these traditional deals, you get no share of the studio's performance monies because you'll be paid directly by the PRO (see page 226 if you don't remember how this works).

Publishing Royalties

While the mainstream publishing industry has done away with the distinction between writer's share and publisher's share, and instead just pays a percentage of total income (as we discussed on page 277), the distinction between writer's share and publisher's share is alive and well in the film world. That's because songwriters generally just get the writer's share of royalties.

As noted above, however, if you have some clout, you can sometimes get a piece of the publisher's share of income. This is typically from 25% to 50% of the publisher's share, along with the same percentage of copyright ownership. So if you get 50% of the publisher's share, you'll get (a) 100% of the writer's share of income, meaning 50% of the total income, or 50¢ for every dollar that comes in; plus (b) 50% of the publisher's share of income (meaning 50% of the remaining 50¢, or 25¢), for a total of 75% of every dollar that comes in (75¢). However, unlike mainstream publishers, who just say you get 75% of the income, most film studios break out the royalties into two calculations: one for your writer's share, and a separate one for your piece of the publisher's share. And in calculating the publisher's share, they may try to deduct an administration fee (see page 278 for what that means). In fact, if the film studio doesn't administer its own publishing company, it will have an administration deal with another publisher, and that other publisher's fees will come out before they split with you.

Some studios will write the deal as 75% of income, and in this case, you'll only get 50% of the publisher's share of performance money (see page 279 if you don't remember why).

There are a few situations, however, where you can't get a share of the publishing unless you're gargantuan, and even then it's difficult. Those are when you write songs for (a) animation films, (b) huge franchise movies like Star Wars or Marvel, and (c) other 900-pound gorillas who like to beat their chests in this area. When traipsing through the ape habitat, get as much front money as you can, to compensate for the fact that you're taking less on the back end.

If your song is based on music in the underscore, getting a share of publishing is trickier. As you'll see in the next chapter, underscore composers typically don't get a share of publishing in the score. Thus, since the song includes underscore, the composer won't have a piece of the publishing. But if you're a lyricist who wrote words for the underscore, you can sometimes get a share of publishing for your piece of the song. For example, if you wrote 50% of the song, and the studio is sharing 50% of publishing with the creators, you get half of that 50% publishing, or 25% of the total publishing. Put another way, you have one-half of the song, and therefore (a) 50% of the writer's share (25¢ out of every dollar), plus (b) 50% of the 50% share of the publishing income, meaning 25% of the publishing income (12.5¢ of every dollar). So the grand total is 37.5% of the total income from the song.

If you're the underscore composer, and the song is separately identifiable from the underscore—in other words, if it has a distinct name and lyrics—you should argue for a share of publishing on the song, even though you don't share in the same music when it's used in the underscore. We'll discuss this more on page 450.

Also, if you're the underscore composer and you write a song that is *not* based on a theme in the underscore, you should be able to get a separate songwriter fee and a percentage of that song's publishing income.

If you do get a share of publishing, the studios want the exclusive administration rights (see page 220 for a discussion of administration). If you've got clout, you may be able to keep co-administration (unless it's the title song, where the studio feels it's so identified with the film that they have to keep control). (Co-administration is discussed on page 299.) Even with co-administration, however, there will be restrictions on sync licenses, as we discussed in connection with masters on page 234 (e.g., you can't license to another film, TV show, or commercial).

If you don't get co-administration, you may still be able to approve certain types of sync licenses (such as commercials), just like in any other songwriter deal (see page 294), but this takes muscle. At a minimum, try for consultation rights on commercials, which means they have to discuss proposed uses with you, but they can make the final decision. Also, try to get paid directly by the soundtrack record company for mechanical royalties, and by your performing rights society for the publisher's piece of performance monies, so you don't have to wait for the money to go through the film company.

Some small-budget films will license songs for very little and let the composer keep all ownership, administration, and income from the songs. However, they'll restrict synchronization licenses, as we've discussed.

Credit

The other major provision in a songwriter deal is credit. Normally, unless you write the title song, and it's performed by a major artist, you get a credit in the "crawl" (see page 436). If this is the case, there's not much to say except that your credit shouldn't be any less prominent than any other songwriter's.

If you do write the main title song, you may be able to get credit on a **single card** (meaning no one else's credit is on the screen at the same time), except that it can be coupled with the song's performer, such as "Title song performed by X, written by Y." Possibly you can get your card in the **main titles** (meaning those listing the stars, director, etc.) and, if so, you should ask for the size to be no less than that of the writer, director, or (film) producer.

If you're a really major writer, you may be able to get credit in the **billing block** of paid ads for the film, but this is extraordinarily hard to come by. (The billing block is that microscopic box of credits down at the bottom of movie ads.)

An exception to these rules is where the film features a number of original songs, and you're the main songwriter (for example, *A Star Is Born*). In that case, you can get credit in the main titles (without sharing with the performer credit), and also in the billing block. However, this credit is usually conditioned on at least four or five of your songs being featured in the film.

Top-level writers may also get a credit in ads for the soundtrack album in *Billboard* and other trades.

30

Composer Agreements

Composers are the guys and gals who write the **underscore.** *Underscore,* also called *score,* is the music underneath the dialogue, action, transitions, etc., that you're not supposed to notice. If you've ever seen a film without music, you know how stark and empty it feels. A good underscore can radically increase the impact of a film, just as a bad one can make a movie feel weird and cheap.

You may be surprised to hear that most film scoring is no longer done by a full orchestra sitting in a recording studio, watching film clips on a giant screen. With the exception of a few old-school composers who don't "do" electronics, most films are first scored electronically (meaning with just a synthesizer), so the director and producer can approve the music. If it's a small-budget film, that electronic score may be it. For bigger-budget films, once the electronic score is locked, the composer brings in an orchestra, clamps headphones over their ears, and has them listen to the electronic score while they overdub their parts (meaning they replace the synthesized violins with real ones, add acoustic instruments, etc.). In some cases, the composer freshly records what was in the electronic score with an orchestra.

DEAL POINTS

Deals for composers are similar to those for songwriters, except that a composer almost never gets any share of the publishing.

Other than extremely low-budget films (where the composer might keep the publishing to compensate for getting little or no fee), the only exception to this publishing ban is where a portion of the underscore is used in a song written for the film (we touched on this on page 448). For example, if you're a composer, and the studio hires a lyricist to write words for one of your underscore themes, you might get some of the publishing for that song. But you only get it if the stars line up correctly, meaning: (1) the music and lyrics constitute a "real song," with its own title, and (2) the lyricist is getting a piece of the publishing on that song (if the lyricist isn't getting a share of publishing, it's much harder for the composer to get any). Assuming all that works out, and you get a publishing piece, it will only be for that melody when it's used in the song. You won't share in the publishing of that melody when it's used in the underscore.

The fee for writing and conducting a major studio theatrical motion picture underscore ranges anywhere from a low of $50,000 to a high of $2,000,000 plus for the superstars. The really big deals are reserved for **tentpole** pictures (basically meaning the massive releases, like *Fast and Furious*, *Avengers*, etc.) or big-budget animated films. The normal range is from $300,000 to $1,000,000, though lower-budget independent films are less.

More and more, studios want to do **package** deals (meaning a lump sum that covers both the fee and recording costs) because that makes it easier for them to manage the film budget. The prices are in the same range as above, but can be $50,000 to $100,000 higher to cover the cost of creating an electronic score. Generally, but not always, the costs of recording live musicians are paid by the studio on top of the package fee.

If you can avoid a package, you'll be better off, though that's not always possible. As we'll discuss in a bit, packages can do some serious damage to the composer's pocketbook if things don't go well.

Because composer prices have drifted downward over the last few years, more and more studios are open to the idea of bonuses based on box-office gross. For example, you might get $50,000 for every $25 million of box office. The size of each bonus, and the levels where you kick in, are very deal specific, depending on the budget of the film, the size of your fee, and that ever-present factor, your clout.

Historically, the bonuses were based only on U.S. box office, but now you can get kickers for worldwide box office. If you do, the worldwide number is around two times the U.S. number (though one studio uses 2.25 times U.S.). In other words, if your bonus is based on $100 million U.S. box-office gross, it would kick in at a worldwide box office of $200 million. You should say that you get your bonus on the first to occur of these (U.S. or worldwide), in case the worldwide distribution is delayed (or the foreign grosses suck).

If your bonuses are based on worldwide gross, by the way, the studio will count only a portion of the gross in China. That's because the government takes a huge tariff on foreign films.

By the way, you can only get worldwide bonuses from studios that own the international distribution rights to the film. Studios sometimes sell off foreign rights to independent distributors (for large guarantees that help finance the film), and in those cases, the studio makes little or no additional money from the foreign grosses. So it can only base your bonus on U.S. and maybe Canadian earnings.

As to other deal points, most of the issues we discussed in Chapter 29 concerning songwriters also apply to composers. However, there are some weird twists that live only in composer-land, so let's take a walk down that crooked path.

Delivery Date.   Interestingly, composer deals have no term. They go on until the composer delivers the score, which could mean the composer works on a film for four or five months, sometimes even years.

The process starts with **spotting,** which means the composer and director determine precisely which "spots" need music, as well as the exact length of each piece needed (measured in tenths of seconds). Historically, spotting happened only when there was a **final cut** of the film, meaning there wouldn't be any more changes. With animation, and with films that add a lot of special effects after they've been shot, it's not uncommon for the composer to get chunks of the film over time. In this case, they do the spotting and composing for each of the pieces as they come.

Whether the film comes to the composer in pieces or in one big glorious package, it's common for directors to keep making changes all along. Which means the music has to keep adjusting. This is more serious than it sounds. A change of even one second in a scene may require a total rewrite of the music because a well-written score moves precisely with the action on screen, and even a slight variation throws everything out of whack. It's like a marching band doing an extra half step between beats. So changes mean the composer goes back to the drawing board, though sometimes a good music editor can creatively edit existing music to the new scene.

Anyway, because there's no end date, you could be tied up for a *looooong* time. Which brings us nicely to our next topic:

Exclusivity.   Composer deals used to be exclusive until delivery of the score, which meant you couldn't do anything else during that time. Since the studios no longer limit how long they can keep you working—it goes until you finish—you have to insist that your deal is **non-exclusive,** meaning you can take other work rather than starve.

The studio will agree to this, but only if you agree that the other work won't prevent you from delivering to them on time.

The studios all require exclusivity at the end, from the time you actually start recording the score until you finish.

Payment Schedule. Historically, before you got any money, the studios made you sign something called a **Certificate of Authorship,** also known to its friends as a **C of A.** This is a one-page document that says they own everything you do, and the problem is that you're giving up ownership without having the deal fully negotiated. So once you sign it, you lose a lot of leverage.

More and more, studios have now adopted a policy of not paying any money until the full contract is signed. Because these deals can be pretty complex, this policy can seriously delay your paycheck. So if you're working for one of these studios, it's a good idea not to do too much work before the contract is signed.

Composers normally get their fees in either thirds or fourths. If it's in thirds, you usually get one-third on spotting, one-third on commencement of recording, and one-third on completion of services. If you're paid in fourths, expect one-fourth upon spotting, one-fourth on commencement of recording, one-fourth on completion of recording, and the balance on completion of services. "Completion of recording" is almost always the same as "completion of services," but occasionally you have to stick around and help with dubbing the music into the picture, editing for the soundtrack album, sweeping the floor, etc.

Major composers can speed up the payment schedule a bit. Here's a recent deal (it's in thirds and sixths, but it could also be fourths as well): one-third on commencement of services and execution of the agreement, one-third on commencement of recording, one-sixth on delivery of the score, and one-sixth on completion of all services.

The studios that pay based on a C of A will hold back some money until signature of the full agreement, which may be well after the services have started (or finished). The range is from 10% to one-third of the total fee.

Orchestrations. It may surprise you to know that many composers don't have the ability to write musical parts for each instrument in their orchestras. (In fact, some composers don't even read music, although this is rare. These guys are known in the trade as "hummers.") Most of us assume that all film composers are like John Williams, who is a premier orchestral arranger, and who understands the subtleties of every instrument. However, many composers only write the melody line for the underscore, then give it to an **orchestrator,** who writes out the parts for the trumpets, oboes, clarinets, violins, etc. Next time you see a film, look for the orchestrator's credit buried among the assistants, makeup people, grips, and gaffers (whatever they are).

Orchestrators aren't used only by composers who are incapable of writing their own instrumental parts. Quite the contrary, virtually all composers use orchestrators, if for no other reason than to save the time and/or tedium of mechanically doing it themselves. However, classically trained composers often sketch out the parts pretty thoroughly, and the orchestrator then becomes more of a copyist. (By the way, I know of one situation where a composer, under extreme time pressure to finish a film, hired three orchestrators at the same time to crank out the parts.)

The orchestrator is of course paid for his or her services. If it's the composer, or a primary orchestrator, they get a negotiated fee, usually in the range of $80 per page of score. Second and third orchestrators are generally paid union scale, but the better-known ones can get more. Scale for orchestrators varies with the size of the orchestra and number of pages of music. If the film is non-union, the per-page fee will usually increase (to about $140 per page) because there are no **residuals.** *Residuals* are royalties that the studios pay to union members when a film is used other than in theaters, such as on television and in streaming. If it's a non-union project, there are no residuals, so the orchestrator loses money and is entitled to more up front.

As a rough guideline, at the time of this writing, the price for *simple* orchestrations is roughly $400 per minute of music (e.g., thirty minutes is $12,000), though complex orchestrations can exceed $30,000 for a film. Orchestrators also can get something called a **booth monitor fee,** which means you get paid to hang out in the recording studio's control booth while the session is being recorded, in case the score needs some last minute help. Booth monitor fees are payable through the AFM (if the project is a signatory to the union), and they're roughly a double-scale payment per session (though if there are two orchestrators, they each get a single-scale payment for booth monitoring).

An important part of your composer deal is to negotiate whether your composer's fee includes orchestrations. Even if the film company knows you aren't capable of doing this job, you may be responsible for paying the orchestrator out of your fee. Conversely, you may be perfectly capable of doing orchestrations but (a) your time doesn't permit it; (b) you're only willing to do the orchestrations if you're paid additional money for the trouble, or (c) you're not in the mood. Either way, you should make sure the orchestration fees are on top of your composer fee (if you don't raise this issue, the film company may try to deduct the cost of orchestrations from your money). Of course, if you're doing a package deal that includes everything (as we'll discuss in a minute), the orchestrator fees are part of the package cost.

Record Royalties. A film composer isn't a performer, so it's not automatic that you get record royalties. Underscore royalties are only paid if you are (a) conducting the orchestra; and/or (b) producing the recordings. Sometimes the composer does neither of those.

Let's look at the royalties separately:

Conducting royalties. When conducting, the composer becomes (in a sense) a recording artist by leading the orchestra. The customary range of these royalties is 6% to 10% (though some studios won't go beyond 9%), pro-rated by the number of cuts (see page 162 for a discussion of pro-ration), and further pro-rated for royalty artists on any particular cut (see page 151 for a discussion of joint recordings).

In the real world, many composers don't actually conduct. Instead, they hire a conductor and "buy out" his or her royalties for a fee payable through the musicians' union (if the project is a signatory to the union). The fee is roughly double- or triple-scale payment per session. Once they pay the actual conductor, the composer then steps into their shoes and gets the conductor royalty.

Producing royalties. If you produce the recordings (see page 125 for what producing is), you can get 3% to 4%. (Note this is independent of conducting royalties; you can produce even if you don't conduct, or vice versa.) Like other producer royalties, these are retroactive to record one after recoupment (see page 127 for a discussion of retroactivity). Historically, "producing" didn't mean much more than remixing the masters, since no one really "produced" music that had already been recorded for the film. However, since a lot of scores are now electronically pre-recorded (as we discussed on page 450), composers are in fact doing more production—they first produce the pre-recorded synthesizer score, then, after the orchestra overdubs the pre-record, they produce and mix the final product.

You can usually insist on producing the underscore for records, but composers have had singularly bad luck imposing themselves as producers of *songs*. This is because artists may simply refuse to work with them. The best you can do is say that the film company must use you as the producer of all songs if the artist and record company approve. Sounds great, but unfortunately, it's almost meaningless—most artists don't want a film composer producing them. (Of course, if a composer is a producer of note in his own right, that's a different story.)

The studios will insist on reducing your royalty if you produce the recordings and then another producer comes in later and reworks your cuts. Try to have this only happen with your permission, and in any event try not to go below 50% of your producing royalty.

Floors.   Major composers can sometimes get a **floor,** meaning that if you do absolutely nothing on the record, you still get a royalty. Usually it's a guarantee of one or two cuts on the album, although they don't really guarantee to include your cuts. They only agree to pay you as if your cuts were included. In other words, if you have a 10% royalty, and there are ten masters on the album, you would be guaranteed 1% or 2%, even if you don't have any recordings on it. You should also argue for an imputed mechanical royalty on those tracks, since you would have been paid one if the tracks were actually included.

A guaranteed minimum is relatively easy to get when the album is mostly underscore, but it gets difficult to impossible if you're working on a film with a number of pop songs (like a Quentin Tarantino movie). The reason is obvious—the company has to pay royalties to a lot of expensive outside artists, and there's no assurance there will even be any score selections on the album (if any).

Because CDs and downloads are fading, and most everything is a single-song stream, the guaranteed minimum issue has become much less relevant. But it's still worth asking for.

Some very major composers get a guarantee that there will be a score album released (many films don't release *score* albums, even if they release *song* albums). However, in recent years, this has been extremely hard to come by, since there are so few soundtrack albums being made and they don't sell very well.

But couldn't the studio just throw out an album on the streaming services to satisfy the composer's ego? What's the big deal?

Well, it's actually very expensive to do that. Can you figure out why?

Score yourself a hundred points if you remembered that you have to pay conversion costs when you put film music in another medium (records in this case), and that can be *really* expensive for an orchestral album. (Conversion costs are discussed on page 440.)

Recoupment. With composers, the record company normally recoups only conversion costs. The argument is over what royalty they're recouped from. The best is to have them recouped from the gross royalty payable to all participants, and the worst is recoupment from your artist/conductor royalty (the bigger the royalty rate that's used for recoupment, the faster you'll get paid).

Most deals say that you won't get paid until the film studio has recouped everything that's charged against the studio's royalty, which could be advances to other folks that can slow you down quite a bit. Your argument is that most of the studio's advances were used to pay artist advances and recording costs, and therefore the studio will be able to recoup those costs from the artists' royalties. Accordingly, it's not fair for them to take these advances and costs out of the overall royalties before paying you. Sometimes you can pull this off, and sometimes the studio will agree only if the record company agrees.

Try to get the record company to pay your royalties directly to you once the conversion costs have been recouped. The studios don't like to do this, so you'll have to fight. But you'll get the royalties faster if they're paid directly to you rather than to the film company, who won't pay them for another accounting period.

Credit

1. **Credit in the Film.** Composers normally get main title, single-card credit. (See page 436 for a discussion of film credits.)
2. **Paid Ads.** All composers can get credit in paid ads where the full billing block of film credits appears. Midlevel to major composers can get credit in ads even if the only credits are the writer, film producer, and director. (See page 449 about paid ads.)
3. **Soundtrack Album Credit.** Composer credit on soundtrack albums has historically been a hot issue, though it's becoming less relevant as CD sales fade.

   As we discussed, the composer isn't really an "artist"—he or she only wrote the music, and maybe conducted it or produced the record. So it's not a foregone conclusion that the composer will get credit on the soundtrack album. Which means you gotta ask.

Ideally, you want credit on the front cover of the soundtrack album (or the digital artwork equivalent). The film company will argue (correctly) that it doesn't control this; it's up to the soundtrack album record company. So you'll probably end up with a commitment for the film company to use its "reasonable efforts" to get you front-cover credit.

Whether you get front-cover credit also depends on the nature of the album. If it's a compilation of songs by major artists, you're not likely to get credit on the front cover—bluntly, your name won't mean as much as the names of the artists. However, if it's a 50% or more score album, front-cover credit shouldn't be too difficult.

You should always insist (and the film company should have no trouble agreeing) that you get credit anywhere that the songwriters and artists are credited.

The exact credit can sometimes be a tussle as well. Composers want the credit "Music by," but if there is other music in the film, the studios want to say "Score by" or "Underscore by" or "Flowers by" (okay, I made up the last one to see if you were sleeping). The composers fight hard for "Music by."

Other Uses.   As we discussed earlier, film companies take the right to use music in more than just the film for which you're hired. As the composer, you pretty much have to go along, but the question is whether you can get more money for any other uses.

As noted in the last chapter, with enormous clout, songwriters can sometimes get paid for sequels, prequels, and spin-offs. However, composers normally don't get additional monies for that or anything else related to the original film, even in situations where the film company gets money (see page 434 for a laundry list). One exception, if you ask, is for ringtones and mastertones (see page 155 for what these are) *if* the film company gets paid. For those, you can get a songwriter royalty for the ringtone mechanicals, and a record royalty (whatever percentage you negotiated) on the mastertone sales.

Travel Expenses.   It's not uncommon for composers to travel to places where it's cheaper to record (like England, Ireland, Czech Republic, Germany, or Canada, or the slightly less exotic Seattle and Salt Lake City). In this case, you should negotiate for reimbursement of your expenses. On a high-class, big-budget picture, this is usually business-class travel (unless you're Godzilla, or unless it's a very long flight, in which case you can sometimes pull off first class), plus something in the neighborhood of $2,000 to $3,500 per week for New York or London. Sometimes you can get first-class accommodations plus $100 to $150 per day for all expenses besides the hotel (this is called a **per diem,** which is Latin for *per day,* but it could also be Slovakian for *You're standing on my flute*). For low-budget flicks, you'll get Greyhound tickets and Motel 6 vouchers.

If you're going to a foreign country, it's important to get your expense money in the local currency, as you don't want to be in the business of speculating whether the dollar is going to be worth more or less than the peso. For example, suppose your London hotel room costs £100 per night, which at the time of your deal is $150. If your deal is $150 per night in dollars, and if the dollar drops against the pound so that your $150 only equals £90, you're in trouble: the room is £100, but you only get £90 for your $150. So you'll be coming up £10 short. If your deal says you get £100, you're covered. For this reason, it's better to require the studio to cover the hotels and give you a per diem on top.

PACKAGE DEALS

As we touched on earlier, some composers do **package** deals, especially in television and low-budget or independent films. As we discussed, a *package* is very much like a fund in record deals (see page 97 for a discussion of funds). In other words, the composer agrees to deliver a completed score for a set dollar amount, and this money includes both the compensation for the composer's services and the costs of recording the score.

Not surprisingly, most package deals are done by composers who create electronic scores. In other words, they use a small number of musicians (sometimes only the composer) to create music on a synthesizer (which, these days, can sound like the Academy of St Martin in the Fields).

There are some score package deals that use real orchestras, but they tend to be for really big money (we'll discuss how big in a minute). In these deals, the composer gets the film's entire music budget, less only an amount the studio thinks it'll need to license existing songs and recordings, and/or to create new songs and recordings.

There is also a hybrid package, which consists of synthesizer recordings mixed with orchestral recordings (see the next section).

Package Prices

The price of packages can be anywhere from $50,000 for a low-budget film up to $1,800,000 or even $2,000,000 plus for a mainstream, big-budget feature (though packages in big-budget films are rare; they are mostly low-budget creatures). The really large packages are most common on films where the film producer requires the score to be recorded outside the United States, which is often done for tax reasons.

Pure electronic scores (or electronic scores with up to maybe ten musicians in a package) for major studio films run around $100,000 to $400,000, sometimes a bit higher for top-level folk. The hybrid packages described above (both synthesizer and score) have (a) a package price of $50,000 to $200,000 for the synthesizer portion, plus (b) a market-rate fee (sometimes as low as union scale) for the composer's orchestration and conducting services, plus (c) the costs of the orchestra and orchestrations, which is paid by the studio on top of the fee (meaning they're not part of the package).

At the lower end, I've seen starving composers do low-budget film scores for a $5,000 to $10,000 package price. In this case you should try to keep the publishing, and sometimes you can get the soundtrack album as well. Even if you can't keep those, you should get a nice chunk of the income from publishing and records, since you're taking so little up front.

Exclusions

If you're going to make a package deal, you have to worry about exactly what you have to deliver in the package. Most contracts just require you to deliver "all music," and the trick is negotiating what's *not* included.

This turns out to be more complicated than you'd think, and through the courtesy of my friend Michael Gorfaine (one of the most experienced film music agents in the business), I bring you the following list of exclusions:

Licensing of Outside Music (i.e., songs not written by the composer for this project). Since most contracts say you must provide "all music," I've seen film companies license an expensive outside tune and expect the composer to pay for it. You can't control the costs of outside songs (indeed, one license could eat half your package fee), so never agree to this.

Note you want the exclusion stated as "songs not written by the composer *for this project.*" Some composers have a "library" of cues they've previously written, and there's an issue whether those should be excluded from the package price. We'll discuss these babies on the next page.

Recording Costs of Outside Music. If the sessions for outside music can't be scheduled during the normal scoring sessions, their costs shouldn't be included in the package.

Re-use Fees. (See page 440 for a discussion of re-use fees). Not your problem. But . . .

(1) You can't exclude re-use fees from the package if you're composing for a non-union film. The reason is that there won't be any union re-use fees for non-union musicians, which is what the film producer wants. Meaning, if you hire a union person, the studio will make you pay their residuals. So watch it . . .

(2) Even if it's a union project, if you make a deal where you own the masters, re-use fees will be your responsibility. That's because your exploiting the masters apart from the movie will trigger a re-use fee, and since the studio doesn't share in that income, they won't bear the expense.

Re-scoring. This is one of the most important and trickiest areas. The concept is to save your rear end if the director says he wants an angelic harp accompanying his scene, which you record and deliver, only to have him decide later that he really meant hip-hop. In other words, if the film people require you to re-record for reasons totally beyond your control (as opposed to your screwup), it should be on them.

Lyricist Expenses. If the studio wants a lyricist to write words to your music, it should be on their nickel.

Vocalist Expenses. As with lyricists, if the company wants somebody to croon your newly created song, they should pay. Note this isn't just about featured artists singing songs in the film; it could also mean a chorus singing along with the underscore.

Music Editor Fees. The music editor's fee should be a film cost, not a music cost. A **music editor** is to film music what a film editor is to film. In other words, he or she is the technical person responsible for getting all the music in the right places. They will create the **spotting notes** (which are detailed notes, down to a tenth of a second, of where music goes), edit music to fit a scene if the film has been cut, help with any technical difficulties, etc.

Mag Stock and Transfer Costs.   Mag stock is the actual soundtrack imprinted on the film, and **transfer costs** are the costs of transferring the music from the recording studio to the film. The purpose of this exclusion is to clarify that you only have to deliver a standard audio recording, and that the cost of physically putting the music into the film is a motion picture cost, and not a package cost.

In truth, with digital sound, there are no more mag stock or transfer costs, but everyone still excludes them from the package, and the words sound so cool that I've left them in the book.

Pre-records.   This is music recorded before shooting, to be lip-synced and/or danced to in the film. Since the on-camera action has to precisely follow the recording, these cuts have to be done in advance. Note these are not demos of themes prior to writing the score (those are customarily included in the package), but rather cuts of finished songs that will actually be in the film.

A package should include the cost of pre-records only if it's specifically negotiated up front. However, for purely electronic scores, pre-records are usually included.

Sidelining.   This is a situation where a musician either gets on camera and pretends to perform, or actually performs. Film companies have been known to charge this cost against the package, which again is a matter of negotiation. It's usually easy to exclude if you ask, because the musician is paid through SAG (Screen Actors Guild) as an actor, and this isn't a music cost.

Excess Musicians.   For a smaller package, where it's clear the intent is to use primarily electronic score, it's a great idea to limit the number of musicians you're required to supply. For a television package, for example, this is usually small—in the range of four or five at the most—and the limit gives you ammunition to ask for more money if the director has a sudden attack of orchestra-itis.

Library Music.   As noted above, there's an issue over licensing music that was written by the composer, but not written for the film.

For example, many composers have built-up "libraries" of music that they own and license to films. If you have such a library, you should try to exclude this music from the package (meaning you can charge them extra if it's used in the film).

The studios push back on this. They think compensation for your library music should be included as part of the package fee. Their argument (not without merit) is that they're paying you to create new music, and if they give you extra money for old stuff, you're likely to toss in a lot of it. The usual compromise is to say they won't have to pay for pre-existing material unless it's used at the film producer's request.

Of course, any of the above exclusions may be included in your package if it's negotiated up front and you budget for it. But be sure they're only in the package price when you expect them, or you may be paying the film company for the privilege of using your music.

CREATIVE FINANCING

In today's world, there are a number of films that use something known loosely as "creative financing" (not really an industry term). That's where an independent studio (or a major studio for that matter) doesn't have the budget to hire the composer they want, and instead comes up with creative ways to snag their dream symphonist for a lower fee. These are things like:

Back-End Participation.   The composer gets a piece of the film's profits, or built-in bonuses at certain box-office levels (the "kickers" we discussed on page 445).

If it's a piece of the film's profits (maybe you'll get 1% or so), that looks great on paper. Unfortunately, the reality is that you're not likely to ever see any money. Film company accountants are far more creative than record company accountants, and film profits are defined in a way that makes them virtually nonexistent. Still, if the best you can do is to get a share of profits, try to get the same profit definition as the director or producer, and hope they had enough clout to get something decent.

Because of this little accounting game, you'll be better off with box-office bonuses, which we discussed on page 451. The advantage of box-office bonuses as compared to a share of profits is that box-office numbers are specific figures, published in industry trades, so there's no question whether or not you're entitled to the money. Also, box-office bonuses are usually paid faster—you get them within thirty days after the box-office number is reached, while shares of profits are only accounted every six months.

Percentage of Publishing.   As we discussed, film companies normally own all the publishing for the underscore. In these creative deals, the composer might get ownership and/or administration. Or if not, certainly a share of the publishing income. Sometimes the composer gets a large percentage of publishing until they make a certain sum, then a lesser amount for a while, maybe dropping to zero at some earnings level.

Soundtrack Record Goodies.   The composer gets a higher-than-normal record royalty, or sometimes the right to own the soundtrack album itself, subject to paying the film company a small royalty. If you own it, try to keep all non-film rights, such as ringtones, commercial licenses, etc.

Adding the Advance.   The composer's fee or package price is increased by some or all of the advance (less conversion costs) that the film company gets for the soundtrack album, or for its publishing. In these deals, the additional monies are almost always recoupable from the composer's royalties.

If the composer gets several of the above goodies, there's often a ceiling on the dough. For example, once the composer has made $1 million from all sources (including the fee), the participations drop out. However, the improved record provisions usually go on forever.

TELEVISION COMPOSERS

Network and basic cable television composers live in a different world from film composers. The time they have to compose and deliver is shorter because, as I'm sure you know, television programs are cooked up like batches of cookies right before they go on the air. Also, the budgets to produce TV shows are substantially lower than motion picture budgets, so the music budgets get squashed down along with everything else. Thus the composer's fees and the money available for recording costs are much less than those for theatrical films.

The exceptions are things like HBO, Netflix, and the premium streaming services, where there can be a long lead time before the project has to be finished, and many of these programs want real orchestras for most or all of the shows (think *Game of Thrones* as the extreme). These deals have substantially higher package fees, or even fees plus the cost of the orchestra on top.

The good news is that, even though the fees are lower, the performance monies generated by television programs (see page 225) can be substantial—much more than for films—because programs may be shown over and over, forever. However, a lot of the reruns are now on streaming services, where the composer earns much less performance money than on broadcast television. But at least that money will keep coming for a long time.

Background Score

Because of the short time frame and lower budgets, television music is tailor-made for electronic score packagers (the folks who get an all-in amount that includes both their fee and the recording costs, as we discussed on page 459). In fact, almost all television deals are packages.

Typical package fees (which include recording costs) are around $2,000 to $5,000 for a half-hour television episode, with a few going as high as $7,000. One-hour programs are from $12,000 to $22,000, but the higher end is only paid for shows with really big budgets, lots of music, and expectations of orchestral elements, or for shows that have been on the air a long time (the longer they're on the air, the more money the networks pay for them).

Very few TV projects use an orchestra anymore, so the above package fees are for a synthesizer score. If there is an orchestra, it's usually a big-budget production, and the deal is structured as a fee (in the range of $25,000 to $30,000) plus recording costs. In the case where a package includes an orchestra, the orchestra is usually only part of the music (for example, half of it), with synthesizer making up the rest. In this case, the package fee will of course be higher, in the range of $45,000 per episode. But any kind of orchestra is rare today, probably less than 10% of television music.

Before a show is sold for a series, the TV producer first makes either a **pilot** (meaning a single episode of a TV show that's produced in hopes of selling the show to a network), or something called a **sales version** or **pilot presentation** (which may only be a ten-minute pitch, never intended to be aired). Sales versions are becoming more and more common these days, for the simple reason that they're cheaper than pilots.

For a sales version, studios pay a very small fee, from $500 for 30 minutes to as much as $5,000 for 60 minutes, including all recording costs and musicians. For these Dollar Store prices, they get a quick electronic score, or cues from the composer's library. For a fully scored pilot, before it's sold as a series, the package fees are between $3,000 and $6,000.

Even though all these fees are low, the producers insist on owning any new material created for these programs (though they shouldn't own any preexisting library material).

If the series is picked up by a network, usually one of two things happens:

1. The composer is hired to do the full season of the series, and the pilot becomes one of those episodes. In this case, the composer gets an episodic fee for the pilot (actually, she gets the difference between the fee for the pilot/sales version and the episodic fee); or
2. The composer is hired only for the pilot, in which case they score any new footage and finish up the material they previously scored. In this case, the composer gets either an additional package fee in the same amount as the sales version, or an additional fee that brings the total price up to (or a little under) the episodic fees we just discussed.

There are, however, some kinds of shows that run above these figures. For example, shows that are very music intensive (meaning there's music under almost the entire show) pay more because the composer has to deliver so much more. A well-known composer might get a package fee of about $150,000 for an hour show that's music heavy.

Another example of higher fees would be a long-running show with a well-known TV composer and heavy orchestra. That might have a package fee of about $45,000.

A two-hour movie-of-the-week package is about $35,000 to $90,000, though for major composers it can be a *fee* of $30,000 to $90,000 *plus* recording costs.

Miniseries deals are mostly done for a per-episode fee (rather than a total amount for the entire series). If it's a package, the fee is about the same as the sixty-minute episodic package fees we talked about. If they're done as a fee deal (with the producer paying the costs on top), the range is about $30,000 to $50,000 for the entire series. If you're doing a package for the whole series, it's in the range of $100,000 to $300,000, with the higher numbers being for a series with more episodes. For a miniseries with an orchestral score, the package amount can be as high as that of a major motion picture.

Usually the TV production studio hires the music editor (see page 461 for what that means), but some composers like to hire the editor directly. In this case the composer includes the cost of the music editor in their package, which typically raises the per-episode fee by $2,000 to $4,000 to cover the cost.

If you want to give somebody a good chuckle, just ask the TV people if you can have a piece of the publishing. In the television industry, the producer's commandment to hold on to publishing isn't just carved in stone, it's tattooed on their foreheads. (Remember all that lovely performance money? The TV guys figured that out, too.) The only exceptions are some non-studio shows (miniseries, HBO, TNT, Netflix), or really big-name TV composers, where, if you have major clout, you can sometimes get a piece of the publishing income (though almost never a piece of the copyright, and usually no administration rights).

If you think it's bad enough that the television people want to take your publishing, get a load of this. Some of the smaller TV producers, but also some cable and streaming networks that produce their own shows, are not only taking publishing, but are also trying to take your *writer's* share of royalties. Under these deals, you don't get any of the performance monies I talked about in the previous section. In fact, you don't get any money for *any* use of the score (besides your fee), even if they put your music in other shows, license it to a motion picture, use it in ads to sell dog food, etc.

Fight back hard on this. Usually you can keep your writer's share of performance monies, but I've seen a few situations where they try to buy those out as well.

And by the way, the fees for these deals aren't any higher than the fees for deals where you keep your writer's royalties!

BE VERY WARY OF THIS. Sometimes you don't know that's what they want until the contract arrives, so you have to be clear up front that you expect writer's royalties. If they absolutely refuse, it may be worthwhile to give up writer's royalties when you first get started (to get credits under your belt), but as soon as you have any clout, fight fiercely to hang on.

Other deal points are the payment schedule (usually half on start and half on completion); record royalties (which are usually left to good-faith negotiations, unless the producer knows in advance there will be a record); and credit. Prominent credits are getting harder to come by, but give it a whirl. A half-hour show credit is usually in the end title crawl no matter what. For one hour or more, try for a main title or Act One credit, single card, shared only with the theme composer (our next topic), but the recent trend (if you can get a single card at all) is for the card to be in the end titles. (See page 436 for what all this credit stuff means.)

TV Themes

Composers sometimes write the **main title theme** for a television show (meaning the theme at the beginning of the show).

This is almost always done as a package. If it's instrumental only, the package is in the range of $15,000 to $40,000, leaning toward the higher end if you include orchestral elements. If the theme has both music and lyrics, the package price is more like $30,000 to $60,000.

Studios won't give up publishing on TV themes, but sometimes non-studio players will.

Occasionally the producers hire a Big Name Writer to compose the television theme, and someone else (cheaper) to write the weekly score. Big Name gets the high end of the scale we just discussed. If it's not a package, they'll get a fee of $10,000 to $20,000, and the TV producer pays the costs on top. Big Name can also get a royalty on records close to what film composers get (see page 455).

There's also a trend for producers to license a well-known song for a theme. We discussed those rates on page 243.

If the composer is doing the underscore, the fee usually includes writing an end title theme.

VIDEO GAME COMPOSERS

In recent years, a number of composers have written scores for video games. In days past, video game scores were predominantly done on a synthesizer. Nowadays, some of them use live orchestras.

Unlike films, where the action moves linearly, video game composers have to pick the right music for every possible twist and turn in the game. In addition to all this juggling, the composers have to write a lot more music. A typical film score has thirty to forty minutes of music, while a typical video game has more like eighty to a hundred minutes, or even more—some battle games can run into hundreds of minutes of music.

These deals look very much like the deals for motion pictures—the music is written as a work for hire, the composer usually gets songwriter royalties, etc. Unlike films, however, historically there have been very little performance monies, for the simple reason that video games weren't played on television or in theaters. As games have moved to the online and mobile environment, things are looking a bit brighter on the performance side. Video gaming sites like Twitch pay performance royalties, and while it's not yet significant money, it's growing.

Some game companies take a much tougher stance and refuse to pay writer royalties at all (though the writer can collect performance monies from the performing rights societies). Others take a little softer stance and agree to pay the writer a share of mechanicals (not for video game sales; only if the song is exploited on records). However, they won't pay the writer for anything else, even if the game company licenses the songs (and gets money) for third-party uses.

Fees for video games were historically smaller than film fees, but they're getting closer. While a few deals are the composer's fee plus costs, most of them are done as packages (meaning the fee includes recording costs). These deals are sometimes a flat fee for the entire game, but most commonly they're a dollar amount for each minute of music. It's typically $1,000 to $2,000 per minute, though for big names, it can get up to $3,000, occasionally a bit more. The packages usually include all music costs except third-party music licenses, re-scoring after delivery, and any musicians requested by the game company (for example, if they request an orchestra, that would be a separate budget and fee).

If you're on the *Advanced Overview Track*, go to the
Conclusion, on page 489.
Experts: Onward!

31

Licensing Existing Recordings and Existing Songs for Motion Pictures

This chapter deals with licensing existing masters and songs (records and songs *not* created for the film).

MASTER LICENSES

Record Company Masters

Most of the licenses to use masters in motion pictures and television are, not surprisingly, from record companies. The rest are individual owners of recordings, which we'll deal with a little later. With record company masters, you'll only be involved in the deals as a secondary player because the contracting parties are your record company and the film company, who make a deal with each other. The money is paid to your record company, who promptly pockets half and treats the balance as artist royalties under your deal.

If your record contract says they need your consent to license masters into films and TV (see page 150), they'll call up and ask you to bless the deal. If the record company doesn't need your consent, they may not even call you, although most will as a courtesy. (By the way, even if you don't have the right to consent in your record deal, if you wrote the song and control the publishing, you can block the deal—remember, the right to use the master is only the right to use the physical recording itself. The record company can't give a film company the right to use the musical composition [they don't have these rights], so the film company has to make a deal with *both* the record company and the publisher to get a full set of rights. Therefore, if you're the publisher, you can control the deal through the side door even if you can't do it through the front door. We'll talk about publishing deals in a minute.)

Because you may be asked to consent to these deals, and because you share in the income, you should know how they work. So let's take a look.

A record company/film company master license has two main elements:

1. How much is the fee to synchronize the master in the film (and for advertising/marketing if the film company wants that as well)?
2. If the master is also going on a soundtrack album or released as a single track, what's the royalty?

Master License Fees

The fee to use a master in the film varies directly with the importance of the song in its own right (was it a number one single, or an obscure album cut?), the stature of the artist, and how it's used in the film. The highest fees go for uses of masters that are integrated with the on-screen action (for example, the actors are dancing to it, or singing along), so that it takes on dramatic content and moves the story forward. Also at the high end are licenses to play the recording over the main titles, or the license of a cut that's the title of the film (think *Bohemian Rhapsody*). At the low end, a master might be playing on a radio in the background for ten seconds while people are talking, so that you need a truffle-sniffing pig to even know it's there.

Obviously, there are all shades of variations in between, and sometimes it's just a question of how much the producer has fallen in love with a particular cut. The range of fees is the same as what's paid for use of the song that's embodied in the master, which we discussed on page 243, and in fact you should insist that your fee is **most favored nations** (meaning no less than) what the film company pays for the publishing. By the way, the publishers will be asking for the same **MFN** as the fee for the master.

You should always ask the record company to pay through your half of the fee if you're unrecouped, on the age-old theory of "Hey, no harm in asking." Most of the time you won't get it, so don't let that affect your self-esteem.

Royalties

If the deal also grants record rights, the range of royalties paid to the record company is 11% to 14% for each track, which would be pro-rata if there's an album (see page 162 for what pro-rata means). You'll get half of this from your record company, unless you can bludgeon more out of them. Of course, if your record company is releasing the soundtrack album or the track, you should get 100% of your normal royalty.

If your master is the key master in the album (meaning, for example, it's the only song in an album of underscore, or it's the only hit in an album of obscure toads), or if it's the theme song or the title of the film or TV show, then the royalty should be higher, as we discussed for artists (in Chapter 28). In addition, your record company can usually get a most favored nations treatment for the master, at least insofar as other *existing* masters are concerned. The film company usually wants to reserve the right to pay higher royalties for recordings that are created for the film.

Since the film company didn't pay the recording costs, the only things that can be recoupable are the union re-use fees (see page 440), and this too is negotiable. The fee paid to use the recording in the film or television program should *not* be recoupable.

Film companies sometimes pay a small advance for the record use.

Other Master License Deal Points

The other deal points are about consent: the AFM (American Federation of Musicians) and you.

AFM Consent. There is an obscure rule in the AFM labor agreement that requires not only the payment of re-use fees, but also the consent of the AFM to put existing masters in a motion picture or television program. The theory is that the union won't put musicians out of work (i.e., by not requiring a new recording session) unless it's such a unique master that a new recording won't do justice to the film. An example would be a Buddy Holly master, which can't be duplicated since Buddy isn't available. In actual practice, however, I've never seen the union object to any licensing—in fact, this rule is almost always ignored and no one even asks. If you do ask, their consent is a rubber stamp.

You. Since the licensing deal is between your record company and the film company, you're not directly involved. But once the deal gets under way, the record company will call up your manager and ask if you're okay with the use of your master in a particular film. How do you evaluate this?

On the financial side, you should review the deal and decide if you think it's fair. The above criteria should give you a pretty good feel for it. If the deal sounds okay, then proceed to the next step, which is just as important, but often overlooked: You should find out precisely what's going on in the film when your song is being played. I have avoided a number of disasters with this simple question. For example, a film company once wanted to use a recording of one of my clients during a scene where kids were shooting drugs. Or perhaps it's a graphic sexual sequence (which, depending on your image, could be a plus). Remember, it's your music and your career, so be careful about the creative aspects.

Non–Record Company Masters

As we discussed in the section on record deals, artists don't usually end up owning their own masters, and even when they do, they often license the rights to a record company for a number of years. On the other hand, there are artists whose careers are, shall we say, "taking a holiday"—they might have been huge in the eighties or nineties, but they don't mean as much today. Often these artists are "between deals" and have recorded stuff that they own. The same holds true for other artists whose deals have expired, and they've decided they can make more money by recording and distributing their own records.

An important sub-category of this is where the older artists have re-recorded their major hits after the re-recording restrictions expired (see page 170 for re-recording restrictions). That way they can license the re-recorded version and keep all the money, rather than share it with the record label. This was possible under older deals, because the re-recording restrictions were much looser in those days. Today the contracts say you can never duplicate your old masters, even after the re-recording restrictions expires, for exactly this reason.

When these artist-owned masters are licensed for movies, the deals are pretty much the same as those outlined above, except of course there's no record company in the middle. Meaning you keep all the money. Which I guess is no small "except" . . .

Another type of master license is made by composers who've built up a library of instrumental song masters that they license into small films. The film companies take these tracks and hire someone to sing over them. This is similar to the underscore library music we discussed on page 462, but they're more than instrumental cues—they're actual song masters without the vocals. These library songs go for anywhere from $500 to $5,000.

LICENSING EXISTING MUSICAL COMPOSITIONS FOR FILMS

As we just discussed, the money paid to use a master goes to your record company. This means two things:

1. Right off the top, they get half of it.
2. If you're unrecouped, you never see the other half.

Not such an appetizing proposition. But remember that the film also needs a synchronization license for the *song* in the master. So if you wrote the song and own the publishing, they now need to make a deal directly with you, and this side of the equation looks very different in one aspect:

You get much more of the money.

Your publisher of course takes a chunk, and will also use it to recoup any advance. But as we discussed, publishers typically keep 25% or less (as opposed to the record company's 50%).

Fees

We discussed the fees for song synchronization licenses on page 242. You should provide that the fee is most favored nations with the fee paid for the master side.

FILM MUSIC QUIZ

You're an independent film company that's producing a teenage motion picture. The music supervisor called Capitol Records and got a license to use the Beatles recording "She Loves You" in the film, for a payment of $10,000. The license is fully signed, the money has been paid to Capitol, and the master has been dubbed into the film.

Assuming you're now aware of everything that's been done, are there any problems in going forward and distributing the film? If so, what?

Answer to quiz:

Here's what's wrong: They haven't licensed the *song* for the film, only the recording. Thus they can't use the track until they make a deal with the publisher. (See page 242 if you want a refresher.)

And there's one other thing that's wrong: the Beatles haven't licensed anything for $10,000 since 1962.

32

Music Supervisors

ROLE

A **music supervisor,** as the job title implies, coordinates the music for a film or TV series. They primarily focus on the choice of songs (music and lyrics), though they may be involved in the underscore as well.

First, he or she sits down with the producer and director to work out the type of music they want, ideally before production. If the film is a musical, or one that relies heavily on music (such as a dance film), the music supervisor *must* be involved in advance. This is because songs performed on camera have to be **pre-recorded,** meaning they're made in a recording studio before the start of photography of the film and then lip-synched or danced to on film. As you can imagine, it's difficult to dance to a song not yet recorded.

Actually, I was once involved in a situation where the opposite happened. A dance scene had been shot to a specific song, but after the film was finished, the writer of the song refused to make a deal with the film company, and the song had to be scrapped. A client of mine then wrote a new song for the dance sequence (obviously having to match the beat precisely), which ended up being a number one hit.

After meeting with the director and producer, the music supervisor comes up with suggestions for artists, songwriters, composers, etc., for the film. The director and producer decide what they want, then the supervisor works with the studio's music department to make the deals happen. He or she contacts the creative people, arranges for meetings with the film personnel, and supervises the recording sessions.

Done properly, being a music supervisor is one of the most difficult jobs on planet Earth. For example:

1. Other than pre-recorded music (which we discussed above, and which is a tiny fraction of film music), most of the music

can't be finalized until the film is finished (see page 452 for why). The studio has millions of dollars riding on a specific film release date, and music is at best considered a minor element in the overall production, even if it's a central element in the film. (The cost of a *major* music budget is maybe a bit over $2,000,000, while most major studio films run $40 million to $100 million, not to mention the multimillions for advertising and marketing. And $2,000,000 is a huge music budget. More typically, music budgets for major films run about $500,000 to $1,000,000.)

2. As we discussed (on page 429), each piece of music in a film can represent eight or more deals (see page 430 for what they are), and because music comes in last, complicated deals have to be made under enormous time pressure, which geometrically increases the likelihood of mistakes.

It's the music supervisor's job to keep all these competing interests satisfied and to ensure a happy ending. So good music supervisors are worth their weight in gold (maybe platinum). They call on their relationships to pull favors and smooth out difficult situations, getting music into pictures that couldn't be there any other way. Music supervisors are in a sense "marriage brokers." They creatively marry music and films, which is no easy process, and they also have to marry the film and music industries on a business level (which can be even more difficult).

MOTION PICTURE SUPERVISOR FEES AND ROYALTIES

Film music supervisors can get fees of $25,000 to $100,000 per picture. For some very big projects—for example, a live action musical (think *Greatest Showman*)—they can work for multiple years and can get up to $400,000 or more. The top supervisors also have royalties on the soundtrack album, usually in the range of 1% to 2% non-pro-rated. There may also be escalations of .25% or .5% for STEAs of 500,000 and 1,000,000 units (see page 90 if you don't remember what STEA means). These royalties are payable prospectively after recoupment of all costs, at the same time the film studio recoups.

In addition, there may be box-office bonuses based on the picture's gross, just like the deals for composers we discussed on page 451.

TELEVISION SUPERVISORS

Over the years, a few television shows have licensed extensive amounts of existing music to create a "cool vibe" for the show. Because of the rushed time frame in television, and the smaller budgets, and the fact that television producers' music departments simply aren't equipped to deal with the complicated clearance issues we've discussed, this is a seriously tough thing to pull together.

Stepping in to save the day are music supervisors who work on television shows. The fees are pretty small—$3,500 to $5,500 for a half-hour episode, up to maybe $8,000 for an hour. These supervisors also get a record royalty of about 1%, sometimes with TSEA escalations. However, producers that churn out tons of programs (television production companies and streaming services) often hire in-house music supervisors to take care of this, and those folks work for a salary with no royalties.

A recent trend in this area is for music supervisors to troll indie labels, music blogs, SoundCloud, YouTube, and similar sites, looking for unknown artists with cool material. They then approach the artist or label and say, "We love your song. We'd like to put it on a TV show, which is a great way to promote your career. And if you wrote the song, you'll even get performance money when it's aired. Oh, by the way, we pay almost nothing."

The artists are usually thrilled, because it can mean massive exposure for their music.

33

Soundtrack Record Deals

As an artist, you have nothing to do with the deal to distribute soundtrack records—not even consent or consultation. These contracts are made between the film company and a record company, and in a sense are "none of your business." However, they affect the types of deals you can make with the film company, so you should know about them.

Once the film company has acquired the bundle of rights we discussed in Chapters 27 through 31, they turn them over to a record company to put out a soundtrack album. There are two different kinds of soundtrack albums—score albums and song albums—and the deals are very different.

SCORE ALBUMS

A score album is an album wholly of underscore (i.e., with no songs), often because the only music in the film is underscore. Unless there's something extraordinary about the situation (for example, the film looks like it's going to be garganzo), the soundtrack album deal is relatively modest or, more commonly, nonexistent. The reason is simple— pure underscore albums don't usually sell or stream very well (in the days of sales, anything over 10,000 copies was unusual). At first blush, it doesn't seem like it'd be any big deal to just throw a soundtrack album out on the streaming services, but don't forget the conversion costs we discussed on page 440, which can be substantial for an orchestra. So for this reason, many record companies aren't interested in this product at all, and will only put out a score album if someone forces them. (For example, a film company may put out a score album just to satisfy the ego of a film producer or composer.) However, there are a couple of companies (like Varèse Sarabande, or the classical divisions of major companies) who specialize in score albums.

Assuming someone is interested, the deal for pure score albums is usually an advance equal to the conversion costs, though sometimes there is no advance at all (which means the film company has to pay the conversion costs). The royalty on these albums is usually in the range of 17% to 18%, but it can climb higher for major event films.

SONG ALBUMS

At the other end of the spectrum is an album of songs by major artists, often a combination of preexisting songs and songs written for the film. The deals for these albums are bigger if (a) the album is finished before they make the record deal (so the record company can hear them); and (b) the new songs sound like hits.

For these albums, the price escalates dramatically. If a lot of companies are chasing the deal, song albums can get advances up to $500,000 (sometimes even more if the record company is really frothing at the mouth), but usually the advances are in the range of $100,000 to $300,000. (These prices include conversion costs.) The royalty on song albums is also higher, usually in the range of 18% to 20%, and sometimes with escalations to 21% and 22% at sales/streaming levels equivalent to one to two million albums (United States). In addition, or sometimes instead of a royalty, the film company may get a piece of the record company's profits.

More commonly, these deals are made before the music is actually in existence. Depending on what everyone believes the music will be, and to a large degree depending on the reputation of the film director or producer (and the director/producer's prior history with soundtrack albums), the advances can still be high.

The record company will try to get some marketing requirements from the film company (for example, a contribution to promotional videos, screen credit for the soundtrack album, use of the soundtrack music in ads for the film, and so forth). The record company will also want the film company to use a minimum number of their artist's recordings in the film (anywhere from one to six, or sometimes half the masters used in the film).

OTHER ISSUES

The other major issues in soundtrack album deals:

Release Timing

The record has to be released in coordination with the film. The film company wants maximum promotion for its film, and the record company wants maximum promotion for its record, all from the cross-advertising and cross-marketing of the film and album, streaming and radio play of the record, etc. Thus both sides are extraordinarily touchy about delivery and release dates.

If there is an original single, or what's called a **tie-in** (meaning a track from an artist's upcoming album that's used in the film), the film and record companies want the track released about six weeks ahead of the film. This allows the single to gather steam by the time the film hits the theaters. Both the record and film company want the album released right around the same time as the release of the film, or maybe a short time before.

A major reason for screwing up this ideal timing is the film company's changing its release date, based on a variety of film-related issues (for example, they have other films that are scheduled for release around the same time, the director isn't finished, etc.).

Film Release

The record company wants a guaranteed release of the film. They argue (quite rightly) that their album isn't worth much without a film to go with it. Film companies are very reluctant to do this, since they never guarantee a film release to any of the actors, producers, directors, etc. For some film companies, it's an absolute no-no. For others, they'll work out some compromise.

The record companies also want to know how big a release it's going to be. Will it be a small release, in 200 to 400 theaters, to see how it goes? Or a major release (called a **wide release**), on 2,000 to 4,000 screens? The film companies almost never guarantee a number of theaters, but they'll give an indication of what's happening "off the record."

Who Owns the Masters?

There are obviously two choices: the film company or the record company. The film company argues that it paid for the little darlings and thus should own them. The record company argues that the advance it pays under the soundtrack album deal pays for the masters, and thus the record company should own them. The record companies are particularly touchy when the master is recorded by one of their exclusive artists; they can't stand the idea of someone else owning that recording. So the record companies want to own the masters and license them back to the filmmaker, while film companies want to own them and license them to the record company.

Compromises run all over the map, but most often the record company owns the masters and licenses them to the film company. Occasionally they split the ownership—meaning the film company owns the recordings for the film and other non-record rights, while the record company owns them for phonograph records.

To me, the real issue isn't so much ownership as who controls the masters outside of the film, the soundtrack album, and singles. This means things like synchronization rights (for other films, television programs, commercials, etc.), and usages on records other than the soundtrack album and singles, like the artist's album, etc. Both sides have legitimate arguments, and the answer depends solely on bargaining power. However, regardless of who ends up with the ownership and control, all film companies will insist (and the record companies will agree) that the film company has some level of control over licensing the masters for use in other films, television programs, advertising, etc. They correctly argue that these usages dilute the film company's right to have the song identified exclusively with their movie.

Note, by the way, that if the film company owns the publishing of any of the songs, they have a back-door control of the ancillary uses, since the non-record uses require the publisher's consent.

Related to the issue of control is the question of who gets the money from usages outside the film and records. If the record company ends up with the rights, then the monies are split between it and the film company (or credited to the film company's account if unrecouped). If the film company keeps the rights, then it usually keeps the money (but not always). Results here also vary in proportion to bargaining power.

Videos

Who makes the promo videos and how are the costs recouped? The film company almost always supplies film footage without additional charge. The real question is whether the film company pays for part of the videos.

Credit

What type of credit will the record company have in the film? Will it be in film ads as well as on-screen? What credit will the film company get on the records and in record company ads?

Advertising

Will either company guarantee advertising of the album and/or the film?

Marketing

Will the film company pay any money for marketing, promotion, etc.? Will the record company? This is heavily negotiated, to make sure each side gets the most bang out of the other.

Skip to the Conclusion on page 489 unless (a) you were once under (or you're the heir to) a really old contract that's based on the retail price of records, or (b) you enjoy pain.

Appendix

Ye Olde Royalty Calculations

The following is how royalties were computed up in the olden days. If you were once under an older recording contract (or you're the heir to someone who was), you'll need to understand how these Byzantine provisions work. But if you don't fit into that category, feel free to skip to the Conclusion on page 489.

Historically, the artist royalty was a percentage of the **suggested retail list price** (also called *SRLP*). The SRLP had absolutely nothing to do with what you paid at your local record store. It was just a way to compute royalties.

From this price, the company first deducted a **packaging charge** (also called a **packaging deduction** or **container charge**). In *theory*, this was the cost of the "package," and it was deducted because the artist should get a royalty only on the record, not the package. In *reality*, it was a charge of much more than any package actually cost, and thus was just an artificial way to reduce the artist's royalty.

The *packaging charge* was stated as a percentage of the SRLP, and the industry norm was 25% for compact discs and other "new configurations," 20% for cassettes, and 10% for vinyl.

The result of this (i.e., the SRLP after deducting the packaging charge) was called a **base price** or **royalty base.** This was the figure against which you applied your royalty percentage.

Here's an example of a royalty base computation using easy (not real-world) numbers:

Retail price of CD	$10.00
Less: Packaging (25% of $10.00)	– 2.50
ROYALTY BASE	**$ 7.50**

Thus, in this example, if an artist had a 10% royalty, he or she got 75¢ (10% of $7.50).

Phony Free Goods

If you liked the special program and promotional free goods we discussed on page 83, you'll positively *love* the phony free goods that record companies used when computing royalties based on SRLP.

Before I tell you how this works, you need to know about my soft-drink stand.

When I was ten years old, I had a soft-drink stand in front of our house. I don't mean a card table with lemonade; I mean a serious soft-drink stand made out of genuine pine (by my stepfather), with Dr Pepper and Coca-Cola signs that, if I'd kept them, would be worth more than my first car. Anyway, I stumbled on the brilliant idea of delivering soft drinks to the workmen at a construction site about a block away, using my little wagon. Instead of selling the drinks for a nickel, like everyone else, I would sell them for a dime (delivery labor, you know).

But for every two drinks they bought, they'd get two free. (Even though I thought I was putting one over on the workmen, I have a feeling they really knew I was selling the drinks for a nickel each and using mirrors.)

My idea for a soft-drink scam was taken to dizzying heights by the early record company accounting magicians. First, they figured out

Figure 10. The author invents free goods.

that selling one hundred records at 85¢ each was the same as selling eighty-five records for $1 each and giving the customer fifteen "free" records for every eighty-five they bought (the retailer gets one hundred records either way, and the company gets $85 either way). Then they realized that, because fifteen of these records were "free," they didn't have to pay the artist for the free records—I mean, how could you have the gall to ask for royalties on a record for which the company wasn't being paid? So by raising the price and giving away records for "free," the companies saved royalties on fifteen records out of every one hundred while making the same money. (Remember, the artist's royalty was based on retail, so the artist didn't get any benefit from an inflated wholesale price.) Nifty, eh?

It took the workmen who bought my soft drinks about thirty seconds to figure out that the price of my drinks was 5¢ each. But it took recording artists more than twenty years to figure out that these "free" records were hardly free, because the economics to the company were exactly the same as if all the records had been sold at a lesser price. Got it?

In the last years of this old system, only a few companies actually gave away 15% of the records they shipped. Where it was done, those "free" records were known as **phony free goods** because, like my soft drinks, they were nothing more than a cute way of discounting the purchase price. (Technically, they were called **standard free goods,** or **normal distributor free goods.**) And in fact the companies that used this practice charged a higher wholesale price than those who didn't, and the difference (not surprisingly) was the percentage of "free goods." (By the way, even though it sounds like you would, you didn't get more royalties from the companies without free goods, as we'll see in a minute.)

Let's go back to our example:

Retail price of CD	$10.00
Less: Packaging (25% of $10.00)	– 2.50
ROYALTY BASE	**$ 7.50**

Using a 10% (75¢) royalty, and assuming sales of 100,000 CDs, the artist's earnings would be $75,000. However, since the company "gave away" 15% (or 15,000 of the 100,000 units in this example) for "free," these 15,000 units didn't bear any royalties. Thus, the artist was only paid on 85,000 units, and instead of getting $75,000, the artist only got $63,750 (75¢ × 85,000 units), which is 85% of $75,000.

As noted before, most of the companies did away with the fiction of these phony free goods. But did you get more royalties? No; instead of free goods, they only paid on 85% of the sales. So the result was exactly the same as it was with free goods. It looked like this:

Units shipped	100,000
Royalty-bearing percentage	× 85%
Royalty-bearing units	85,000
Times: Royalty	× 75¢
AMOUNT PAYABLE	**$63,750**

These normal distributor free goods were in addition to the special program and promotional free goods that were on top of them (and in fact alive and well today).

"90% of Net Sales"

In the really early days, records were made of shellac, and were therefore breakable. So the record companies developed a practice of paying the artist on only 90% of the shipment, keeping the remaining 10% to cover their breakage.

Records haven't been made of shellac since the 1950s, but the practice of paying on 90% of net sales persisted until the late 1990s. There was no logical reason for this—it was a total rip-off that arbitrarily reduced your royalty by 10%. Thus, where a company paid on 90%, you were being paid on 90% (for "breakage") of 85% (for free goods), resulting in payment on only 76.5% of shipments! And they took special program and promotional free goods out of the balance!

Aren't you sorry you missed all this fun?

One last tidbit: If you have one of these old deals, there was a time that some companies applied these crazy calculations to digital downloads. In other words, they based the price on retail, then took a packaging and free goods reduction before applying your royalty rate. Even though there is no package and there are no free goods in the digital world. I understand this has mostly gone away, but watch out for it.

Conclusion

This concludes the informational portion of our program.

Congratulations! Whichever track you took through the book, you now have a better overview of the music business than 98% of your colleagues (or at least 97.63%). Despite my informal style of writing, I've given you a lot of info. In fact, you now have everything you need to go as far as your music and drive will take you, without being pillaged and plundered along the way (or at least you can only get zapped with your eyes open).

To get the most from this book, I suggest you keep it handy as a reference. It was important for you to read it through as a solid framework on which to build, but it will be even more valuable as you apply it to specific situations in your life. When you get involved in a particular deal, look up that section and read it again. Seeing it for the second time, you'll pick up things you might have missed before. And it'll be far more meaningful in practice than it was in theory. Sort of like reading a book on flying when you're home in bed, then reading it again just before you pilot an airplane.

Now you're ready for takeoff, so . . .

Go get 'em!

Index

About the Author

Donald S. Passman is the author of *All You Need To Know About the Music Business* and a graduate of the University of Texas and Harvard Law School. He practices law with the Los Angeles firm of Gang, Tyre, Ramer, Brown & Passman and has specialized in the music business for more than forty years.

Don has lectured extensively on the music industry, including at Harvard Law School, Yale Law School, USC Gould School of Law, UCLA School of Law, the Los Angeles Copyright Society, and the Beverly Hills Bar Association. He is also the author of three novels: *The Amazing Harvey*, *The Visionary*, and *Mirage*.

Don has been listed in the Best Lawyers in America for more than twenty years, as well as the Top 100 Lawyers in California, the Top 500 Attorneys in America, *Billboard*'s Power 100, *Hollywood Reporter*'s Top 100 Entertainment Attorneys, *Billboard*'s Music's Most Powerful Attorneys, and Southern California's Super Lawyers.

Check out Don's website at www.donpassman.com.